A MAHĀBHĀRATA COMPANION

A
MAHĀBHĀRATA
COMPANION

Arthur Farndell

ST JAMES PUBLISHING

First published by St James Publishing in 2003

St James Publishing
c/o St James Independent Schools
Earsby Street
London W14 8SH

Tel: 0870-870 8797   Fax: 0870-870 8798
email: stjamespublishing@stjamesschools.co.uk

© Arthur Farndell 1978

Produced by Bookchase (UK) Ltd.

Typeset by Alacrity
Banwell Castle, Weston-super-Mare

ISBN 1-903843-15-4

A record for this book is available from the British Library

No part of this publication may be reproduced,
stored in a retrieval system or transmitted
in any form or by any means, electronic,
mechanical, photocopying, recording or otherwise,
without prior permission of the Publisher.

CONTENTS

Acknowledgements		vii
Foreword		ix
A Note on Pronunciation		xi
Locating the Parvas		xiii
The Mahābhārata at a Glance		xiv
PART ONE	**Summary of the Mahābhārata**	1
	Adi Parva	3
	Sabha Parva	34
	Vana Parva	41
	Virata Parva	74
	Udyoga Parva	81
	Bhishma Parva	102
	Drona Parva	114
	Karna Parva	136
	Salya Parva	147
	Sauptika Parva	155
	Stree Parva	158
	Santi Parva	161
	Anusasana Parva	207
	Aswamedha Parva	226
	Asramavasika Parva	236
	Mausala Parva	241
	Mahaprasthanika Parva	242
	Swargarohanika Parva	243
PART TWO	**Where's What in the Mahābhārata**	245
PART THREE	**Who's Who in the Mahābhārata**	315

ACKNOWLEDGEMENTS

THANKS GO TO friends and mentors who have given their encouragement in this work; to Mr Nathan David for his drawing of the head of Krishna; to Jean Desebrock, Elaine Marigold and Sandra Woodward for overseeing and typing a difficult manuscript; and to my wife, Phyllis, for her forbearance.

FOREWORD

ANY ATTEMPT to read the *Mahābhārata* can prove a daunting and humbling experience. This was the case in the late 1970s, when the first 70 pages were perceived as an incomprehensible mass of verbiage. The books were set aside for a few months, while courage was gathered for a second onslaught. The first 70 pages remained as intractable as ever, and the books were again put away, in a spirit of despondency, perhaps for ever.

But it was not to be so. Some months later a clear sound entered the mind and formulated itself into English as: 'If you are finding this work difficult, so are others. What can you do to help them?' This formulation immediately switched the emotional approach from a desire to gain mastery over something to a willingness to be of service. At that moment the complete method was laid out with astonishing clarity and simplicity: 'Read the first section. Write down a summary of it. Read the second section. Write down a summary of it. Read each section in turn. Do not proceed to a new section until a summary of the current section has been written down. When all the summaries are complete, produce from them two indexes, one of topics and one of people.'

This method was a joy to follow. The work flowed quickly through the 12 volumes and no problem was encountered that did not speedily resolve itself.

The two indexes, both incorporated in this present volume, were first printed many years ago and it is now felt that the summary on which they are based should also be published. It is presented in its pristine innocence, with the prayer that its sole function may be to encourage the reader to have recourse to the *Mahābhārata* itself, of which this summary is the palest of reflections.

ARTHUR FARNDELL
2003

A NOTE ON PRONUNCIATION

THIS WORK is based upon the excellent English translation of the *Mahābhārata* published under the name of Pratap Chandra Roy.* The summary preserves Mr Roy's renderings of Sanskrita names and technical terms, although these show neither vowel length nor mouth position.

To help the reader with correct pronunciation some of the more important examples that are open to serious mispronunciation are listed on the following page in the forms in which this work presents them, together with their Devanāgarī forms.

---

*The Mahābhārata of Krishna-Dwaipayana Vyasa, translated by Pratap Chandra Roy, published by Munshiram Manoharlal. Third Edition, September 1972. 12 volumes. Although Pratap Chandra Roy was both instigator and publisher of the first edition of this translation of the *Mahābhārata* (11 volumes, 1883-1896), almost the entire translation was done by Kisari Mohan Ganguli. Subsequent editions, as the above, have erroneously credited the translation to Mr Roy.

Anusasana	अनुशासन	Pandu	पाण्डु
Ashtavakra	अष्टावक्र	Parasara	पराशर
Aswatthaman	अश्वत्थामन्	Parvati	पर्वती
Bharadwaja	भरद्वज	Prajapati	प्रजापति
Bhimasena	भीमसेन	Pritha	पृथा
Bhishma	भीष्म	Ravana	रावण
Chekitana	चेकितान	Sachi	शची
Damayanti	दमयन्ती	Sakra	शक्र
Dansa	दंश	Santi	शान्ति
Dasaratha	दशरथ	Santanu	शान्तनु
Dhritarashtra	धृतराष्ट्र	Saraswati	सरस्वती
Draupadi	द्रौपदी	Sesha	शेष
Drona	द्रोण	Sikhandim	शिखण्डिन्
Gandhari	गान्धारी	Sisupala	शिशुपाल
Ganga	गङ्गा	Sita	सीता
Hiranyakasipu	हिरण्यकशिपु	Siva	शिव
Kaikeyi	कैकेयी	Sree	श्री
Karna	कर्ण	Swetaketu	श्वेतकेतु
Kripa	कृप	Uma	उमा
Krishna	कृष्ण	Vasishtha	वसिष्ठ
Kunti	कुन्ती	Virata	विराट
Narada	नारद	Viswamitra	विश्वामित्र
Narayana	नारायण	Vyasa	व्यास
Pandavas	पाण्डवाः	Yajnavalkya	याज्ञवल्क्य

LOCATING THE PARVAS

THE EDITION of the *Mahābhārata* on which this summary is based is the 12-volume set published in 1972 by Munshiram Manoharlal, New Delhi. To help locate the Parvas within this edition or a similar one, the following table is provided:

Adi Parva		Volume I
Sabha Parva		Volume II
Vana Parva	Sections I-CXIII	Volume II
	Sections CX1V-CCCXIII	Volume III
Virata Parva		Volume IV
Udyoga Parva		Volume IV
Bhishma Parva		Volume V
Drona Parva		Volume VI
Karna Parva		Volume VII
Salya Parva		Volume VII
Sauptika Parva		Volume VII
Stree Parva		Volume VII
Santi Parva	Sections I-CLXXIII	Volume VIII
	Sections CLXXIV-CCCI	Volume IX
	Sections CCCII-CCCLXV	Volume X
Anusasana Parva	Sections I-XXXV	Volume X
	Sections XXXVI-CLXVIII	Volume XI
Aswamedha Parva		Volume XII
Asramavasika Parva		Volume XII
Mausala Parva		Volume XII
Mahaprasthanika Parva		Volume XII
Swargarohanika Parva		Volume XII

THE MAHĀBHĀRATA AT A GLANCE

ADI PARVA
Mahābhārata: its composition.
Creation of the universe.
Ancestry and birth of the principal characters.
Beginnings of hostility between the sons of Pandu and the sons of Dhritarashtra.
Draupadi marries the five sons of Pandu.

SABHA PARVA
The citizens flourish under Yudhishthira, eldest son of Pandu.
Jealousy afflicts Duryodhana, eldest son of Dhritarashtra.
The dice game: Yudhishthira loses.
Draupadi is insulted.
The sons of Pandu prepare for 13 years of exile.

VANA PARVA
The sons of Pandu, with Draupadi, go to the forest for 12 years.
Arjuna spends five years in heaven being trained in warfare.
Story of Nala and Damayanti.
Hanuman: the story of Rama, Sita, and Ravana.

VIRATA PARVA
The last year of exile is spent in disguise in a royal city.

UDYOGA PARVA
Duryodhana is asked to grant half the kingdom to Yudhishthira.
Duryodhana rejects all pleas, including Krishna's.
The two sides draw up their battle lines at Kurukshetra.

BHISHMA PARVA
Battle preparations.
The *Bhagavadgita* [Sections XXV-XLII].
The battle rages for ten days.
Bristling with arrows, Bhishma falls but does not die.

DRONA PARVA
Widespread carnage on the battlefield.
Death of Drona.

KARNA PARVA
Wholesale slaughter.
Death of Karna.

SALYA PARVA
Duryodhana, his army exterminated, is defeated in mace-combat by Bhima.

SAUPTIKA PARVA
Death of Duryodhana.

STREE PARVA
Lamentations from Dhritarashtra and the Kuru ladies.

SANTI PARVA
A month of mourning.
Yudhishthira is installed on the throne.
Bhishma's words from his bed of arrows.

ANUSASANA PARVA
More teaching from Bhishma.
His death.

ASWAMEDHA PARVA
Yudhishthira rules.
Krishna and Arjuna enjoy the time of peace.
Teaching from Krishna.
The horse-sacrifice.

ASRAMAVASIKA PARVA
Dhritarashtra and his wife, Gandhari, set off to the forest.
They die in a conflagration.

MAUSALA PARVA
Krishna leaves the body.

MAHAPRASTHANIKA PARVA
The five sons of Pandu, with Draupadi and a dog, retire from the world.
They all fall to the ground, apart from Yudhishthira and the dog.

SWARGAROHANIKA PARVA
All's well that ends well.

PART ONE

SUMMARY OF THE MAHĀBHĀRATA

ADI PARVA

I

Ugrasrava (also known as Sauti, also known as son of Lomaharshana) addresses a group of sages in the forest of Naimisha. The sages have attended the twelve years' sacrifice of Saunaka (also known as Kulapati) and are 'desirous of hearing that history also called *Bharata*, the holy composition of the wonderful Vyasa, which dispelleth the fear of evil, just as it was cheerfully recited by the Rishi Vaisampayana, under the direction of Dwaipayana himself, at the snake-sacrifice of Raja Janamejaya.'

Sauti begins: How creation developed from the mighty egg. The ancestors of the Kurus, the Yadus, and Bharata. The detailed form and the abridged form of the *Bharata*. The Puranas, composed by Vyasa. How Ganesa was commissioned to write down the *Mahābhārata*. 'As the full moon by its mild light expandeth the buds of the water-lily, so this Purana, by exposing the light of the Sruti hath expanded the human intellect. By the lamp of history, which destroyeth the darkness of ignorance, the whole mansion of nature is properly and completely illuminated.'

Picture of the *Mahābhārata* as a tree. Vyasa becomes the father of Dhritarashtra, Pandu, and Vidura. 'It was not till after these were born, grown up, and departed on the supreme journey, that the great Rishi Vyasa published the *Bharata* in this region of mankind; when being solicited by Janamejaya and thousands of Brahmanas, he instructed his disciple Vaisampayana, who was seated near him; and he, sitting together with the Sadasyas, recited the *Bharata*, during the intervals of the ceremonies of the sacrifice, being repeatedly urged to proceed.'

The different versions of the *Mahābhārata*, this being the one with 100,000 verses.

Picture of Yudhishthira as a tree. How Pandu 'killed a stag coupling with its mate, which served as a warning for the conduct of the princes of his house as long as they lived. Their mothers, in order that the ordinances of the law might be fulfilled, admitted as substitutes to their embraces the gods Dharma, Vayu, Sakra, and the divinities the twin Aswins.'

Summary of the *Mahābhārata*.

'The study of the *Bharata* is an act of piety. He that readeth even one foot, with belief, hath his sins entirely purged away.'

'In former days, having placed the four Vedas on one side and the *Bharata* on the other, these were weighed in the balance by the celestials assembled for that purpose. And as the latter weighed heavier than the four Vedas with their mysteries, from that period it hath been called in the world *Mahābhārata*.'

II

Sauti: How Rama formed Samanta-panchaka in the interval between the Treta and the Dwapara Yugas, and how 'in the interval between the Dwapara and the Kali Yugas there happened at Samanta-Panchaka the encounter between the armies of the Kauravas and the Pandavas.'

The constitution of an Akshauhini.

In praise of the *Mahābhārata*. 'There is not a story current in this world but doth depend upon this history even as the body upon the food that it taketh.'

Composition of the *Mahābhārata*: Vyasa composed a hundred Parvas, which Sauti redistributed into eighteen Parvas.

Two further summaries of the *Mahābhārata*, together with the number of slokas in each Parva.

III

Sauti: How the brothers of Janamejaya are cursed by Sarama (= the celestial bitch) for unjustly beating her offspring. How Janamejaya chooses for his Purohita Somasrava (=son of the Rishi Srutasrava).

The story of the Rishi Ayoda-Dhaumya and the tests endured by his three disciples (= Upamanyu, Aruni, and Veda. How Aruni came to be called Uddalaka; how Upamanyu was cured of his blindness. [In praise of the twin Aswins. 'Having created the Sun, ye weave the wondrous cloth of the year by means of the white thread of the day and the black thread of the night!' Picture of the Wheel of Time, with seasons and the signs of the Zodiac]; how Veda's disciple Utanka obtained ear-rings from the Queen of King Paushya, and how these were stolen by Takshaka (= the king of the serpents), and how they were recovered. Utanka's vision of the Wheel of Time. How Utanka came to Hastinapura and exhorted King Janamejaya to avenge his (the monarch's) father's death (at the fangs of Takshaka) by holding a snake-sacrifice.

IV

Sauti waits for Saunaka to rejoin the Rishis.

ADI PARVA

V

Sauti: The beginning of the race of Bhrigu. How Puloma (= Bhrigu's wife) was carried off by the Rakshasa Puloma (*sic*).

VI

Sauti: How the Rakshasa died; why Chyavana (= Bhrigu's son) was so called; and why Bhrigu decided to curse Agni.

VII

Sauti: How Agni withdrew himself from all places until comforted by Brahma.

VIII

Sauti: How Ruru (= grandson of Chyavana) was due to marry Pramadvara on 'the day when the star Varga-Daivata (Purva-phalguni) would be ascendant', and how Pramadvara was killed by a snakebite.

IX

Sauti: How Ruru gives half of his own life in order that Pramadvara might live. Ruru's vow to kill all serpents. One day Ruru is about to kill a Dundhuba snake.

X

Sauti: The snake explains that it used to be a Rishi named Sahasrapat, who was cursed by a Brahmana.

XI

Sauti: The sight of Ruru restores the snake to its previous form of the Rishi Sahasrapat.

XII

Sauti: Before disappearing, Sahasrapat tells Ruru that he will hear from Brahmanas how King Janamejaya was intent upon killing snakes and how Astika saved the snakes.

XIII

At Saunaka's request, Sauti begins the long story of King Janamejaya and the Rishi Astika:
    Jaratkaru (= father of Astika), alarmed at seeing his ancestors hanging head first into a hole, decides to marry and beget offspring.

XIV
Sauti: How Jaratkaru marries Jaratkaru (*sic*) (= sister of Vasuki).

XV
Sauti: How Astika frustrates the purposes of Janamejaya's snake-sacrifice.

XVI
Sauti: The story of Astika in detail:
In the Golden Age, Kasyapa granted boons to his two wives: Kadru becomes the mother of a thousand snakes, and Vinata becomes the mother of Surya's charioteer and of Garuda.

XVII
Sauti: Description of Mount Meru. Here Narayana advises the gods to churn the Ocean to obtain Amrita.

XVII
Sauti: How the gods used Mount Mandara and Vasuki to churn the Ocean, from which proceed the Moon, Lakshmi, Soma, the Steed Uchchaishravas, the gem Kaustubha, Dhanwantari holding the vessel of Amrita, the Elephant Airavata, and the poison called Kalakuta. To protect the creation, Siva swallows the poison and holds it in his throat — hence his name Nilakantha.

XIX
Sauti: The Asuras fight the gods for the possession of Lakshmi and the Amrita. Rahu manages to drink some Amrita, but he is recognised as a Danava by Surya and Soma and he is beheaded by Narayana before the Amrita can go further than his throat. Rahu's head rises into the sky. 'And from that time there is a long-standing quarrel between Rahu's head and Surya and Soma. And to this day it swalloweth Surya and Soma.' The gods, headed by Nara and Narayana, defeat the Danavas and Daityas. The vessel of Amrita is given to Narayana for safe keeping.

XX
Sauti: Why Kadru and Vinata lay a wager on Uchchaishravas, and why Kadru puts a curse upon her snake-sons, saying, 'During the snake-sacrifice of the wise King Janamejaya of the Pandava race, Agni shall consume you all.'

XXI
Sauti: Striking description of the Ocean:
'It becomes the bed of the lotus-naveled Vishnu when at the

termination of every Yuga that deity of immeasurable power enjoys Yoga-nidra, the deep sleep under the spell of spiritual meditation.'

XXII

Sauti gives another striking description of the Ocean.

XXIII

Sauti: How Vinata is deceived and put into slavery by Kadru. The birth of Garuda. In praise of Garuda.

XXIV

Sauti: Why Surya decided to consume the world, and how Aruna (= son of Kasyapa and Vinata) prevented disaster by becoming Surya's charioteer.

XXV

Sauti: Why Garuda carries Kadru's snake-sons near the Sun. Kadru's words in praise of Indra. Divisions of time.

XXVI

Sauti: Indra causes a downpour of rain.

XXVII

Sauti: Kadru's snake-sons, refreshed by the rain, tell Garuda that only by bringing Amrita can he and his mother be free from their slavery.

XXVIII

Sauti: Garuda flies off to bring the Amrita. He devours thousands of Nishadas in the midst of the Ocean.

XXIX

Sauti: Garuda, still hungry, meets his father, Kasyapa, who advises him to eat an enormous elephant and tortoise, who used to be two brothers called Vibhavasu and Supritika. Garuda seizes the two creatures, but when he alights on a large tree to devour them, the branch breaks.

XXX

Sauti: Garuda protects the Rishis who are hanging in penance from the branch and then disposes of the branch on a distant mountain, where he eats the elephant and the tortoise. Portents in the celestial regions; the gods prepare to defend the Amrita. Origin of Garuda's name.

XXXI

Sauti: The story behind Garuda's birth. Why Indra became frightened after insulting some Rishis whose bodies were of the measure of a thumb.

XXXII

Sauti: Graphic account of how Garuda defeated the gods and extinguished the fire around the Amrita.

XXXIII

Sauti: How Garuda obtained the Amrita; how he became Vishnu's flagstaff device; how he became immortal; how he was struck by Indra's thunderbolt; and why he came to be called Suparna.

XXXIV

Sauti: How Indra makes friends with Garuda; how snakes are given to Garuda for food; how Garuda deceives the snakes and allows Indra to recover the Amrita; why the tongues of snakes are divided in twain; why Kusa grass is holy. Vinata is freed from slavery.

XXXV

Sauti: The names of the principal snakes, Sesha being the firstborn and Vasuki being second.

XXXVI

Sauti: How Sesha (= the lord Ananta) came to 'live underneath the Earth, alone supporting the world at the command of Brahman'.

XXXVII

Sauti: How the assembled snakes suggest expedients for frustrating the predicted snake-sacrifice of King Janamejaya.

XXXVIII

Sauti: Elapatra tells the other snakes that the virtuous snakes will be rescued by Astika.

XXXIX

Sauti: The snakes await the opportunity of marrying Vasuki's sister Jaratkaru to the Rishi Jaratkaru.

XL

Sauti: How King Parikshit insulted the Rishi Samika (who was the father of Sringin) by placing a dead snake across his shoulders.

XLI

Sauti: Sringin curses Parikshit, but Samika condemns his son's action and speaks of the importance of kingship.

XLII

Sauti: Samika informs Parikshit of the curse:
'Within seven nights hence, shall (the snake) Takshaka cause thy death'. Parikshit takes defensive measures.

XLIII

Sauti: Kasyapa hopes to obtain wealth by protecting Parikshit, but instead he accepts the wealth offered by Takshaka. How Takshaka kills Parikshit.

XLIV

Sauti: Takshaka departs, 'coursing through the blue sky like a streak of the hue of the lotus, and looking very much like the vermilion-coloured line on a woman's crown dividing the dark masses of her hair in the middle'. Janamejaya is crowned and marries Vapushtama.

XLV

(This section appears as a repeat of XIII, but with a more graphic account of the precarious condition of Jaratkaru's ancestors.)

XLVI

Sauti: Vasuki offers his sister to Jaratkaru.
(Cf. XIV.)

XLVII

Sauti: Jaratkaru marries Vasuki's sister on condition that she does nothing to offend him. Shortly after his wife has conceived, the Rishi Jaratkaru leaves her because she has failed to keep the marriage condition.

XLVIII

Sauti: The abandoned wife goes back to Vasuki. Why her son is called Astika. Astika studies the Vedas with Chyavana, the son of Bhrigu.

XLIX

Sauti: Janamejaya's ministers speak in praise of Parikshit.

L

Sauti: The ministers give Janamejaya a full account of Parikshit's death.

LI
Sauti: Janamejaya resolves to perform the snake-sacrifice.

LII
Sauti: The sacrifice begins, and thousands of snakes perish in the fire.

LII
Sauti: The names of the priests.

LIV
Sauti: Astika goes to the sacrifice to save the snake-race.

LV
Sauti: Astika speaks in praise of Janamejaya.

LVI
Sauti: Janamejaya grants Astika a boon. Just as Takshaka is about to fall into the fire, Astika asks for the sacrifice to be stopped.

LVII
Sauti: The names of the principal snakes that perished in Janamejaya's sacrifice.

LVIII
Sauti: How Astika stopped the sacrifice and saved Takshaka.

LIX
Saunaka wants to hear 'that sacred history called the *Mahābhārata*, spreading the fame of the Pandavas, which Krishna-Dwaipayana, asked by Janamejaya, caused to be duly recited after the completion of the sacrifice'.

Sauti promises to give a full account.

LX
Sauti: Vyasa's parentage and training.

How Vyasa came to the sacrifice of Janamejaya, who asked him to relate the history of the Kurus and the Pandavas. Vyasa instructs his disciple Vaisampayana to give the narrative.

LXI
Sauti: Vaisampayana gives a summary of the *Mahābhārata*.

LXII

Sauti: Janamejaya says, 'I am not satisfied with hearing in a nutshell the great history'. Vaisampayana speaks in praise of the *Mahābhārata*, and promises to begin a full account.

LXIII

[This is where the story really begins!]

Sauti: Vaisampayana: The story begins with King Vasu. Why Vasu was also called Uparichara. Born in the Paurava race, he became the King of Chedi. Why Indra is worshipped around a pole planted in the ground.

Vasu's five sons: Vrihadratha (= Maharatha), Pratyagraha, Kusamva (= Manivahana), Mavella, and Yadu.

How twins were born from the River Suktimati embraced by the Kolahala Mountain: Vasu makes the boy his commander-in-chief and marries the girl (= Girika).

How a fish (in fact, an Apsara under a curse) gave birth, from Vasu's seed, to twins: the girl Satyavati and the boy Matsya.

How Vyasa is begotten upon Satyavati by the Rishi Parasara. Why he is called Vyasa and why he is called Dwaipayana.

Bhishma 'was born in the womb of Ganga through King Santanu'.

How Dharma, cursed by the Rishi Animandavya, 'was born a Sudra in the form of the learned Vidura'.

Birth of Karna by Surya from Kunti.

Birth of Krishna by Vasudeva from Devaki.

In praise of Krishna.

Satyaki and Kritavarma 'had their births from Satyaka and Hridika'.

Why Drona is so called.

'From the seed of Gautama, fallen upon a clump of reeds, were born two that were twins, the mother of Aswatthaman (called Kripi), and Kripa of great strength.'

Dhrishtradyumna was born from the sacrificial fire.

Draupadi was born from the sacrificial altar.

Sakuni was born from Suvala, as was Gandhari.

'And from Krishna [= Vyasa] was born, in the soil of Vichitravirya, Dhritarashtra, the lord of men, and Pandu of great strength. And from Dwaipayana was also born, in the Sudra caste, the wise and intelligent Vidura.'

Pandu's five sons, and their real fathers:

Yudhishthira < Dharma (= Yama, the god of Justice);

Bhima < Marut (the wind god);

Dhananjaya < Indra;

Nakula and Sahadeva < the twin Aswins.

LXIV

Vaisampayana: After Rama had twenty-one times made the Earth bereft of Kshatriyas, the Rishis and Brahmanas raised up the race upon the Kshatriya ladies. Righteous community living in the Krita Age.

'And the sons of Diti (Daityas) being repeatedly defeated in war by the sons of Aditi (celestials) and deprived also of sovereignty and heaven, began to be incarnated on the Earth'. The Earth groans under the weight of the Asuras, and Brahman (= Isa, = Sambhu = Prajapati) commands the gods to become incarnate and strive against the Asuras.

LXV

Vaisampayana: The gods become incarnate and slay many of the Asuras. The names of

>Brahman's six spiritual sons
>Daksha's thirteen daughters
>The twelve Adityas (sons of Aditi)
>Diti's son (= Hiranyakasipu)
>Hiranyakasipu's five sons
>Prahlada's three sons
>Virochana's son (= Vali)
>Danu's forty sons
>Danayu's four sons
>Vinata's sons
>Kadru's sons
>Muni's sons
>etc.

LXVI

Vaisampayana: The names and/or description of

>the eleven Rudras
>Angiras' three sons
>Pulastya's sons
>Pulaha's sons
>Kratu's sons
>Daksha's fifty daughters
>Dharma's ten wives
>the wives of Soma (= the Nakshatras)

(Manu = Brahman's son) Manu's son (= Prajapati)
>Prajapati's eight sons (= the Vasus)
>Dhruva's son (= Kala = Time)
>Soma's son (= Varchas)

[Prabhasa begets Viswakarman (= the founder of all arts) upon the sister of Vrihaspati]

The three sons of Dharma (= son of Brahman)

Marichi's son (= Kasyapa)

Kasyapa's offspring (= the gods and the Asuras)

Tvashtri begets the twin Aswins upon Savitri.

The thirty-three gods are the eight Vasus, the eleven Rudras, the twelve Adityas, Prajapati, and Vashatkara.

Bhrigu is a son of Brahman.

Bhrigu's son is Sukra, who became a planet and also the spiritual guide of the Daityas and the gods.

Bhrigu's son Chyavana begot Aurva upon Arushi (= the daughter of Manu).

Aurva begot Richika.

Richika begot Jamadagni.

Jamadagni begot Rama (= Parasurama)

Brahman's sons Dhatri and Vidhatri

and their sister Lakshmi.

'And Adharma (Sin) was born when creatures (from want of food) began to devour one another. And Adharma always destroys every creature. And Adharma hath Niriti for his wife, whence the Rakshasas who are called Nairitas (offspring of Niriti).

Etc, etc, etc.

'Thus hath the genealogy of all the principal creatures been fully described by me.'

Origins of many zoological species and botanical species.

LXVII

Vaisampayana now gives the names of the celestial beings and their earthly counterparts:

Viprachitti	>	Jarasandha
Hiranyakasipu	>	Sisupala
Samhlada	>	Salya
Anuhlada	>	Dhrishtaketu
Sivi	>	Druma
Vashkala	>	Bhagadatta
Ketumat	>	Amitaujas
Swarbhanu	>	Ugrasena
Aswa	>	Asoka
Aswapati	>	Hardikya

Vrishaparvan	>	Dirghaprajna
Ajaka	>	Salwa
Aswagriva	>	Rochamana
Sukshma	>	Vrihadratha
Tuhunda	>	Senavindu
Ishupa	>	Nagnajita
Ekachakra	>	Pritivindhya
Virupaksha	>	Chitravarman
Hara	>	Suvahu
Suhtra	>	Munjakesa
Nikumbha	>	Devadhipa
Sarabha	>	Paurava
Kupatha	>	Suparswa
Kratha	>	Parvateya
Salabha	>	Prahlada
Chandra	>	Chandravarman
Arka	>	Rishika
Mritapa	>	Pascimanupaka
Garishtha	>	Drumasena
Mayura	>	Kalakirti
Chandrahantri	>	Sunaka
Chandravinasana	>	Janaki
Dhirghajihva	>	Kasiraja
Rahu (?)	>	Kratha
Vikshara	>	Vasumitra
Valina	>	Paundramatsyaka
Vritra	>	Manimat
Krodhahantri	>	Danda
Krodhavardhana	>	Dandadhara
Kukshi	>	Parvatiya
Krathana	>	Suryaksha
Surya	>	Darada
Kalanemi	>	Kansa
Portion of Vrihaspati	>	Drona
Dwapara (= the third Yuga)	>	Sakuni
Varchas	>	Abhimanyu

The names of Dhritarashtra's hundred sons.

Soma, father of Varchas, found it hard to part with his son and asked that the youth should be returned in his sixteenth year as Abhimanyu.

Portion of Agni	>	Dhrishtadyumna
A Rakshasa	>	Sikhandin

Sura was the father of Vasudeva and a daughter called Pritha. Sura gives Pritha as a daughter to Kuntibhoja, who has no offspring. Surya begets Karna upon Pritha (= Kunti).

Portion of Narayana	>	Vasudeva
Portion of Sesha	>	Valadeva
Portion of Sri	>	Rukmini
Portion of Sachi	>	Draupadi
Siddhi	>	Kunti
Dhriti	>	Madri
Mati	>	Gandhari

LXVIII

Vaisampayana: The founder of the Paurava line was Dushmanta. The people lived righteously while he was king.

LXIX

Vaisampayana: How Dushmanta went hunting.

LXX

Vaisampayana: Striking description of the forest.
Dushmanta is welcomed at the sacred asylum of Kasyapa.

LXXI-LXXII

Vaisampayana: Dushmanta meets Sakuntala, who tells him how she was begotten by Viswamitra upon the Apsara Menaka and brought up by the Rishi Kanwa as his own daughter. Viswamitra's great achievements.

LXXIII

Vaisampayana: Dushmanta marries Sakuntala, who has agreed on condition that her son becomes the heir apparent. Dushmanta departs, promising to send a royal escort for Sakuntala.
The eight kinds of marriage.

'As the swine always look for dirt and filth even when in the midst of a flower garden, so the wicked always choose the evil out of both evil and good that others speak. Those, however, that are wise, on hearing the speeches of others that are intermixed with both good and evil, accept only what is good, like geese that always extract the milk only, though it be mixed with water' — Quotation from the following section, i.e. Section LXXIV.

LXXIV

Vaisampayana: When her son is three years old, Sakuntala takes him to the palace, but Dushmanta refuses to acknowledge them. When the truth is uttered by a great voice, Dushmanta accepts them, having received the confirmation he felt was necessary for his people. Why the child is called Bharata. 'It is that Bharata from whom have emanated so many mighty achievements' — the founder of the Bharata race.

In praise of wives.
In praise of sons.
In praise of Truth.

LXXV

Vaisampayana: More genealogies.

Prachetas
|
Daksha
 \
  daughter + Kasyapa
  |
  Vivaswat (the Sun)
  |
  Manu
  |
  All human beings (= Manavas)

How King Yayati exchanged his decrepitude for the youth of his son Puru, realised that appetites are insatiable, restored Puru's youth, and set Puru on the throne, saying, 'In the world shall my race be known by thy name'.

Manu → Ila → Pururavas → Ayus → Nahusha → Yayati → Puru.

LXXVI

Vaisampayana: How the Brahmana Kacha (= son of Vrihaspati) was hacked to pieces, fed to jackals and wolves, and revived by Sukra (= Kavya = Usanas), who knew the science of Sanjivani.

How Kacha, though pounded to paste by the Danavas and mixed with the ocean, was revived by Sukra.

How Kacha, even inside Sukra's stomach, is revived, and how he in turn revives Sukra.

LXXVII

Vaisampayana: Kacha, having learned the science of re-vivification, now returns to the gods, who had originally commissioned him to learn this science.

LXXVIII

Vaisampayana: How Devayani (= daughter of Sukra) quarrelled with Sarmishtha (= daughter of the Asura chief Vrishaparvan).

LXXIX

Vaisampayana: Sukra fails to console his offended daughter.

LXXX

Vaisampayana: How Sarmishtha with her thousand maids becomes the waiting-maid of Devayani.

LXXXI

Vaisampayana: How King Yayati comes to marry Devayani.

LXXXII

Vaisampayana: How Yayati begets a son upon Devayani and a son upon Sarmishtha.

LXXXIII

Vaisampayana: Devayani's sons by Yayati are Yadu and Turvasu. Sarmishtha's sons by Yayati are Drahyu, Anu and Puru. Sukra puts the curse of decrepitude upon Yayati.

LXXXIV

Vaisampayana: Puru exchanges his youth for his father's decrepitude.

LXXXV

Vaisampayana: After a thousand years Yayati takes back his decrepitude and gives Puru his youth and the kingdom. 'The progeny of Puru are the Pauravas.'

LXXXVI

Vaisampayana: Yayati practises austerities in the forest, after which he ascends to heaven.

LXXXVII

Vaisampayana: The advice given by Yayati to Puru when the latter became king.

LXXXVIII

Vaisampayana: Why Yayati fell from heaven and hovered in the welkin.

LXXXIX

Vaisampayana: Yayati's conversation with the royal sage Astaka:
Acts and their fruits. 'Insects and worms, all oviparous creatures, vegetable existences, all crawling animals, vermin, the fish in the water,

XC

Vaisampayana: Yayati to Ashtaka: The Hell called Bhauma; re-birth; the sin of vanity.

XCI

Vaisampayana: Yayati to Ashtaka: The characteristics of a Muni.

XCII

Vaisampayana: Yayati speaks of instantaneous realisation for the man of knowledge.

Ashtaka and Pratardana give their merits to Yayati.

XCIII

Vaisampayana: Vasumat and Sivi (= son of Usinara) give their merits to Yayati, whereupon all five (i.e. the four donors and Yayati) ascend to Heaven.

XCIV

Vaisampayana: A list of 'the heroic kings in Puru's line'.

XCV

Vaisampayana: A full genealogy from Daksha to Arjuna's great-great-great-grandson.

The curse upon Pandu: Pandu's death.

Why Santanu was so called.

Bhishma = Devavrata.

XCVI

Vaisampayana: The background to the birth of Bhishma begins.

Why King Mahabhisha was cursed in heaven and why Ganga would be reborn on Earth, and why the Vasus were cursed by Vasishtha.

XCVII

Vaisampayana: The birth of Santanu. Why he is called Santanu. (This is King Mahabhisha reborn.)

Santanu is made king, while his father Pratipa retires to the woods.

XCVIII

Vaisampayana: Santanu marries the human form of Ganga. Ganga throws her first seven children into the river, but Santanu prevents her from throwing in the eighth, who will be called Gangadatta.

XCIX

Vaisampayana: Before departing from Santanu, Ganga explains why the Vasus were cursed by the Rishi Apava and why Dyu (= one of the Vasus) has to live on Earth as her child (= Gangadatta = Gangeya = Devavrata = Bhishma). Ganga now departs with her son.

C

Vaisampayana: Description of Santanu and his virtues.

'And during the rule of the best of Kurus — of that King of kings — speech became united with truth, and the minds of men were directed towards liberality and virtue.'

How Bhishma relinquished his right to the throne and vowed to die childless, in order that his father, Santanu, might marry Satyavati (= the fisherman's supposed daughter).

Why Bhishma is so called.

CI

Vaisampayana: Santanu begets upon Satyavati two sons, Chitrangada and Vichitravirya. On Santanu's death, Chitrangada is made king, but is killed by a Gandharva also called Chitrangada. Vichitravirya becomes king.

CII

Vaisampayana: How Bhishma defeats the assembled kings of the Earth at a self-choice ceremony and carries off three maidens, two of whom (= Ambika and Ambalika) marry Vichitravirya. While still young, Vichitravirya dies of phthisis, leaving no children.

CIII

Vaisampayana: Satyavati begs Bhishma to rule and raise a family, but Bhishma adheres to his vow. 'I would renounce three worlds, the empire of heaven, anything that may be greater than that, but truth I would never renounce. The Earth may renounce its scent, water may renounce its moisture, light may renounce its attribute of exhibiting forms, air may renounce its attribute of touch, the Sun may renounce his glory, fire its heat, the Moon his cooling rays, space its capacity of generating sound, the slayer of Vritra his prowess, the god of Justice his impartiality; but I cannot renounce truth.'

CIV

Vaisampayana: Bhishma tells Satyavati why Dirghatamas, still in the womb of Mamata, was cursed with blindness by Vrihaspati, and how Dirghatamas, now a great Rishi, perpetuated the royal line of Vali.

CV

Vaisampayana: Vyasa agrees to raise children to his brother Vichitravirya. Why he is called Krishna.

CVI

Vaisampayana: Vyasa begets Dhritarashtra upon Amvika, Pandu upon Ambalika, and Vidura upon Amvika's maid. Why Dhritarashtra and Pandu are so called.

CVII-CVIII

Vaisampayana: Why the god of Justice was cursed by Mandavya and obliged to be born in the Sudra order.

CIX

Vaisampayana: The prosperity of the Kurus. Description of a well-run society. Why Pandu becomes king. 'And the children, having passed through the usual rites of their order, devoted themselves to vows and study. And they grew up into fine young men skilled in the Vedas and all athletic sports.'

CX

Vaisampayana: Dhritarashtra marries Gandhari (= daughter of King Suvala), who has obtained from Siva a boon that she will have a hundred sons.

Sakuni = brother to Gandhari.

CXI

Vaisampayana: Pandu marries Pritha (= Kunti = adopted daughter of Kuntibhoja), who has received from the Rishi Durvasa a mantra for invoking the gods. Surya begets Karna upon Pritha. How Karna is brought up by Radha and her husband. Why he is called Karna and why he is called Vasusena.

CXII

Vaisampayana: How Pritha came to choose Pandu as her husband. Description of Pandu.

CXIII

Vaisampayana: How Pandu married Madri (= sister to the King of Madra), and subjugated many countries.

CXIV

Vaisampayana: How Pandu, accompanied by Kunti and Madri, leads the life of a hunter in the woods. Vidura marries the daughter of King Devaka and begets 'many children like unto himself in accomplishments.'

CXV

Vaisampayana: How Dhritarashtra's one hundred sons are born in pots. 'As soon as Duryodhana was born, he began to cry and bray like an ass.' Dhritarashtra begets Yuyutsu upon one of Gandhari's maids.

CXVI

Vaisampayana: How Gandhari's daughter (= Duhsala) was born.

CXVII

Vaisampayana: The names of Dhritarashtra's sons in order of birth. Duhsala marries Jayadratha, King of Sindhu.

CXVIII

Vaisampayana: Why a deer (which is really a Muni called Kindama) curses Pandu.

CXIX

Vaisampayana: Pandu and his two wives decide to undergo penances in the woods.

CXX

Vaisampayana: The childless Pandu feels he will not be admitted to Heaven. The twelve kinds of sons. Pandu tells Kunti how the daughter of Saradandayana obtained children for her husband by soliciting a Brahmana.

CXXI

Vaisampayana: Kunti tells Pandu how King Vyushitaswa died of phthisis contracted from sexual excess and how his corpse begot seven children upon his wife Bhadra.

CXXII

Vaisampayana: Pandu refers to the ordinance of marriage established by Swetaketu (= the son of Uddalaka). Kunti informs Pandu of the mantra which she received from the Rishi Durvasa.

CXXIII

Vaisampayana: The god of Justice begets Yudhishthira upon Kunti. He was born 'at the eighth Muhurta called Abhijit, of the hour of noon of that very auspicious day of the seventh month (Kartika), viz., the fifth of the lighted fortnight, when the star Jyeshtha in conjunction with the Moon was ascendant'.

Vayu begets Bhima upon Kunti. Bhima is born on the same day as Duryodhana. Sakra begets Arjuna upon Kunti.

CXXIV

Vaisampayana: The twin Aswins beget Nakula and Sahadeva upon Madri. 'And the five Pandavas and the hundred sons of Dhritarashtra — that propagator of the Kuru race — grew up rapidly like a cluster of lotuses in a lake.'

CXXV

Vaisampayana: How Pandu and Madri die.

CXXVI

Vaisampayana: The citizens of Hastinapura are informed of the deaths of Pandu and Madri.

CXXVII

Vaisampayana: The funeral rites for Pandu and Madri.

CXXVIII

Vaisampayana: The death of Satyavati.

How the youthful Bhima showed his prowess in sporting with the sons of Dhritarashtra. The beginning of Duryodhana's hostility towards Bhima. How Bhima was poisoned and thrown into the river and how he gained the strength of ten thousand elephants.

CXXIX

Vaisampayana: Duryodhana, Karna and Sakuni make numerous attempts on the lives of the Pandavas. Dhritarashtra appoints Gautama (= Kripa) as preceptor to the Kuru princes.

CXXX

Vaisampayana: The birth of Kripa and why he was so called.

CXXXI

Vaisampayana: Drona teaches the science of arms to the Kauravas and the Pandavas.

The birth of Drona (= son of Bharadwaja) and why he was so called.

Drona marries Kripi (= twin sister of Kripa) and begets Aswatthaman. Why Aswatthaman is so called. How Rama (= son of Bhrigu) gives all his weapons to Drona.

CXXXII

Vaisampayana: Drupada (= King of the Panchalas) repudiates Drona's offer of friendship.

CXXXIII

Vaisampayana: How Drona amazes the young princes by bringing up a ball and a ring from the bottom of a dry well.

CXXXIV

Vaisampayana: Arjuna's special devotion to Drona and to the science of arms. How Arjuna and Aswatthaman receive extra tuition from Drona.
Why Prince Ekalavya paid Drona a tuition fee of his own right thumb.
'And amongst all the princes, Arjuna alone became an Atiratha.'

CXXXV

Vaisampayana: How Arjuna shot the head from the bird.
Drona gives Arjuna the Brahmasira weapon.

CXXXVI

Vaisampayana: How the princes display their prowess at a tournament.

CXXXCVII

Vaisampayana: A tournament mace-combat between Bhima and Duryodhana.
Arjuna shows his prowess:
'And having performed the propitiatory rites, the youthful Phalguna, equipped with the finger protector and his quiver full of shafts and bow in hand, donning his golden mail, appeared in the lists even like an evening cloud reflecting the rays of the setting sun and illuminated by the hues of the rainbow and flashes of lightning.'
Arjuna uses the Agneya weapon, the Varuna weapon, the Vayavya weapon, the Parjanya weapon, the Bhauma weapon, the Parvatya weapon, and the Antardhana weapon. 'And Drona stood, surrounded by the five brothers, the sons of Pritha, and looked like the Moon in conjunction with the five-starred constellation Hasta.'

CXXXVIII

Vaisampayana: Karna emulates Arjuna's feats.
Karna sides with Duryodhana.

CXXXIX

Vaisampayana: As the spectators disperse, they, like the exhibitors, have already fallen into opposing camps.

CXL

Vaisampayana: How the Pandavas bring Drona his preceptorial fee:

Drupada, King of Panchala! Drona gives Drupada his life and half his kingdom, while Drona takes the other half.

CXLI

Vaisampayana: Dhritarashtra installs Yudhishthira as heir apparent.

Arjuna and the Kshura, Naracha, Vala and Vipatha weapons.

The fee which Drona demands of Arjuna:

'O sinless one, thou must fight with me when I fight with thee.'

'Sahadeva obtained the whole science of morality and duties from (Vrihaspati) the spiritual chief of celestials.'

When he hears of the prowess of the Pandavas, 'Dhritarashtra's sentiments towards the Pandavas became suddenly poisoned.'

CXLII

Vaisampayana: Kanika's advice to Dhritarashtra:

The duties of a king. The story of the jackal, the tiger, the mouse, the wolf, and the mongoose.

CXLIII

Vaisampayana: Duryodhana begins to plot.

CXLIV

Vaisampayana: The plot thickens.

CXLV

Vaisampayana: Dhritarashtra suggests that the Pandavas go to a festival in Varanavata; the Pandavas set out.

CXLVI

Vaisampayana: On Duryodhana's orders, his counsellor Purochana constructs a house of lac in Varanavata.

CXLVII

Vaisampayana: Vidura warns the Pandavas.

'The Pandavas set out on the eighth day of the month of Phalguna when the star Rohini was in the ascendant.'

CXLVIII

Vaisampayana: The Pandavas live in the house of lac.

CXLIX

Vaisampayana: The secret underground passage is dug.

CL

Vaisampayana: How the burning house kills Purochana and a Nishada woman with her five sons.

How the Pandavas escape with Kunti.

CLI

Vaisampayana: The fugitives cross the Ganga.

CLII

Vaisampayana: In Varanavata and Hastinapura there is mourning for the Pandavas (presumed dead).

CLIII

Vaisampayana: That night in the forest Bhima utters an eloquent lament over his sleeping mother and brothers.

CLIV

Vaisampayana: How Hidimva (= the sister of the Rakshasa Hidimva) falls in love with Bhima.

CLV

Vaisampayana: How Bhima wrestles with the Rakshasa.

CLVI

Vaisampayana: How Bhima slays the Rakshasa.

CLVII

Vaisampayana: How Bhima begets Ghatotkacha upon the Rakshasa woman Hidimva. Why Ghatotkacha is so called.

CLVIII

Vaisampayana: The fugitives study 'the Rik and the other Vedas and also all the Vedangas as well as the sciences of morals and politics.'

Vyasa advises the fugitives to dwell in the town of Ekachakra.

CLIX

Vaisampayana: The fugitives live with a Brahmana in Ekachakra. Kunti learns of the Brahmana's distress.

CLX

Vaisampayana: The Brahmana's wife offers her life.

CLXI

Vaisampayana: The Brahmana's daughter offers her life, and the tiny son declares that he will kill the Rakshasa.

CLXII

Vaisampayana: Kunti learns the full story:
This family has to give a human being as food for a Rakshasa named Vaka.

CLXIII

Vaisampayana: Kunti promises to send Bhima instead.

CLXIV

Vaisampayana: Kunti persuades Yudhishthira that her action is a good one.

CLXV

Vaisampayana: How Bhima grapples with Vaka.

CLXVI

Vaisampayana: Bhima slays Vaka. The gratitude of the citizens.

CLXVII

Vaisampayana: Another Brahmana comes to lodge with the family.

CLXVIII

Vaisampayana: The visitor speaks of the birth of Drona, Drupada's repudiation of Drona's friendship, and Drona's revenge upon Drupada.

CLXIX

Vaisampayana: The visitor: How Drupada obtained a twin boy and girl (= Dhrishtadyumna and Krishna) from the sacrifice performed by the Brahmanas Yaja and Upayaja. Meaning of the name Dhrishtadyumna.
Celestial voice: 'This prince hath been born for the destruction of Drona.'

CLXX

Vaisampayana: Kunti suggests a visit to Panchala.

CLXXI

Vaisampayana: While still at Ekachakra, the fugitives are visited by Vyasa, who tells them how Mahadeva once promised five husbands to a Rishi's daughter and how that lady has now been born as Krishna in the line of Drupada.

CLXXII

Vaisampayana: On their way to Panchala, the fugitives encounter Angaraparna (= King of the Gandharvas). Arjuna overpowers Angaraparna, who speaks of Chakshushi (= the science of producing illusions) and who offers Arjuna celestial horses in exchange for the weapon of fire.

The Gandharva speaks of the importance of a priest to a king.

CLXXIII

Vaisampayana: The Gandharva explains why he addresses Arjuna as Tapatya; how Tapati (= daughter of the god Vivaswat) met King Samvarana (= son of Riksha).

CLXXIV

Vaisampayana: The Gandharva: How Samvarana and Tapati fall in love.

CLXXV

Vaisampayana: The Gandharva: How Samvarana, with the help of Vasishtha, married Tapati. (Importance of the priest.) Tapati gives birth to a son named Kuru (= ancestor of Arjuna, etc.)

CLXXVI

Vaisampayana: The Gandharva: Vasishtha = 'Brahma's spiritual (lit. mind-born) son and Arundhati's husband'.

CLXXVII

Vaisampayana: The Gandharva: The story of Viswamitra (= son to King Gadhi and grandson to Kusika). How Viswamitra tries to take the cow Nandini from Vasishtha; how Nandini protects herself, and how Viswamitra becomes an ascetic.

CLXXVIII

Vaisampayana: The Gandharva: How King Kalmashapada, cursed by Saktri (= son of Vasishtha), becomes a Rakshasa and devours Saktri himself and all the other sons of Vasishtha. Vasishtha tries in vain to kill himself.

CLXXIX

Vaisampayana: The Gandharva: Vasishtha is delighted to discover that his daughter-in-law Adrisyanti is bearing a child. How Vasishtha frees Kalmashapada from his curse. Adrisyanti gives birth to a son named Asmaka.

CLXXX

Vaisampayana: The Gandharva: Why Asmaka was also called Parasara.

Vasishtha begins a story to Parasara:

Why the Kshatriyas once tried to exterminate the Brahmanas, and how a Brahmana baby blinded some Kshatriyas.

CLXXXI
Vaisampayana: The Gandharva: Vasishtha continues his story:
Why the baby was called Aurva, and how the Pitris pleaded with Aurva not to consume the three worlds.

CLXXXII
Vaisampayana: The Gandharva: Vasishtha: How Aurva casts the fire of his wrath into the sea. 'And that fire, which consumeth the waters of the great ocean, became like unto a large horse's head which persons conversant with the Vedas call by the name of Vadavamukha.'

CLXXXIII
Vaisampayana: The Gandharva: How Parasara, until stopped by Pulastya, performed a sacrifice for the destruction of Rakshasas.

CLXXXIV
Vaisampayana: The Gandharva explains why King Kalmashapada appointed Vasishtha to beget a son upon his queen.

CLXXXV
Vaisampayana: How the fugitives appoint Dhaumya as their priest.

CLXXXVI
Vaisampayana: The fugitives journey to Panchala.

CLXXXVII
Vaisampayana: Kings from all over the world assemble at Panchala, hoping for the hand of Draupadi. (Draupadi = Krishna. Yajnasena = Drupada.)

CLXXXVIII
Vaisampayana: Dhrishtadyumna lists some of the great kings assembled for the contest.

CLXXXIX
Vaisampayana: The heroes of the world fail to string the great bow. Karna strings it, but Draupadi refuses him.

CLXL
Vaisampayana: How Arjuna strings the bow, hits the mark, and is chosen by Draupadi.

CLXLI

Vaisampayana: The enraged monarchs attack Drupada and Draupadi, and the Pandavas step in to defend them. Krishna (= Vasudeva) is delighted to recognise the Pandavas.

CLXLII

Vaisampayana: Arjuna overpowers Karna, and the attack stops.

CLXLIII

Vaisampayana: How Draupadi becomes the common wife of the five Pandavas.
(Ajatasatru = Yudhishthira.)

CLXLIV

Vaisampayana: How Dhrishtadyumna learns the true identity of the Pandavas, who are disguised as Brahmanas.

CLXLV

Vaisampayana: Drupada is delighted to learn the identity of the five 'Brahmanas'.

CLXLVI

Vaisampayana: The marriage feast begins.

CLXLVII

Vaisampayana: Drupada's joy is ruffled by the news that Draupadi should be the common wife of all the brothers.

CLXLVIII

Vaisampayana: The awkward situation is discussed.
Vyasa arrives.

CLXLIX

Vaisampayana: Vyasa gives Drupada a very powerful account of how five Indras, as a punishment from Mahadeva, had to be born as men. He explains how Devaki gave birth to Krishna from a black hair of Narayana's body and how Rohini gave birth to Valadeva (= Rama) from a white hair of Narayana's body. 'Thus, O king, they who have been born as the Pandavas are none else than those Indras of old. And the celestial Sri herself who had been appointed as their wife is this Draupadi of extraordinary beauty.' Vyasa gives Drupada celestial sight, to see the celestial forms of the Pandavas. (Why Arjuna is called Savyasachin.)

CC

Vaisampayana: How Draupadi marries the five sons of Pandu. 'This day the Moon has entered the constellation called Pushya.'

CCI

Vaisampayana: The joyous alliance of King Drupada with the Pandavas. The gifts from Krishna to the Pandavas.

CCII

Vaisampayana: Duryodhana begins to plot.

CCIII

Vaisampayana: Duryodhana suggests various stratagems.

CCIV

Vaisampayana: Karna suggests the use of force against the Pandavas.

CCV

Vaisampayana: Bhishma suggests the gift of half the kingdom to the Pandavas.

CCVI

Vaisampayana: Drona supports Bhishma, and Karna opposes them both.

CCVII

Vaisampayana: Vidura supports Bhishma and Drona and points out that the Pandavas are invincible.

CCVIII

Vaisampayana: Dhritarashtra sends Vidura to the Pandavas as an ambassador of peace and reconciliation.

CCIX

Vaisampayana: Dhritarashtra gives half the kingdom to the Pandavas, who establish a magnificent city at Khandavaprastha.

CCX

Vaisampayana: Narada begins telling the Pandavas the story of the two brothers Sunda and Upasunda.

CCXI

Vaisampayana: Narada continues: On account of their ascetic penances, Brahman grants the two brothers total immunity — except from each other.

CCXII

Vaisampayana: Narada continues: 'When the constellation Magha was in the ascendant', the brothers begin their conquest of the three worlds.

CCXIII

Vaisampayana: Narada continues: Implored by the gods, the Grandsire orders Viswakarman to create a most beautiful damsel: why she is called Tilottama. How Mahadeva came to have four faces and a thousand eyes.

CCXIV

Vaisampayana: Narada concludes: Sunda and Upasunda kill each other over Tilottama.

Narada suggests: 'Make some such arrangements that you may not quarrel with one another for the sake of Draupadi.'

The agreement made by the Pandavas.

CCXV

Vaisampayana: How Arjuna breaks the agreement and goes to live in the forest for twelve years.

CCXVI

Vaisampayana: How Arjuna spends a night with Ulupi (= daughter of the King of the Nagas).

CCXVII

Vaisampayana: How Arjuna begets a son upon Chitrangada (= daughter of King Chitravahana).

CCXVIII

Vaisampayana: How Arjuna meets five crocodiles that are really Apsaras under a Brahmana's curse.

CCXIX

Vaisampayana: How Arjuna released the Apsaras from the curse. By this time the son (= Vabhrurapana) begotten upon Chitrangada is now on the throne in the city of Manipura.

CCXX

Vaisampayana: How Arjuna meets Krishna and receives a hero's welcome in Dwaraka.

CCXXI

Vaisampayana: How Arjuna falls in love with Bhadra (= sister of Krishna). [Revati = wife to Valarama, who is also known as Haladhara.]

CCXXII
Vaisampayana: How Arjuna seizes Bhadra (= Subhadra) for himself.

CCXXIII
Vaisampayana: How Krishna approves of this action. Arjuna marries Subhadra and spends a year in Dwaraka. The last year of his twelve-year exile he spends 'in the sacred region of Pushkara'.

Arjuna begets Abhimanyu upon Subhadra. Upon Draupadi Yudhishthira begets Prativindhya, Bhima Sutasoma, Arjuna Srutakarman, Nakula Satanika, and Sahadeva Srutasena; the reason for the names of the six sons. 'A second tie always relaxeth the first one upon a faggot!'

CCXXIV
Vaisampayana: The magnificence of Yudhishthira's reign.

'In consequence of Yudhishthira's influence, the good fortune of all the monarchs of the Earth became stationary, and their hearts became devoted to the meditation of the Supreme Spirit, and virtue itself began to grow every way all round.'

CCXXV
Vaisampayana: How Agni drank clarified butter for twelve years at the sacrifice of King Swetaki.

CCXXVI
How Agni asked the help of Krishna and Arjuna in fulfilling his desire to burn the forest of Khandava.

CCXXVII
Vaisampayana: How Arjuna received the marvellous chariot made by Viswakarman and the bow Gandiva; how Krishna received the discus and a mace called Kaumodaki.

CCXXVIII
Vaisampayana: How the forest of Khandava was burned.

CCXXIX
Vaisampayana: How Arjuna and Krishna rout the celestials; the weapons of the gods:
  Yama: mace
  Kuvera: spiked club
  Varma: noose and missile
  Skanda: lance

Dhatri: bow
Jaya: club

CCXXX

Vaisampayana: The forest is consumed by Agni. How the Asura Maya escapes.

CCXXXI

Vaisampayana: Why Agni agreed to spare the Sarngaka birds (= offspring of the Rishi Mandapala).

CCXXXII

Vaisampayana: How the birds' mother (= Jarita) seeks to protect them.

CCXXXIII

Vaisampayana: How Jarita finally abandons her offspring.

CCXXXIV

Vaisampayana: The songs of praise to Agni, sung by the baby birds. How Agni spares them.

CCXXXV

Vaisampayana: How Mandapala and Jarita and the four baby birds are reunited.

'Arundhati insulted even the wise Muni (= Vasishtha) amongst the (celestial) seven. In consequence of such insulting thoughts of hers, she has become a little star, like fire mixed with smoke, sometimes visible and sometimes invisible, like an omen portending no good (amongst a constellation of seven bright stars representing the seven Rishis).'

CCXXXVI

Vaisampayana: Agni is gratified.

Indra is gratified and offers boons to Arjuna and Krishna. Arjuna asks for all of Indra's weapons; Krishna asks for eternal friendship with Arjuna.

END OF ADI PARVA

SABHA PARVA

I

Vaisampayana: Maya, pleased at being spared from the fire, begins to construct a marvellous palace for the Pandavas.

II

Vaisampayana: Krishna goes home to Dwaraka. He 'set out at an excellent moment of a lunar day of auspicious stellar conjunction.'

III

Vaisampayana: How Maya gives a marvellous club to Bhima and the conch Devadatta to Arjuna.

(Mahadeva has his abode on the peak called Hiranya-sringa.) How Maya completes the palace.

IV

Vaisampayana: The official opening of the palace (= the Sabha).

V

Vaisampayana: Narada arrives. Striking list of Narada's attainments. The art of kingship.

VI

Vaisampayana: How Yudhishthira asks the well-travelled Narada if he has ever seen an assembly hall like this one.

VII

Vaisampayana: Narada describes 'the celestial assembly room of Sakra'.

VIII

Vaisampayana: Narada describes the assembly house of Yama.

IX

Vaisampayana: Narada describes the assembly house of Varuna.

X

Vaisampayana: Narada describes the assembly house of Kuvera.

XI
Vaisampayana: Narada describes the assembly house of Brahma.

XII
Vaisampayana: How Yudhishthira decides to perform the Rajasuya sacrifice so that his father Pandu may attain (like King Harishchandra) to the region of Indra.

XIII
Vaisampayana: How the citizens flourished under the rule of Yudhishthira, who always said, 'Give unto each what is due to each'. Government.

XIV
Vaisampayana: Krishna gives his verdict: 'thou wilt not be able to celebrate the Rajasuya sacrifice as long as the mighty Jarasandha liveth'.

XV
Vaisampayana: Krishna relates the prowess of King Jarasandha.

XVI
Vaisampayana: Arjuna is prepared to oppose Jarasandha:
   'Concentration of attention, exertion and destiny exist as the three causes of victory.'

XVII-XVIII
Vaisampayana: Krishna speaks of Jarasandha's strange birth and the reason for his name.

XIX
Vaisampayana: How Jarasandha became a king.

XX
Vaisampayana: Krishna, Arjuna, and Bhima, dressed as Brahmanas, set off for Magadha.

XXI
Vaisampayana: How Krishna, Arjuna, and Bhima break down the Chaityaka peak and confront Jarasandha.

XXII
Vaisampayana: Jarasandha is challenged.

XXIII

Vaisampayana: How Jarasandha and Bhima wrestle together for thirteen days.

XXIV

Vaisampayana: How Bhima slays Jarasandha, and how Krishna releases the kings imprisoned by Jarasandha. Krishna receives Jarasandha's celestial car and flagstaff.

XXV

Vaisampayana: Arjuna conquers the North, Bhima the East, Sahadeva the South, and Nakula the West.

XXVI

Vaisampayana: Details of some of Arjuna's conquests.

XXVII

Vaisampayana: More details of Arjuna's conquests.

XXVIII

Vaisampayana: Details of some of Bhima's conquests.

XXIX

Vaisampayana: More details of Bhima's conquests.

XXX

Vaisampayana: Details of Sahadeva's conquests.
How Agni married the daughter of King Nila. Agni's other names and the reasons for some of them. Sahadeva's hymn of praise to Agni.

XXXI

Vaisampayana: Details of Nakula's conquests.

XXXII

Vaisampayana: The state of a country under good rule. Yudhishthira makes preparations for the Rajasuya sacrifice.

XXXIII

Vaisampayana: Many kings gather for the sacrifice.

XXXIV

Vaisampayana: The sacrifice gets under way.

XXXV
Vaisampayana: The last day of the sacrifice. The Arghya is offered to Krishna.

XXXVI
Vaisampayana: King Sisupala censures this act of worship towards Krishna.

XXXVII
Vaisampayana: Bhishma speaks in praise of Krishna.

XXXVIII
Vaisampayana: Sisupala (= Sunitha) stirs up the other kings against the Vrishnis and the Pandavas.

XXXIX
Vaisampayana: Bhishma reassures Yudhishthira.

XL
Vaisampayana: Sisupala mocks Bhishma's words and tells the story of 'The Hypocritical Old Swan'.

XLI
Vaisampayana: Bhishma restrains the wrathful Bhima.

XLII
Vaisampayana: Bhishma speaks of Sisupala's birth and the prophecy concerning his death.

XLIII
Vaisampayana: Sisupala's harsh words.

XLIV
Vaisampayana: Krishna slays Sisupala, and the sacrifice ends successfully.

XLV
Vaisampayana: Vyasa appears and prophesies the destruction of all the Kshatriyas.

XLVI
Vaisampayana: How Duryodhana burns with jealousy and how he is laughed at for his mistakes in Yudhishthira's assembly room.

XLVII

Vaisampayana: Sakuni puts the idea of the dice match into Duryodhana's mind.

XLVIII

Vaisampayana: Dhritarashtra reluctantly approves of the dice match, but Vidura (= his adviser) speaks against it.

XLIX

Vaisampayana: Dhritarashtra seeks to dissuade Duryodhana.

L-LII

Vaisampayana: Duryodhana describes the varied wealth of the Pandavas.

LIII

Vaisampayana: Dhritarashtra seeks to cool his son's jealousy.

LIV

Vaisampayana: Duryodhana's jealousy continues unabated.

LV

Vaisampayana: Dhritarashtra weakly yields to his son and orders a gaming house to be constructed.

LVI

Vaisampayana: Dhritarashtra speaks of the inevitability of the decrees of Fate.

LVII

Vaisampayana: The Pandavas come to the gaming house.

LVIII

Vaisampayana: The pros and cons of gambling.

LIX

Vaisampayana: The game begins.

LX

Vaisampayana: Yudhishthira loses much of his wealth.

LXI

Vaisampayana: Vidura's wise advice to Dhritarashtra:
   'For the sake of a family a member may be sacrificed; for the sake of

a village a family may be sacrificed; for the sake of a province a village may be sacrificed; and for the sake of one's soul the whole Earth may be sacrificed.'

LXII
Vaisampayana: Vidura speaks of the evils of gambling.

LXIII
Vaisampayana: Altercation between Duryodhana and Vidura.

LXIV
Vaisampayana: Yudhishthira loses his wealth, his brothers, himself, and Draupadi.

LXV
Vaisampayana: Vidura reproves Duryodhana.

LXVI
Vaisampayana: Draupadi is dragged in and insulted by Dussasana and others.

LXVII
Vaisampayana: How Dussasana pulls hundreds of robes from Draupadi. Bhima's oath to slay Dussasana. Questions of morality. Is Draupadi won or not?

LXVIII
Vaisampayana: Draupadi's laments.

LXIX
Vaisampayana: Draupadi laments and Bhima fumes.

LXX
Vaisampayana: Duryodhana insults Draupadi, and Bhima vows to break his thighs. When Dhritarashtra offers Draupadi a boon, she chooses and receives the freedom of her five husbands.

LXXI
Vaisampayana: Bhima's wrath.

LXXII
Vaisampayana: Dhritarashtra gives the Pandavas leave to return to Khandavaprastha with their wife and their wealth.

LXXIII

Vaisampayana: Dhritarashtra is persuaded to summon the sons of Pandu back for another dice game.

LXXIV

Vaisampayana: Gandhari seeks in vain to dissuade Dhritarashtra.

LXXV

Vaisampayana: The sons of Pandu lose the second game of dice.

LXXVI

Vaisampayana: The sons of Pandu prepare for their thirteen years of exile.

LXXVII

Vaisampayana: Vidura gives his farewell blessing to the Pandavas.

LXXVIII

Vaisampayana: Kunti bids farewell to Draupadi and the Pandavas.

LXXIX

Vaisampayana: Vidura tells Dhritarashtra how the Pandavas, with Draupadi and the Brahmana Dhaumya, left Hastinapura. The destruction of the Kurus is foretold.

LXXX

Vaisampayana: Portents. Dhritarashtra fears the worst.

END OF SABHA PARVA

VANA PARVA

I

Vaisampayana: The citizens go out to bid a sad farewell to the exiles.

II

Vaisampayana: The Brahmana Saunaka gives wise teaching to the exiles:
'Sensible physicians first seek to allay the mental sufferings of their patients by agreeable converse and the offer of desirable objects. And as a hot iron bar thrust into a jar maketh the water therein hot, even so doth mental grief bring on bodily agony'. Desire. 'When any of the six senses findeth its particular object, the desire springeth up in the heart to enjoy that particular object. And thus when one's heart proceedeth to enjoy the objects of any particular sense, a wish is entertained which in its turn giveth birth to a resolve. And finally, like unto an insect falling into a flame from love of light, the man falleth into the fire of temptation, pierced by the shafts of the object of enjoyment discharged by the desire constituting the seed of the resolve! And thenceforth blinded by sensual pleasure which he seeketh without stint, and steeped in dark ignorance and folly which he mistaketh for a state of happiness, he knoweth not himself!'

III

Vaisampayana: Dhaumya shows how 'the food that supporteth the lives of creatures is instinct with solar energy'. The 108 names of the Sun. The hymn of praise to the Sun. 'Those versed in chronology say that thou art the beginning and thou the end of a day of Brahma, which consisteth of a full thousand Yugas.'

Vivaswan grants Yudhishthira a copper vessel with an inexhaustible supply of food.

IV

Vaisampayana: Vidura seeks in vain to persuade Dhritarashtra to adopt a virtuous course of action.

V

Vaisampayana: Vidura tells the forest exiles of Dhritarashtra's stubborn attitude.

VI

Vaisampayana: Dhritarashtra obtains Vidura's forgiveness.

VII

Vaisampayana: The enraged Duryodhana, with Karna and others, intend to slay the exiles, but Vyasa appears and forbids them.

VIII

Vaisampayana: Vyasa reproves Dhritarashtra.

IX

Vaisampayana: Vyasa speaks on 'The Value of a Son'.

X

Vaisampayana: How the Rishi Maitreya curses Duryodhana.

XI

Vaisampayana: Vidura tells Dhritarashtra how Bhima slew the Rakshasa Kirmira (= brother to Vaka).

XII

Vaisampayana: Arjuna recites the feats achieved by Krishna in former lives.

Krishna to Arjuna: 'Thou art mine and I am thine, while all that is mine is thine also! He that hateth thee hateth me as well, and he that followeth thee followeth me! ... O Partha, thou art from me and I am from thee! O bull of the Bharata race, no one can understand the difference that is between us!'

Draupadi: 'One's own self is begotten on one's wife, and therefore it is that the wife is called Jaya. A wife also should protect her lord, remembering that he is to take his birth in her womb.'

Draupadi laments what has happened.

XIII

Vaisampayana: Krishna explains that these things would not have happened if he had been present at the dice match. He speaks of the evils of dice-gaming.

XIV

Vaisampayana: Krishna explains that he was absent because he was destroying Salwa, who was angry because Krishna had slain King Sisupala.

XV

Vaisampayana: Krishna gives details of how Salwa attacked the city of Dwaravati (= ? Dwaraka). (Details of fortification and defensive works.)

XVI

Vaisampayana: Krishna gives an account of the skirmishing that took place outside his city.

XVII

Vaisampayana: Krishna speaks of the combat between his son Pradyumna and Salva.

XVIII

Vaisampayana: Krishna: Pradyumna upbraids his charioteer for taking him unconscious from the battlefield.

XIX

Vaisampayana: Krishna: How Pradyumna is asked to leave Salwa for Krishna to slay.

XX-XXI

Vaisampayana: Krishna tells of his encounter with Salwa.

XXII

Vaisampayana: Krishna tells how he destroyed Salwa and his city of Saubha.
Krishna bids farewell to the Pandavas.

XXIII

Vaisampayana: The citizens of Kurujangala lament the plight of the exiles.

XXIV

Vaisampayana: The exiles visit the sacred lake called Dwaitavana.

XXV

Vaisampayana: The exiles receive a brief visit from the Rishi Markandeya.

XXVI

Vaisampayana: The Rishi Vaka tells Yudhishthira how important it is for Kshatriyas to be associated with Brahmanas.

XXVII
Vaisampayana: Draupadi expresses her grief.

XXVIII
Vaisampayana: Draupadi quotes the words of Prahlada to his grandson Vali: On forgiveness.

XXIX
Vaisampayana: Yudhishthira speaks on anger and forgiveness.

XXX
Vaisampayana: Draupadi speaks of the perverse ways of God to man.

XXXI
Vaisampayana: Yudhishthira speaks of Virtue and Atheism.

XXXII
Vaisampayana: Draupadi speaks of Exertion.

XXXIII
Vaisampayana: Bhima speaks of virtue, wealth, and pleasure and advocates the use of force against Duryodhana.

XXXIV
Vaisampayana: Yudhishthira adheres to his agreement.

XXXV
Vaisampayana: Bhima expresses his impatience.

XXXVI
Vaisampayana: Vyasa appears and imparts to Yudhishthira the science called Pratismriti. Vyasa suggests that Arjuna should receive weapons and instruction from the gods.

XXXVII
Vaisampayana: Yudhishthira imparts the knowledge of Pratismriti to Arjuna. Arjuna meets Indra, who promises to give Arjuna the celestial weapons when Arjuna has obtained a sight of Siva.

XXXVIII
Vaisampayana: The austerities practised by Arjuna.

XXXIX

Vaisampayana: Arjuna's single combat with Mahadeva, who is in the guise of a Kirata. Arjuna's song of praise to Mahadeva, who embraces Arjuna.

XL

Vaisampayana: Arjuna asks for the Brahmasira weapon. Mahadeva gives him the Pasupata weapon.

XLI

Vaisampayana: Yama gives Arjuna his mace. Varuna gives Arjuna some Varuna weapons. Kuvera gives Arjuna his Antarddhana weapon.

XLII

Vaisampayana: Arjuna rides in Indra's chariot through self-effulgent regions. 'And in that region there was no Sun or Moon or fire to give light, but it blazed in light of its own, generated by virtue of ascetic merit.'

Matali (= Indra's charioteer) to Arjuna: 'These, O son of Pritha, are virtuous persons stationed in their respective places. It is these whom thou hast seen, O exalted one, as stars, from the Earth.' Arjuna reaches Amaravati (= the city of Indra).

XLIII

Vaisampayana: Description of Amaravati. Arjuna shares Indra's seat:

'And seated on one seat, the father and son enhanced the beauty of the assembly, like the Sun and Moon beautifying the firmament together on the fourteenth day of the dark fortnight.'

XLIV

Vaisampayana: Arjuna spends five years in heaven. From Chitrasena he learns dancing and 'the instrumental music that is current among the celestials and which existeth not in the world of men'.

XLV

Vaisampayana: Indra orders the beautiful Apsara Urvasi to use her wiles upon Arjuna.

XLVI

Vaisampayana: Arjuna treats Urvasi with the respect due to a mother. Urvasi curses Arjuna: he will pass his time among females like a eunuch. Indra decrees that this curse will operate only for the thirteenth year of exile.

XLVII

Vaisampayana: Indra instructs the Rishi Lomasa to guide and protect Yudhishthira and his brothers.

XLVIII

Vaisampayana: Dhritarashtra expresses his despondency to his charioteer Sanjaya.

XLIX

Vaisampayana: Dhritarashtra is anxious about the impending revenge from the Pandavas.

L

Vaisampayana: How the four sons of Pandu shoot deer for food.

LI

Vaisampayana: Dhritarashtra expresses his despair. Sanjaya informs him that Krishna has promised to be Arjuna's charioteer and to restore the kingdom to Yudhishthira.

LII

Vaisampayana: Yudhishthira explains his state of exile to the Rishi Vrihadaswa.

LIII

Vaisampayana: Vrihadaswa begins the long story of King Nala, 'a prince more miserable than thyself'. How Nala and the Princess Damayanti fall in love and how a swan carries messages between them.

LIV

Vaisampayana: Vrihadaswa: On his way to Damayanti's Swayamvara Nala is accosted by the gods.

LV

Vaisampayana: Vrihadaswa: Nala is obliged to tell Damayanti that Indra, Agni, Varuna, and Yama all desire to marry her.

LVI

Vaisampayana: Vrihadaswa: Damayanti expresses her love for Nala.

LVII

Vaisampayana: Vrihadaswa: At her Swayamvara Damayanti chooses Nala in preference to even the celestials. She sees the gods as 'unmoistened with perspiration, with winkless eyes, and unfading garlands, unstained with dust, and staying without touching the ground. And Naishadha (= Nala) stood revealed to his shadow, his fading garlands, himself stained with dust and sweat, resting on the ground with winking eyes'. Nala begets upon Damayanti a son and daughter, both called Indrasena.

LVIII
Vaisampayana: Vrihadaswa: Why the god Kali seeks to ruin Nala.

LIX
Vaisampayana: Vrihadaswa: How Kali begins to ruin Nala through a game of dice.

LX
Vaisampayana: Vrihadaswa: How Damayanti makes sure that the twins are taken to safety.

LXI
Vaisampayana: Vrihadaswa: Utterly ruined, Nala and Damayanti become exiles in the woods.

LXII
Vaisampayana: Vrihadaswa: How Nala, under the influence of Kali, deserts his wife in the woods.

LXIII
Vaisampayana: Vrihadaswa: How a hunter who kills a snake which has seized Damayanti himself falls dead after trying to force his attentions upon her.

LXIV
Vaisampayana: Vrihadaswa: Damayanti's eloquent lament and wild search for Nala.

LXV
Vaisampayana: Vrihadaswa: After some harrowing adventures Damayanti receives a comforting welcome from the royal family in the city ruled by Suvahu.

LXVI
Vaisampayana: Vrihadaswa: Meanwhile Nala receives help from a snake he has freed from a curse.

LXVII

Vaisampayana: Vrihadaswa: How Nala takes service with King Rituparna.

LXVIII

Vaisampayana: Vrihadaswa: How the Brahmana Sudeva, sent in search of Damayanti by her father, discovers Damayanti.

LXIX

Vaisampayana: Vrihadaswa: The queen mother who has looked after Damayanti turns out to be her aunt! How Damayanti is reunited with her father. The search for Nala now begins.

LXX

Vaisampayana: Vrihadaswa: How a messenger thinks he might have found Nala in the city of Ayodhya.

LXXI

Vaisampayana: Vrihadaswa: In Ayodhya a second Swayamvara for Damayanti is announced. King Rituparna orders his charioteer (= Nala under the pseudonym of Vahuka) to this Swayamvara.

LXXII

Vaisampayana: Vrihadaswa: During the journey Rituparna imparts to Nala the whole science of dice, whereupon Kali comes out of Nala's body, 'incessantly vomiting from his mouth the virulent poison of Karkotaka'.

LXXIII

Vaisampayana: Vrihadaswa: How Damayanti begins to suspect that Vahuka is really Nala.

LXXIV

Vaisampayana: Vrihadaswa: How Damayanti's suspicion grows.

LXXV

Vaisampayana: Vrihadaswa: How Damayanti's suspicion moves towards certainty.

LXXVI

Vaisampayana: Vrihadaswa: How Nala admits his identity, regains his proper form, and is reunited with his wife (in the fourth year after the loss of his kingdom).

LXXVII

Vaisampayana: Vrihadaswa: General rejoicing. Nala imparts to Rituparna 'the mysteries of equestrian science'.

LXXVIII

Vaisampayana: Vrihadaswa: How Nala, through a game of dice, regains his kingdom.

LXXIX

Vaisampayana: Vrihadaswa concludes the story, imparts to Yudhishthira the full science of dice, and departs for a bath.

LXXX

Vaisampayana: The four brothers lament the absence of Arjuna.

LXXXI

Vaisampayana: The Rishi Narada appears and begins to quote the words of Pulastya on the subject of tirthas and shrines.

LXXXII

Vaisampayana: Pulastya: The merits attaching to tirthas. Numerous tirthas named.

LXXXIII

Vaisampayana: Pulastya: As for LXXXII. The story of Mankanaka and the vegetable juice emitted by his finger.

LXXXIV-LXXXV

Vaisampayana: Pulastya: As for LXXXII.

LXXXVI

Vaisampayana: Yudhishthira expresses his dependence on Arjuna in the coming battle.

LXXXVII-LXXXIX

Vaisampayana: Dhaumya lists some tirthas and 'sacred asylums'.

XC

Vaisampayana: As for LXXXVII. The absolute pre-eminence of the asylum called Vadari.

XCI

Vaisampayana: The Rishi Lomasa arrives and tells the four brothers how Arjuna is faring in heaven.

XCII

Vaisampayana: Lomasa reports that he has been sent by Indra and Arjuna to conduct the four brothers on a pilgrimage to the tirthas.

XCIII

Vaisampayana: The pilgrimage begins 'on the day following the full moon of Agrahayana in which the constellation Pushya was ascendant'.

XCIV

Vaisampayana: Lomasa speaks on Virtue and Vice.

XCV

Vaisampayana: The pilgrimage proceeds.

XCVI

Vaisampayana: Lomasa begins the story of the Rishi Agastya:
How he slew Vatapi, younger brother of the Asura Ilwala.

XCVII

Vaisampayana: Lomasa: How Agastya marries Lopamudra.

XCVIII

Vaisampayana: Lomasa: How Agastya goes in search of wealth.

XCIX

Vaisampayana: Lomasa: How Agastya obtains wealth from the Asura Ilwala and begets a son called Dridhasyu (also called Idhmavaha) upon Lopamudra.
Lomasa also tells the story of Rama (= the son of Dasaratha), who was Vishnu incarnate, and Rama of Bhrigu's line:
The stringing of the bow and the humbling of Rama of Bhrigu's line.

C

Vaisampayana: Lomasa: How Twashtri made the Vajra weapon from the bones of the Rishi Dadhicha for the destruction of the Asura Vritra.

CI

Vaisampayana: Lomasa: How Indra slays Vritra with the Vajra weapon, and how the other Asuras make the ocean their fortress.

CII

Vaisampayana: Lomasa: How the Asuras terrorise the universe.

CIII
Vaisampayana: Lomasa: How the celestials ask Agastya for help.

CIV
Vaisampayana: Lomasa: How Agastya previously helped by preventing the expansion of Mount Vindhya, who was jealous of Mount Meru and had said to the Sun:

'As thou every day goest round Meru and honourest him by thy circumambulations, do thou even the same by me, O maker of light!'

CV
Vaisampayana: Lomasa: How Agastya drinks up the ocean, and how the gods vanquish the Asuras.

CVI
Vaisampayana: Lomasa: How Siva promises offspring to King Sagara.

CVII
Vaisampayana: Lomasa: How Sagara begets sixty thousand sons from one wife and one son from another. How the sixty thousand are slain. (All part of an involved account about the refilling of the ocean.)

CVIII
Vaisampayana: Lomasa: Description of the Himalayas.

CIX
Vaisampayana: Lomasa: How Ganga, granting the request of King Bhagiratha, 'running in three streams, was brought down to the Earth for filling the sea'. How Siva broke Ganga's fall after her leap from heaven.

CX
Vaisampayana: Lomasa: How Rishyasringa was born of a hind and why he was so called.

CXI
Vaisampayana: Lomasa: How Rishyasringa is tempted.

CXII
Vaisampayana: Lomasa: Rishyasringa speaks about the temptation to his father Vibhandaka.

CXIII
Vaisampayana: Lomasa: How Rishyasringa marries Santa (= daughter of King Lomapada), and how the drought ceases in Lomapada's country.

CXIV

The saint, Lomasa, conducts the sons of Pandu and the daughter of Drupada to the River Vaitarani. He explains why Rudra receives the best portions of sacrifices and tells how the goddess Earth was given to Kasyapa.

CXV

Akritavrana tells Yudhishthira of the birth of Jamadagni: 'to him, rivalling in lustre the author of light, came spontaneously and without instruction the knowledge of the entire military art and of the fourfold missile arms'.

CXVI

Akritavrana tells of Jamadagni's marriage to Renuka, of their five sons (of whom Rama is the youngest), of Renuka's death at Rama's hands, of her resuscitation, of Rama's combat with Arjuna ('the mighty lord of the Haihaya tribe'), and of Jamadagni's death.

CXVII

Akritavrana tells how Rama cremates his father's body and wreaks vengeance upon the entire military caste. Rama appears to the sons of Pandu, who worship him before starting their journey towards the southern regions.

CXVIII

The sons of Pandu perform ablutions at the bathing-places along the sea. They receive a reverential visit from Valarama and Krishna, the leaders of the Vrishni tribe.

CXIX

Valarama puts this question to Krishna: Why are the virtuous suffering, while the vicious flourish?

CXX

Satyaki wishes to help the Pandavas in battle, but to Yudhisthira 'truth seems to be the first consideration, above that of my sovereign power itself'.

CXXI

The Pandavas perform ablutions in the holy Payosini River. Lomasa says '... this period is the junction between the Treta and the Kali Age'.

CXXII

Lomasa tells the story of Chyavana and his austerities. He became an anthill and his eyes were pierced by the Princess Sukanya. To obtain forgiveness the princess became his bride.

CXXIII
Chyavana has youth and beauty bestowed upon him by the twin Aswins.

CXXIV
Chyavana is forbidden by Indra to offer Soma juice to the Aswins. He paralyses Indra's arm and creates a huge demon called Mada to devour the god.

CXXV
Indra quickly gives the Aswins the right to the Soma juice, and Chyavana distributes Mada 'piecemeal in drinks, in women, in gambling, and in field sports'.

CXXVI
Lomasa tells the story of Mandhata ['Me he shall suck'], who was born to his own father Yuvanasva (alias Saudyumni).

Indra put his forefinger into the baby's mouth, saying, 'He will suck me.' The boy grew to be a mighty and virtuous king.

CXXVII
Lomasa tells the story of King Somaka, who had only one son (Jantu) but wanted a hundred.

CXXVIII
Somaka's priest sacrifices Jantu, and a hundred sons are born, Jantu being reborn as the eldest. Somaka's gratitude to his priest and their common sufferings in hell.

CXXIX
The Pandavas bathe in the sacred lake near the field of the Kurus.

CXXX
Lomasa points out more sacred rivers and lakes.

CXXXI
Lomasa tells the story of King Usinara, whose virtues were tested and approved by Indra and Agni, who appeared unto him in the form of a hawk and a pigeon. [Cf. Section CLXVI.]

CXXXII

Lomasa begins the story of Swetaketu and his nephew Ashtavakra, who was born crooked in eight parts of his body after being cursed by his father Kahoda, who is later drowned after being defeated in debate by Vandin.

CXXXIII

With the object of defeating Vandin in debate, Ashtavakra gains admittance to the court of King Janaka. Janaka says:

'He alone is a truly learned man who understandeth the significance of the thing that hath thirty divisions, twelve parts, twentyfour joints, and three hundred and sixty spokes.'

CXXXIV

Ashtavakra, though only ten years old, defeats Vandin in magnificent debate, establishing the unity of the Supreme Being. Vandin is drowned, Kahoda is restored to life, and Ashtavakra's limbs are all made straight.

CXXXV

Lomasa begins the story of Bharadwaja's son, Yavakri, and his practice of the severest austerities in order to gain direct knowledge of Vedic lore for himself and for his father. Bharadwaja, attempting to curb his son's pride, tells him the story of Valadhi and his son Medhavi, who died when the mountains which were the instrumental cause of his life were shattered by buffaloes.

CXXXVI

On account of his insulting behaviour, Yavakri is killed by the power of the sage Raivya.

CXXXVII

Grieved by his son's death, Bharadwaja enters 'a full-blazing fire'.

CXXXVIII

Raivya is accidentally killed by his son Paravasu, but the austerities of his other son Arvavasu restore him to life, together with Bharadwaja and Yavakri.

CXXXIX

Lomasa takes the Pandavas to a dangerous stage of their journey: 'here flow before thee the seven Gangas. This spot is pure and holy. Here Agni blazeth forth without intermission. No son of Mann is able to obtain a sight of this wonder.'

CXL

Yudhisthira re-affirms the purpose of their journey: 'Those only that are impure meet with flies, gadflies, mosquitoes, tigers, lions, and reptiles, but the pure never come across them. Therefore, regulating our fare, and restraining our senses, we shall go to the Gandhamadana [Mountain], desirous of seeing Dhananjaya.'

CXLI

Lomasa tells how Naraka was slain by Vishnu; he also tells how the Earth in the Krita Yuga sank to the nether regions on account of overpopulation and how it was lifted up by Vishnu in the form of a huge boar with one tusk.

CXLII

On their way to the Gandhamadana Mountain the Pandavas encounter a dust storm and a thunderstorm which causes floods.

CXLIII

Draupadi becomes faint and has to be nursed by the Pandavas and the Brahmanas. Bhima summons his mighty Rakshasa son Ghatotkacha — merely by thinking of him.

CXLIV

Carried aloft by Rakshasas, the whole company soon reach the hermitage of Nara and Narayana beside the Kailasa Mountain. Description of the mighty jujube tree. Warm reception by the sages.

CXLV

To please Draupadi Bhima scours the Gandhamadana Mountain in search of a particular species of flower. Eventually his way is barred by his brother Hanuman, of whom there is a fine description.

CXLVI

Bhima cannot so much as lift Hanuman's tail. Reference to the *Ramayana*. Hanuman begins to tell the story of Rama and of the abduction of his queen by Ravana.

CXLVII

Hanuman recounts his leap across the ocean and the destruction of Lanka and Ravana. 'Then Rama recovered his wife even like the lost Vaidic revelation.' The boon granted to Hanuman was that he should live as long as Rama's fame.

CXLVIII
Hanuman teaches Bhima the characteristics of the four Yugas.

CXLIX
On Bhima's insistence, Hanuman reveals something of the mighty form he had at the time of his leap across the ocean. Hanuman instructs Bhima on the duties of the four orders.

CL
Bhima receives guidance and support from Hanuman, who makes further reference to Rama, 'who delighted the heart of the world; and who was as the Sun in regard to the lotus face of Sita, and also to that darkness — Ravana'.

CLI
At last Bhima reaches the mighty river where the special flowers grow.

CLII
At the lotus lake Bhima is challenged by the Rakshasa guards stationed there by Kuvera, the high-souled King of the Yakshas.

CLIII
Bhima vanquishes the guards and begins to gather the Saugandhika lotuses. Natural law and free land!

CLIV
Dreadful omens of battle bring Yudhishthira and company to the lotus lake.

CLV
Yudhishthira wants to go to 'the sacred abode of Vaisravana', but he is gainsaid by an aerial voice, which suggests a different route. In obedience, the Pandavas return to Vadari, the hermitage of Nara and Narayana.

CLVI
Once, Bhima being absent, Yudhishthira, the twins, and Draupadi are all carried off by the Rakshasa Jatasura. The king instructs the unheeding Rakshasa in virtue, pointing out that 'the gods, the Pitris, the Siddhas, the Rishis, the Gandharvas, the brutes and even the worms and ants depend for their lives on men'. Bhima arrives and kills the Rakshasa after a fierce encounter.

CLVII

The Pandavas have been in the woods for four years. In the fifth year they are due to rejoin Arjuna at 'the excellent cliff Sweta'. So they travel to the slopes of the Gandhamadana Mountain. Description of flora, fauna, and minerals. They approach the hermitage of 'the royal sage Arshtishena'.

CLVIII

Arshtishena questions Yudhishthira about his conduct, informs him of the ceremonies practised during the Parvas, and concludes: '... thou wilt at length rule the Earth, having conquered it by the force of thy arms'.

CLIX

Single-handed, Bhima clears the whole area of Rakshasas and destroys the Rakshasa Maniman. Description of the palace of Vaisravana, 'the Lord of Treasures' and 'Lord of the Rakshasas'.

CLX

Vaisravana (or Kuvera) comes out to meet Bhima and his brothers. Instead of being angry, he is delighted, for Bhima's action has ended an ancient curse laid upon Kuvera by the Rishi Agastya.

CLXI

Kuvera gives some instruction on 'propriety regarding place and time'. Reference to the Krita Yuga. Kuvera promises full support to the Pandavas. He refers to Arjuna as Phalguna, Dhananjaya, Jishnu, and Gudakesa.

CLXII

Dhaumya instructs Yudhishthira in 'geography', referring to Mandara, Mahameru, and the work of the Sun and Moon. 'O Bharata, dividing time into day and night, and Kala, and Kashtha, that lord, the Sun, dealeth life and motion to all created things'.

CLXIII

Arjuna, having studied the science of arms for five years in Vasava's abode and having obtained all the celestial weapons, comes to the Gandhamadana.

CLXIV

The Pandavas and Krishna rejoice to be reunited with Arjuna, who is referred to as Kiriti.

CLXV

The Pandavas are blessed with a short visit from Purandara, or Sakra, 'that graceful king of the immortals'.

CLXVI

Arjuna relates his combat with the disguised Shiva, 'the god Tryamvaka'. The god grants Arjuna his wish 'to learn all the weapons that are with thy god-head'. Various weapons mentioned by name.

CLXVII

Arjuna continues: From the base of the Himalaya Mountain I was taken by Matali, Sakra's charioteer, to Indra's abode, Amaravati. When I had acquired proficiency in weapons, Indra asked me to pay the preceptor's fee: the conquest of thirty million Danavas, called Nivata-Kavachas, living in the womb of the ocean. The gods gave me the conch Devadatta.

CLXVIII

Arjuna continues: With Matali as my charioteer I began the conflict with the Nivata-Kavachas.

CLXIX

Arjuna continues: The battle waxed fierce.

CLXX

Arjuna continues: The enemy used fearful illusions.

CLXXI

Arjuna continues: After defeating the enemy, I entered their marvellous city, which had formerly belonged to Purandara.

CLXXII

Arjuna continues: At Matali's bidding, and using the weapon called Raudra, I destroyed the aerial city called Hiranyapura. Purandara was well pleased with my exploits.

CLXXIII

Arjuna concludes his account of how the gods equipped him for battle.

CLXXIV

Arjuna begins to display the celestial weapons to his brothers. This has a devastating effect on all creatures, and the immortals hasten to stay Arjuna's hand.

CLXXV
After spending four years at the abode of Vaisravana (making a total of ten years in exile), the Pandavas begin to retrace their steps.

CLXXVI
They continue their return journey, spending a year in the forest of Visakhayupa.

CLXXVII
Bhima is seized and overpowered by a mighty snake.

CLXXVIII
The snake is really the royal sage, Nahusha, under a curse from Agastya.

CLXXIX
Nahusha was an ancestor of the Pandavas, and 'the son of Ayu and fifth in descent from the Moon'. Yudhishthira engages the snake in conversation about the nature of a Brahmana.

CLXXX
Yudhishthira questions the snake on the virtues and on the means of salvation. This releases Nahusha from the curse, and he leaves his serpentine form to return to heaven.

CLXXXI
A description of the rainy season and of autumn.

CLXXXII
The company is honoured by a visit from Krishna and his consort Satyabhama. Krishna is variously referred to as Hari, the son of Devaki, the slayer of Madhu, the leader of the Dasarha tribe, and Kesava. Another visitor is the deathless sage Markandeya, who delivers a discourse on the effects of men's actions.

CLXXXIII
Markandeya tells a story to show that death has no power over the Rishis.

CLXXXIV
Markandeya tells the story of Atri and how he praised King Vainya as 'the foremost of sovereigns'. Sanatkumara's words on sovereignty and the titles of kings.

CLXXXV

Markandeya tells of Tarksha's question about virtue and repeats the answer given by Saraswati, with its emphasis upon giving.

CLXXXVI

Markandeya tells the 'Legend of the Fish'. It concerns Manu, universal flood, and salvation in an ark towed by a great fish and settling on Mount Naubandhana. 'Manu will create (again) all beings', says the fish (Brahma in the shape of a fish).

CLXXXVII

Markandeya speaks of the Yugas, of the universal dissolution which he has witnessed, and of the boy whose stomach contains all creation.

CLXXXVIII

Markandeya repeats the boy's wonderful speech and his teachings on the Yugas.

CLXXXIX

Markandeya lists the signs of the end of the Yuga, and tells how Kalki, 'commissioned by Time' ... 'will inaugurate a new Yuga'.

CLXL

Markandeya speaks of the establishment of virtue in the new age. He instructs Yudhishthira in kingly duty.

CLXLI

To illustrate the greatness of Brahmanas, Markandeya tells the story of King Parikshit, the frog-princess, Vamadeva, and the Vami steeds.

CLXLII

Markandeya speaks of the meeting between Indra and the royal sage Vaka.

Vaka answers the question: 'What are the sorrows and joys of those that lead deathless lives?'

CLXLIII

To illustrate the greatness of the royal Kshatriyas, Markandeya tells how King Suhotra and King Sivi blocked each other's way and how Narada solved the problem by speaking of virtuous conduct.

CLXLIV

Markandeya tells the story of King Yayati and his gift of a thousand kine to a Brahmana.

CLXLV

Markandeya tells the story of King Vrishadarba and King Seduka.

CLXLVI

Markandeya tells how King Sivi was put to the test by Indra and Agni, who appeared as hawk and pigeon. The story is an exact parallel to that of Section CXXXI.

CLXLVII

Markandeya tells the story of four brothers — King Ashtaka, King Pratardana, King Vasumanas, King Sivi — and their conversation with Narada on virtuous conduct.

CLXLVIII

Markandeya tells how King Indradyumna lost and regained heaven. The story involves an owl, a crane, and a tortoise, and is ideal for retelling to children.

CLXLIX

Markandeya expatiates on virtue, morality and the practice of making gifts. Auspicious times connected with constellations are mentioned at the end of this section.

CC

Markandeya begins the story of how the royal Kuvalaswa of Ikshvaku's race changed his name to Dhundhumara:

The Rishi Utanka through penances obtains a boon from Vishnu (to whom there is a beautiful hymn).

CCI

The story continues: Utanka beseeches King Vrihadaswa to slay a Danava chief called Dhundhu who plans to conquer the celestials and the three worlds.

CCII

The story continues: Vrihadaswa, who has devoted himself to asceticism, tells Utanka that his son, Kuvalaswa, will slay Dhundhu.

The story backtracks: When the creation came to its end the Danavas

Madhu and Kaitabha were slain by Hari (= Govinda = Kesava = Vishnu).

[A striking account of inter-creation activity.]

CCIII

The story concludes: Dhundhu, the son of Madhu and Kaitabha, is slain by Kuvalaswa, who is known henceforth as Dhundhumara.

CCIV

King Yudhishthira beseeches Markandeya to discourse on the subtle truths of morality, and particularly on 'the high and excellent virtue of women'.

CCV

Markandeya tells how the Brahmana Kausika, having destroyed a she-crane which has fouled him, has to wait at a house while the lady serves her husband first. The lady's beautiful discourse on virtue appeases Kausika's wrath.

CCVI

The story continues: Kausika, on the lady's advice, goes to the city of Mithila and seeks out a fowler. The latter expatiates on virtuous conduct and refers to the duties of the four orders of men. 'Our mental faculties have their proper play when their foundation is laid in truth.'

CCVII

The story continues: The fowler expatiates on food and the question of flesh-eating, on Karma, on injury and non-injury. 'It is said authoritatively that herbs and vegetables, deer, birds and wild animals constitute the food of all creatures.'

CCVIII

The story continues: The fowler expatiates on Karma:

'It is the immemorial tradition that the soul is eternal and everlasting, but the corporeal frame of all creatures is subject to destruction here (below). When therefore life is extinguished, the body only is destroyed, but the spirit, wedded to its actions, travels elsewhere.'

CCIX

The story continues: The fowler expatiates on vice and virtue and on the seventeen qualities:

'This whole universe unconquerable everywhere and abounding in great elements, is Brahma, and there is nothing higher than this.'

CCX

The story continues: The fowler expatiates on the elements and the subjugation of the senses:

'Man's corporeal self has been compared to a chariot, his soul to a charioteer and his senses to horses.'

CCXI

The story continues: The fowler expatiates on sattwa, rajas, and tamas and their influence upon men.

CCXII

The story continues: The fowler speaks of Prana, Purusha, Samana, Apana, Udana, Vyana, purification, and Moksha. Biological information. 'Leniency is the best of virtues, and forbearance is the best of powers, the knowledge of our spiritual nature is the best of all knowledge, and truthfulness is the best of all religious obligations.'

CCXIII

The story continues: The fowler introduces the Brahmana to his parents and declares:

'These my father and mother, O Brahmana, are my supreme gods.'

CCXIV

The story continues: The fowler urges the Brahmana to return home and care for his parents. The fowler starts to speak of a former existence in which, as a Brahmana, he was cursed by a Rishi whom he had accidentally shot.

CCXV

The story concludes: The Brahmana takes his leave of the fowler and goes home to serve his parents. 'These wise men whose knowledge has made them happy and contented, and who are indifferent to happiness and misery alike, are really happy.'

CCXVI

Markandeya tells how Angiras became accepted as the son of Agni.

CCXVII

Markandeya lists the offspring of Angiras from his wife Subha.

CCXVIII

Markandeya gives the names of other descendants of Angiras, all connected with fire and sacrifice.

CCXIX

Markandeya speaks of Uktha and his son, and again of fire and sacrifice.

CCXX

Markandeya gives further genealogies of fire-gods and speaks of the sacrifices associated with them.

CCXXI

Markandeya concludes: 'I have thus described to thee the history of the great race of Agni who when duly worshipped with the various hymns, carry the oblations of all creatures to the gods.'

CCXXII

Markandeya tells how Indra rescued a lady by slaying an Asura named Kesin.

CCXXIII

The story continues: The lady is Devasena, a daughter of Prajapati. She beseeches Indra to find her an invincible husband. Indra refers the matter to Brahma, who promises that a husband for her will arise from the present conjunction of the Sun, the Moon, and Agni.

CCXXIV

The story continues: Swaha, in love with Agni, assumes the forms of various ladies beloved by Agni, and the result is a godlike being variously named Skanda, Guha, and Mahasena.

CCXXV

The story continues: The celestials, daunted by the prowess of Skanda, ask Vasava (Sakra) to destroy him. When Sakra refuses, the gods make the same request of the Mothers of the Universe. The Mothers consider Skanda to be invincible and they act as wet-nurses to him.

CCXXVI

The story continues: The gods, led by Sakra (= Vasava = Indra), come to attack Skanda, but they soon succumb and seek Skanda's protection.

CCXXVII

The story continues with a confusing account, partly to do with Skanda's offspring.

CCXXVIII

The story continues: Indra offers the lordship of the three worlds to

Skanda, who refuses this offer, but accepts the generalship of the celestial forces. A description of Skanda's appearance and his inborn virtues. He marries Devasena, whose other names are: Shashthi, Lakshmi, Asa, Sukhaprada, Sinivali, Kuhu, Saivritti, and Aparajita.

CCXXIX

The story continues: More beings give their allegiance to Skanda. Markandeya describes the evil spirits that mould the destinies of men: these include spirits that cause abortion and 'the evil spirits presiding over the destinies of young children, and until children attain their sixteenth year, these spirits exercise their influence for evil, and after that, for good.' All these are known as 'the spirits of Skanda'.

CCXXX

The story continues: Skanda grants Swaha her boon that she should forever be associated with Pavaka (= Agni). The story concludes with a terrific battle between the gods and the Danavas. The gods are eventually victorious, after Skanda slays Mahisha, the enemy leader. Markandeya lists the many names of Skanda and prays to Skanda with an enumeration of his other titles.

CCXXXI

Krishna (Draupadi) tells Satyabhama of her self-sacrifice in the service of the sons of Pandu. 'The husband is the wife's god, and he is her refuge.' Wifely duty.

CCXXXII

Draupadi continues her exposition of wifely duty.

CCXXXIII

Before departing with Kesava (= Krishna = Vasudeva), Satyabhama bids an encouraging farewell to Draupadi.

CCXXXIV

Dhritarashtra, hearing of the fortunes of the Pandavas, falls prey to gloomy forebodings.

CCXXXV

Sakuni and Karna suggest to Duryodhana a visit to the Pandavas, in order to deepen the latter's grief and their own happiness.

CCXXXVI

Duryodhana feels that Dhritarashtra will withhold permission, and so

Karna and Sakuni propose that the visit be made under the pretext of supervising the cattle stations.

CCXXXVII

Dhritarashtra reluctantly grants permission, and Duryodhana sets off with a magnificent retinue for the lake and forest named Dwaitavana, where the Pandavas are dwelling.

CCXXXVIII

Duryodhana's way to the lake is barred by Gandharvas, whose king has come to that region in search of amusement.

CCXXXIX

A mighty encounter takes place between the Gandharvas, led by their king Chitrasena, and the Kurus, prominent among whom is Karna.

CCXL

Duryodhana and many of his following are made captive by the Gandharvas, while the rest of his men seek the protection and help of the sons of Pandu. Bhima is sarcastic.

CCXLI

Yudhishthira instructs Arjuna to lead a party and procure the release of Duryodhana and his followers.

CCXLII

The Pandavas engage the Gandharvas in battle.

CCXLIII

After a great onslaught, the Gandharvas are subdued, and Arjuna converses with his friend Chitrasena.

CCXLIV

Chitrasena explains that his attack on Duryodhana (= Suyodhana) was to help Arjuna. At Yudhishthira's request Duryodhana is released and returns to his capital.

CCXLV

Duryodhana makes his way despondently towards Hastinapura and meets up with Karna, who is unaware of the intervention and rescue made by the sons of Pandu.

CCXLVI
Duryodhana tells Karna (= Radheya = the ruler of the Angas) of his defeat, captivity, and liberation.

CCXLVII
Sunk in misery, Duryodhana resolves not to return to Hastinapura and asks his brother Dussasana to be king in his stead.

CCXLVIII
Karna seeks to dissuade Duryodhana from his resolve to remain immobile and forgo all food.

CCXLIX
Duryodhana adheres to his vow of starvation. This alarms the Daityas and the Danavas, whose cause would be weakened by the king's death. By mantras and rituals they summon him to the infernal regions.

CCL
The Daityas and Danavas persuade Duryodhana to return in magnificent procession to Hastinapura.

CCLI
With Duryodhana's consent, Karna sets out to re-conquer the Earth for his master.

CCLII
Karna subdues the Earth and raises Duryodhana's hopes.

CCLIII
Duryodhana prepares to celebrate the Vaishnava sacrifice.

CCLIV
Duryodhana celebrates the Vaishnava sacrifice. The sons of Pandu are invited, but decline on account of their vow.

CCLV
Duryodhana receives general acclaim. Karna vows to slay Arjuna.

CCLVI
The sons of Pandu move from the Dwaita woods to the forest of Kamyakas, near Lake Trinavindu.

CCLVII

Vyasa visits the sons of Pandu and speaks to them of virtue, and of happiness and misery, declaring that there is nothing harder to practise than charity.

CCLVIII

Vyasa tells the story of Mudgala and the drona of corn:
How Mudgala passed the test set by the Muni Durvasa.

CCLIX

Vyasa concludes his story: Mudgala hears from a celestial messenger of the advantages and disadvantages of heaven and also of the region known as Para Brahma, the supreme seat of Vishnu. 'Misery after happiness, and happiness after misery, revolve by turns round a man even like the point of a wheel's circumference round the axle.' Vyasa departs.

CCLX

The irascible Muni Durvasa, pleased with the reception given him by Duryodhana, offers him a boon: Duryodhana requests him to visit the Pandava, hoping that the latter will be exposed to the Muni's curses.

CCLXI

After supper Durvasa descends on the Pandavas with ten thousand disciples. Draupadi, unable to feed them, prays to Krishna, who satiates all the visitors and extricates the Pandavas from a difficult situation.

CCLXII

One day, when Draupadi is alone, Jayadratha, the King of Sindu, is struck by her beauty and sends the Prince Kotika to question her on his behalf.

CCLXIII

Kotika introduces himself and the rest of the company to Draupadi.

CCLXIV

Draupadi, observing all decorum, welcomes the travellers as guests.

CCLXV

Draupadi is outraged by Jayadratha's offer of marriage.

CCLXVI

Jayadratha abducts the indignant Draupadi.

CCLXVII
The sons of Pandu overtake Jayadratha and his army.

CCLXVIII
The sons of Pandu open fire.

CCLXIX
Jayadratha's army is defeated, but he himself flees the battlefield, pursued by Bhima and Arjuna.

CCLXX
Jayadratha's life is spared by the mercy of Yudhishthira. The wicked Jayadratha seeks from the god Hara the power to defeat all the five sons of Pandu. He is told that this is impossible, but he will, for a single day, be able to subdue the four brothers (Arjuna excepted). Teaching on the cycle of the ages and the 'interval' between cycles. The meaning of the name 'Narayana'. Teaching on Vishnu. The story of 'The Incarnation of the Dwarf'.

CCLXXI
Yudhishthira asks Markandeya: 'Is there any one who is more unfortunate than I am?'

CCLXXII
Markandeya begins the story of Rama:
The birth of Rama and Sita and their parentage.

CCLXXIII
The story continues: The birth of Ravana, and how he gained the sovereignty of Lanka. The meaning of the name 'Ravana'.

CCLXXIV
The story continues: At the request of Brahma, Vishnu and all the celestials are incarnated on Earth to bring about Ravana's downfall.

CCLXXV
The story continues: The wiles of Queen Kaikeyi cause Rama's exile, while her son Bharata becomes ruler of Ayodhya. Rama provokes Ravana by mutilating his sister Surpanakha.

CCLXXVI
The story continues: At Ravana's instigation, his friend Maricha, disguised as a golden deer, lures away Rama and allows Ravana to carry off Sita. The abduction is watched by Jatayu the vulture.

CCLXXVII

The story continues: Jatayu attacks Ravana, but is mortally wounded. Sita is taken to Lanka. Rama and Lakshmana put off in pursuit, receiving direction from the dying vulture. They slay a headless Rakshasa, from whose body emerges a resplendent Gandharva named Viswavasu, who tells them to seek the aid of Sugriva, the brother of the monkey-king Vali.

CCLXXVIII

The story continues: Rama allies himself with Sugriva and slays Vali. Sita is guarded by Rakshasa women, through one of whom, Trijata, she receives news that Rama is on his way.

CCLXXIX

The story continues: Sita's rejects Ravana's advances.

CCLXXX

The story continues: Sugriva's monkeys search the Earth for Sita. Hanuman returns to say that with the help of Sampati, Jatayu's eldest brother, he has discovered Sita in Lanka.

CCLXXXI

The story continues: The monkey hosts assemble and march to the rescue. They cross the Ocean, who appears to Rama as Sagara, over a bridge built by the monkey Nala, the son of Tashtri, 'the divine artificer of the Universe'.

CCLXXXII

The story continues: When Angada, the monkey envoy to Ravana, is abused, Rama launches the attack on Lanka.

CCLXXXIII

The story continues: Ravana launches his counter-attack.

CCLXXXIV

The story continues: When his forces are repulsed, Ravana wakes his long-sleeping brother Kumbhakarna and sends him to the attack.

CCLXXXV

The story continues: Kumbhakarna is slain by Lakshmana.

CCLXXXVI

The story continues: Indrajit, the son of Ravana, joins the battle and wreaks havoc among the invaders.

CCLXXXVII
The story continues: After a fearful encounter, Lakshmana slays Indrajit. The enraged Ravana prepares to do battle himself.

CCLXXXVIII
The story continues: After a mighty conflict Rama slays Ravana.

CCLXXXIX
The story concludes: The gods and the elements persuade Rama to accept Sita again; the slain monkeys are restored to life; Rama's exile of fourteen years is over, and he joyfully receives the kingdom from his brother, Bharata, who has acted as regent.

CCLXL
Markandeya comforts Yudhishthira.

CCLXLI
Markandeya begins the story of King Aswapati and his beautiful daughter Savitri, named after the goddess who had bestowed her. The father sends his daughter out in search of a husband, for all are overawed by her beauty and celestial energy.

CCLXLII
The story continues: Savitri chooses as husband a man of excellent virtue named Satyavan, who has (according to Narada) but one year to live.

CCLXLIII
The story continues: Satyavan's father, the ascetic Dyumatsena, agrees to the marriage, and Savitri lives in the forest with her husband and her parents-in-law.

CCLXLIV
The story continues: The day dawns when Satyavan is doomed to die. Savitri, after a three-day fast and filled with anguish, accompanies her husband into the woods.

CCLXLV
The story continues with a most moving account: Yama takes away the vital essence of Satyavan and moves south, accompanied by Savitri, whose devotion and utterances on morality and righteousness move Yama to granting her four boons: 1) sight to the blind Dyumatsena; 2) restoration of kingdom to Dyumatsena; 3) a hundred sons to her father, Aswapati; 4) a hundred sons to herself and Satyavan. As a final boon she receives the life of her husband: the two start to return to the

hermitage. (Yama's other names and titles, with explanations, are given here.)

CCLXLVI
The story continues: Savitri relates everything to her anxious parents-in-law.

CCLXLVII
The story concludes with the fulfilment of the four boons.

CCLXLVIII
In the thirteenth year of the Pandavas' exile Sakra plans to ask Karna for his earrings. Surya warns Karna of the plan, but Karna is determined to keep his vow of giving to superior persons whatever they ask. He utters notable words on fame.

CCLXLIX
Surya repeats his warning to Karna.

CCC
Karna remains adamant to his vow — 'Death itself is not fraught with such terrors for me as untruth!' — but is persuaded to offer his earrings in exchange for an infallible weapon.

CCCI
Vaisampayana begins to tell Janamejaya of the secret which Surya did not reveal to Karna. King Kuntibhoja welcomes a Brahmana to his palace and offers his adopted daughter Pritha to be the Brahmana's attendant.

CCCII
The princess serves the Brahmana as if he were a very god.

CCCIII
After a year of being well served, the Brahmana gives Pritha 'those mantras which are recited in the beginning of the Atharvan Veda' and which can put any deity, when invoked, under the power of the speaker.

CCCIV
Out of curiosity, Pritha summons the sun-god Surya whom she has seen accoutred in mail and adorned with earrings. Surya offers to father a son similarly accoutred upon Pritha, but the latter refuses.

CCCV
At last Pritha succumbs to Surya's requests, but she remains a virgin.

CCCVI

Pritha gives birth to a son cased in mail and adorned with earrings. She consigns him in a wicker basket to the River Aswa, which carries him to the Ganga, via the Charmanwati and the Yamuna.

CCCVII

Karna is found and brought up by a charioteer named Adhiratha and his wife Radha. The child was also known as Vasusena and Vrisha. He learned arms from Drona, formed a friendship with Duryodhana, and was always challenging Arjuna to a fight.

CCCVIII

Karna exchanges his mail and earrings for 'a dart incapable of being baffled' from Indra. Origin of the name 'Karna' is given.

CCCIX

The Pandavas move from the woods of Kamyaka to the woods of Dwaitavana. There a deer entangles his antlers with the fire-sticks and churning-staff of a Brahmana and runs off with them. The Pandavas give chase, but the deer becomes invisible.

CCCX

Searching for water, Nakula, then Sahadeva, then Arjuna, then Bhima come to a lake guarded by a Yaksha. In defiance of his words they drink and drop dead.

CCCXI

Yudhishthira answers the Yaksha's questions (pages of riddles with deep significance) and regains the lives of his four brothers.

CCCXII

The Yaksha reveals himself as Yudhishthira's father, Dharma, the Lord of Justice. He grants a number of boons, including non-recognition of the Pandavas during their thirteenth year of exile, and the return of the fire-sticks and churning-staff, for he was the deer as well.

CCCXIII

Dhaumya tells the Pandavas of numerous occasions when the gods disguised themselves in order to overcome their foes, and then the brothers prepare for their year of non-recognition.

END OF VANA PARVA

VIRATA PARVA

I

The Pandavas decide to spend their thirteenth year in the city of Virata, King of the Matsyas. Yudhishthira will disguise himself as a dice-loving courtier and Brahmana named Kanka.

II

Bhima plans to work in the palace as a cook and wrestler under the name of Vallabha. Arjuna (= Dhananjaya = Gudakesa = Vibhatsu) will go as one of the neuter sex under the name of Brihannala and will instruct the women of Virata's palace in singing and dancing.

III

Under the name of Granthika, Nakula will act as keeper of the horses to King Virata. Under the name of Tantripal, Sahadeva will act as royal cowherd. Draupadi will act as a royal waiting woman in the service of Virata's queen, Sudeshna.

IV

Before taking his leave, Dhaumya expatiates on the conduct of a person in royal service. [Kingship and service.]

V

The brothers conceal their weapons on a mighty tree.

VI

Yudhishthira utters a beautiful invocation to the goddess Durga (= Kali), who appears and promises her protection. Explanation of the name Durga.

VII

Yudhishthira receives a most cordial welcome from Virata, who treats him as a friend.

VIII

Bhima receives a most cordial welcome from Virata, who appoints him superintendent of the royal kitchens.

IX
Draupadi enters the service of Queen Sudeshna.

X
Sahadeva is employed as chief of the royal cowherds.

XI
Arjuna is appointed royal dancing-master.

XII
Nakula becomes chief keeper of the royal horses.

XIII
In their respective capacities, the Pandavas give great delight to King Virata.

XIV
Kichaka, commander of Virata's forces, makes improper proposals to Draupadi.

XV
Draupadi invokes Surya and obtains the protection of an invisible Rakshasa.

XVI
Kichaka's advances are repulsed.

XVII
Draupadi urges Bhima to avenge her.

XVIII
Draupadi bewails the results of Yudhishthira's dicing.

XIX
Draupadi bewails the present plight of her husbands.

XX
Draupadi bewails her present plight. Her thoughts on Destiny.

XXI
Draupadi again exhorts Bhima to avenge her. Why the wise call a wife 'Jaya'.

XXII

Bhima slays Kichaka.

XXIII

Bhima rescues Draupadi from Kichaka's relatives, who want to cremate her along with the corpse.

XXIV

The populace, frightened by these acts of violence, hold Draupadi in awe.

XXV

Duryodhana's spies return to report their belief that the exiles have perished without trace.

XXVI

Karna suggests a renewed search.

XXVII

Drona supports the motion.

XXVIII

Bhishma declares that wherever the Pandavas are dwelling will be a place full of contentment and virtue.

XXIX

Kripa advises appraisal of one's present forces and those of allies.

XXX

Susarman, King of the Trigartas, advocates allied invasion of Virata's country; the attack begins.

XXXI

The year of non-discovery passes, and the Pandavas join Virata's army against the invaders.

XXXII

A fierce battle ensues.

XXXIII

Without revealing who they are, the Pandavas bring victory to Virata's forces over the Trigartas.

XXXIV
Virata praises the prowess of the Pandavas, but does not yet know their true identity.

XXXV
Meanwhile Bhishma, Drona, Karna, and Kripa have invaded Virata's domains and are driving off huge herds of cattle.

XXXVI
Back in the palace, Arjuna offers to act as charioteer to Virata's son Bhuminjaya (= Uttara), so that the latter may repulse the invading Kurus.

XXXVII
Uttara and Arjuna get ready for the fray. Knockabout comedy from Arjuna.

XXXVIII
More comedy, as Uttara, frightened by the prospect of the battle, jumps out of the chariot and runs off with Arjuna in pursuit. Arjuna seizes him and drags him back. Arjuna will fight and Uttara will be the charioteer.

XXXIX
Drona warns his side that they will be fighting Arjuna, but Karna welcomes the opportunity.

XL
Arjuna asks Uttara to fetch the bows of the Pandavas down from the tree where they have been hidden.

XLI
After some hesitation Uttara climbs the tree.

XLII
Uttara finds the weapons and asks about the owners. Details of individual bow, arrows, swords.

XLIII
Arjuna names the owners and gives more details of the weapons, including the history of the Gandiva. [A surname of Arjuna is Swetavahana.]

XLIV
To Uttara Arjuna reveals the true identity of himself and his four brothers. He states his ten names [Arjuna, Falguna, Jishnu, Kiritin,

Swetavahana, Vibhatsu, Vijaya, Krishna, Savyasachin, Dhananjaya] and gives their origin.

XLV
With Uttara as charioteer, Arjuna prepares to fight the Kurus.

XLVI
The sound of Arjuna's conch terrifies Uttara and confirms Drona's suspicion that Arjuna is here. Record of ill omens.

XLVII
Duryodhana thinks, but is not certain, that the year of non-recognition is not yet over.

XLVIII
Boasting of his own prowess, Karna declares that he will slay Arjuna.

XLIX
Kripa praises Arjuna and disparages Karna.

L
Aswatthaman disparages Karna and praises Arjuna.

LI
Bhishma supports Drona, but manages to heal the rift developing in the Kuru leadership.

LII
Bhishma calculates that the 13th year is well past and he draws up his battle-line [references to the divisions of time and their calculation], having sent Duryodhana back towards the city.

LIII
Arjuna turns aside from the opposing army to seek out the king.

LIV
The battle develops into a duel between Arjuna and Karna (= Vikartana's son), who eventually retires from the fray.

LV
Wreaking havoc among the Kuru ranks, Arjuna strives to approach Duryodhana.

LVI
The heaven becomes filled with all the celestials, who have come to watch the combat.

LVII
A fierce encounter between Arjuna and Kripa ends in the latter's overthrow.

LVIII
A fierce encounter between Arjuna and Drona [= the son of Bharadwaja] ends in the latter's withdrawal. Arjuna's description of Drona's virtues.

LIX
A fierce encounter between Arjuna and Drona's son Aswatthaman (in which the latter actually severs the bowstring of the Gandiva) ends when Aswatthaman's supply of arrows becomes exhausted.

LX
A fierce encounter between Arjuna and Karna ends in the latter's retreat.

LXI
Arjuna raises Uttara's drooping spirits, and wishing to fight with Bhishma (= Santanu's son = the son of Ganga), he re-enters the fray.

LXII
Arjuna's prowess creates a great river of blood, described in the most graphic terms.

LXIII
A mighty combat between Arjuna and Bhishma ends in the withdrawal of the latter.

LXIV
A mighty conflict between Arjuna and Bhishma ends in the flight of the latter.

LXV
With his weapon Sanmohana, Arjuna stupefies his foes. In rout they return to their city, and the celestials return to their respective abodes.

LXVI
The weapons of the Pandavas are again hidden in the tree, the cattle are

brought back, and Arjuna re-enters the city as Vrihannala, giving all the glory to Uttara.

LXVII

After the defeat of the Trigartas, Virata returns to his city, overjoyed at the news of the defeat of the Kurus. Angered by Yudhishthira's praise of Vrihannala, Virata strikes Yudhishthira on the face, causing blood to flow.

LXVIII

Uttara reproves his father, who then obtains Yudhishthira's pardon. Virata praises Uttara for his astounding victory.

LXIX

Uttara claims no glory, but assigns the full credit to 'the son of a deity' who appeared and disappeared.

LXX

The true identity of Yudhishthira is revealed and his virtues enumerated by Arjuna.

LXXI

The true identity of the other brothers and of Draupadi is revealed, and an alliance is made between the Matsya and the Bharatas.

LXXII

The marriage ceremony between the Princess Uttara, daughter of Virata, and Abhimanyu, son of Arjuna, takes place amid general rejoicing.

THE END OF VIRATA PARVA

UDYOGA PARVA

I

The following morning, in the council chamber of King Virata, Krishna proposes sending an ambassador to Duryodhana to request that half the kingdom be given to Yudhishthira.

II

Baladeva (Krishna's elder brother) supports 'the elder brother of Gada' and suggests that the ambassador should strive to pacify the Kurus.

III

Satyaki (= Yuyudhana) recommends that the ambassadors be sharp arrows.

IV

Drupada recommends an allied onslaught on the Kurus.

V

The Pandavas and the Kurus begin to gather their forces.

VI

Drupada sends his priest as envoy to the Kurus.

VII

Both Duryodhana and Arjuna go to the city of Dwaraka to solicit Krishna's aid. Given the choice, Arjuna selects Krishna as a non-combatant charioteer, while Duryodhana is delighted to receive ten crores of Narayanas to fight for him.

VIII

Salya, leader of mighty forces, is beguiled into agreeing to be commander of Duryodhana's armies. Salya pays his respects to his nephew Yudhishthira and promises that when he is driving Karna's chariot he will act in Arjuna's favour.

IX

Salya tells Yudhishthira a story:

Once Twashtri, 'the lord of creatures and the foremost of celestials', created a three-headed son to oppose Indra, who slew this being with his thunderbolt. In anger Twashtri created Vritra to kill Indra.
[Origin of the yawn.]

X

The story continues: With the help of Vishnu, Vritra is destroyed, but Indra becomes overpowered by the sin of Brahmanicide (the slaughter of the three-headed being), and the whole of creation suffers. [The attributes of Vishnu: notes on friendship.]

XI

The story continues: Nahusha is appointed King of the Gods, but his mind turns to sensuality. His designs on Sachi, Indra's queen, cause her to take refuge with Vrihaspati, the son of Angiras.

XII

The story continues: Creation suffers again, and the gods ask for Sachi to go to Nahusha. Vrihaspati suggests delaying tactics. [Morality: what happens if one abandons a person seeking protection.]

XIII

The story continues: Sachi asks Nahusha for time. At Vishnu's direction a horse-sacrifice is made to wipe out Indra's sin of Brahmanicide, but Indra becomes invisible. Sachi beseeches Night, the goddess of Divination.

XIV

The story continues: The goddess of Divination takes Sachi to where Indra (= Purandara) is hiding in the fibres of a lotus-stalk.

XV

The story continues: On Indra's advice Sachi asks Nahusha to have a palanquin made to himself, to be borne by Rishis. Vrihaspati sends Agni to search for Indra. In vain Agni searches, for he is unwilling to enter water:

'Fire rose from water, the military caste rose from the priestly caste; and iron had its origin in stone. The power of these which can penetrate all other things, hath no operation upon the sources from which they spring.'

XVI

The story continues: Vrihaspati enumerates Agni's attributes. Agni finds out Indra; the gods gather and request Indra to slay Nahusha. To Kuvera

Indra assigns sovereignty over the Yakshas and all the wealth of the world; to Yama, sovereignty over the Pitris; and to Varuna, sovereignty over the waters.

XVII
The story continues: The ascetic Agastya arrives and relates how Nahusha, for following the path of unrighteousness and turning Rishis into draught-animals, has become a snake, forced to roam the Earth for 10,000 years. General rejoicing.

XVIII
The story concludes with Indra's reinstatement as chief of the celestials, and Salya bids farewell to the Pandavas.

XIX
Many kings bring their troops to support the Pandavas.

XX
Drupada's priest goes to the Kurus and sues for peace and half the kingdom.

XXI
Dhritarashtra promises to send Sanjaya to convey his decision to the Pandavas.

XXII
Dhritarashtra instructs Sanjaya to parley with the Pandavas in fully conciliatory tones.

XXIII
Sanjaya (son of Gavalgana) and Yudhishthira exchange courtesies.

XXIV
Sanjaya speaks of peace.

XXV
Sanjaya sues for peace.

XXVI
Yudhishthira agrees to peace, provided that he is granted Indraprastha for his kingdom.
[Yudhishthira = Ajatasatru.]

XXVII

Sanjaya suggests that aggression from the Pandavas would be a grave sin under any circumstances.

XXVIII

Yudhishthira speaks of morality and duty in times of distress and other times. [Vabhru, the King of Kasi = the brother of (Sri) Krishna.]

XXIX

(Sri) Krishna speaks of the significance of work, the duties of the four castes, and the duties of a king. He supports the Pandavas.

XXX

Yudhishthira asks for his respects — instructive in their detailed nature — to be conveyed to the Kurus, together with his challenge to Duryodhana: 'Give me back my own Indraprastha or fight with me!'

XXXI

Yudhishthira again asks Sanjaya to convey his message of reconciliation.

XXXII

Sanjaya conveys the message to Dhritarashtra and refers to King Vali's consideration that the eternal Essence is the cause of everything. 'The eye, the ear, the nose, the touch, and the tongue, these are the doors of a person's knowledge. If desire be curbed, these would be gratified by themselves.'

XXXIII

Vidura (= Kshatri) instructs Dhritarashtra (= son of Ambika) in the attributes of wisdom and foolishness, and in the power of forgiveness; Vidura's words are strongly reminiscent of certain passages in Proverbs, and they are related to number. 'Discriminating the two by means of the one, bring under thy subjection the three by means of four, and also conquering the five and knowing the six, and abstaining from the seven, be happy.' ... 'That Being who is One without a second ... is Truth's self, and the Way to heaven, even like a boat in the ocean.' Vidura enjoins a just sharing of the kingdom.

XXXIV

More 'Wisdom' teaching from Vidura. 'One's body, O king, is one's car; the soul within is the driver; and the senses are its steeds.' Teaching on the nature of action.

XXXV

Vidura gives more 'Wisdom' teaching and tells the story of Virochana and Sudhanwan, suitors for the hand of Kesini. The destructive power of lies, the worst being lies for the sake of land.

XXXVI

Vidura speaks of the attributes of high families, and of the value of friendship.

XXXVII

Vidura teaches the principles of social morality: kings, masters, servants. [Dhritarashtra + son of Vichitravirya.]

XXXVIII

Vidura, still addressing Dhritarashtra, expatiates on morality: treatment of guests, administration of households and kingdoms.

XXXIX

Vidura gives many further epigrams on morality, urging Dhritarashtra to show justice to the Pandavas. The importance of a right attitude towards one's relatives.

XL

More Wisdom teaching from Vidura. 'Idleness, inattention, confusion of the intellect, restlessness, gathering for killing time, haughtiness, pride, and covetousness — these seven constitute, it is said, the faults of students in the pursuit of learning.'

'The person cast into the funeral pyre is followed only by his own acts.' The respective duties of the four castes.

XLI

Vidura summons the immortal Rishi Sanat-sujata to overcome the doubt in the mind of Dhritarashtra.

XLII

Sanat-sujata gives Dhritarashtra profound teaching on death, Yama, vice, virtue, rebirth, attainment of celestial regions, knowledge, ignorance.

XLIII

Sanat-sujata instructs Dhritarashtra in asceticism (mauna), the Vedas, the Chhandas, and the knowledge of Brahman. He gives the meaning of the root 'Diksha' ... 'In consequence of one's being able to expound every object (Vyakarana), one is said to be endued with universal knowledge (Vaiyakarana); and, indeed, the science itself is called Vyakarana owing to its being able to expound every object to its very root (which is Brahman).'

XLIV

Sanat-sujata discourses on the four steps of Brahmacharya and on the nature of Brahman.

XLV

Sanat-sujata discourses on morality. More on 'mada'; see also XLIII.

XLVI

Sanat-sujata utters magnificent rhetoric about Brahman; the primary seed called Mahayasas; accidents; the creature-Soul, identified as Iswara; Apana; Prana; will; intellect; picture of the body as chariot, etc.

XLVII

The following morning the Kuru leaders meet to hear Sanjaya's message from the Pandavas.

XLVIII

Sanjaya delivers the Pandavas' challenge, but puts the emphasis on the inevitability of battle, with resulting destruction for the Kurus. Catalogue of Krishna's past exploits. Names of weapons: Sthur-karna, Pasupata, Brahma. Reference to astrology.

XLIX

Bhishma relates ancient exploits of Nara and Narayana and identifies Arjuna and Krishna as these two gods: 'they are one Soul born in twain'. Both Bhishma and Drona strongly advise suing for peace with the Pandavas.

L

Sanjaya gives the Kurus an account of the opposing forces.

LI

Dhritarashtra expresses his overwhelming fear of Bhima and gives a description of Bhima, his exploits, his prowess, and his mace. Even so, Dhritarashtra regards the battle as inevitable. Reference to 'ever-fleeting Time' and 'the Wheel of Time.'

LII

Dhritarashtra expresses his fear of Arjuna and Krishna.

LIII
Dhritarashtra, fearful of the foe, recommends suing for peace.

LIV
Sanjaya censures Dhritarashtra for his previous actions and advises restraint over Duryodhana. Reference to 'the upraised Wheel of Time'.

LV
Duryodhana expresses his confidence in himself, his prowess with the mace, and in Bhishma, Drona, Kripa, and Karna.

LVI
Sanjaya describes the chariots and steeds of the Pandavas. [The celestial artificer is Tashtri = Bhaumana.]

LVII
Sanjaya describes the enemy ranks and shows how each division has been assigned a particular target. Dhritarashtra expresses despair, Duryodhana confidence.

LVIII
Dhritarashtra disowns Duryodhana for disobedience.

LIX
Sanjaya gives an account of the charming way he was received by Krishna and Arjuna. He describes the auspicious marks on Arjuna's feet.

LX
Dhritarashtra expresses his apprehension about the impending battle.

LXI
Duryodhana expresses confidence in his own prowess.

LXII
Karna expresses confidence, yet when aggrieved by Bhishma's words he says he will not fight.

LXIII
Vidura speaks of the characteristics of self-restraint.

LXIV
Vidura tells the story of the fowler and the two birds that quarrelled and talks of the hunters who perished trying to obtain 'immortal' honey. He urges peace.

LXV

Dhritarashtra expresses his apprehension.

LXVI

Sanjaya repeats Arjuna's challenge to the Kurus.

LXVII

The kings retire from council, and Dhritarashtra with his father Vyasa (= Krishna-Dwaipayana) and his queen Gandhari meet for further consultation with Sanjaya.

LXVIII

Sanjaya describes Krishna (= Janardana = Govinda = Kesava = Hari) and his discus. 'Wherever there is truthfulness, wherever virtue, wherever modesty, wherever simplicity, even there is Govinda.' ... 'Endued with divine attributes, Kesava, by the power of his soul causeth the Wheel of Time, the wheel of the Universe, and the wheel of the Yuga, to revolve incessantly.'

LXIX

Sanjaya speaks of his knowledge of Krishna (= Madhava = Hrishikesa = the divine son of Devaki). 'A man of uncontrolled mind can by no means know Janardana whose soul is under perfect command.'

LXX

Sanjaya, now acting as Dhritarashtra's spiritual preceptor, gives the various names of Krishna with their meanings.

LXXI

Dhritarashtra offers a hymn of praise to Krishna and commends himself to his protection.

LXXII

Meanwhile back in the Pandava camp: Yudhishthira speaks of prosperity and poverty; sin, hell, and salvation; the stages of a dogfight. Krishna offers to go to the Kurus to sue for peace.

LXXIII

Krishna speaks to Yudhishthira about the duties of the Kshatriyas. He again offers to go as an envoy, but considers battle inevitable. He lists some omens.

LXXIV
Bhima urges Krishna to address Duryodhana with all gentleness. He considers Duryodhana as typical of the vile individuals that spring up at the end of each Yuga.

LXXV
Krishna chaffs Bhima for his new-found mildness.

LXXVI
The fire in Bhima blazes up at Krishna's provocation.

LXXVII
Krishna praises Bhima and speaks of human actions and Providence.

LXXVIII
Arjuna supports Krishna's idea of going as an ambassador.

LXXIX
Krishna says, '... the wise men of old have said that human affairs are set agoing in consequence of the co-operation of both providential and human expedients.'

LXXX
Nakula supports Krishna's idea of going as an ambassador.

LXXXI
Sahadeva, Satyaki, and many others are eager for battle.

LXXXII
Draupadi pleads for violent revenge.

LXXXIII
Krishna sets off on his embassy. Description of his chariot. His attributes. Names of his steeds. Specific reference to the season, the month, the hour.

LXXXIV
The omens that accompany Krishna's journey.

LXXXV
Dhritarashtra utters the attributes of Krishna. The Kurus prepare a right royal welcome which leaves Krishna totally unimpressed.

LXXXVI

Dhritarashtra again sings the praises of Krishna and prepares to give him a lavish welcome. Reference to China.

LXXXVII

Vidura recommends simplicity of welcome and cautions Dhritarashtra against attempting to alienate Krishna from the Pandavas.

LXXXVIII

Duryodhana horrifies everyone by expressing his wish to imprison Krishna.

LXXXIX

Krishna receives a tumultuous welcome.

XC

Krishna (= Sauri) visits his paternal aunt Pritha (= Kunti), who expresses her pent-up grief about her five sons. Krishna reassures her.

XCI

Krishna refuses the royal banquet, but dines with Vidura. How Krishna speaks 'words that were clear, distinct, correctly pronounced, and without a single letter dropped'.

XCII

Vidura lists Duryodhana's attributes and points out to Krishna the futility of his peace undertaking.

XCIII

Krishna tells Vidura that the impending calamity is due directly to the action of Duryodhana and Karna.

XCIV

The following morning Krishna travels in pomp to the royal court. A delightful section, full of beautiful imagery: e.g. 'And Janardana attired in yellow robes having the complexion of the Atasi flower, sat in the midst of that assembly like a sapphire mountain on gold.'

XCV

Krishna, 'possessing fine teeth and having a voice deep as that of the drum', sues for peace. The function of an assembly with regard to righteousness.

XCVI

Krishna tells the story of King Dambhodbhava, whose pride was curbed by Nara and Narayana. The latter two he identifies with Arjuna and himself. Arjuna's weapons named: Kakudika, Suka, Naka, Akshisantarjana, Santana, Nartana, Ghora, Asyamodaka.

XCVII

The Rishi Kanwa begins the story of Indra's charioteer, Matali, who begot upon his wife, Sudharma, a beautiful daughter called Gunakesi. Matali searches unsuccessfully for a fit son-in-law.

XCVIII

The story continues: The Rishi Narada takes Matali on a conducted tour of the realm of the Nagas. Varuna's son is Pushkara, who has been chosen by Soma's daughter (= Jyotsnakali) for her husband. Matali sees the discus of Vishnu and 'that knotty bow that was created for the destruction of the world', from which Arjuna's bow has taken its name.

XCIX

The story continues: Narada shows Matali the city of Patalam 'in the very centre of the world of the Nagas'. Here is the Asura-fire; here the Amrita was quaffed by the gods; from here the waxing and waning of the Moon are seen; from here Vishnu fills the universe with sound. Description of the vow called 'Go'.

The elephants: Supratika, Airavata, Vamana, Kumuda, Anjana. Matali finds no fit son-in-law.

C

The story continues: Narada shows Matali the city of Hiranyapura. Reference to Daityas, Danavas, Asuras called Kalakhanjas, Rakshasas called Yatudhanas, Danavas called Nivatakavachas. Matali has no wish to choose anyone!

CI

The story continues: Narada shows Matali the region of birds, whose principal names are given. Their guardian deity is Vishnu. They all subsist on snakes and have no compassion.

CII

The story continues: Narada takes Matali to Rasatala, 'the seventh stratum below the Earth'. Surabhi, 'the mother of all kine'; her principal offspring; the Milky Ocean; the Foam-drinkers; the origin of the wine called Varuni, the goddess Lakshmi, Amrita, Uchchhaisrava, the gem Kaustubha.

CIII

The story continues: Narada takes Matali to the city of Bhogavati, ruled over by Vasuki, the King of the Nagas. Description of Shesha. Mention of Swastika. Names of famous Nagas. Matali plumps for the Naga called Sumukha.

CIV

The story continues: Narada asks Aryaka, Sumukha's grandfather, to bestow the young Naga on Matali's daughter. Aryaka hesitates, because Garuda has devoured Chikura, Sumukha's father, and has threatened to devour Sumukha. Narada obtains length of days for Sumukha from Sakra. Sumukha marries Matali's daughter.

CV

The story concludes: Garuda angrily boasts of his prowess before Vishnu, is humbled by the weight of Vishnu's right arm, and is reconciled to everlasting friendship with Sumukha. The story is wasted on Duryodhana, who dismisses it as 'these senseless declamations'.

CVI

Now present in the Kuru council chamber, Narada tells the story of Viswamitra (the only person we know of to rise from a lower order to become a Brahmana by ascetic austerities) and of the obstinacy of his disciple Galava.

CVII

The story continues: Galava is dejected because Viswamitra has asked him to make an impossible gift. Garuda offers assistance.

CVIII

The story continues: Garuda describes the eastern quarter (Purva) and speaks of all the wonderful events connected with it: e.g. 'It was here that the divine Creator of the universe first sang the Vedas ... Here first grew the hundred different branches of OM!'

CIX

The story continues: Garuda gives a similar account of the southern direction (Dakshina), 'the second door of Yama' ... 'It is here that the periods allotted to men are calculated in Trutis and Lavas.' ... 'This region ... is the goal of the acts of the dead.'

CX

The story continues: Garuda gives an account of the west (Paschima). Mention of the origin of the Maruts, and the movements of the Sun, the Moon, and the constellations.

CXI

The story continues: Garuda gives an account of the north (Uttara or Madhyama). [The significance of the names of all four quarters is given.]
Here dwell Krishna, Jishnu, Brahman, Maheswara. Origin of Ganga. The constellation Swati, the Sun, Moon, other luminaries. The abode of Ailavila (= Kuvera). Vishnupala (the footprint of Vishnu) = a place in this quarter.

CXII

The story continues: Garuda and Galava set off towards the east. [Garuda = son of Vinata = Tarkhya = younger brother of Aruna = Suparna.]

CXIII

The story continues: Garuda and Galava alight on the peak of the Rishabha Mountain and are welcomed by an ascetic lady named Sandili. On account of some contempt in his mind Garuda loses his wings, but the lady pardons him and restores his wings. Purity of conduct.

CXIV

The story continues: Garuda speaks of the creation and function of wealth (= Hiranya = Dhana). The constellations Purvabhadra and Uttarabhadra. Garuda takes Galava to King Yayati, son of Nahusha, to ask for help.

CXV

The story continues: Yayati gives his daughter Madhavi to Galava, who then offers her as a wife to Haryyaswa, King of Ayodha.

CXVI

The story continues: Haryyaswa gives 200 prescribed steeds to Galava and begets a fine son upon Madhavi, who then becomes a maiden again. The signs of feminine beauty.

CXVII

The story continues: The process is repeated with Divodasa, King of the Kasis. A list of gods (and others?) with their consorts.

CXVIII

The story continues: The process is repeated with Usinara, King of the Bhojas, who fathers a son named Sivi.

CXIX

The story continues: Galava offers Viswamitra 600 steeds + Madhavi. Viswamitra begets a son named Ashtaka upon Madhavi, who then returns to her father.

CXX

The story continues: Yayati holds a Swayamvara for his daughter, who, choosing the forest as her husband, devotes herself to ascetic austerities. Yayati dies and goes to heaven, where, much later, he is divested of his splendour on account of ignorance, folly, and pride.

CXXI

The story continues: Yayati falls to Earth, and his four grandsons (Pratarddana, Vasumanas, Sivi, Ashtaka) and his daughter Madhavi seek to help him.

CXXII

The story continues: By their merits Yayati returns to heaven.

CXXIII

The story concludes: Yayati is welcomed back in heaven.

CXXIV

Krishna makes a personal plea to Duryodhana.

CXXV

Krishna's plea is supported by Bhishma, Drona, Vidura (= Kshattri), and Dhritarashtra.

CXXVI

Bhishma and Drona repeat their plea.

CXXVII

Duryodhana disparages all advice.

CXXVIII

Duryodhana stalks out. Krishna recommends binding him, Karna, and Sakuni, on the principle, 'For the sake of a family a member may be sacrificed; for the sake of a village a family may be sacrificed; for the sake of a province a village may be sacrificed; and for the sake of one's soul the whole Earth may be sacrificed.'

CXXIX

Gandhari puts her own plea to her son Duryodhana. Her words on kingship.

CXXX

Duryodhana disregards his mother's words. He plans to capture Krishna. Vidura lists some of Krishna's qualities and exploits.

CXXXI

Krishna assumes a terrible form and departs.

CXXXII

Krishna visits his paternal aunt (Kunti). Her words on kingship and the Yugas:

'It is the king that createth the Krita, the Treta, or the Dwapara Age. Indeed, it is the king that is the cause of also the fourth Yuga (viz., the Kali).'

CXXXIII

Kunti begins a story which she would like Krishna to convey to the Pandavas:

The Princess Vidula upbraids her son, who is in depair after defeat. 'He that hath not achieved a great feat forming the subject of men's conversation, only increaseth the number of population. He is neither man nor woman.'

'A man is called Purusha because he is competent to trouble his foe (param).'

CXXXIV

The story continues: Vidula continues to upbraid her son for his lack of manliness.

CXXXV

The story continues: Vidula continues to upbraid her son Sanjaya:

'This will be — with such a belief should one, casting off all sloth, exert and wake up and address himself to every act.'

CXXXVI

Kunti concludes the story: Sanjaya is spurred into effective action.

'This history is called Jaya and should be listened to by everyone desirous of victory.'

CXXXVII
Kunti adds further encouraging words for Krishna to convey to the Pandavas.

CXXXVIII
Bhishma and Drona make a last-ditch plea to Duryodhana. They list the observable portents.

CXXXIX
Bhishma and Drona repeat their plea.

CXL
Krishna's conciliatory words to Karna.

CXLI
Karna shows a level-headed side to his character. He knows that his side will suffer, but that is the side to which he belongs.

CXLII
Krishna decrees that the battle will occur in seven days, the day of the new moon, 'for that day ... is presided over by Indra'. At the time of the battle 'all signs of the Krita, the Treta, and the Dwapara Ages will disappear (but, instead, Kali embodied will be present)'.

CXLIII
Karna speaks of all the omens portending battle. Planets and constellations named. He has had a vision of the defeat of the Kurus.

CXLIV
Kunti visits Karna, who is her son.

CXLV
Kunti reveals herself as Karna's mother and asks him to be reconciled to the Pandavas.

CXLVI
Karna declares his unwavering support of Duryodhana's cause.

CXLVII
Krishna tells the Pandavas what Bhishma has said in the council:
    Bhishma's parentage; his brother Vichitravirya; Santanu; the birth of Pandu and of Dhritarashtra.

CXLVIII
Krishna relates Drona's words spoken in the Kuru council:
Pratipa = father of Santanu. Santanu = father of Bhisma. Bhisma = Devavrata. The historical background to the impending battle. Vidura = younger brother of Dhritarashtra and nephew to Bhishma.

CXLIX
Krishna tells the Pandavas the words spoken by Dhritarashtra in the Kuru council:
A clear account of the origin and earlier history of the Kuru race.

CL
Krishna tells the Pandavas how the assembly ended and how eleven Akshauhinis, led by Bhishma, have marched to Kurukshetra. 'With death waiting before them, they have all become the cause of a universal destruction.' Bhishma = Ganga's son.

CLI
The Pandavas consider how their troops should be organised and, on Krishna's advice, they elect Dhrishtadyumna as their generalissimo.

CLII
The Pandava forces begin to move!

CLIII
The Pandava forces encamp on Kurukshetra. Their weapons, tackle, and supplies.

CLIV
Quick flashback to the gathering of the Kuru forces.

CLV
Krishna advises Yudhishthira that war is now the only course of action left open.

CLVI
The Kuru battle array. Men, beasts, tackle, weapons. Names of units and companies (e.g. Pattis, Gulmas, Ganas).

CLVII
Flashback to the appointment of Bhishma as the commander of the Kurus. The secret of victory. Fierce omens of calamity.

CLVIII
Rama (= Rohini's son = ? Halayudha) pays a brief visit to the Pandavas.

CLIX
Rukmi (= King Hiranyaroman = Bhishmaka's son) offers his fighting services to the Pandavas, but is rejected. His offer to Duryodhana is also rejected. The three celestial bows (Gandiva, Vijaya, Sarnga) and the gods associated with them.

CLX
Dhritarashtra and Sanjaya raise the question of destiny, free-will, sanskara.

CLXI
Duryodhana commissions Uluka to convey to the Pandavas many provoking words, including the story of the cat and the mice.

CLXII
Uluka conveys the message.

CLXIII
The Pandavas, in anger, instruct Uluka to convey a reply to Duryodhana.

CLXIV
The Pandavas give further messages to Uluka. The battle is due to take place tomorrow!

CLCXV
The next day Dhrishtadyumna draws up his battle-line and gives his leading warriors particular targets in the enemy ranks.

CLXVI
Bhishma, confident of victory, tells Duryodhana of the Rathas and the Atirathas in their ranks.

CLXVII
Bhishma names more Rathas in the Kuru ranks.

CLXVIII
Bhishma names more Rathas, Atirathas and Maharathas.

CLXIX
Bhishma names Karna as half a Ratha, and a quarrel breaks out between the two men.

CLXX
Bhishma begins to tell Duryodhana of the Rathas in the Pandava forces.

CLXXI
Bhishma names more Pandava heroes.

CLXXII
Bhishma names more Rathas, Atirathas, and Maharathas among the Pandava ranks.

CLXXIII
Bhishma completes his list of Pandava heroes.

CLXXIV
Bhishma begins to tell Duryodhana the story of why he will never fight with Sikhandin:
When his brother Vichitravirya was on the throne, Bhishma carried off three sisters (Amva, Amvika, Amvalika) as possible brides for Vichitravirya.

CLXXV
Bhishma continues his account: Amva, eldest daughter of the ruler of Kasi, has given her heart to another. She begs leave to go.

CLXXVI
Bhishma continues his account: Amva goes to the man she has chosen — Salwa, ruler of the Salwas — but she is rejected. [Bhishma's mother = Kali = Gandhavati.]

CLXXVII
Bhishma continues: Amva, in despair, seeks help from some ascetics.

CLXXVIII
Bhishma continues: The royal sage Hotravahana (= Amva's grandfather) advises her to seek the guidance of Rama (= Jamadagni's son).
Akritavrana, a friend of Rama, appears.

CLXXIX
Bhishma continues: Rama (= Bhargava = that foremost one of Bhrigu's race) appears. Amva's case is put to him.

CLXXX
Bhishma continues: Rama espouses Amva's cause and takes her to see Bhishma, whose death she now strongly desires.

CLXXXI

Bhishma continues: Rama commands Bhishma to take Amva to himself. Bhishma refuses. Single combat becomes imminent. The four types of weapon in the science of arms. [Bhishma's divine mother = the great River = Ganga.]

CLXXXII

Bhishma continues: In the single combat Rama seems to lose his senses. A superb encounter, showing the high standards of morality.

CLXXXIII

Bhishma continues: Round two! Bhishma swoons, Rama swoons. Weapons named: Vayavya, Guhyaka, Agneya, Varuna.

CLXXXIV

Bhishma continues: Round three! A fierce set-to.

CLXXXV

Bhishma continues: Round four! Bhishma swoons, Rama swoons.

CLXXXVI

Bhishma continues: That night victory is promised to Bhishma. Weapons named: Praswapa, Samvodhana.

CLXXXVII

Bhishma continues: Round five! The combat waxes exceedingly fierce. The Brahma weapon used.

CLXXXVIII

Bhishma continues: Rama submits! [Bhishma's mother = Bhagirathi.]

CLXXXIX

Bhishma continues: Amva, seeking Bhishma's destruction, undergoes ascetic austerities. On account of her perverse aim, half of her becomes a crooked river and the other half lives on as a maiden.

CXC

Bhishma continues: Rudra (= the divine lord of Uma = Kapardin) grants Amva her wish that she will one day slay Bhishma. Amva proceeds to walk into her own funeral pyre.

CXCI

Bhishma continues: To King Drupada (= Prishata) is born a daughter who is treated like a son. She is named Sikhandin.

CXCII

Bhishma continues: Sikhandin grows up and is married to the daughter of Hiranyavarman, King of the Dasarnakas. Hiranyavarman declares war when he discovers that his daughter has married a lady.

CXCIII

Bhishma continues: Drupada, in fear, seeks guidance from his wife.

CXCIV

Bhishma continues: Sikhandin seeks help from a Yaksha called Sthunakarna. [Drupada = Yajnasena.]

CXCV

Bhishma concludes: Sthunakarna and Sikhandin exchange sex, and peace is restored between Hiranyavarman and Drupada. Bhishma therefore refuses to harm Sikhandin, who was once a lady.

CXCVI

Bhishma and others consider how long it would take to annihilate the Pandava army.

CXCVII

The Pandavas take a final stock of forces.

CXCVIII

The Kuru forces encamp at Kurukshetra.

CXCIX

The Pandavas move into battle array.

END OF UDYOGA PARVA

BHISHMA PARVA

I

The two sides lay down combat regulations. Nature produces strange portents. The conches of Krishna and Arjuna are called Gigantes and Theodotes.

II

Vyasa grants celestial vision unto Sanjaya (= son of Gavalgani), that he may narrate all the details of the battle unto Dhritarashtra. 'Manifest or concealed, (happening) by day or by night, even that which is thought of in the mind, Sanjaya shall know everything. Weapons will not cut him and exertion will not fatigue him' Portents. Astronomy.

III

Portents. Astronomy. Power of Time. Signs of a victorious army and of an army in rout.

IV

Sanjaya tells Dhritarashtra of the nature of the Earth and gives a classification of creatures. 'Twenty-four in all, these are described as Gayatri (Brahma).'

V

Sanjaya speaks of the five elements and of the island called Sudarsana.

VI

Sanjaya begins a detailed account of the island of Sudarsana. The names of the seven Varshas. Mount Meru. Ganga (= Bhagirathi) and the names of her streams. Mount Gandhamadana.

VII

Sanjaya continues to describe Sudarsana. The huge Jamvu tree. Mount Malyavat.

VIII

Sanjaya describes more Varshas. The Lord Hari.

IX

Sanjaya describes Bharatvarsha and names its rivers and provinces.

'Earth, if its resources are properly developed according to its qualities and prowess, is like an ever-yielding cow, from which the three-fold fruits of virtue, profit and pleasure, may be milked.'

'If Earth be well looked after, it becometh the father, mother, children, firmament and heaven, of all creatures.'

X
Sanjaya lists the respective qualities of the four Yugas, including the measure of life.

XI
Sanjaya gives an account of Sakadwipa, and the Utopian life there. Rahu, Soma, Surya, the constellation Revati.

XII
Sanjaya describes the islands in the north. Seven more Varshas. The four princely elephants. The dimensions of the planet Swarbhanu, the Moon, the Sun, the planet Rahu.

XIII
Sanjaya reports to Dhritarashtra that Bhishma has been slain by Sikhandin.

XIV
Dhritarashtra's eloquent lament for his father Bhishma.

XV
Sanjaya speaks of the beginning of the battle.

XVI
Sanjaya: The two armies come face to face.

XVII
Sanjaya: Portents. Astronomy. The Kuru battle standards and their devices.

XVIII
Sanjaya: Many Kurus are appointed to protect Bhishma.

XIX
Sanjaya: The Pandava army is put into the battle array known as Vajra. The reason for this array. Portents.

XX

Sanjaya: How the Kurus were arrayed by Bhishma. The Kurus face west; the Pandavas face east.

XXI

Sanjaya: Arjuna tells the secret of victory:
 Truth, compassion, righteousness and energy.

XXII

Sanjaya: More about the Pandava forces.

XXIII

Sanjaya: Arjuna utters his hymn of devotion to Durga (= Kali = wife of Kapala = Mahakali = Uma = Sakambhari = mother of Skanda = Swaha = Swadha = Kala = Kashta = Saraswati = Savitra = Savitri.) Durga assures Arjuna of victory.

XXIV

Sanjaya: The two sides appear equal.

XXV

The Bhagavadgita begins: Sanjaya: Arjuna surveys both sides, is overcome by grief, and will not fight. Names of the Pandava conches.

XXVI

Sanjaya: Krishna encourages Arjuna: The immortality of the soul, the pairs of contraries: 'equanimity is called Yoga'; action and non-attachment; control of the senses.

XXVII

Sanjaya: Krishna speaks of work; sacrifice; duty; nature; desire. 'It hath been said that the senses are superior (to the body which is inert). Superior to the senses is the mind. Superior to the mind is the knowledge. But which is superior to knowledge is He.'

XXVIII

Sanjaya: Krishna speaks of the transmission of system; origin of castes; action; devotion; knowledge; sacrifice; the Pranas. 'Brahma is the vessel (with which the libation is poured); Brahma is the libation (that is offered); Brahma is the fire on which by Brahma is poured (the libation); Brahma is the goal to which he proceedeth by fixing his mind on Brahma itself which is the action.'

XXIX
Sanjaya: Krishna speaks of action; non-attachment.

XXX
Sanjaya: Krishna speaks of devotion and contemplation.

XXXI
Sanjaya: Krishna speaks of his higher nature and lower nature; the man of knowledge; Adhyatma, Adhibhuta, Adhidaiva, Adhiyajna.

XXXII
Sanjaya: Krishna speaks of death; Prana; devotion; the day and night of Brahman; the bright path, the dark path.

XXXIII
Sanjaya: Krishna speaks of his higher nature; worship.

XXXIV
Sanjaya: Krishna speaks of his universal nature.

XXXV
Sanjaya: Arjuna is vouchsafed a glimpse of Krishna's 'supreme form, full of glory, Universal, Infinite, Primeval, which hath been seen before by none save thee.'

XXXVI
Sanjaya: Krishna speaks of devotion.

XXXVII
Sanjaya: Krishna: 'This body ... is called Kshetra. Him who knoweth it, the learned call Kshetrajna.' The Supreme Purusha.

XXXVIII
Sanjaya: Krishna declares 'that supernal science of sciences' ... 'When an observer recognises none else to be an agent save the qualities, and knows that which is beyond (the qualities), he attaineth to my nature.' Description of the realised man.

XXXIX
Sanjaya: Krishna: The eternal Aswattha tree. Krishna's qualities and powers. Paramatman. Purushottama.

XL
Sanjaya: Krishna describes the demoniac nature.

XLI
Sanjaya: Krishna speaks of the three kinds of food; three kinds of sacrifice; penance of the body, penance of speech, penance of the mind; the three-fold designation of Brahma as OM, TAT, SAT.

XLII
Sanjaya: Krishna speaks of renunciation and abandonment and their three-fold nature; the five causes for the completion of all actions; the three-fold nature of knowledge, of action, of agent, of intellect, of constancy, of happiness; the respective duties of the four castes.
The Bhagavadgita Ends.

XLIII
Sanjaya: Arjuna takes Gandiva again, and the Pandavas rejoice. Yudhishthira pays due respects to Bhishma, Drona, Kripa (= Gautama = son of Saradwat), and Salya. Yuyutsu transfers his allegiance to the Pandavas.

XLIV
Sanjaya: The battle begins.

XLV
Sanjaya: The first clash.

XLVI
Sanjaya: The first clash (continued):
'The mighty-armed Bhishma ... with his standard which was made of silver and graced with the device of the palmyra with five stars, setting upon his great car, shone like the lunar orb under the peak of Meru.'

XLVII
Sanjaya: The battle rages.

XLVIII
Sanjaya: The battle rages on, centring on the encounter between Bhishma and Sweta, in which Sweta is slain. Both armies suspend hostilities for the night.

XLIX
Sanjaya gives more details of the first day's fighting.

L

Sanjaya: Krishna comforts the saddened Yudhishthira. Next morning the Pandava army forms a very special battle array known as Krauncharuma.

LI

Sanjaya: Preparations for the second day's battle. The names of the Pandava conches.

LII

Sanjaya: The battle now centres mainly on a well-matched combat between Bhishma and Arjuna.

LIII

Sanjaya: The combat between Drona and Dhrishtadyumna.

LIV

Sanjaya: Bhima single-handed takes on the whole division of the Kalingas. His prowess.

LV

Sanjaya: The battle rages till twilight. The advantage goes to the Pandavas.

LVI

Sanjaya: On the third day of battle the Kurus form the array called Garuda, and the Pandavas make a counter-array in the form of the half-moon.

LVII-LVIII

Sanjaya: The battle rages.

LIX

Sanjaya: Great slaughter. Bhishma exerts his prowess. Krishna sets out to slay Bhishma [a most beautiful description], but is restrained by Arjuna, who then exerts his prowess and releases the Mahendra weapon. End of day's fighting.

LX

Sanjaya: A new day's combat begins. Bhishma fights with Arjuna.

LXI

Sanjaya: The clash of arms. The prowess of Abhimanyu, Arjuna's son.

LXII

Sanjaya: The battle rages. Bhima's prowess in his encounter with ten thousand elephants.

LXIII

Sanjaya: Bhima wreaks havoc upon the entire Kuru army.

LXIV

Sanjaya: Bhima (= Satyaki) continues to wreak havoc. Twice he is struck senseless, one by Duryodhana and once by King Bhagadatta, but is protected by the Rakshasa Ghatotkacha. End of day's fighting; advantage to the Pandavas.

LXV

Dhritarashtra expresses dismay at the turn of the battle against the Kurus. He asks the cause of this. Sanjaya: Duryodhana wonders the same, and Bhishma gives this answer:

Long ago the celestials assembled, and Brahma uttered a hymn to Krishna. The words of the hymn.

LXVI

Sanjaya: Bhishma: Krishna promised that for the good of the Universe he would take his birth among mankind in the family of Vasudeva. More qualities and titles of Krishna. 'He it is who, towards the close of the Dwapara Yuga and the beginning of the Kali Yuga, is sung of with Sankarshana, by believers with devotion. It is that Vasudeva that createth, Yuga after Yuga, the worlds of the gods and the mortals, all cities girt by the sea, and the region of human habitation.'

LXVII

Sanjaya: Duryodhana asks Bhisma about the origin and glory of Vasudeva (= Krishna). Bhishma extols Krishna's infinite glories.

LXVIII

Sanjaya: Bhishma reports what Narada, Markandeya, and Bhrigu have said about Krishna. Duryodhana begins to 'regard highly both Kesava and these mighty car-warriors, viz., the sons of Pandu'. Bhishma again pleads with Duryodhana to seek peace.

LXIX

Sanjaya: The next day sees renewed fighting. The Kurus have a battle array called Makara, while the Pandavas form 'that invincible and prince of arrays called the Syena'.

LXX

Sanjaya: The battle rages.

LXXI

Sanjaya: The battle rages. Gandiva. Panchajanya. Arjuna's prowess. Portents.

LXXII

Sanjaya: The battle rages.

LXXIII

Sanjaya: The battle rages. Prowess of Aswatthaman (= son of Drona).

LXXIV

Sanjaya: Bhurisravas slays the ten sons of Yuyudhana (= Satyaki). The day's fighting ends.

LXXV

Sanjaya: A new day's fighting begins. Prowess of Drona. The Pandavas from the array called Makara.

LXXVI

Dhritarashtra describes his army, its training, its qualities, its weapons.

LXXVII

Sanjaya: Bhima's prowess. The devotion of Dhrishtadyumna (= Prishata's son) to Bhima. Dhrishtadyumna wields the weapon called Pramohana. Drona (= Bharadwaja's son) counters with the weapon called Prajna. The battle array called Suchimukha. Drona's prowess.

LXXVIII

Sanjaya: Prowess of Duryodhana and Bhima.

LXXIX

Sanjaya: Prowess of Abhimanyu.

LXXX

Sanjaya: Bhima wounds Duryodhana. Prowess of Abhimanyu. Dushkarna is slain. The day's fighting ends.

LXXXI

Sanjaya: Duryodhana is disconsolate. Bhishma comforts him by promising to exert himself to the utmost.

LXXXII

Sanjaya: The next day's battle begins. The Kurus form the Mandala array. The Pandavas form the Vajra array. Bhishma cures Duryodhana's wound with a herb. Arjuna's prowess. Arjuna invokes the Aindra weapon.

LXXXIII

Sanjaya: The battle rages. Drona slays Sankha, son of Virata.

LXXXIV

Sanjaya: The battle rages. The prowess of Bhagadatta, King of the Pragjyotishas. Nakula and Sahadeva vanquish their maternal uncle, Salya.

LXXXV

Sanjaya: The battle rages. Yudhishthira vanquishes King Srutayush. The wrath of Yudhishthira described.

LXXXVI

Sanjaya: The battle rages. Sikhandin wields the Varuna weapon.

LXXXVII

Sanjaya: The battle rages. Combat between Bhishma and Yudhishthira. End of day's fighting.

LXXXVIII

Sanjaya: Next day the battle is renewed. The Pandavas form the Sringataka array.

LXXXIX

Sanjaya: Bhima slays these sons of Dhritarashtra: Aparajita, Kundadhara, Panditaka, Visalaksha, Mahodara, Adityaketu, Vahvasin.

XC

Sanjaya: The battle rages.

XCI

Sanjaya: The prowess and death of Arjuna's son Iravat, begotten upon the daughter of the King of the Nagas.

XCII

Sanjaya: Combat between Duryodhana and the Rakshasa Ghatotkacha.

XCIII

Sanjaya: Ghatotkacha wreaks havoc among the Kurus.

XCIV
Sanjaya: The battle rages.

XCV
Sanjaya: The battle rages till sunset.

XCVI
Sanjaya: The battle rages. Prowess of King Bhagadatta and his elephant, Supratika.

XCVII
Sanjaya: Bhima slays these sons of Dhritarashtra: Vyudoroksha, Kundalin, Anadhriti, Kundabhedin, Virata, Dirghalochana, Dirghavahu, Suvahu, Kanykadhyaja. Deep night stops the fighting.

XCVIII
Sanjaya: Duryodhama tries to persuade Bhishma to leave the battle, so that Karna can go into action.

XCIX
Sanjaya: Bhishma promises: 'Tomorrow I will fight a fierce battle about which men will speak as long as the world lasts.' Next day the armies confront each other again.

C
Sanjaya: The Kurus form the Sarvatobhadra array. Portents.

CI
Sanjaya: The prowess of Abhimanyu, son of Arjuna and Subhadra. The Rakshasa Alamvusha (= the son of Rishyasringa) wreaks havoc among the Pandavas.

CII
Sanjaya: Abhimanyu vanquishes Alamvusha. Comparisons between the combatants and the heavens: Rahu, the Sun, the Moon, the planets Budha and Sukra (= Mercury and Venus).

CIII
Sanjaya: Combat between Arjuna and Drona. 'Shot by those two warriors, O king, the shafts looked beautiful in the welkin like cranes in the autumnal sky.' Arjuna wields the Vayavya weapon; Drona the Saila weapon.

CIV

Sanjaya: Bhishma's prowess. The battle rages. The warriors of the Kuru forces blame Dhritarashtra and Duryodhana.

CV-CVI

Sanjaya: The battle rages.

CVII

Sanjaya: Bhishma wreaks havoc among the Pandavas. Krishna prepares to slay him, but is restrained by Arjuna. Krishna's skill as a charioteer.

CVIII

Sanjaya: The day's fighting ends. At night Krishna and the sons of Pandu visit Bhishma (= Devavrata = the son of Ganga and Santanu). Bhishma tells them that he can be slain only by Arjuna shielded by Sikhandin.

CIX

Sanjaya: A new day's fighting begins. Sikhandin attacks Bhishma.

CX

Sanjaya: This is the tenth day of battle. Bhishma slays hundreds of thousands.

CXI

Sanjaya: The battle rages around Bhishma. Combat between Arjuna and Dussasana (= son of Dhritarashtra).

CXII

Sanjaya: The battle rages around Bhishma.

CXIII

Sanjaya: Drona speaks of the portents; the constellation called Parigha; his own sadness.

CXIV

Sanjaya: The prowess of Bhimasena.

CXVI

Sanjaya: The battle rages around Bhishma.

CXVII

Sanjaya: The battle rages around Bhishma. Bhishma's prowess.

CXVIII
Sanjaya: The battle rages around Bhishma. Arjuna's prowess.

CXIX
Sanjaya: The battle focuses more and more upon Bhishma.

CXX
Sanjaya: Bristling with arrows, Bhishma falls! His father granted him two boons: he would be incapable of being slain in battle, and his death would depend on his own choice. Since it is now the southern declension, he will hold on to life until the northern declension. 'The valiant and intelligent Bhishma, the son of Santanu, having recourse to that Yoga which is taught in the great Upanishads and engaged in mental prayers, remained quiet, expectant of his hour.'

CXXI
Sanjaya: A turning-point in the battle. The Kurus and the Pandavas go to Bhishma to pay their respects.

CXXII
Sanjaya: With three arrows Arjuna fashions a fitting pillow for Bhishma. Skilled surgeons are brought, but Bhishma asks for them to be dismissed.

CXXIII
Sanjaya: The next day all go to honour Bhishma. Arjuna shoots an arrow into the ground to provide a special jet of water for Bhishma. Bhishma's praise of Arjuna's qualities. Bhishma's plea for peace is unheeded by Duryodhana.

CXXIV
Sanjaya: Reconciliation between Bhishma and Karna (= Vrisha). Bhishma's balanced account of Karna's character. Karna feels he still has to fight, and he obtains Bhishma's permission to fight.

END OF BHISHMA PARVA

DRONA PARVA

I
Vaisampayana to Janamejaya: Sanjaya to Dhritarashtra: With the fall of Bhishma all the hopes of the Kurus turn to Karna.

II
Sanjaya: Karna pays tribute to Bhishma and takes up the challenge. Reference to the permanent presence of Lakshmi in the Moon.

III
Sanjaya: Karna represents Arjuna's prowess unto Bhishma.

IV
Sanjaya: Bhishma encourages Karna to be the champion of the Kurus.

V
Sanjaya: The Kurus rejoice at Karna's appearance.
Karna recommends that Drona should now lead the Kurus.

VI
Sanjaya: Duryodhana asks Drona to lead.

VII
Sanjaya: Drona accepts the leadership. Portents. The Kurus form the Sakata array. The Pandavas form the Krauncha array. Battle recommences. (Drona = son of Bharadwaja.)

VIII
Sanjaya: The prowess of Drona (= 'the pot-born'). He wreaks havoc among the Pandavas. He is slain by Dhristadyumna. [The remainder of the Drona Parva appears to be Sanjaya's account of the events leading to Drona's death.]

IX
Dhritarashtra lists Drona's virtues and grieves over his death.

X

Dhritarashtra swoons. On regaining his senses, he enquires about the battle.

XI

Dhritarashtra lists Krishna's qualities and achievements. How Krishna obtained the conch called Panchajanya, the discus called Sudarsana, and the celestial flower called Parijata.

XII

Sanjaya: Duryodhana commissions Drona to capture Yudhishthira alive. Drona promises to achieve this, provided that Arjuna is not protecting Yudhishthira.

XIII

Sanjaya: Yudhishthira learns of Drona's promise. Arjuna promises protection. Battle. 'Protected by Drona and Arjuna, both the hosts seemed to stand inactive like two blossoming forests in the silence of the night.'

XIV

Sanjaya: The prowess of Drona. Extended analogy between the battlefield and a river. Prowess of Abhimanyu.

XV

Sanjaya: A perfectly matched combat with maces between Bhima and Salya (= Artayani = the ruler of the Madras). Advantage to the Pandavas.

XVI

Sanjaya: The battle rages. Drona slays Vyaghradatta (= the Prince of the Panchalas) and Singhasena, and Kumara. End of day's fighting.

XVII

Sanjaya: Many warriors take a most solemn oath to slay Arjuna or die. This will leave Drona free to capture Yudhishthira. They challenge Arjuna to fight in the southern part of the field. Arjuna accepts, leaving Satyajit to protect Yudhishthira.

XVIII

Sanjaya: The combat begins. The blare of Devadatta. 'Then those thousands of arrows fell upon Arjuna, like swarms of bees upon a flowering cluster of trees in the forest.' Advantage to Arjuna.

XIX

Sanjaya: The combat continues. Arjuna slays thousands. He releases the Tvashtra weapon. Krishna becomes 'covered with sweat, and much weakened'. Arjuna uses the Vayavya weapon.

XX

Sanjaya: Meanwhile Drona puts his forces into Garuda formation. A fierce encounter around Yudhishthira. Striking similes.

XXI

Sanjaya: Drona's prowess. He wreaks havoc among the Pandavas. He slays Satyajit, Satanika (= the younger brother of the ruler of the Matsyas), King Kshema, Vasudeva, the Prince Panchala.

XXII

Sanjaya: An attack on Drona is led by Bhima.

XXIII

Sanjaya: A description of the horses and standards belonging to the Pandava heroes. Sutasoma is a son of Arjuna. Abhimanyu is 'regarded as superior to Krishna or Partha one and a half times in battle'. The names of bows: Vayavya (Bhima); Vaishnava (Nakula); Aswina (Sahadeva); Paulastya (Ghatotkacha); Raudra, Agneya, Kauverya, Yamya, Girisa (the five sons of Draupadi). Many fierce encounters around Drona. (Nakula's son is called Satanika). Salwa is slain by Bhimaratha (= brother of Duryodhana). Satanika slays Bhutakarman (= Sabhapati).

XXIV

Sanjaya: Combat between Bhima and Duryodhana. Bhagadatta (= the King of the Pragjyotisha) with his elephant (= Supratika) causes havoc among the Pandava forces. Even Bhima fails to overcome Supratika. Bhima slays the ruler of the Angas. Bhagadatta slays Ruchiparvan (= Kriti's son).

XXV

Sanjaya: Arjuna fights with his fourteen thousand opponents. 'Then Janardana became deprived of his senses and perspired greatly.' Arjuna shoots the Brahma weapon and slays his opponents.

XXVI

Sanjaya: Arjuna is now able to join the main battle and redress the balance.

XXVII

Sanjaya: Combat between Arjuna (= Indra's son) and Bhagadatta. Krishna protects Arjuna from the Vaishnava weapon hurled by Bhagadatta. Krishna tells the history of the Vaishnava weapon and speaks of his own four forms. Arjuna slays Supratika and Bhagadatta.

XXVIII

Sanjaya: Arjuna's prowess. He slays Vrishaka and Achala (= sons of the King of Gandhara). He uses the Jyotishka weapon and the Aditya weapon.

XXIX

Sanjaya: The battle rages around Drona.
   Aswatthaman slays Nila.

XXX

Sanjaya: The battle rages. Arjuna slays Satrunjaya and Vipatha (= brothers of Karna).

XXXI

Sanjaya: Abhimanyu is slain.

XXXII

Sanjaya: The qualities of Yudhishthira, Bhima, Arjuna, Nakula, and Sahadeva. The qualities of Abhimanyu.

XXXIII

Sanjaya: The events leading to Abhimanyu's death. While Arjuna is again called away to fight on the southern part of the battlefield, Abhimanyu prepares to penetrate the circular array of the Kuru forces.

XXXIV

Sanjaya: Abhimanyu penetrates the array and wreaks havoc upon the Kuru army.

XXXV

Sanjaya: Abhimanyu holds the entire Kuru army in check. He slays Sushena, Drighalochana, Kundavedhin, and the ruler of the Asmakas. He shocks Karna and causes Salya to faint.

XXXVI

Sanjaya: Abhimanyu slays the younger brother of Salya and turns back the foe. 'Only his trembling bow drawn to a circle could be seen on every side, looking like the blazing disc of the autumnal Sun.'

XXXVII
Sanjaya: Duhsasana (= son of Dhritarashtra) encounters Abhimanyu.

XXXVIII
Sanjaya: Abhimanyu causes Duhsasana to faint and distresses Karna.

XXXIX
Sanjaya: Abhimanyu slays the younger brother of Karna.

XL
Sanjaya: The Pandavas are checked by Jayadratha (= the ruler of the Sindhus) on account of a boon conferred upon him by the god Mahadeva.

XLI
Sanjaya: Prowess of Jayadratha. His chariot and standard.

XLII
Sanjaya: Prowess of Abhimanyu. He slays Vasatiya.

XLIII
Sanjaya: Abhimanyu slays Rukmaratha (= the son of Salya). He uses the Gandharva weapon. He turns back Duryodhana.

XLIV
Sanjaya: Abhimanyu (= the grandson of Dhritarashtra) slays Lakshmana (= grandson of Dhritarashtra) and the son of Kratha.

XLV
Sanjaya: Abhimanyu slays Vrindaraka and Vrihadvala (= the ruler of the Kosalas).

XLVI
Sanjaya: Abhimanyu slays the ruler of the Magadhas, Aswaketu, the Bhoja Prince of Martikavata, Satrunjaya, Chandraketu, Mahamegha, Suvarchas, Suryabhasa. He is deprived of his bow, his chariot, his sword, his shield. He attacks with a chariot wheel.

XLVII
Sanjaya: Abhimanyu is slain by Duhsasana's son.

XLVIII
Sanjaya: End of day's fighting. 'Then came that wonderful hour

intervening between day and night.' The battlefield at dusk: the carrion creatures.

XLIX
Sanjaya: Yudhishthira laments the death of Abhimanyu.

L
Sanjaya: Yudhishthira is visited by the great Rishi Krishna Dwaipayana. Yudhishthira asks him about the nature of Death. The Rishi begins the story of King Akampana, whose son Hari was slain in battle. Narada appears and, to comfort the grieving Akampana, tells this story:

Brahma became angry because the creation showed no sign of decay: his very anger begins to burn the universe, and Hara (= Sthanu = Siva) approaches Brahma to seek a boon.

LI
Sanjaya: Vyasa (= Krishna Dwaipayana): Narada: Sthanu (= Rudra = Mahadeva) beseeches Brahma to show mercy on the creatures. From Brahma's pent-up wrath emerges a lady called Death. Brahma commands her to slay the creatures. She is distressed and weeps.

LII
Sanjaya: Vyasa: Narada: The lady wishes no harm to the creatures and she practises severe austerities (measured in billions of years), but Brahma insists that she slay the creatures, saying that her tears will be diseases. (Origin and nature of disease and death.)

King Akampana is consoled by the story. Vyasa urges Yudhishthira to be consoled as well.

LIII
Sanjaya: Vyasa: The story of King Srinjaya (= son of King Switya). Srinjaya gave his daughter to the Rishi Narada, who was then cursed by the Rishi Parvata. Constitution of marriage. A son called Suvarnashthivin (= 'of golden excreta') is born to Srinjaya, but the boy is later slain by robbers. Narada consoles Srinjaya by telling him how even King Marutta (= son of Avikshit) had to die. [The four cardinal virtues are ascetic penances, truth, compassion, liberality.]

[The numbers LIV and LV do not appear, the next section being numbered LVI.]

LVI
Sanjaya: Vyasa: Narada: Even King Suhotra, noted for his endless gifts of gold, had to die.

LVII

Sanjaya: Vyasa: Narada: Even King Paurava had to die.

LVIII

Sanjaya: Vyasa: Narada: Even King Sivi (= son of Usinara) had to die.

LIX

Sanjaya: Vyasa: Narada: Even Rama had to die. (Rama's defeat of Ravana: the Utopian conditions in Rama's kingdom.)

LX

Sanjaya: Vyasa: Narada: Even King Bhagiratha, whom Ganga adopted as her father, had to die.

LXI

Sanjaya: Vyasa: Narada: Even King Dilipa (= son of Ilavila) had to die. 'In the abode of Dilipa, called also Khattanga, these five sounds were always to be heard, viz., the sound of Vedic recitations, the twang of bows, and Drink, Enjoy, and Eat!'

LXII

Sanjaya: Vyasa: Narada: Even King Mandhatri (delivered surgically by the twin Aswins from the womb of his father *(sic)* Yuvanaswa) had to die.

LXIII

Sanjaya: Vyasa: Narada: Even King Yayati (= son of Nahusha) had to die.

LXIV

Sanjaya: Vyasa: Narada: Even King Amvarisha (= son of Nabhaga) had to die.

LXV

Sanjaya: Vyasa: Narada: Even King Sasavindu had to die.

LXVI

Sanjaya: Vyasa: Narada: Even King Gaya (= son of Amartarayas) had to die.

LXVII

Sanjaya: Vyasa: Narada: Even King Rantideva (= son of Srinjaya) had to die.

LXVIII

Sanjaya: Vyasa: Narada: Even King Bharata (= son of Dushmanta) had to die.

LXIX

Sanjaya: Vyasa: Narada: Even King Prithu (= son of Vena) had to die. The bow of Siva, called Ajagava or Pinaka. The meaning of the words 'Kshatriya' and 'Raja'. How the Earth was milked.

LXX

Sanjaya: Vyasa: Narada: Even Rama (= son of Jamadagni) will have to die. 'Rooting out all evils from the Earth, he caused the primeval Yuga to set in.' Rama's gift of the Earth to Kasyapa (= Marichi).

Thus ends 'this sacred history of sixteen kings'.

LXXI

Sanjaya: Vyasa: Srinjaya is consoled by Narada's accounts. His son is restored to life.

Sanjaya: Vyasa consoles Yudhishthira and departs.

LXXII

Sanjaya: Krishna and Arjuna adore the goddess Twilight. Arjuna's lament over Abhimanyu.

LXXIII

Sanjaya: Arjuna vows to slay Jayadratha.

LXXIV

Sanjaya: When Jayadratha hears of Arjuna's vow, he seeks either protection or permission to leave the Kuru camp. Duryodhana and Drona promise him their full protection.

LXXV

Sanjaya: Krishna upbraids Arjuna for not consulting him prior to the vow.

LXXVI

Sanjaya: Arjuna re-affirms his vow.

LXXVII

Sanjaya: Krishna tries to console his sister Subhadra. Portents.

LXXVIII

Sanjaya: Subhadra's lament for her son Abhimanyu. 'Alas, O hero, thou hast been to me like a treasure in a dream that is seen and lost.'

LXXIX

Sanjaya: Bed-time preparations for Arjuna and Krishna. Krishna resolves to fight. He instructs his own charioteer, Daruka, to be ready. His mace called Kaumodaki. Panchajanya will emit the shrill Rishava note [the second note of the Hindu gamut].

LXXX

Sanjaya: That night Arjuna dreams: Arjuna travels with Krishna. They visit the god Bhava (= Sarva = Rudra = Kapardin = Mahadeva = Bhima = 'the Three-eyed' = Isana = the wielder of Pinaka = the father of Kumara = Sankara = Siva). Their hymn of adoration to the god. They request the weapon called Pasupata.

LXXXI

Sanjaya: Arjuna's dream: Siva (= 'the god having the bull for his mark') grants their request. Arjuna leans how to use the Pasupata weapon.

LXXXII

Sanjaya: Yudhishthira's morning ablutions and devotions as a king. Names of musical instruments. Swastikas.

LXXXIII

Sanjaya: Krishna promises Yudhishthira his assistance in the fulfilment of Arjuna's vow.

LXXXIV

Sanjaya: Arjuna prepares for battle. Good portents. Soma, Budha, Sukra.

LXXXV

Dhritarashtra bewails the present situation.

LXXXVI

Sanjaya attributes the present situation to Dhritarashtra's past actions.

LXXXVII

Sanjaya: Drona puts his forces into an array part Sakata and part a circle, 'full forty-eight miles long and the width of its rear measured twenty miles' ... 'In the rear of that array was another impenetrable array of the form of lotus. And within that lotus was another dense array called the needle.'

LXXXVIII
Sanjaya: Battle begins. Arjuna wreaks havoc among the Kurus.

LXXXIX
Sanjaya: Arjuna wreaks havoc.

XC
Sanjaya: Drona temporarily delays Arjuna in his progress towards Jayadratha. Drona even stuns Arjuna for a moment.

XCI
Sanjaya: Prowess of Drona. King Srutayudha, 'the son of Varuna, having for his mother that mighty river of cool water called Parnasa', is slain by his own mace. Arjuna slays Sudakshina, the Prince of the Kamvojas.

XCII
Sanjaya: Arjuna swoons from a lance thrown by Srutayus. Arjuna slays Srutayus, Achyutayus, and Srutayus *(sic)* (= the ruler of the Amvashthas).

XCIII
Sanjaya: Drona equips Duryodhana to fight against Arjuna by fastening the king's golden armour with special mantras. Drona tells the story of Siva, who gave these mantras (with armour) to Sakra to enable him to overcome the Asura named Vritra. (Vritra had been created by Tvashtri, the divine artificer, and had defeated the celestials.) Sakra, the lord of the celestials, slew Vritra and gave the mantras to Angiras, who gave them to his son Vrihaspati, who gave them to Agnivesya, who gave them to Drona.

XCIV
Sanjaya: The battle rages. Prowess of Drona and Dhrishtadyumna.

XCV
Sanjaya: The battle rages.

XCVI
Sanjaya: Widespread carnage. Dhrishtadyumna leaps upon Drona's chariot-shaft and fights with sword and shield. Satyaki, the Vrishni hero, rescues Dhrishtadyumna from Drona.

XCVII

Sanjaya: Combat between Drona and Satyaki (= Yuyudhana = Sini's grandson). All other warriors stop to watch. Prowess of Satyaki. Drona invokes the Agneya weapon; Satyaki invokes the Varuna weapon.

XCVIII

Sanjaya: Description of Arjuna's arrows. Their range is two miles. The chariot moves as fast as the arrows. Arjuna slays Vinda and Anuvinda, 'the two heroic brothers of Avanti'. Krishna stops the chariot to tend the steeds. Arjuna holds the entire opposition at bay and at the same time creates a lake to water the steeds and an arrowy hall.

XCIX

Sanjaya: Arjuna's prowess. 'Although staying on the ground, and alone, he succeeded yet in baffling all those kings on their cars, like that one fault, avarice, destroying a host of accomplishments.' When the steeds have been groomed and watered, the two Krishnas proceed towards Jayadratha.

C

Sanjaya: Picture of the two Krishnas painted by many literary images and similes. As they come within range of Jayadratha, they find their way barred by Duryodhana.

CI

Sanjaya: Arjuna and Duryodhana prepare to fight each other.

CII

Sanjaya: Arjuna, unable to harm Duryodhana, kills his charioteer and steeds and destroys his chariot. The battle rages. 'Kesava meanwhile forcibly and very loudly blew his conch Panchajanya, his face covered with dust.'

CIII

Sanjaya: The battle rages around Arjuna. Bhurisravas 'cut off the goad in Krishna's hand'.

CIV

Sanjaya describes Arjuna's standard and nine standards belonging to Kuru heroes.

CV

Sanjaya: Encounter between Drona and Yudhishthira. They both invoke the Brahma weapon. Advantage to Drona.

CVI

Sanjaya: Vrihatkshatra slays Kshemadhurti. Dhrishtaketu slays Viradhanwan. Satyaki slays Vyaghradatta, 'that Prince of the Magadhas'.

CVII

Sanjaya: The son of Yudhishthira slays Saumadatti (= son of Somadatta). Encounter between Bhima and the Rakshasa Alamvusha. Bhima uses the Tvashtri weapon. Advantage to Bhima.

CVIII

Sanjaya: Ghatotkacha slays Alamvusha.

CIX

Sanjaya: Yudhishthira urges Satyaki to rush to Arjuna's assistance. He relates Arjuna's praise of Satyaki.

CX

Sanjaya: Satyaki objects that he is under command from Arjuna to stay and protect the king. Yudhishthira repeats his instruction.

CXI

Sanjaya: Satyaki decides to obey Yudhishthira. He charges Bhima to protect the king.

CXII

Sanjaya: Satyaki cuts his way through the Kuru ranks.

CXIII

Dhritarashtra bewails the present situation.
Sanjaya: The battle rages. Prowess of Kritavarman (= son of Hridika), who 'held in check all the Parthas with their followers'.

CXIV

Sanjaya: Satyaki slays Jalasandha, 'the heroic ruler of the Magadhas'.

CXV

Sanjaya: Combat between Duryodhana and Satyaki (= Madhava = Satwata). Advantage to Satyaki. Combat between Satyaki and Kritavarman. Advantage to Satyaki.

CXVI

Sanjaya: Satyaki vanquishes Drona!

CXVII

Sanjaya: Satyaki slays Sudarsana.

CXVIII

Sanjaya: Satyaki makes his way through the Kuru ranks with terrible carnage.

CXIX

Sanjaya: Amazing prowess of Satyaki, 'surpassing Arjuna himself'.

CXX

Sanjaya: Satyaki vanquishes 'the mountaineers who battle with stones'.

CXXI

Sanjaya: Drona slays Viraketu (= the Prince of Panchala). Mighty conflict between Drona and Dhristadyumna. Advantage to Drona.

CXXII

Sanjaya: Satyaki vanquishes Duhsasana (= son of Dhritarashtra).

CXXIII

Sanjaya: Duryodhana penetrates the Pandava ranks.

CXXIV

Sanjaya: Drona slays Vrihatkshatra, Dhrishtaketu (= son of Sisupala), the son of Jarasandha, Kshatradharman, the son of Dhrishtaketu. 'The venerable Drona, full five and eighty years of age, dark in hue and with white locks descending to his ears, careered in battle like a youth of sixteen.'

CXXV

Sanjaya: Yudhishthira, anxious for the safety of Arjuna and Satyaki, decides to send Bhima to their rescue. Physical description of Arjuna.

CXXVI

Sanjaya: Bhima slays these sons of Dhritarashtra: Kundabhedin, Sushena, Dirghanetra, Vrindaraka, Abhaya, Raudrakarman, Durvimochana, Vinda, Anuvinda, Suvarman, Sudarsan.

CXXVII

Sanjaya: Bhima meets up with Arjuna and Satyaki. Their leonine roars reassure Yudhishthira.

CXXVIII
Sanjaya: Bhima vanquishes Karna.

CXXIX
Sanjaya: Conflict between Duryodhana and the two Panchala princes (the two brothers), Yudhamanyu and Uttamaujas.

CXXX
Sanjaya: Again Bhima vanquishes Karna.

CXXXI
Sanjaya: Another encounter between Bhima and Karna. 'Shafts equipped with vulturine feathers, shot by those two heroes, looked like rows of excited cranes in the autumn sky.'

CXXXII
Sanjaya: As Bhima gains the upper hand, he is attacked by Durjaya (= son of Dhritarashtra). Bhima slays Durjaya.

CXXXIII
Sanjaya: Bhima vanquishes Karna and slays Durmukha (= son of Dhritarashtra).

CXXXIV
Sanjaya: Bhima slays Durmarshana, Duhsaha, Durmada, Durdhara, and Jaya (all sons of Dhritarashtra).

CXXXV
Sanjaya: Bhima slays Chitra, Upachitra, Charuchitra, Sarasan, Chitrayudha, and Chitravarman (all sons of Dhritarashtra).

CXXXVI
Sanjaya: Bhima slays seven sons of Dhritarashtra: Satrunjaya, Satrusaha, Chitra, Chitrayudha, Dridha, Chitrasena, and Vikarna.

CXXXVII
Sanjaya: Renewed conflict between Bhima and Karna.

CXXXVIII
Sanjaya: After a terrific encounter Karna gains the advantage over Bhima. (Karna = Vrisha.)

CXXXIX

Sanjaya: Satyaki slays King Alamvusha.

CXL

Sanjaya: The prowess of Satyaki in his progress towards Arjuna.

CXLI

Sanjaya: Bhurisravas (= son of Somadatta) is about to slay Satyaki when Arjuna lops off the right arm of Bhurisravas.

CXLII

Sanjaya: Bhurisravas immediately takes to an ascetic way of life, but he is slain by Satyaki. Question of morality on the battlefield.

CXLIII

Sanjaya explains the previous episode by referring to an earlier event involving Sini and Somadatta.

CXLIV

Sanjaya: Arjuna vanquishes Karna. Arjuna invokes the Varuna weapon.

CXLV

Sanjaya: Arjuna causes widespread carnage. He invokes the Aindra weapon. Krishna produces an illusion of darkness; the Kurus relax a little, thinking it to be sunset; Arjuna cuts off Jayadratha's head and sends it right off the battlefield to land in the lap of Vriddhakshatra (= father of Jayadratha), who is saying his evening prayers. When the latter rises, the head falls to the ground and Vriddhakshatra's own head shatters into a hundred pieces, according to his own curse.

CXLVI

Sanjaya: Arjuna drives Kripa and Aswatthaman from the battlefield. Combat between Karna and Satyaki, with Satyaki on Krishna's own chariot, which is driven so skilfully by Daruka. Advantage to Satyaki.

'Thirty one of thy sons have been slain by Bhimasena.'

CXLVII

Sanjaya: Arjuna vows to slay Karna. Krishna gives a most striking description of the battlefield after sunset. 'The lords of the Earth, slain for the sake of Earth, are slumbering on the Earth clasping with their limbs the Earth like a dear wife.'

CXLVIII

Sanjaya: Yudhishthira offers a hymn of praise to Krishna:
'In the beginning, this universe, enveloped in darkness, had been one vast expanse of water. Through thy grace, O mighty-armed one, the universe became manifest, O best of men!'

CXLIX

Sanjaya: Duryodhana expresses his despair:
'I am covetous and sinful and a transgressor against righteousness.'

CL

Sanjaya: Drona ascribes the present situation to the disobedience of Duryodhana, but he promises to exert himself against the Pandavas. 'Having said these words, Drona proceeded against the Pandavas and set himself to override the energy of the Kshatriyas like the Sun overshadowing the light of the stars.'

CLI

Sanjaya: Karna speaks to Duryodhana about the power of Fate:
'Fate, ever intent on its own purposes, is awake when all else sleeps.'

CLII

Sanjaya: The battle continues after sunset. Duryodhana's prowess. 'Resolved to go to the other world, the Panchalas and the Kauravas fought with one another for admission into the swelling domains of Yama.'

CLIII

Sanjaya: The battle rages through the pitch dark night. 'Indeed, on that night, Drona alone pierced with his shafts, elephants in thousands and cars in tens of thousands and millions of millions of foot-soldiers and steeds.'

CLIV

Sanjaya: Drona slays King Sivi. Bhima slays the son of the ruler of the Kalingas and his brother Dhruva. Bhima slays Durmada and Dushkarna (= sons of Dhritarashtra).

CLV

Sanjaya: Aswatthaman vanquishes Ghatotkacha and slays Anjanaparvan (= Ghatotkacha's son = Bhima's grandson), a full Akshauhini of Rakshasa troops, Suratha and Satrunjaya (= sons of Drupada), Valanika,

Jayanika, Jaya, Prishdhra, Chandrasena, the ten sons of Kuntibhaja, and Srutayus. The Vajra weapon and the Vayavya weapon.

CLVI

Sanjaya: Bhima slays Valhika (= Pratipa's son and Somadatta's father). Bhima slays these sons of Dhritarashtra: Nagadatta, Dridharatha, Viravahu, Ayobhuja, Dridha, Suhasta, Viragas, Pramatha, Ugrayayin. Bhima slays Satachandra and Sakuni's five brothers: Gavaksha, Sarabha, Bibhu, Subhaga, Bhanudatta. Combat between Drona and Yudhishthira. Weapons: Vayavya, Varuna, Yamya, Agneya, Tvashtra, Savitra, Aindra, Prajapatya, Mahendra, Brahma.

CLVII

Sanjaya: Kripa (= son of Saradwat) criticises Karna for empty boastfulness. 'Kshatriyas evince their eminence by means of their arms; Brahmanas, by means of speech; Arjuna evinces his by means of the bow; but Karna, by the castles he builds in the air.'

CLVIII

Sanjaya: Arjuna vanquishes Karna.

CLIX

Sanjaya: Aswatthaman vanquishes Dhrishtadyumna.

CLX

Sanjaya: The battle rages. The Vayavya weapon.

CLXI

Sanjaya: Satyaki slays Somadatta. Combat between Yudhishthira and Drona. The Vayavya weapon.

CLXII

Sanjaya: Both sides carry lamps to illumine the dark battlefield.

CLXIII

Sanjaya: The battle continues.

CLXIV

Sanjaya: Kritavarman vanquishes Yudhishthira. 'Yudhishthira's armour, decked with gold, cut off by Hridika's son with his shafts, dropped down from his body, O king, like a cluster of stars dropping down from the firmament.'

CLXV
Sanjaya: Satyaki slays Bhuri. Combat between Aswatthaman and Ghatotkacha. Bhima vanquishes Duryodhana.

CLXVI
Sanjaya: Karna vanquishes Sahadeva.

CLXVII
Sanjaya: The ruler of the Madras slays Satanika (= brother of King Virata). Description of Alamvusha's chariot. Arjuna vanquishes Alamvusha.

CLXVIII
Sanjaya: The nocturnal battle rages on. Allusion to Mercury and Venus.

CLXIX
Sanjaya: Nakula vanquishes Sakuni (= Suvala's son). Kripa vanquishes Sikhandin. (Kripa = Gotama's son = Gautama).

CLXX
Sanjaya: Dhrishtadyumna slays Drumasena.
Combat between Satyaki and Karna.

CLXXI
Sanjaya: Satyaki vanquishes Duryodhana.
Advantage to the Pandavas.

CLXXII
Sanjaya: The nocturnal battle rages.

CLXXIII
Sanjaya: Karna wreaks havoc among the Pandavas. Arjuna asks Ghatotkacha to engage in single combat with Karna.

CLXXIV
Sanjaya: Ghatotkacha slays the Rakshasa Alamvusha (= son of Jatasura) and throws his head upon Duryodhana's chariot.

CLXXV
Sanjaya: Description of Ghatotkacha and his chariot. Combat between Ghatotkacha and Karna. The Vayavya weapon.

CLXXVI
Sanjaya: Duryodhana's army is reinforced by a great company of

Rakshasas, headed by Alayudha, who is seeking revenge for the death of Vaka and Kirmira and Hidimva at the hand of Bhima.

CLXXVII
Sanjaya: Combat between Bhima and Alayudha.

CLXXVIII
Sanjaya: Ghatotkacha slays Alayudha.

CLXXIX
Sanjaya: Karna slays Ghatotkacha with the infallible weapon called Naikartana which Sakra had given to him in exchange for his earrings. On falling, Ghatotkacha slays a full Akshauhini of his foes by his sheer weight.

CLXXX
Sanjaya: Krishna is delighted! He explains to the sorrowing Pandavas: Karna is now capable of being slain by Arjuna! Meaning of 'Vaikartana' and 'Vrisha'.

CLXXXI
Sanjaya: Krishna explains how Jarasandha and the ruler of the Chedis and Ekalavya were slain for the benefit of the Pandavas. Birth of Jarasandha and meaning of his name.

Krishna tells the truth about Ghatotkacha: 'Because he was a destroyer of sacrifices and of a sinful soul, therefore hath he been thus slain.'

CLXXXII
Sanjaya: Both sides wonder why Karna did not cast the weapon at Arjuna. Krishna (= Devaki's son) explains that he always stupefied Karna, adding, 'I do not regard my sire, my mother, yourselves, my brothers, ay, my very life, so worthy of protection as Vibhatsu in battle.'

CLXXXIII
Sanjaya: Yudhishthira mourns Ghatotka. Vyasa appears and promises Yudhishthira: 'On the fifth day from this, the Earth will be thine.'

CLXXXIV
Sanjaya: When midnight comes, both sides, taking their cue from Arjuna, cease fire and lie down to sleep. 'Elephants, heavy with sleep, made the Earth cool with the breath of their nostrils, that passed through their snake-like trunks spotted with dust.' ... 'That slumbering host,

deprived of sense and sunk in sleep, then looked like a wonderful picture drawn on canvas by skilful artists.'

'Then the Moon, that delighter of eye and lord of lilies, of hue white as the cheeks of a beautiful lady, rose, adorning the direction presided over by Indra. Indeed, like a lion of the Udaya hills, with rays constituting his manes of brilliant yellow, he issued out of his cave in the east, tearing to pieces the thick gloom of night resembling an extensive herd of elephants.'

CLXXXV

Sanjaya: Battle is renewed.

CLXXXVI

Sanjaya: Drona slays the three grandsons of Drupada, Drupada himself, and Virata. 'The east was soon reddened with the red rays of the Sun that resembled a circular plate of gold.'

CLXXXVII

Sanjaya: The Sun (= the thousand-rayed Aditya) rises. Duryodhana vanquishes Nakula.

CLXXXVIII

Sanjaya: Combat between Duhsasana and Sahadeva. Combat between Bhima and Karna. Combat between Arjuna and Drona. Weapons: Aindra, Pasupata, Tvashtra, Vayavya, Yamya, Brahma.

[The serial enumeration 'Section CLXXXIX' appears to have been omitted in the printed book.]

CXC

Sanjaya: The battle rages. Types of arrow regarded as improper.

CXCI

Sanjaya: To cause Drona's downfall, Bhima and Yudhishthira, encouraged by Krishna, tell untruths! The Brahma weapon.

CXCII

Sanjaya: Drona, now desperate, overcomes Dhrishtadyumna. Prowess of Satyaki. The Brahma weapon.

CXCIII

Sanjaya: Portents. Death of Drona at the hands of Dhrishtadyumna! 'Endued with great effulgence and possessed of high ascetic merit, he had fixed his heart on that Supreme and Ancient Being, viz., Vishnu. Bending his face slightly down, and heaving his breast forward, and closing his eyes, and resting on the quality of goodness, and disposing his heart to contemplation, and thinking on the monosyllable OM, representing Brahma, and remembering the puissant, supreme, and indestructible god of Gods, the radiant Drona of high ascetic merit, the preceptor (of the Kurus and the Pandavas) repaired to heaven that is so difficult of being attained even by the pious.'

CXCIV

Sanjaya: The Kuru army flees in total rout. Aswatthaman hears of the slaughter of his father.

CXCV

Dhritarashtra highly commends Aswatthaman's prowess.

CXCVI

Sanjaya: Aswatthaman vows to slay Dhristadyumna. How Aswatthaman was given the Narayana weapon.

CXCVII

Sanjaya: The Kuru forces rally. Meaning of Aswatthaman's name. Arjuna upbraids Yudhishthira for his untruth to Drona.

CXCVIII

Sanjaya: Bhima and Dhristadyumna speak in support of the actions leading to Drona's death.

CXCIX

Sanjaya: Dhrishtadyumna and Satyaki have a violent quarrel about Dhrishtadyumna's slaughter of Drona. Questions of battle morality.

CC

Sanjaya: Aswatthaman wreaks havoc among the Pandavas by invoking the Narayana weapon. Krishna explains that the only way to escape this weapon is to stand 'weaponless on the Earth'. But Bhima boldly goes into the attack, and the Narayana weapon falls upon his head!

CCI

Sanjaya: Krishna and Arjuna rescue Bhima from the Narayana weapon, which can be used once only. The battle recommences. Aswatthaman vanquishes Satyaki and slays Sudarshana and Paurava and the ruler of the Chedis. Combat between Bhima and Aswatthaman. 'At that time, Aswatthaman looked like the meridian sun of blazing rays in an autumnal day.' Bhima retreats when his driver falls unconscious. Arjuna attacks, and Aswatthaman invokes the Agneya weapon, which Arjuna baffles with the Brahma weapon.

Fleeing from the battlefield, Aswatthaman meets Vyasa, 'the abode of Saraswati, the compiler of the Vedas, the habitation of those scriptures, unstained by sin, and of the hue of rain-charged cloud.' Aswatthaman asks why his Agneya weapon was baffled. Vyasa explains: Narayana (= Vasudeva = Sauri) was once granted a boon by Rudra (= Hara = Sambhu) that he would have total invulnerability and absolute prowess in battle. Description of Rudra and his nature. 'From Narayana's asceticism was born a great Muni of the name of Nara, equal to Narayana himself. Know that Arjuna is none else than that Nara. Those two Rishis, said to be older than the oldest gods, take their births in every Yuga for serving the purposes of the world.' In a former life Aswatthaman was 'endued with great wisdom and equal to a god.' ... 'The Lord Kesava always worshippeth Siva in the phallic emblem as the origin of all creatures.' Aswatthaman now has the highest regard for Krishna. Aswatthaman withdraws the Kuru troops for the night, and the Pandavas also retire.

CCII

Sanjaya: Arjuna meets Vyasa. Arjuna says that another person continually preceded him in battle and actually defeated the foe.

Vyasa: This is Sankara = Isana = Mahadeva = Rudra = Hara = Sthanu = Sambhu = Sarva = Parumesthin = Siva = Maheswara = Purusha = Bhava = Parjanya = Surya = Varuna = Kala = Antaka = Mrityu = Yama = Dhatri = Vidhatri = Vahurupa = Durjjati = Viswarupa = Tryamvaka = Vyomakesa = Vrishakapi. 'In the Vedas the excellent hymn called Sata Rudriya, hath been sung in honour of that great god called the infinite Rudra.'

Vyasa explains the meanings of many of these names and lists some of Rudra's exploits, notable among which is his conquest of the Asuras in their triple city. For this conquest Rudra made of the Earth an astonishing chariot, possessing, among its many unique features, the Sun and Moon for its wheels, the four Vedas for its steeds, and the syllable OM for its whip. The whole description would sound superb side by side with Shakespeare's description of Queen Mab's coach!

CCIII

Sanjaya: 'The fruits that arise from a study of the Vedas arise from a study of this Parva also.'

END OF DRONA PARVA

KARNA PARVA

I

Vaisampayana (to Janamejaya): The Kurus make Karna their commander-in-chief. After two days of fighting, Karna is slain by Arjuna.

II

At Hastinapura, Sanjaya converses with Dhritarashtra, who is in great distress.

III

Sanjaya: With great energy Karna takes command of the Kurus until he is slain by Arjuna.

IV

Sanjaya (to Dhritarashtra): Vaikartana and Dussasana have been slain.

V

Dhritarashtra longs to know who is dead. Sanjaya gives the current battle-toll: Bhishma, Drona, Karna, Prince Vivingsati, Vikarna (= son of Dhritarashtra), Vinda, Anuvinda, Jayadratha, Bhurisravas, King Srutayus, Dussasana (= son of Dhritarashtra), Sudakshina, Chitrasena (= son of Dhritarashtra), Vrishasena, Rukmaratha, King Bhagiratha, Vrihatkshatra, Valhika (grandsire to Dhritarashtra), Jayatsena, Durmukha and Dussaha (= sons of Dhritarashtra), Durmarshana, Durvisaha, Durjaya, Kalinga, Vrishaka, Vrishavarman, King Paurava, etc, etc, etc.

VI

Sanjaya: The toll among the Pandavas: Satyajit, King Virata, King Drupada, Abhimanyu, the son of Amvashtha, Vrihanta, King Manimat, King Dandadhara, Ansumat, Chitrasena, Nila, Vyaghradatta, Chitrayudha, Chitrayodhin, Janamejaya, the brothers Rochamana, Purujit, Kuntibhoja, Abhibhu, Yudhamanyu, Uttamaujas, Mitravarman, Kshatradeva (= Sikhandin's son), Suchitra, Chitravarman, Vardhakshemi, Senavindu, Dhrishtaketu, Satyadhritri, Suketu, Sankha, Uttara, Satyadhriti, Madiraswa, Suryadatta, Srenimat, Vasudana, etc, etc, etc.

VII

Sanjaya gives a list of the great warriors who are still alive.

VIII

Dhritarashtra praises Karna and is unable to understand how he came to be slaughtered. 'Amongst steeds, Uchchaisravas is the foremost; [amongst] Yakshas, Vaisravana is the foremost; amongst celestials, Indra is the foremost; amongst smiters, Karna was the foremost.'

IX

Dhritarashtra is distraught by the enigma of Karna's death.

X

Sanjaya now begins the long account of events leading to Karna's death. Karna is installed as commander of the Kuru forces.

XI

Sanjaya: Karna puts his troops into the Makara array. The Pandavas form the half-moon.

XII

Sanjaya: Bhima slays Kshemadhurti (= the King of the Kulutas).

XIII

Sanjaya: Satyaki slays Vinda and Anuvinda of the Kaikayas (not to be confused with the two brothers previously slain by Arjuna).

XIV

Sanjaya: Srutakarman slays Chitrasena.
    Prativindhya slays Chitra.

XV

Sanjaya: Combat between Bhima and Aswatthaman.
    (Mars and Mercury.)

XVI

Sanjaya: Combat between Arjuna and Aswatthaman. 'An incorporeal voice said, "These viz., Kesava and Arjuna, are those two heroes that always possess the beauty of the moon, the splendour of fire, the force of the wind and the radiance of the sun."'

XVII

Sanjaya: Aswatthaman retreats from before Arjuna.
    The planets Sukra and Vrihaspati.

XVIII

Sanjaya: Arjuna slays Dandadhara, his brother Danda, and their elephants. The headless planet Ketu.

XIX

Sanjaya: Arjuna wreaks havoc among the Kurus. (The planet Mercury.) Krishna describes the battlefield to Arjuna. 'Behold, the Earth possessing the effulgence of the bright Moon and diversified as if with myriads of stars, looks like the autumnal firmament bespangled with stellar lights.' Arjuna and Krishna find Pandya destroying the Kuru host.

XX

Sanjaya: 'That force, swelling with cars and steeds and teeming with foremost of foot-soldiers, struck by Pandya, began to turn round like the potter's wheel.' Aswatthaman slays Pandya.

XXI

Sanjaya: The battle rages. 'The faces and the limbs of those slain in that dreadful battle looked like crushed lotuses and faded floral wreaths.'

XXII

Sanjaya: The battle rages.

XXIII

Sanjaya: Sahadeva vanquishes Dussasana.

XXIV

Sanjaya: Karna vanquishes Nakula and spares his life. Prowess of Karna.

XXV

Sanjaya: Uluka vanquishes Yuyutsu. Sakuni vanquishes Sutasoma.

XXVI

Sanjaya: Kripa vanquishes Dhrishtadyumna. Kritavarman (= Hridika's son) vanquishes Sikhandin.

XXVII

Sanjaya: Satyasena pierces Krishna's left arm with a lance. Arjuna slays Satyasena, King Satrunjaya, the son of Susruta, Chandradeva, Chitravarman, Mitrasena, and thousands more! The Aindra weapon.

XXVIII

Sanjaya: The battle rages. Elephants.

XXIX

Sanjaya: Yudhishthira vanquishes Duryodhana and spares his life.

XXX

Sanjaya: The battle rages. The day's fighting ends. 'Strewn with human heads that were adorned with white teeth and fair faces and beautiful eyes and goodly noses, and graced with beautiful diadems and earrings, and everyone of which resembled the lotus, the Sun, or the Moon, the Earth looked exceedingly resplendent.'

XXXI

Sanjaya: Karna vows to slay Arjuna the next day. Karna's bow, Vijaya: its manufacture and history.

XXXII

Sanjaya: Salya, the ruler of the Madras, condescends to be the charioteer of Karna. The origin and function of the four orders of men. Meaning of Salya's name and of his other name, Artayani.

XXXIII

Sanjaya: Duryodhana tells Salya a story:

The Daityas and the Danavas once built three cities — in Heaven, in the Welkin, on the Earth — which could be destroyed only by a single shaft which pierced through all three. They then oppress everyone else. The celestials seek the protection of the three-eyed god Sthanu. Their hymn of praise to Sthanu.

XXXIV

Sanjaya: Duryodhana: The celestials create a wonderful chariot, using all the parts of the universe. With Brahman as his charioteer, Sthanu destroys the three cities with one shaft. Why Sthanu came to be called Mahadeva. Description of chariot. Duryodhana tells Salya a second story:

Bidden by Maheswara (= Sthanu etc), Rama (= the son of Jamadagni) once vanquished the assembled Danavas. As a result, Rama received all the celestial weapons from Maheswara and passed the whole science of weapons to Karna. [Why horses are without teats, and why animals of the bovine species have cloven hooves.]

XXXV

Sanjaya: The meaning of Salya's name.

He agrees to become Karna's charioteer provided that he may speak whatever he wishes.

XXXVI
Sanjaya: Karna and Salya prepare for battle.

XXXVII
Sanjaya: Portents. 'The seven great planets including the Sun seemed to proceed against one another (for combat).' Karna proceeds to battle, while Salya speaks harsh words to him.

XXXVIII
Sanjaya: Karna promises great wealth to the Pandava soldier that will indicate Arjuna to him.

XXXIX
Sanjaya: Salya's harsh words to Karna. 'Thou art always a jackal, and Dhananjaya always a lion.'

XL
Sanjaya: Karna makes many insulting remarks about Salya and the Madrakas.

XLI
Sanjaya: Salya tells Karna the story of the crow and the swan.

XLII
Sanjaya: Karna speaks of two curses put upon him — one by Rama and one by a Brahmana.

XLIII
Sanjaya: Karna upbraids Salya for his harsh words.

XLIV
Sanjaya: Karna makes more disparaging remarks about the Madrakas.

XLV
Sanjaya: Karna makes further disparaging remarks.
    Immorality: intoxication, adultery, abortion, theft.

XLVI
Sanjaya: The two armies clash in battle.
    Portents. The Sun is eclipsed by Ketu.

XLVII
Sanjaya: The battle rages.

XLVIII

Sanjaya: The battle rages. Bhima slays Bhanusena (= a son of Karna).

XLIX

Sanjaya: Karna vanquishes Yudhishthira.
The Kurus begin to retreat. Karna invokes the Brahma weapon. The constellation Punarvasu. The slain heroes are received in the sky by heavenly choristers and taken towards the region of Indra.

L

Sanjaya: Bhima vanquishes Karna.

LI

Sanjaya: Bhima slays Vivitsu, Vikata, Saha, Nanda, Upananda (= sons of Dhritarashtra). Bhima encounters Karna. Bhima slays a thousand elephants, three thousand horses, etc, etc.

LII

Sanjaya: The battle rages.

LIII

Sanjaya: Arjuna and Krishna are assailed at close quarters. Arjuna uses the Naga weapon, which causes snakes to fetter the legs of the foe. Susarman invokes the Sauparna weapon, which causes birds to devour the snakes. Arjuna is stunned by Susarman. The Aindra weapon. Arjuna slays 27,000 warriors and 3,000 elephants.

LIV

Sanjaya: Kripa slays Suketu (= son of Shitraketu).

LV

Sanjaya: Yudhishthira retreats from before Aswatthaman.

LVI

Sanjaya: Dhrishtadyumna overcomes Duryodhana.
Karna slays Jishnu, Jishnukarman, Devapi, Chitra, Chitrayudha, Hari, Singhaketu, Rochamana, Salabha. Aswatthaman holds Arjuna and Krishna in check! Arjuna vanquishes Aswatthaman.

LVII

Sanjaya: Aswatthaman vows to slay Dhrishtadyumna.

LVIII

Sanjaya: Krishna gives Arjuna a beautiful description of the whole battlefield.

LIX

Sanjaya: Arjuna rescues Dhrishtadyumna from the hands of Aswatthaman.

LX

Sanjaya: Krishna describes to Arjuna the actions occurring all over the battlefield.

LXI-LXII

Sanjaya: The battle rages.

LXIII

Sanjaya: Yudhishthira, 'exceedingly mangled with shafts', retreats to the Pandava camp.

LXIV

Sanjaya: Arjuna causes great carnage. The Aindra weapon. Karna wreaks havoc with the Bhargava weapon.

LXV

Sanjaya: Arjuna and Krishna visit Yudhishthira in the camp.

LXVI

Sanjaya: Assuming that Karna has been slain, Yudhishthira is overjoyed.

LXVII

Sanjaya: Arjuna gives Yudhishthira the facts and promises to slay Karna.

LXVIII

Sanjaya: Yudhishthira accuses Arjuna of cowardice, etc. The heavenly words spoken of Arjuna seven days after his birth.

LXIX

Sanjaya: Arjuna draws his sword to slay Yudhishthira! Krishna interposes. Krishna speaks of the five kinds of sinless falsehood. Morality. Krishna tells the story of Valaka and the blind beast, and the story of Kausika 'living among the rivers'.

LXX

Sanjaya: To keep a vow, Arjuna, urged by Krishna, upbraids Yudhishthira and vaunts his own prowess.

LXXI

Sanjaya: Yudhishthira and Arjuna are reconciled to each other. Arjuna again vows to slay Karna.

LXXII

Sanjaya: Arjuna proceeds to the attack! 'All the points of the compass, O king, became serene. Kingfishers and parrots and herons, O king, wheeled around the son of Pandu.' Krishna's assessment of Karna.

LXXIII

Sanjaya: Krishna gives Arjuna a summary of the battle since its inception seventeen days ago. Krishna exhorts Arjuna to slay Karna.

LXXIV

Sanjaya: Arjuna determines to slay Karna.

LXXV

Sanjaya: The battle rages. Uttamaujas slays Sushena (= son of Karna).

LXXVI

Sanjaya: Visoka (= charioteer to Bhima) gives Bhima a check-list of remaining weapons with their quantities. The constellation Chitra.

LXXVII

Sanjaya: Prowess of Arjuna.
Prowess of Bhima: 'Bhima came out of the press like a fish coming out of a net, having slain ten thousand unretreating elephants, two hundred thousand and two hundred men, O Bharata, and five thousand horses, and a hundred car-warriors.' Bhima vanquishes Sakuni.

LXXVIII

Sanjaya: Prowess of Karna.

LXXIX

Sanjaya: Karna's sober estimate of Arjuna. How Arjuna received his bow Gandiva, his chariot, his steeds, his inexhaustible quivers, his conch Devadatta, the weapon Pasupata, etc.
Prowess of Arjuna: 'Having arrows for his fierce rays, the Arjuna sun,

with Gandiva drawn to its fullest stretch constituting his corona, looked resplendent, as he scorched his foes, like the Sun himself between the months of Jyaishtha and Ashadha, within his bright corona.'

LXXX

Sanjaya: Prowess of Arjuna.

LXXXI

Sanjaya: Prowess of Arjuna. Prowess of Arjuna with his mace.

LXXXII

Sanjaya: The grandson of Sini slays Prasena (= son of Karna). Karna slays Visoka (= the Kaikaya prince). Karna slays the son of Dhrishtadyumna. Dussasana stuns Bhima.

LXXXIII

Sanjaya: Bhima slays Dussasana and quaffs his blood. Yudhamanyu slays Chitrasena (= brother to Karna).

LXXXIV

Sanjaya: Partha (= Bhima? or Arjuna?) slays these sons of Dhritarashtra: Nishangin, Kavachin, Pasin, Dundadhara, Dhanurgraha, Alolupa, Saha, Shanda, Vatavega, Suvarchasas. Combat between Nakula and Vrishasena (= son of Karna). Prowess of Nakula.

LXXXV

Sanjaya: The battle rages. Arjuna slays Vrishasena.

LXXXVI

Sanjaya: Krishna describes Karna's chariot and standard.

LXXXVII

Sanjaya: Everything (lists are given) in the universe chooses to be either on Arjuna's side or on Karna's side. Brahman and Isana tell Maghavat (= the chief of the celestials) that victory will go to Arjuna; they identify Arjuna and Krishna with Nara and Narayana and speak of their greatness. The planets Rahu and Ketu. The elephant's rope on Karna's standard and the ape on Arjuna's standard battle with each other.

LXXXVIII

Sanjaya: The two armies fight. Aswatthaman, in vain, makes a final plea for peace to Duryodhana.

LXXXIX

Sanjaya: The combat between Karna and Arjuna begins! Weapons: Varuna, Vayavya, Bhargava, Brahma.

Krishna encourages Arjuna: 'That patience with which, Yuga after Yuga, thou hadst slain persons having the quality of darkness for their weapons, as also terrible Kshatriyas, and Asuras born of pride, in many a battle — with that patience do thou slay Karna today.'

Yudhishthira has been made whole by surgeons using mantras and drugs.

XC

Sanjaya: The combat rages between Arjuna and Karna. In the lull, 'Both of them were then fanned with excellent and waving fans made of young (palm) leaves and sprinkled with fragrant sandal-water by many Apsaras staying in the welkin. And Sakra and Surya, using their hands, gently brushed the faces of these two heroes.'

The snake Aswasena becomes united with Karna's most terrible weapon and is fired at Arjuna. Krishna presses Arjuna's chariot one cubit into the Earth, and the snaky weapon removes Arjuna's diadem (about which details of manufacture and history) and destroys it. Arjuna slays Aswasena. In accordance with the Brahmana's curse, Karna's chariot begins to sink into the Earth. Karna's armour is struck off by Arjuna. When Karna heaves up his chariot, the whole Earth rises 'with her seven islands and her hills and waters and forests.' Karna asks for time to raise his chariot. The Brahma weapon.

XCI

Sanjaya: Arjuna slays Karna! Weapons: Brahma, Vayavya, Anjalika. 'The head also of that commander of the (Kaurava) army, endued with splendour equal to that of the risen sun and resembling the meridian sun of autumn, fell down on the Earth like the sun of bloody disc dropped down from the Asta hills.' ... 'The beautiful head, graced with a face that resembled a lotus of a thousand petals, of Karna whose feats were like those of the thousand-eyed Indra, fell down on the Earth like the thousand-rayed Sun as he looks at the close of day.'

XCII

Sanjaya: The Kuru forces are all distraught.

XCIII

Sanjaya: Bhima slays 25,000 opponents. Duryodhana alone fights all the Pandavas united together.

XCIV

Sanjaya: Salya describes the battlefield to Duryodhana. Both sides retire for the night.

Tribute to Karna: 'He left the world, taking away with him that blazing glory of his own which he had earned on Earth by fair fight ... When Karna fell, the rivers stood still ...'

Other portents. Mercury, Jupiter, the constellation Rohini. 'Upon the slaughter of Karna in that dreadful battle, the gods, Gandharvas, human beings, Charanas, great Rishis, Yakshas, and great Nagas, worshipped Krishna and Arjuna with great respect and wished them victory (in all things).'

XCV

Sanjaya: The Kuru forces withdraw.

XCVI

Sanjaya: Yudhishthira rejoices at news of Karna's death.

Dhritarashtra swoons.

The merit obtained from reading this Parva 'without malice'.

END OF KARNA PARVA

SALYA PARVA

I

Vaisampayana to Janamejaya: Sanjaya reports to Dhritarashtra the deaths of Salya, Sakuni, Uluka, Duryodhana, Dhrishtadyumna, Sikhandin, Uttamauja, Yudhamanyu, Vrishasena. Indeed, there are only three warriors left alive on one side: Kripa, Kritavarman, Aswatthaman, and seven on the other side: the five Pandava brothers, Vasudeva, Satyaki.

II

Vaisampayana: Dhritarashtra laments his dead sons. Destiny. He asks Sanjaya to narrate the whole episode.

III

Vaisampayana: Sanjaya: The battle flares up again. Prowess of Duryodhana.

IV

Sanjaya: Kripa presents Duryodhana with an eloquent appraisal of the present situation and a plea for reconciliation with Yudhishthira. 'Preserve thy own self now, for self is the refuge of everything.'

V

Sanjaya: Duryodhana appreciates Kripa's words but declares his determination to continue the fight.

VI

Sanjaya: Physical description of Aswatthaman, and his other qualities. Salya accepts the position of commander of the Kuru forces.

VII

Sanjaya: Salya is installed as commander. Krishna tells Yudhishthira that only he (= Yudhishthira) is able to slay Salya.

VIII

Sanjaya: The next day the battle recommences.

IX

Sanjaya: The battle rages.

X

Sanjaya: Nakula slays Chitrasena and two sons of Karna: Satyasena and Sushena.

XI

Sanjaya: Portents. Conjunction of Venus, Mars, and Mercury. Description of Bhima's mace. (Salya = Artayani.)

XII

Sanjaya: A mace-combat between Bhima and Salya ends in a double knockout. Duryodhana slays Chekitana.

XIII

Sanjaya: The prowess of Salya.

XIV

Sanjaya: Combat between Arjuna and Aswatthaman. Aswatthaman slays Suratha.

XV

Sanjaya: The battle rages.

XVI

Sanjaya: Bhima causes Duryodhana to faint. Yudhishthira vanquishes Salya. The planet Saturn.

XVII

Sanjaya: Yudhishthira slays Salya with a special dart forged by Tashtri. Yudhishthira slays Salya's younger brother. Satyaki vanquishes Kritavarman.

XVIII

Sanjaya: The battle rages. The Pandavas form the Madhyama array.

XIX

Sanjaya: Strong advantage to the Pandavas. Bhima slays 21,000 foot-soldiers.

XX

Sanjaya: Salwa, King of the Mlechchhas, is slain by Satyaki, and his huge elephant is slain by Dhrishtadyumna.

XXI

Sanjaya: Satyaki slays King Kshemakirti. Combat between Satyaki and Kritavarman (= son of Hridika). Duryodhana's army is routed.

XXII

Sanjaya: Prowess of Duryodhana.

XXIII

Sanjaya: The battle rages. Portents. Terrific carnage.

XXIV

Sanjaya: The battle rages. Arjuna decides to exterminate the opposition. (Sakuni = son of Suvala.)

XXV

Sanjaya: The battle rages.

XXVI

Sanjaya: Bhima slays these sons of Dhritarashtra: Durmarshana, Srutanta, Jayatsena, Jaitra, Ravi, Bhurivala, Durvimochana, Dushpradharsha, Sujata, Durvishaha, Srutarvan.

XXVII

Sanjaya: Arjuna slays Satyakarman, Susarman, and Satyeshu. Bhima slays Sudarsana (= son of Dhritarashtra). Duryodhana is now the sole surviving son of Dhritarashtra.

XXVIII

Sanjaya: Sahadeva slays Sakuni and Uluka (= son of Sakuni).

XXIX

Sanjaya: His army exterminated, Duryodhana takes refuge in a lake. Sanjaya, who has been taken prisoner by the Pandavas, is released on the instructions of Vyasa.

XXX

Sanjaya: The Pandavas, hearing (from some hunters) of Duryodhana's concealment, proceed to the lake (which is called Dwaipayana).

XXXI

Sanjaya: Yudhishthira challenges Duryodhana to come out and fight.

XXXII

Sanjaya: Duryodhana emerges and prepares for a single combat with the mace.

XXXIII

Sanjaya: Bhima accepts the challenge.

XXXIV

Sanjaya: Rama comes to watch the combat. He says, 'Two and forty days have passed since I left home. I had set out under the constellation Pushya and have come back under Sravana.' (Rama = Rohini's son = Kesava's elder brother.)

XXXV

Vaisampayana to Janamejaya: Rama has been on a pilgrimage to the sacred places (tirthas) on the Saraswati. He set out under the constellation Pushya, under the conjunction of the asterism called Maitra. (Rama = Valadeva = Baladeva.)

The tirtha Prabhasa: Origin of its name. Story of Daksha, his twenty-seven daughters, Soma (= Sasin = Chandramas = Virochana), Rohini, and the wasting disease (phthisis). Astronomy.

XXXVI

Vaisampayana: The tirtha Udapana. The story of Ekata, Dwita and Trita (= sons of Gautama): the sacrifice made in imagination by Trita after falling into a deep hole. (Vrihaspati = the preceptor of the gods.)

XXXVII

The tirthas Vinasana, Subhumika, Gargasrota, and the origin of their names. Time. Astronomy. (Rama = Vala.) The Dwaita lake and the tirtha Nagadhanwana. Why the River Saraswati moved her course eastwards into the forest of Naimisha during the Krita Age.

XXXVIII

How the Saraswati came to have seven forms called Suprava, Kanchanakshi, Visala, Manorama, Oghavati, Surenu, Vimalodaka. The seven forms unite at Sapta-Saraswat. The story of Mankanaka (= son of the wind-god and Sukanya). From Mankanaka and Saraswati sprang seven Rishis, and from these Rishis sprang the 49 Maruts. Mankanaka and the vegetable juice. Mankanaka's hymn of praise to Mahadeva.

XXXIX

The tirtha Usanasa and why it is also called Kapalamochana:

The story of a Rakshasa's head sticking to the thigh of Mahodara the great Rishi. How Rushangu cast off his aged body.

XL

How Arshtishena acquired mastery of the Vedas in the Krita Age. How Viswamitra (= the son of Gadhi; Gadhi = Kausika) attained Brahmanhood.

XLI

How the great ascetic Dalvya-vaka began to destroy Dhritarashtra's kingdom and why he stopped. Why the tirtha Yayata is so called.

XLII

Why the tirtha Vasishthapavaha is so called. How the Saraswati managed to obey both Viswamitra and Vasishtha and why her waters became blood for a year. Vasishtha's hymn to Saraswati.

XLIII

How some Rishis freed Saraswati from the curse of Viswamitra. The types of food reserved for Rakshasas and to be avoided by learned men. The origin of the Aruna, a tributary of the Saraswati. How Indra was purified from Brahmanicide by bathing in the Aruna. Why the tirtha Soma is so called.

XLIV

From Maheswara and Agni springs Skanda (= Kartikeya = Gangeya.) Skanda's wonderful powers as a child.

XLV

At Samanta-Panchaka on the banks of the Saraswati, Skanda is installed by Brahman as the generalissimo of the celestial forces. Long list of gods and powers in creation. The companions given to Skanda sound exactly like monsters depicted in modern comics. (Skanda = Kumara.) 'Some had mouths on their stomachs, some on their backs, some on their cheeks, some on their calves', etc, etc.

XLVI

Long list of the mothers who became Skanda's companions. Gifts offered to Skanda (= Guha). Skanda slays the Daityas, the Rakshasas, and the Danavas. He pierces the Krauncha Mountain with his dart. Why the Krauncha Mountain is so called.

XLVII

The installation, in a former Kalpa, of Varuna as lord of all aquatic creatures. Agnitirtha: Why Agni hid in the entrails of the Sami wood. The tirtha called Kauvera, where Ailavila (= Kuvera) was installed as lord of all treasures.

XLVIII

The tirtha Vadarapachana: How Sruvavati, the daughter of Bharadwaja, burned her feet to boil five jujubes for the Rishi Vasishtha (who was really Sakra in disguise). How Arundhati cooked jujubes for twelve years while fasting and listening to the sacred discourses of Mahadeva.

XLIX

Indra-tirtha: Why Indra is also called Satakratu.

L

The story of the two ascetics Jaigishavya and Asita-Devala, and how the latter adopted the Moksha religion.

LI

How Saraswat, born of the sage Dadhicha and the River Saraswati, taught the Vedas to 60,000 Rishis who had forgotten the scriptures. How Dadhicha, son of the Rishi Bhrigu, and the strongest creature in the world, gave his bones (as weapons) to Sakra for vanquishing the Asuras.

LII

Why the daughter of the Rishi Kuni-Garga gave half of her ascetic merits to the man who would marry her.

LIII

Why Kurushetra is so called; how Kuru tilled the plain. Sakra's verse:
   'The very dust of Kurukshetra, borne away by the wind, shall cleanse persons of wicked acts and bear them to heaven.' ... 'The space between the Tarantuka and the Arantuka and the lakes of Rama and Shamachakra, is known as Kurukshetra. Samantapanchaka is called the northern (sacrificial) alter of Brahman, the Lord of all creatures.'

LIV

In the hermitage called Plakshaprasravana, on the slope of the Himavat Mountain, Rama hears from Narada of the impending combat between Bhima and Duryodhana. Rama's hymn about the Saraswati.
   [This really takes us back to where we were in Section XXXIV.]

LV

On Rama's advice, Bhima and Duryodhana prepare to start their combat at Samantapanchaka.

LVI

Portents. 'Rahu swallowed the Sun most untimely, O monarch!' After a verbal exchange, the combat begins.

LVII

Sanjaya: The mace-combat.

LVIII

Sanjaya: Krishna favours deception. Bhima fractures Duryodhana's thighs. Portents.

LIX

Sanjaya: Yudhishthira reproves Bhima for putting his foot on Duryodhana's head.

LX

Sanjaya: Rama, furious that Bhima has struck below the navel, rushes to attack Bhima, but is prevented by Krishna: 'Those two foremost heroes of Yadu's race, the one dark in complexion and the other fair, looked exceedingly beautiful at that moment, like the Sun and the Moon, O king, on the evening sky!'

Krishna lists the six kinds of advancement a person may have. Morality, Profit, Pleasure. Rama leaves in wrath, and Krishna supports Bhima's actions. Krishna says: 'Know that the Kali Age is at hand.'

LXI

Sanjaya: Duryodhana bitterly accuses his foes, and Krishna in particular, of using unfair means. Krishna supports the use of 'contrivances and means', citing the actions of the gods as antecedents.

LXII

Sanjaya: The Pandavas go to the derelict Kuru camp. When Krishna descends from the chariot, the Ape vanishes and the whole chariot disintegrates into ashes, having been previously destroyed by the Brahma weapon and having been maintained by Krishna's presence. The Pandavas spend the night by the sacred stream Oghavati, but Krishna is despatched to Hastinapura, to comfort Gandhari.

LXIII

Vaisampayana: Krishna comforts Gandhari, while Vyasa comforts Dhritarashtra. Krishna, suddenly aware of an evil plan in Aswatthaman's mind, quickly returns to the Pandavas. The power of Time. Destiny.

LXIV

Sanjaya: Duryodhana's lamentations. Portents.

LXV

Sanjaya: Aswatthaman, Kripa, and Kritavarman visit Duryodhana on the battlefield.

Aswatthaman waxes eloquent on the reverses brought by Time. Aswatthaman vows to slay the Pandavas. Kripa installs Aswatthaman as the generalissimo.

END OF SALYA PARVA

SAUPTIKA PARVA

I

Sanjaya: Aswatthaman, Kripa, and Kritavarman prepare to spend the night in a forest. 'The firmament, bespangled with planets and stars, shone like an ornamented piece of brocade and presented a highly agreeable spectacle.'

Aswatthaman, seeing an owl attack the sleeping crows, has the idea of slaying the sleeping Pandavas. Morality.

II

Sanjaya: Kripa cannot approve of Aswatthaman's idea and wants to seek advice from Vidura. Morality. 'All men are subjected to and governed by these two forces, viz., Destiny and Exertion.'

III

Sanjaya: Aswatthaman maintains his position. Morality. Standards of understanding. The four divisions of men.

IV

Sanjaya: Kripa and Aswatthaman maintain their respective positions.

V

Sanjaya: Kripa speaks of the persons who should never be slain. Morality. But Aswatthaman sets out to slaughter the sleeping Pandavas, and Kripa and Kritavarman follow him.

VI

Sanjaya: Aswatthaman's way is barred by a huge figure, against which his weapons have no effect.

VII

Sanjaya: Aswatthaman's hymn to Siva (= Girisha). An altar appears, accompanied by myriads of marvellous beings — 'the lords of the lords of the three worlds. Always engaged in merry sports, they are thorough masters of speech and are perfectly free from pride.' Aswatthaman offers himself as a sacrifice and Siva enters his body.

VIII

Sanjaya: Aswatthaman enters the enemy camp and slays Dhrishtadyumna, Uttamaujas, Yudhamanyu, Prativindhya, Sutasoma, Satanika, Srutakarman, Srutakirti, Sikhandin; Aswatthaman and Kripa and Kritavarman slay everybody there, including the sons of Draupadi.

IX

Sanjaya: The three return to Duryodhana, who is in a terrible plight, and report what has happened. Destiny. Death of Duryodhana.
  (Sanjaya loses the spiritual sight which the Rishi gave him.)

X

Vaisampayana: Yudhishthira's lament. Striking metaphor of the Drona-ocean.

XI

Vaisampayana: Draupadi's distress at the news of her sons' death. Bhima, vowing vengeance, sets off in pursuit of Aswatthaman.

XII

Krishna recalls a time when Aswatthaman asked Krishna for his discus. Krishna granted it, but Aswatthaman was unable to budge it! Since Aswatthaman has control over the Brahmasira weapon, Krishna recommends protection for Bhima.

XIII

Names of Krishna's horses. Aswatthaman fires his celestial weapon.

XIV

At Krishna's bidding, Arjuna fires a celestial weapon in opposition. Two Rishis, 'Narada who is the soul of every creature' and Vyasa, appear and stand between the two weapons.

XV

Arjuna withdraws his weapon, but Aswatthaman is unable to withdraw his. Vyasa censures Aswatthaman and asks him to give to the Pandavas the gem (properties described) which was in his head at birth. Aswatthaman throws his weapon into the wombs of the Pandava women.

XVI

Krishna promises that, in spite of this, there will be born to Virata's daughter (= daughter-in-law to Arjuna) a son called Parikshit, who will rule the Earth for 60 years. Krishna's curse upon Aswatthaman.

Aswatthaman hands over the gem, which is subsequently given to Yudhishthira.

XVII
Krishna gives an account of Siva and creation.

XVIII
Krishna completes the account. The Krita Yuga. The four kinds of sacrifice. How Siva's bow was made and how its string broke.

END OF SAUPTIKA PARVA

STREE PARVA

I

Vaisampayana: Dhritarashtra's laments.

II

Vidura consoles Dhritarashtra. 'As regards living creatures, they are non-existent at first. They exist in the period that intervenes. In the end they once more become non-existent.'
   The power of Time. The fruits of one's acts.

III

Vidura continues: The fruits of one's acts. 'Creatures obtain weal or woe as the fruit of their own acts.'

IV

Dhritarashtra asks about 'the wilderness of this world.' Vidura gives a striking statement about gestation and birth and about the difficulties which beset one in this life.

V

Vidura tells the story of the man who fell into a hole in the forest.

VI

Vidura explains the story.

VII

Vidura gives the picture of the chariot, the steeds, traces, and driver. 'This body is called the car of Yama.' He also gives a different picture of the chariot of man's soul.

VIII

Vyasa (= son of Satyavati) tells Dhritarashtra how the Earth once came to the court of Indra because she was oppressed by the weight of creatures; the gods promise that a great slaughter would occur on account of Duryodhana.

IX

Vidura speaks to Dhritarashtra about the inevitable effects of Time.

X
Widespread grief in Hastinapura.

XI
After slaying the sleeping Pandavas, Kripa goes to Hastinapura, Kritavarman to his own kingdom, and Aswatthaman to the asylum of Vyasa.

XII
The five brothers come to console Dhritarashtra, who is longing to kill Bhima, but who instead destroys an iron statue of Bhima which Krishna presents.

XIII
Reproved by Krishna, Dhritarashtra becomes fully reconciled to the five sons of Pandu.

XIV
The son of Satyavati tries to placate the wrath of Gandhari, who declares that the only thing inciting her to fury is the unjust action of Bhima in striking Duryodhana below the navel.

XV
Bhima and his brothers ask for forgiveness, and Gandhari is reconciled to them, but only after she has produced a sore nail on Yudhishthira's foot.

XVI
The Kuru ladies go to the battlefield. Their laments over the corpses.

XVII
Gandhari's eloquent lament over Duryodhana.

XVIII
Gandhari's grief for her daughters-in-law, who are wandering over the grisly battlefield.

XIX
Gandhari laments her dead relatives.

XX
Uttara laments her husband Abhimanyu.

XXI

Karna's wives lament their husband.

XXII

More laments from the ladies on the battlefield.

XXIII

More eloquent laments. Drona's body is burned on the funeral pyre. (Kripi = wife of Drona.)

XXIV

More eloquent laments.

XXV

More laments from the ladies.

Gandhari curses Krishna: 'On the thirty-sixth year from this, O slayer of Madhu, thou shalt, after causing the slaughter of thy kinsmen and friends and sons, perish by disgustful means within the wilderness.'

XXVI

Yudhishthira to Dhritarashtra: 'One billion six hundred and sixty million and twenty thousand men have fallen in this battle. Of the heroes that have escaped, the number is twenty-four thousand one hundred and sixty-five.'

Yudhishthira speaks of the celestial regions which the slain have attained. Yudhishthira holds funeral rites for all the dead.

XXVII

At the Ganga, Yudhishthira performs the water-rite for the dead. Kunti's lament for Karna shows Yudhishthira that Karna was Kunti's son.

END OF STREE PARVA

SANTI PARVA

I

During the mourning period, which lasts a month, the sons of Pandu, with Vidura, Dhritarashtra and all the Bharata ladies, stay on the banks of the Ganges. They are visited by many Rishis, including Vyasa, Narada, Devala, Devasthana, and Kanwa. Yudhishthira divulges his grief, enormously increased by the knowledge that Karna was his uterine brother.

II

Narada tells Yudhishthira the truth about the birth of Karna, how Karna gained favour with Rama, and the curse put upon Karna by the Brahmana whose cow Karna had slain; how Karna deceived Rama into believing him to be a Brahmana and how Karna thus obtained from Rama knowledge of the Brahma weapon and other weapons.

III

Narada: Details of how Rama realised that Karna was not a Brahmana. The worm biting Karna was an Asura named Dansa put under a curse by Bhrigu in the Krita Age; now Rama, of Bhrigu's race, has freed him from the curse. Rama dismisses Karna, saying that when death is at hand Karna will have no control over the Brahma weapon.

IV

Narada: How Karna's might enabled Duryodhana to carry off a princess at a self-choice ceremony in the city of Rajapura.

V

Narada: Karna's combat with Jarasandha. The contributory factors in Karna's death.

VI

Yudhishthira, stricken by grief, curses all the women of the world: 'Henceforth no woman shall succeed in keeping a secret.'

VII

Yudhishthira's lamentations. He proposes to live as an ascetic, leaving the kingdom to Arjuna.

VIII

Arjuna discourses on Wealth, Kingship, and 'the great path called Dasaratha'.

IX

Yudhishthira re-affirms his intention. Acts, and their consequences.

X

Bhima raises objections to Yudhishthira's proposal.

XI

Arjuna recites the story of the young Brahmanas and the golden bird (= Indra), which expounds the virtues of a life of domesticity.

XII

Nakula praises the life of domesticity. 'The four different modes of life were at one time weighed in the balance. The wise have said, O king, that when domesticity was placed on one scale, it required the three others to be placed on the other for balancing it.'

Kingly virtues.

XIII

Sahadeva: 'The word mama (mine), consisting of two letters, is Death's self; while the opposite word na-mama (not mine), consisting of three letters, is eternal Brahma.' ... 'They that look upon all creatures as their own selves escape from the great fear (of destruction).'

XIV

Draupadi adds her plea. Duties of kings. Duties of Brahmanas.

'The man that treads along the path of madness should be subjected to medical treatment by the aid of incense and collyrium, of drugs applied through the nose, and of other medicines.'

XV

Arjuna: The importance of chastisement. The rod of chastisement. The respective punishments for the four orders of men. 'Chastisement was ordained by the Creator himself for protecting religion and profit, for the happiness of all the four orders, and for making them righteous and modest.'

XVI

Bhima urges Yudhishthira to overcome his doubts and to govern the Earth. Mental and physical diseases: causes and nature thereof. The three attributes of the body. The three attributes of the mind.

XVII

Yudhishthira remains unmoved. He quotes a verse sung of old by Janaka:
  'My treasures are immense, yet I have nothing! If again the whole of Mithila were burnt and reduced to ashes, nothing of mine will be burnt!'

XVIII

Arjuna: How Janaka decided to adopt a life of mendicancy and how his wife pleaded with him to remain king.

XIX

Yudhishthira praises the value of ascetic penances.

XX

Devasthana tells Yudhishthira about wealth and sacrifice:
  'The Supreme Ordainer created wealth for sacrifice, and He created man also for taking care of that wealth and for performing sacrifice. For this reason the whole of one's wealth should be applied to sacrifice.'

XXI

Devasthana: The words of Vrihaspati to Indra: 'Contentment is the highest heaven, contentment is the highest bliss. There is nothing higher than contentment. Contentment stands as the highest. When one draws away all his desires like a tortoise drawing in all its limbs, then the natural resplendence of his soul soon manifests itself.'
  The words of 'the self-create Manu': 'Abstention from injury, truthfulness of speech, justice, compassion, self-restraint, procreation (of offspring) upon one's own wives, amiability, modesty, patience — the practice of these is the best of all religions.'

XXII

Arjuna: The duties of Brahmanas. The duties of Kshatriyas.

XXIII

Arjuna is described as having curly hair. Vyasa speaks of the duties of Kshatriyas.
  Vyasa tells the story of the two brothers Sankha and Likhita, and how Likhita was punished by King Sudyumna for stealing from his brother. The rod of chastisement.

XXIV

Krishna-Dwaipayana tells Yudhishthira the story of Hayagriva, the dutiful king, who is now enjoying bliss in heaven.

XXV

Vyasa: The importance of Time (eloquent passage).

The old story of King Senajit. Duties of a king.

XXVI

Yudhishthira to Arjuna: Distinction between Vedic study and Yoga penances. The faults inherent in the possession of wealth.

XXVII

Yudhishthira blames himself for the deaths of Bhishma, Drona, Karna, and Abhimanyu. Yudhishthira vows he will starve to death, but Vyasa forbids him.

XXVIII

Vyasa quotes the marvellous words of Asma to King Janaka, beginning: 'Immediately after the formation of a man's body, joys and griefs attach themselves to it.'

The power of Time and Destiny. 'The union with brother, mother, father, and friend is like that of travellers in an inn.' Passing references to medicine and chemistry.

XXIX

Krishna tells of King Marutta and the Viswasrij sacrifice; King Suhotra the son of Atithi and the gold given him by Maghavat; Vrihadratha the King of the Angas and the sacrifices he performed; King Sivi, the son of Usinara, and his sacrifices; King Bharata, the son of Dushmanta and Sakuntala, and his sacrifices; King Rama, the son of Dasaratha, and his flourishing reign of eleven thousand years ('The very women did not quarrel with one another, what need then be said of the men?'); King Bhagiratha of Ikshvaku's race and how Ganga (also named Bhagirathi) came to be called Urvasi; King Dilipa and how he gave away the entire Earth and how at his sacrifices Viswavasu 'played on his Vina the seven notes according to the rules that regulate their combinations. Such was the character of Viswavasu's music that every creature (whatever he might be) thought that the great Gandharva was playing to him alone ... These three sounds never ceased in Dilipa's abode, viz., the voice of Vedic recitations, the twang of bows, and cries of Let it be given'; King Mandhatri and how he was born in the stomach of his father Yuvanaswa and how he sucked Indra's finger; King Yayati, son of Nahusha, and his sacrifices; King Amvarisha, the son of Nabhaga, and how he gave away a million kings (sic); King Sasavindu, the son of Chitrasena, and his sacrifices; King Gaya, the son of Amurtarayas, and his sacrifices; King Rantideva, son of Sankriti, and his sacrifices, and how the River

Charmanwati was produced; King Sagara, of Ikshvaku's race, and why the ocean was also called Sagara; King Prithu, the son of Vena, and why he was called Prithu and the meaning of 'Kshatriya' and 'Raja'. [All the above appears to be the speech of Narada to Srinjaya, whose son has died, and Krishna has quoted the whole account to Yudhishthira.]

XXX

Krishna tells the story of Narada and his nephew Parvata; how they cursed each other, then released each other, and how Narada married Sukumari, the daughter of Srinjaya. It so happens that Narada is now present, i.e., among the mourners beside the Ganges.

XXXI

Narada himself concludes the story: To Srinjaya is born a son called Suvarnashthivin. According to Parvata's words, the latter dies when still a boy; Narada tells Srinjaya all the accounts listed in Section XXIX and then brings Suvarnashthivin back to life.

XXXII

Vyasa to Yudhishthira: The duties of Kshatriyas.
  Actions, their causes and results.

XXXIII

Vyasa: The power of Time. How the gods fought the Asuras for 32,000 years. 'If by slaying an individual a family may be saved, or, if by slaying a single family the whole kingdom may be saved, such an act of slaughter will not be a transgression.'

XXXIV-XXXV

Vyasa gives a long list of acts that require expiation and refers to others that do not incur sin.

XXXVI

Vyasa gives details of how various sins may be expiated. 'Women, by leading a regulated life for one year, become cleansed of all their sins.' ... 'Persons conversant with the scriptures do not take into account the sins that women may commit at heart. Whatever their sins (of this description), they are cleansed by their menstrual course like a metallic plate that is scoured with ashes.'

XXXVII

Vyasa quotes the words of Manu on many aspects of morality,

including food suitable for Brahmanas. (These words were first spoken by Manu to an assembly of Rishis in the Krita Age.)

XXXVIII
Yudhishthira at last shakes off his grief and enters Hastinapura.
   Vyasa: Bhishma 'saw with his physical eyes all the gods with Indra at their head'. Details of Bhishma's birth and life.

XXXIX
Yudhishthira receives a royal welcome in Hastinapura. Charvaka (= a Rakshasa and a friend of Duryodhana) disguises himself as a Brahmana, but is slain by the true Brahmanas with the sound 'Hun'.

XL
Krishna fills in the background to the story of Charvaka. The Krita Age.

XLI
Yudhishthira is installed on the throne. Swastikas.

XLII
Yudhishthira urges everyone to be obedient to Dhritarashtra and gives duties to his brothers, to Vidura, Yuyutsu, and Sanjaya.

XLIII
Yudhishthira performs the Sraddha rites for those who have died in the battle.
   'Freed from foes and having conquered the whole Earth, King Yudhishthira began to enjoy great happiness.'

XLIV
Yudhishthira's hymn of praise to Krishna. The constellation Purnarvasu.

XLV
The victors all sleep in the royal palaces.

XLVI
Next morning Yudhishthira approaches Krishna. Dhaumya = Yudhishthira's priest.

XLVII
Yudhishthira finds Krishna in a state of meditation and describes what he observes. Krishna explains that since Bhishma has been thinking of

him, his mind has centred on Bhishma. Details of Bhishma's qualities. Urged by Krishna, Yudhishthira prepares to visit Bhishma on the battlefield.

XLVIII
Bhishma's long marvellous hymn to Krishna: 'Roots with all kinds of affixes and suffixes are thy limbs. The Sandhis are thy joints. The consonants and the vowels are thy ornaments. The Vedas have declared thee to be the divine word. Salutations to thee in thy form as the word!'

XLIX
Yudhishthira asks Krishna about the extermination of the Kshatriyas (in days of old) by Rama. (Krishna = Baladeva's younger brother and Gada's elder brother.)

L
Krishna: The strange way in which were born Jamadagni and Viswamitra; how Rama was begotten by Jamadagni; how Arjuna, the thousand-armed son of Kritavirya, became a great emperor; why Arjuna was cursed by the Rishi Apava; why Rama lopped off Arjuna's arms; how Rama began to exterminate the Kshatriyas; why Ocean created the region called Surparaka; 'When anarchy sets in on Earth, the weak are oppressed by the strong, and no man is master of his own property'; why the Earth came to be called Urvi; how the sage Kasyapa gathered the remaining Kshatriyas, who thus became the ancestors of all successive Kshatriyas.

LI
Yudhishthira and Krishna reach Bhishma. Krishna speaks in praise of Bhishma, who praises Krishna in turn.
Krishna: 'Six and fifty days, O foremost one of Kuru's race, still remain for thee to live! ... When thou, O Bhishma, wilt leave this world for that, all Knowledge, O hero, will expire with thee.'

LII
Krishna grants Bhishma a clear mind and full alleviation from pain. Yudhishthira and Krishna return to Hastinapura for the night. 'Gladdening that great host, the divine Chandramas rose before it in the firmament, once more inspiring with moisture, by his own force, the terrestrial herbs and plants whose juice had been sucked up by the Sun.'

LIII

The following day Krishna and the Pandava brothers pay a second visit to Bhishma.

LIV

Krishna urges Bhishma to speak of 'high morality'.

LV

Bhishma: The duties of Kshatriyas.

LVI

Bhishma: The duties of a king. 'There is nothing which contributes so much to the success of kings as Truth.' ... 'Fire hath sprung from water, the Kshatriya from the Brahmana, and iron from stone. The three (viz., fire, Kshatriya and iron) can exert their force on every other thing, but coming into contact with their respective progenitors, their force becomes neutralised.' ... 'Among the six kinds of citadels indicated in the scriptures, indeed among every kind of citadel, that which consists of (the ready service and the love of the) subjects is the most impregnable.'

LVII

Bhishma: The duties of a king. 'The happiness of their subjects, observance of truth, and sincerity of behaviour are the eternal duty of kings.'

Manu, the son of Prachetas, sang: 'These six persons should be avoided like a leaky boat on the sea, viz., a preceptor that does not speak, a priest that has not studied the scriptures, a king that does not grant protection, a wife that utters what is disagreeable, a cow-herd that likes to rove within the village, and a barber that is desirous of going to the woods.'

LVIII

Bhishma: The prime duty of a king is protection of the subjects. How this is done. The importance of exertion.

Krishna and the five brothers return to Hastinapura for the night.

LIX

The next day Yudhishthira asks Bhishma what is special about a king and why the many bow down to one.

Bhishma: There was no sovereignty at first, but it began in the Krita Age when righteousness and the Vedas were lost. The Grandsire composed 'a treatise consisting of a hundred thousand chapters', of encyclopaedic breadth and dealing with 'the histories of all past events, the origin of the great Rishis, the holy waters, the planets and stars and asterisms, the duties in respect of the four modes of life, the four kinds of Homa, the characteristics of the four orders of men, and the four branches of learning', etc, etc. This treatise was repeatedly abridged by gods and Rishis until it was reduced to a thousand lessons. Prithu is cited as the ideal king. Origin of 'Prithivi'. Origin of 'Nishadas'. The various names of this treatise are 'Dandaniti', 'Vaisalakasha', 'Vahudantaka', and 'Varhaspatya'.

'A person, upon the exhaustion of his merit, comes down from Heaven to Earth, and takes birth as a king conversant with the science of chastisement. Such a person becomes endued with greatness and is really a portion of Vishnu on Earth.'

LX

Bhishma: The duties, general and particular, of the four orders of men. The importance of sacrifice.

LXI

Bhishma: The four modes of life laid down exclusively for Brahmanas: Vanaprastha, Bhaikshya, Garhasthya, Brahmacharya.

LXII

Bhishma: The effects of past actions. The power of Time.

LXIII

Bhishma: The Bhikshu mode of life.
The importance of Kshatriya duties. 'If the science of chastisement disappears, the Vedas will disappear.'

LXIV

Bhishma cites an ancient conversation between Indra and Mandhatri. Indra explains why Kshatriya duties are the foremost of all duties. Bhishma: 'If the functions of royalty are disturbed, all creatures are overtaken by evil.'

LXV

Bhishma: Indra stresses the supremacy of Kshatriya duties. 'After the expiry of this the Krita Age, a confusion will set in, regarding the different modes of life, and innumerable Bhikshus will appear with sectarian marks of different kinds.'

LXVI

Bhishma: How virtue accrues to the dutiful king:

'That king who duly adheres to the duties laid down by the Creator, obtains the blessed merits of all the modes of life.'

'A king can easily cross the ocean of the world, with kingly duties as his boat possessed of great speed, urged on by the breeze of gifts, having the scriptures for its tackle and intelligence for the strength of its helmsman, and kept afloat by the power of righteousness.'

LXVII

Bhishma: The duties of a kingdom:

'The (election and) coronation of a king is the first duty of a kingdom.' ... 'The Srutis declare that in crowning a king, it is Indra that is crowned (in the person of the king).'

'There is no evil greater than anarchy.'

How Manu, in a time of anarchy, set men to their respective duties.

LXVIII

Bhishma quotes the words of Vrihaspati to Vasumanas, King of Kosala, on the duties and nature of a king:

'No one should disregard the king by taking him for a man, for he is really a high divinity in human form.' How the king assumes the forms of Agni, Aditya, Mrityu, Vaisravana, and Yama to meet different occasions.

'The king is the heart of his people; he is their great refuge; he is their glory; and he is their highest happiness.'

LXIX

Bhishma: Miscellaneous duties of the king, including espionage, warfare, internal and external policies, and the great science of chastisement. 'Whether it is the king that makes the age, or it is the age that makes the king, is a question about which thou shouldst not entertain any doubt. The truth is that the king makes the age. When the king rules with a complete and strict reliance on the science of chastisement, the foremost of ages called Krita is then said to set in ... When the king relies upon only three of the four parts of the science of chastisement, leaving out a fourth, the age called Treta sets in ... When the king observes the great science by only a half, leaving out the other half, then the age that sets in is called Dwapara ... When the king, abandoning the great science totally, oppresses his subjects by evil means of diverse kinds, the age that sets in is called Kali.'

Characteristics of the four ages. What happens to the king who produces the four ages.

LXX
Bhishma: The thirty-six virtues which a king should observe.

LXXI
Bhishma: Details of the king's duty to protect his subjects. Taxation and the true source of royal revenue. 'Imitate the example, O king, of the flowerman and not of the charcoal-maker.'

LXXII
Bhishma quotes the words of Matariswan, the god of Winds, to King Pururavas, the son of Aila: The creation and duty of the four orders of men.

LXXIII
Bhishma quotes the words of Kasyapa to Aila: The king and the priest should have mutual trust. Rudra as the god of Vengeance.

LXXIV
Bhishma relates how King Muchukunda and his priest Vasishtha joined their forces to rule the Earth, much to the surprise of Vaisravana (= the Lord of Alaka = the Lord of Treasures).

LXXV
Bhishma: Kingly duties.

LXXVI
Bhishma: Brahmanas, dutiful and neglectful.

LXXVII
Bhishma: The king is responsible for the actions of his subjects. The story of the Rakshasa and the King of the Kaikeyas.

LXXVIII
Bhishma: How the different orders of men should act in changing circumstances.

LXXIX
Bhishma: The qualities of a priest.
The question of giving Dakshina at a sacrifice. Penances.

LXXX
Bhishma: The king's ministers. The four friends of the king.

LXXXI
Bhishma quotes an old conversation between Narada and Vasudeva at a time when the Bhojas and the Vrishnis were threatened with destruction.

LXXXII
Bhishma tells the old story of the sage Kalakavrikshiya, his crow, and Kshemadarsin, King of Kosala.

LXXXIII
Bhishma: The men that make good legislators, ministers of war, courtiers, generalissimos, and counsellors.

LXXXIV
Bhishma cites a conversation between Vrihaspati and Sakra:
'Agreeableness of speech, O Sakra, is the one thing by practising which a person may become an object of regard with all creatures and acquire great celebrity.'

LXXXV
Bhishma: What kinds of ministers should be appointed. The administration of justice.
'Refusal to trust anyone has been said to be one of the highest mysteries of kingcraft.'

LXXXVI
Bhishma: The fortification of citadels.

LXXXVII
Bhishma: The internal administration of a kingdom. Taxation. Levies at time of invasion. How the king should treat the Vaisyas.

LXXXVIII
Bhishma: Taxation. How the king should treat his various subjects.

LXXXIX
Bhishma: How a king should treat his subjects.
'Agriculture, cattle-rearing, and trade, provide all men with the means of living. A knowledge of the Vedas, however, provides them with the means of obtaining heaven. They, therefore, that obstruct the study of

the Vedas and the cause of Vedic practices, are to be regarded as enemies of society. It is for the extermination of these that Brahman created Kshatriyas.'

XC

Bhishma quotes the words of Utathya (of Angirasa's race) to Mandhatri: The king and righteousness. Etymology of 'Rajan', 'Vrishala', and 'Dharma'. The king and Pride. Portents. 'When the king does not restrain vice, a confusion of castes follows, and sinful Rakshasas, and persons of neutral sex, and children destitute of limbs or possessed of thick tongues, and idiots, begin to take birth in even respectable families.'

XCI

Bhishma: Utathya: The awesome responsibilities of the king. The amazing power of Weakness.

XCII

Bhishma quotes the words of the great Rishi Vamadeva to King Vasumanas: Righteousness and the king.

XCIII

Bhishma: Vamadeva: The duties of a king:

'Do not give harsh answers when questioned by anybody. Do not utter undignified speeches. Never be in a hurry to do anything. Never indulge in malice. By such means is a foe won over.'

XCIV

Bhishma: Vamadeva: 'The king should win victories without battles. Victories achieved by battles are not spoken of highly, O monarch, by the wise.'

XCV

Bhishma: Rules of combat. 'Manu himself, the son of the Self-born (Brahman), has said that battles should be fought fairly.'

XCVI

Bhishma: More rules of combat. How the king should conduct himself towards his foes.

XCVII

Bhishma reconciles the slaughter caused by a king with the goodness of the king. How a Kshatriya should die.

XCVIII

Bhishma quotes the ancient conversation between Indra and King Amvarisha, who, having gone to heaven, finds that his generalissimo is enjoying higher regions of felicity than he himself! A magnificent description of battle as sacrifice.

XCIX

Bhishma quotes the words of Janaka, King of Mithila, to his troops on the eve of battle: he lays before them heaven and hell.

'This world rests on the arms of heroes like a son on those of his sire. He, therefore, that is a hero deserves respect under every circumstance. There is nothing higher in the three worlds than heroism. The hero protects and cherishes all, and all things depend upon the hero.'

C

Bhishma: Army tactics and manoeuvres. 'Keeping the constellation called Ursa Major behind them, the troops should fight taking up their stand like hills. By this means, one may vanquish even foes that are irresistible. The troops should be placed in such a position that the wind, the Sun, and the planet Sukra should blow and shine from behind them. As means for ensuring victory the wind is superior to the Sun, and the Sun is superior to Sukra, O Yudhishthira ... That king, who having attended to all these considerations, sets out under a proper constellation and on an auspicious lunation, always succeeds in obtaining victory by properly leading his troops.' (A footnote states that the seven stars of Ursa Major are supposed to be the seven great Rishis, viz., Marichi, Atri, Angira, Pulastya, Pulaha, Kratu, and Vasishtha.

CI

Bhishma: The characteristics of fighters linked to their physical appearance.

CII

Bhishma: The indications of the future success of an army. The use of severity and mildness.

CIII

Bhishma quotes the words of Vrihaspati to Indra: How a king should behave towards his foe. The characteristics of the wicked man.

CIV

Bhishma quotes the words of Kalakavrikshiya to Kshemadarsin: The conduct of a king who has lost his kingdom.

CV

Bhishma: Kalakavrikshiya: The conduct of a king who has lost his kingdom. (Method 2.)

CVI

Bhishma: Kalakavrikshiya. (Method 3.)

CVII

Bhishma: Relationship between aristocracy and monarchy.

CVIII

Bhishma: The most important of all duties:

'The worship of mother, father, and preceptor is most important according to me ... They are the three worlds. They are the three modes of life. They are the three Vedas. They are the three sacred fires ... By serving the father with regularity, one may cross this world. By serving the mother in the same way, one may attain to regions of felicity in the next. By serving the preceptor with regularity one may obtain the region of Brahma ... He who honours these three is honoured in all the worlds ... The father and the mother, O Bharata, only create the body. The life, on the other hand, that one obtains from one's preceptor, is heavenly ... He who favours a person by imparting to him true instruction, by communicating the Vedas, and giving knowledge which is immortal, should be regarded as both a father and a mother.'

CIX

Bhishma: Questions of truth, falsehood, morality, and righteousness. 'Righteousness (Dharma) is so called because it upholds all creatures.'

CX

Bhishma: How a person may overcome all difficulties. In praise of Krishna.

CXI

Bhishma: The story of the jackal and the tiger.

CXII

Bhishma: The story of the camel and his long neck.

CXIII

Bhishma: The story of the Ocean and the Rivers.

CXIV

Bhishma: How to behave when abused by the ignorant.

CXV

Bhishma: The qualities the king's servants should have.

CXVI

Bhishma: The story of the Muni and the dog. (Part I.)

CXVII

Bhishma: The story of the Muni and the dog. (Conclusion.)

CXVIII

Bhishma: The king and his ministers.

CXIX

Bhishma: The importance of appointing ministers to the right office.

CXX

Bhishma: A summary of kingly duties.

CXXI

Bhishma: The many names and multiform appearance of Chastisement and his wife Morality.

'That upon which all things depend is called Chastisement. Chastisement is that by which righteousness is kept up. He is sometimes called Vyavahara.' ... 'This eternal universe is impartial Chastisement's self.'

Law. The words spoken first by Manu (and so known as 'the first words'): 'He who protects all creatures, the loved and the odious equally, by impartially wielding the lord [ADF suggests 'rod'] of Chastisement, is said to be the embodiment of righteousness.'

CXXII

Bhishma quotes the words of King Vasuhoma to King Mandhatri:

How Brahman created the priest Kshupa; how the goddess Saraswati created Danda-niti (science of chastisement); how Vishnu 'made the divine Indra of a thousand eyes the ruler of the deities. Yama the son of Vivaswat was made the lord of the Pitris. Kuvera was made the lord of treasures and of all the Rakshasas. Meru was made the king of the mountains, and Ocean was made the lord of the rivers. The puissant Varuna was installed into the sovereignty of the waters and the Asuras. Death was made the lord of life and all living things, and Fire was appointed as the lord of all things possessed of energy. The puissant Isana the high-souled and eternal Mahadeva, of three eyes, was made the lord of the Rudras. Vasishtha was made the lord of the Brahmanas, and Jatavedas was made the chief of the Vasus. Surya was made the lord of all luminous bodies, and Chandramas was made the king of Stars and constellations. Ansumat was made the lord of all herbs, and the puissant and foremost of deities, viz., Kumara or Skanda, of twelve arms, was made the chief of all the spirits and ghostly beings (that wait upon Mahadeva). Time, possessing the seeds of both destruction and growth, was made the sovereign of all creatures as also of the four portions of Death (viz., weapons, diseases, Yama, and acts) and lastly of grief and joy.' The line of descent of the rod of Chastisement from Kshupa to the Kshatriyas.

CXXIII

Bhishma: The interrelations of Virtue, Wealth, and Pleasure, and their connection with Will and Emancipation and Knowledge of Self. The words of the Rishi Kamandaka to King Angaristha.

CXXIV

Bhishma quotes the conversation between Duryodhana and Dhritarashtra at the time of Duryodhana's envy towards Yudhishthira:

Dhritarashtra: 'There is nothing impossible of attainment by persons of virtuous behaviour. Mandhatri conquered the whole world in course of only one night, Janamejaya, in course of three; and Nabhaga, in course of seven. All these kings were possessed of compassion and of virtuous behaviour.'

Dhritarashtra: How Indra regained his sovereignty from Prahlada, the Daitya chief. The supreme importance of behaviour.

CXXV

Bhishma: Hope. Beginning of the story about the king and the deer.

CXXVI

Bhishma: The story (continued). Hope.

CXXVII

Bhishma: The story (continued): The Rishi Rishabha tells the king another story:

The Rishi Tanu speaks about hope to King Viradyumna, who has lost his son, Bhuridyumna. Hope.

CXXVIII

Bhishma: The story (concluded). Hope.

CXXIX

Bhishma quotes the ancient conversation between Gotama and Yama. Behaviour.

CXXX

Bhishma: How a king may act in times of distress.

CXXXI

Bhishma: The actions open to a weak king when oppressed by the foe.

CXXXII

Bhishma: How the Brahmana should behave in times of distress.
    Morality. 'When slanderous converse goes on, one should close one's ears or leave the place outright.'

CXXXIII

Bhishma: The king's treasury. Treatment of robbers.

CXXXIV

Bhishma: The duties of a Kshatriya. Interrelations of Power, Righteousness, and Truth.

CXXXV

Bhishma: The fine morality of Kayavya the robber.

CXXXVI

Bhishma: How the king should fill his treasury.

CXXXVII

Bhishma: The story of the three Sakula fish. Divisions of time.

CXXXVIII

Bhishma: The story of Palita the mouse, Lomasa the cat, and Chandraka the owl.

CXXXIX

Bhishma: The story of King Brahmadatta and the bird Pujani.

CXL

Bhishma: The conversation between King Satrunjaya and the Rishi Bharadwaja:
    How a king should behave in times of distress. 'It is better, O

monarch, that a king should blaze up for a moment like charcoal of ebony wood than that he should smoulder and smoke like chaff for many years.'

CXLI

Bhishma tells a story set 'towards the end of Treta and the beginning of Dwapara':

The story of the twelve-year drought, the great Rishi Viswamitra, and the haunch of dog's meat. 'The planet Vrihaspati began to move in a retrograde course, and Soma, abandoning his own orbit, receded towards the south.'

CXLII

Yudhishthira expresses his stupefaction at the paradoxical standards of morality suggested by Bhishma's words.

Bhishma: 'Righteousness sometimes takes the shape of unrighteousness. The latter also sometimes takes the shape of the former.'

CXLIII

Bhishma recounts a story which Rama the son of Bhrigu originally told to King Muchukunda:

The story of 'The Fowler and the Pigeon' (Part I).

CXLIV

Bhishma: 'The Fowler and the Pigeon' (Part II). In praise of a good wife.

CXLV

Bhishma: 'The Fowler and the Pigeon' (Part III).

CXLVI

Bhishma: 'The Fowler and the Pigeon' (Part IV). The pigeon's sacrifice.

CXLVII

Bhishma: 'The Fowler and the Pigeon' (Part V). The fowler's remorse.

CXLVIII

Bhishma: 'The Fowler and the Pigeon' (Part VI). In praise of a good husband.

CXLIX

Bhishma: 'The Fowler and the Pigeon' (conclusion). The protection of a suppliant.

CL

Bhishma begins the story of King Janamejaya (= son of Parikshit) and Indrota (= Saunaka = son of Sunaka). Janamejaya commits Brahmanicide.

CLI

Bhishma continues the story: Against all tradition, Indrota begins to instruct Janamejaya.

CLII

Bhishma concludes the story: Indrota speaks of purification. The cleansing power of Prithudaka (= a tirtha on the Saraswati). Indrota helps Janamejaya to perform the horse-sacrifice. The king, cleansed of sin, returns in splendour to his kingdom.

CLIII

Bhishma: The jackal, the vulture, and the boy who was restored to life by the great god Sankara.

CLIV

Bhishma begins the story of Pavana and the huge Salmali tree.

CLV

Bhishma continues the story: The Salmali declares itself to be far stronger than Pavana, the god of the Wind.

CLVI

Bhishma continues the story: Pavana challenges the Salmali, who inwardly acknowledges the superior might of the Wind.

CLVII

Bhishma concludes the story: The Salmali's remorse.

CLVIII

Bhishma: Covetousness as the source of sin.
  Description of the virtuous person.

CLIX

Bhishma: Ignorance. Its relation to covetousness.

CLX

Bhishma: The man of self-restraint. 'As the track of birds along the sky or of fowl over the surface of water cannot be discerned, even so the track of such a person (on Earth) does not attract notice.'

CLXI

Bhishma: Penance.

CLXII

Bhishma: Truth and its thirteen forms.

CLXIII

Bhishma: The thirteen vices; their origin and how they may be subdued.

CLXIV

Bhishma: The malevolent person.

CLXV

Bhishma: The method of expiation for various sins, especially if committed by Brahmanas.

CLXVI

Bhishma answers Nakula's question about the origin of the sword with an account of creation: 'In ancient times the universe was one vast expanse of water, motionless and skyless, and without this Earth occupying any space in it. Enveloped in darkness, and intangible, its aspect was exceedingly awful. Utter silence reigning all over, it was immeasurable in extent.'

In the sacrifice performed by the Grandsire, a sword emerges from the fire, to be wielded first by Rudra in his defeat of the Danavas. All the others who has been custodians of this sword. The eight names of the sword. 'The constellation under which the sword was born is Krittika. Agni is its deity, and Rohini is its Gotra. Rudra is its high preceptor.' ... 'Of all weapons, O son of Madravati, the sword is the foremost.'

The bow was created by Prithu.

CLXVII

Returning home, the Pandavas and Vidura discuss Virtue, Wealth, Desire and Emancipation.

CLXVIII

Bhishma: Those one should not have as friends. Those one should have as friends. The story of Gautama, the Brahmana who lived like a robber (Part I).

CLXIX

Bhishma continues the story: Gautama finds himself in the abode of Rajadharman (= Nadijangha = a prince of cranes).

CLXX

Bhishma continues the story: Rajadharman befriends Gautama and introduces him to Virupaksha, 'a mighty King of the Rakshasas'.

CLXXI

Bhishma continues the story: Gautama receives a large quantity of gold from Virupaksha.

CLXXII

Bhishma continues the story: Gautama slays Rajadharman and is himself slain by Virupaksha.

CLXXIII

Bhishma concludes the story: Rajadharman is restored to life, and, at his request, so is Gautama, upon whom falls a dire curse.
  Ingratitude. Friendship.

CLXXIV

Bhishma: How to overcome grief. The account of King Senajit, whose son had died. The striking words of Pingala when she awoke.

CLXXV

Bhishma quotes the words of Medhavin to his father on how to behave when one sees that Death and Decrepitude are assailing everything. 'In Truth is immortality.' ... 'Seek thy Self which is concealed in a cave.'

CLXXVI

Bhishma quotes the words of Sampaka on Renunciation.

CLXXVII

Bhishma quotes the words of Manki on the Extirpation of Desire. Destiny and Exertion.

CLXXVIII

Bhishma quotes the words of Janaka and of Vodhya on Freedom from Attachments. 'Unlimited is my wealth. At the same time I have nothing. If the whole of (my kingdom) Mithila be consumed in a conflagration, I shall incur no loss.'

CLXXIX
Bhishma quotes the words of Ajagara to King Prahlada: Tranquillity.

CLXXX
Bhishma quotes the words of Indra (in the form of a jackal) to Kasyapa: Contentment; the human form; hands. (Astrology.)

CLXXXI
Bhishma: Acts and their fruits. 'As a calf recognises and approaches its parent in the midst of even a thousand kine, even so the acts of a past life recognise and visit the doer in his new life.'

'A creature while still in the mother's womb enjoys or suffers the happiness or the misery that has been ordained for him in consequence of his own acts. In childhood or youth or old age, at whatever period of life one does an act good or bad, the consequences thereof are sure to visit him in his next life at precisely the same period.'

CLXXXII
Bhishma quotes the words of Bhrigu to Bharadwaja:

An account of creation; Manasa; Mahat; Consciousness; a divine Lotus; Brahma(n); description of the Universe.

CLXXXIII
Bhishma: Bhrigu: A most beautiful account of the creation of the elements (given originally to Rishis in the Brahmakalpa).

CLXXXIV
Bhishma: Bhrigu: The five elements as the constitution of all creatures. The example of the tree. The five Pranas and their names. Physiology. The nine kinds of scents. The six kinds of taste. The sixteen kinds of form constituting the property of vision. The eleven properties appertaining to the wind. The seven kinds of sound (i.e. the seven original notes: their seven names).

CLXXXV
Bhishma: Bhrigu: The Pranas and their respective functions within the body. Motion. Digestion. Heat. Circulation.

CLXXXVI
Bhishma: Bharadwaja asks questions about the dissolution of creatures.

CLXXXVII
Bhishma: Bhrigu distinguishes the living agent from the five elements

which compose the body. 'The whole universe is composed of water. Water is the form of all embodied creatures. In that water is the Soul which is displayed in the mind. That Soul is the Creator Brahman who exists in all things. When the Soul becomes endued with vulgar attributes, it comes to be called Kshetrajna. When freed from those attributes, it comes to be called Paramatman or Supreme Soul. Know that Soul. He is inspired with universal benevolence. He resides in the body like a drop of water in a lotus.' ... 'The man of wisdom, living on frugal fare, and with heart cleansed of all sins, devoting himself to Yoga meditation, succeeds every night, before sleep and after sleep, in beholding his Soul by the aid of his Soul.'

CLXXXVIII

Bhishma: Bhrigu: All the classes of created beings, beginning with the Prajapatis. The four colours associated with the four orders of men. How the four orders of men are all Brahmanas in pursuit of varied activities. The eternal creation, and the creation produced by the great Rishis.

CLXXXIX

Bhishma: Bhrigu: The respective qualities of the four orders of men. Renunciation.

CXC

Bhishma: Bhrigu: Truth and untruth.
Happiness as the highest object of acquisition.

CXCI

Bhishma: Bhrigu: The four modes of life. (*Not* the four orders of men.)

CXCII

Bhishma: Bhrigu: The life of the forest recluses; the life of the Parivrajakas. The region called 'the other world', which is to the north of Himavat.

CXCIII

Bhishma: Conduct.

CXCIV

Bhishma: Adhyatma. The Creation and Destruction of the Universe. The five elements. The senses. The three Gunas. Mind. Intelligence. The Soul. 'A gnat and a fig may be seen to be united with each other. Though united, each however is distinct from the other. Similarly, Intelligence and Soul, though distinguished from each other, by their respective natures, yet they may always be seen to exist in a state of union. A fish and water exist in a state of union. Each, however, is different from the other. The same is the case with Intelligence and Soul ... The understanding or Intelligence creates all the qualities. The Soul only beholds them (as a witness).' Knowledge of Truth. Emancipation.

CXCV
Bhishma: Meditation. 'As a drop of water on a (lotus) leaf is unstable and moves about in all directions, even so becomes the yogin's mind when first fixed on the path of meditation.'

CXCVI
Bhishma: Meditation and 'silent Reciters of sacred mantras'.

CXCVII
Bhishma: 'Listen ... to the end that silent Reciters attain, and to the diverse kinds of hell into which they sink.'

CXCVIII
Bhishma explains that, compared with the region of the Supreme Soul, the regions of the gods are hells. Description of the region of the Supreme Soul.

CXCIX
Bhishma: The Brahmana, King Ikshvaku, Dharma, Mrityu, Yama, and Time.

CC
Bhishma: The conclusion of the story.
Attainment to the region of Brahman.

CCI
Bhishma quotes the words of Manu to his disciple Vrihaspati:
Emancipation. Acts and their fruits. The Absolute.

CCII
Bhishma: Manu: Account of creation.
The Self. The Soul. Acts and their fruits. Rebirth. The five elements. The senses.

'As a person by taking up an axe cannot, by cutting open a piece of wood, find either smoke or fire in it, even so one cannot, by cutting open the arms and feet and stomach of a person, see the principle of knowledge, which, of course, has nothing in common with the stomach, the arms and the feet. As again, one beholds both smoke and fire in wood by rubbing it against another piece, so a person of well-directed intelligence and wisdom, by uniting (by means of yoga) the senses and the soul, may view the Supreme Soul which, of course, exists in its own nature.'

CCIII

Bhishma: Manu: The Soul. The three states of consciousness.

'Nobody has seen the other side of the Himavat mountains, nor the reverse of the Moon's disc.'

CCIV

Bhishma: Manu: The Soul. 'Upon the appearance of Knowledge, one beholds one's Soul in one's understanding even as one sees one's own reflection in a polished mirror.'

'All objects that the mind apprehends through the senses are capable of being withdrawn into the mind; the mind can be withdrawn into the understanding; the Understanding can be withdrawn into the Soul, and the Soul into the Supreme.'

CCV

Bhishma: Manu: Grief and its remedy.

Attainment to Brahma. The primary creation and the secondary creation.

CCVI

Bhishma: Manu: The Soul. Emancipation.

'When the fivefold attributes are united with the five senses and the mind, then is Brahma seen by the individual like a thread passing through a gem. As a thread, again, may lie within gold or pearl or a coral or any object made of earth, even so one's soul, in consequence of one's own acts, may live within a cow, a horse, a man, an elephant, or any other animal, or within a worm or an insect.'

'Water is superior to the Earth in extension; Light is superior to Water; Wind is superior to Light; Space is superior to Wind; Mind is superior to Space; Understanding is superior to Mind; Time is superior to Understanding. The divine Vishnu, whose is this universe, is superior to Time. That god is without beginning, middle, and end.'

CCVII

Bhishma: The achievements of Vishnu (= Govinda = Narayana = Hrishikesa = Kesava = etc). Account of Creation. How Krishna came to be called Madhusudana. Daksha's offspring: thirteen daughters (married to Marichi's son Kasyapa) + ten daughters (married to Dharma) + twenty-seven daughters (married to Soma). The creation of the four orders of men. The different methods of procreation in the four ages.

CCVIII
Bhishma: Account of creation. Pedigrees of the Prajapatis and of the deities that rule the three worlds and of the great Rishis.

CCIX
Bhishma quotes the words of Kasyapa: The qualities and prowess of Krishna (= Vishnu). How Krishna, in the form of a boar, conquered the Daityas and Danavas.

CCX
Bhishma: The Preceptor to his Disciple: The attributes of Krishna. Creation-account. Cycle of celestial Yugas. 'At the end of every (celestial) Yuga (when universal destruction sets in) the Vedas and all other scriptures disappear (like the rest). In consequence of the grace of the Self-born, the great Rishis, through their penances, first re-acquire the lost Vedas and the scriptures. The Self-born (Brahman) first acquired the Vedas. Their branches called the Angas were first acquired by (the celestial preceptor) Vrihaspati. Bhrigu's son (Sukra) first acquired the science of morality that is so beneficial for the universe. The science of music was acquired by Narada; that of arms by Bharadwaja; the history of the celestial Rishis by Gargya; that of medicine by the dark-complexioned son of Atri. Diverse other Rishis, whose names are connected therewith, promulgated diverse other sciences such as Nyaya, Vaiseshika, Sankhya, Patanjala, etc.'

The eight constituents of primordial Prakriti. The sixteen constituents of a creature.

The Soul: why it is called Purusha. 'As a lamp discovers all objects great or small (irrespective of its own size), after the same manner the Soul dwells in all creatures as the principle of knowledge (regardless of the accidents or attributes of those creatures).'

CCXI
Bhishma: The wheel of existence.

'As the wind is truly separate from the dust it bears away, even so, the man of wisdom should know, is the connection between that which is called existence or life and the Soul.' ... 'Seeds that are scorched by fire do not put forth sprouts. After the same manner, if everything that contributes to misery be consumed by the fire of true knowledge, the Soul escapes the obligation of rebirth in the world.'

The immortality of the Soul.

CCXII

Bhishma: Emancipation. Ignorance. The characteristics of the three Gunas. 'As a house made of earth is plastered over with earth, even so this body which is made of earth is kept from destruction by food which is only a modification of earth.'

CCXIII

Bhishma: The Soul. The cycle of birth and death. The characteristics linked to the three Gunas. Emancipation. 'By their nature, women are Kshetra, and men are Kshetrajna in respect of attributes ... Indeed, women are like frightful mantra-powers. They stupefy persons reft of wisdom. They are sunk in the attribute of Passion. They are the eternal embodiment of the senses.' ... 'It should be known that sorrow springs from the very fact of acceptance of body (in the womb).'

CCXIV

Bhishma: How to practise Brahmacharya.

'The juices that are yielded by food, the duct called Manovaha, and the desire that is born of imagination — these three are the causes that originate the vital seed which has Indra for its presiding deity. The passion that aids in the emission of this fluid is, therefore, called Indriya.'

The ten principal ducts in the body.

CCXV

Bhishma: The means of Emancipation.

CCXVI

Bhishma: The nature of dreams. Emancipation.

CCXVII

Bhishma: 'As a weaver drives his threads into a cloth by means of his shuttle, after the same manner the threads that constitute the fabric of the universe are woven by the shuttle of Desire. He who properly knows transformations of Prakriti, Prakriti herself and Purusha, becomes freed from Desire and attains to Emancipation.'

CCXVIII

Bhishma quotes the words of Panchasikha (= Kapileya) to King

Janadeva of Mithila: Speculations on existence and non-existence, on cause and effect.

CCXIX
Bhishma quotes more words of Panchasikha to Janadeva: Emancipation. The senses or organs of action. The five elements. The qualities of the three Gunas.

CCXX
Bhishma: Self-restraint.

CCXXI
Bhishma: True penance. Vegetarianism. Fasting.

CCXXII
Bhishma quotes the words of Prahlada to Indra: Is man to be regarded as the doer of acts? The work of Nature.

CCXXIII
Bhishma begins the story of Indra and Vali (= Virochana's son), the former king who was now in the form of an ass.

CCXXIV
Bhishma continues the story: Vali explains that he feels no grief, for he attributes all activities to the work of Time. 'Time cooks everything.'

CCXXV
Bhishma continues the story: The goddess of Prosperity (= Sree = Duhshaha = Vidhitsa = Bhuti = Lakshmi) deserts Vali. Indra divides her portions equally among the Earth, the Waters, Fire, and good men. Vali predicts a great battle, in which he will be victor, at the time when the Sun 'will shine only upon the region of Brahma situated in the middle of Sumeru.'

CCXXVI
Bhishma quotes the words of Namuchi to Indra: The wise man never regards himself as the actor.

CCXXVII
Bhishma quotes the eloquent words of Vali addressed to Indra: Who is really the actor? 'I am not the actor. Thou art not the actor.' Time is the cause of all effects. 'Time, getting at him who says, "This I will do today

but this other act I will do tomorrow" sweeps him away.' The divisions of Time. 'All things are being cooked in Time's cauldron.'

CCXXVIII

Bhishma: How Sree (=Padma = Swaha = Swadha) deserted the Asuras and came to live with Indra in the celestial regions; how Sree was welcomed by Narada, and the blessings showered upon the Earth. Description of Sree. Powerful description of how society degenerates from a good state to a bad one; characteristics of each state.

CCXXIX

Bhishma quotes the words of Jaigishavya to Asita-Devala: The means to Emancipation.

CCXXX

Bhishma quotes the words of Krishna to Ugrasena: The good qualities of Narada.

CCXXXI

Bhishma quotes the words of Vyasa to his son Suka: The divisions of Time, including the lengths of the Yugas in celestial years.

'On the expiry of His night, Brahman, waking up, modifies the indestructible chit by causing it to be overlaid with Avidya. He then causes Consciousness to spring up, whence proceeds Mind which is identical with the Manifest.'

CCXXXII

Bhishma: Vyasa: Account of Creation. Mahat. Elements and senses. The Yugas and their characteristics.

CCXXXIII

Bhishma: Vyasa: The process of the withdrawal of creation when the night of Brahma(n) comes. Chandramas = Sankalpa.

CCXXXIV

Bhishma: Vyasa: The duties of a Brahmana. 'A life of domesticity is said to be the root of all the other modes of life.' The merit acquired by monarchs who have been magnanimous towards Brahmanas.

CCXXXV

Bhishma: Vyasa: The duties of a Brahmana. The great River of Time. The knowledge called 'Trayi'. The sciences called 'Varna' and 'Akshara'.

CCXXXVI

Bhishma: Vyasa: Emancipation according to the Sankhya system and according to the Yoga system. Mastery over the elements. Eloquent description of the body as a chariot. The two souls.

The seven kinds of Dharana (= one-pointed attention).

CCXXXVII

Bhishma: Vyasa: Wisdom. Hierarchy of created beings.

CCXXXVIII

Bhishma: Vyasa: Questions of existence and non-existence. Characteristics of the four Yugas. The work of Time. Four orders of men.

'The men of the Treta, the Dwapara, and the Kali Yugas are inspired with doubts.'

CCXXXIX

Bhishma: Vyasa: The elements. Senses. The Soul.

'In the feet (of living creatures) is Vishnu. In their arms is Indra. Within the stomach is Agni desirous of eating. In the ears are the points of the horizon (or the compass) representing the sense of hearing. In the tongue is speech which is Saraswati.' ... 'One occupies that much of the Supreme Soul as is commensurate with what is occupied in one's own soul by Vedic sound.' ... 'Time, of its own power, cooks all entities within itself. No one, however, knows That in which Time, in its turn, is cooked.'

CCXL

Bhishma: Vyasa: Contemplation according to the Yoga doctrine. 'He that has subdued his mind beholds in his own self, by the aid of his own knowledge, the Uncreate, Ancient, Undeteriorating, and Eternal Brahma(n)'.

CCXLI

Bhishma: Vyasa: Knowledge. Soul. Jiva. (Vyasa = son of Parasara.)

CCXLII

Bhishma: Vyasa: The life of the Brahmacharin.

CCXLIII

Bhishma: Vyasa: The life of the householder.

CCXLIV

Bhishma: Vyasa: The life of the forest recluse.

CCXLV
Bhishma: Vyasa: The fourth mode of life (= Sannyasa).

'The Supreme Soul is the capacious unconsciousness of dreamless slumber.'

CCXLVI
Bhishma: Vyasa: The Soul.

'This discourse, O son, intended for thy instruction, is the essence of all the Vedas ... By churning the wealth that is contained in all religious works and in all discourses based on truth, as also the ten thousands Richs, this nectar hath been raised. As butter from curds and fire from wood, even hath this been raised for the sake of my son — this that constituteth the knowledge of all truly wise men.'

CCXLVII
Bhishma: Vyasa: Adhyatma. The elements. Senses. Characteristics associated with each of the gunas.

CCXLVIII
Bhishma: Vyasa: Soul. Understanding. Mind.

'The mind must make a lamp of the senses for dispelling the darkness that shuts out the knowledge of the Supreme Soul.' ... 'The gnat born within a rotten fig is really not the fig but different from it. Nevertheless, as the gnat and the fig are seen to be united with each other, even so are Sattwa and Kshetrajna.'

CCXLIX
Bhishma: Vyasa: Understanding. Knowledge of the Soul. Emancipation.

CCL
Bhishma: Vyasa: 'The withdrawal of the mind and the senses from all unworthy objects and their due concentration (upon worthy objects) is the highest penance. That is the foremost of all duties.'

Eloquent picture of the river of life.

CCLI
Bhishma: Vyasa: How to become a truly regenerate person. Emancipation. 'There is only one kind of bondage in this world, viz., the bondage of Desire, and no other.'

CCLII
Bhishma: Vyasa: Elements and senses. 'The mind has doubt for its essence. The understanding discriminates and causes certainty.'

CCLIII
Bhishma: Vyasa: How to behold the Soul.

CCLIV
Bhishma: Vyasa: Eloquent picture of Desire as a tree in the heart of man. Picture of the body as a city.

CCLV
Bhishma: Elements and their properties. The sixty properties of the Understanding.

CCLVI
Bhishma begins to quote Narada's words to Anukampaka, a king in the Krita Age whose son Hari had been slain in battle:
How the Grandsire began to consume the creatures (whose numbers were increasing so as to make the universe uncomfortable).

CCLVII
Bhishma: Narada: Sthanu begs the Grandsire to stop the wholesale destruction of creatures. The Grandsire decides to institute birth and death. From the outlets of his body appears Death — a lady in black and red.

CCLVIII
Bhishma: Narada: The Grandsire instructs Death to slay the creatures. She weeps in grief and only after billions of years of penance does she reluctantly agree. Her tears become human diseases, and she uses Desire and Wrath to stop the life-breaths.

CCLIX
Bhishma: Righteousness. Morality. Conduct.

CCLX
Yudhishthira wants to know whether there be an absolute standard of righteousness.

CCLXI
Bhishma begins the story of Jajali, who became proud of the ascetic penances which he had performed: He once allowed a family of birds to be reared on his head.

CCLXII

Bhishma continues the story: Jajali is sent to a trader called Tuladhara, who instructs Jajali in the practice of harmlessness.

Slavery. Ploughing. Agriculture.

CCLXIII

Bhishma continues the story: Tuladhara speaks of the nature of Sacrifice.

CCLXIV

Bhishma concludes the story: Tuladhara speaks of Faith.

CCLXV

Bhishma quotes the words of King Vichakhy on the practice of harmlessness.

CCLXVI

Bhishma tells the story of Chirakarin; why he was called Chirakarin; what he did when commanded by his father (Gautama) to slay his own mother. In praise of Father. In praise of Mother.

CCLXVII

Bhishma tells the dialogue between Prince Satyavat and his father (= King Dyumatsena): Crime and punishment in society throughout the ages, with particular reference to capital punishment.

CCLXVIII

Bhishma begins the story of Kapila and the cow and the Rishi Syumarasmi who enters the form of the cow. The seventeen limbs of sacrifice.

CCLXIX

Bhishma continues the story: Questions about action and the renunciation of action. The studies comprised by the term 'Agama'.

CCLXX

Bhishma concludes the story: Emancipation. Good conduct. 'To the man of knowledge this (all that is perceived) is both *sat* and *asat*.'

CCLXXI

Bhishma tells the story of the Brahmana who became devoted to duty through the grace of the Cloud called Kundadhara. 'In wealth there may be a very little happiness but in virtue the measure of happiness is very great.'

CCLXXII
Bhishma tells the story of the Brahmana Satya and his wife Pushkara-dharini: The practice of harmlessness.

CCLXXIII
Bhishma: Sin, Righteousness, Renunciation, Emancipation.

CCLXXIV
Bhishma: The means to Emancipation. 'That path which leads to the Eastern Ocean is not the path by which one can go to the Western Ocean.'

CCLXXV
Bhishma quotes the words of Asita-Devala to Narada: The origin and destruction of all creatures. Elements, senses, organs of action, states of consciousness, rebirth.

CCLXXVI
Bhishma quotes the words of the ruler of the Videhas to Mandavya: Emancipation.

CCLXXVII
Bhishma quotes the words of Medhavin to his father: Devotion to Truth. 'When the soldiers that compose Death's army are on their march, nothing can resist them, except that one thing, viz., the power of Truth, for in Truth alone immortality dwells.'

CCLXXVIII
Bhishma: The life of Renunciation as the means to Emancipation.

CCLXXIX
Bhishma begins to quote the discourse between Vritra (= a Danava prince) and his preceptor Usanas: Actions and their fruits.

More names of Narayana: Vaikuntha, Purusha, Ananta, Sukla, Vishnu, Sanatana, Munjakesa, Harismasru, 'the Grandsire of all creatures'.

CCLXXX
Bhishma: Sanatkumara joins in the discourse: In praise of Vishnu. A new way to calculate the length of the life of one creation. How the six colours proceed from different guna-mixtures, with white as the foremost colour. How the Jiva may pass from the Dark Colour to White during a period measured in thousands of Kalpas.

Bhishma speaks of Krishna in relation to the Highest Deity 'who lies at the Root' and of the mutability of Krishna at the end of every Kalpa.

Bhishma predicts the future of the Pandavas: 'Living happily as long as the creation lasts, all of you at the next new creation will be admitted among the gods, and enjoying all kinds of felicities ye will at last be numbered among the Siddhas.'

CCLXXXI

Bhishma begins an account of the conflict between Indra and Vritra.

CCLXXXII

Bhishma: How Indra slew Vritra and became afflicted by the personified form of Brahmanicide. How the Grandsire took Brahmanicide from Indra and divided her equally among Agni, vegetation, the Apsaras, and water.

CCLXXXIII

Bhishma: The origin of Fever (from one drop of sweat on Mahadeva's forehead). How Mahadeva came to be granted a share in sacrificial offerings. Uma = Parvati = daughter of Himavat and wife of Siva or Mahadeva.

CCLXXXIV

Vaisampayana to Janamejaya: How the sacrifice made by Daksha was destroyed by the wrath of Siva. Daksha's prayer and Siva's mercy. Short but striking picture of the rivers of milk.

CCLXXXV

Bhishma quotes the hymn sung by Daksha and containing the 1,008 names of Siva. This is the foremost of all hymns. The 'auspicious religion called Pasupata'.

CCLXXXVI

Bhishma: The science of Adhyatma. Senses, elements, Mind, Soul, gunas, Understanding, Knowledge.

CCLXXXVII

Bhishma quotes the words of Samanga to Narada: Emancipation.

CCLXXXVIII

Bhishma quotes the words of Narada to Galava: The pursuit of excellence.

CCLXXXIX
Bhishma quotes the words of Arishtanemi to Sagara: Emancipation.

CCXC
Bhishma: Why Usanas (= Kavi) entered the stomach of Mahadeva; how Usanas acquired the name of Sukra and became Uma's son; the origin of Mahadeva's Pinaka, and why it was so called.

CCXCI
Bhishma quotes the words of Parasara to King Janaka: Acts and their fruits.

CCXCII
Bhishma: Parasara: Acts and their fruits.

CCXCIII
Bhishma: Parasara: Duties.

CCXCIV
Bhishma: Parasara: The duties of the four orders of men.

CCXCV
Bhishma: Parasara: The rise and fall of morality.

CCXCVI
Bhishma: Parasara: Penance.

CCXCVII
Bhishma: Parasara: The origin and duties of the four orders of men.

CCXCVIII
Bhishma: Parasara: Death and rebirth.

CCXCIX
Bhishma: Parasara: Acts and their fruits. 'Like a snake devouring air, Death wanders in this world made up of days and nights in the form of Decrepitude and devours all creatures.'

CCC
Bhishma quotes the words of Brahma(n) (in the form of a golden swan) to the Sadhyas: Morality.

CCCI

Bhishma: The Yoga system compared to the Sankhya system.

CCCII

Bhishma: The Sankhya system. Striking picture of the Ocean of Life. In praise of the knowledge contained in the Sankhya system.

CCCIII

Bhishma quotes the words of Vasishtha (= Maitravaruni) to King Karala: The Destructible and the Indestructible. Measures of time. Account of creation. Sambhu (= Isana) > Hiranyagarbha > Mahan (= Virat).

Chetana. Prakriti. The three colours. How Akshara (the Indestructible), by union with the unmanifest (Prakriti), becomes transformed into Kshara (destructible).

CCCIV

Bhishma: Vasishtha: Eloquent description of how the Soul surrounds itself with multifarious illusions. Cycle of birth and death. 'Although the Soul is not subject to modification of any kind and is the active principle that sets Prakriti in motion, yet entering a body that is united with the senses of knowledge and action, he regards all the acts of those senses as his own.'

CCCV

Bhishma: Vasishtha: 'the nature of Jiva when invested with ignorance'. The sixteen portions of Jiva compared to the sixteen portions of Chandramas.

CCCVI

Bhishma: Vasishtha: 'An intelligent man regards the unity of Jiva-soul with the Supreme Soul as consistent with the scriptures and as perfectly correct, while the man destitute of intelligence looks upon the two as different from each other.'

'Akshara is Oneness or Unity, while multiplicity or variety is said to be Kshara.'

CCCVII

Bhishma: Vasishtha: How one may behold the Supreme Soul through Yoga Contemplation and through the Sankhya system. Why the Soul is called the Presider and Kshetrajna and Purusha.

CCCVIII

Bhishma: Vasishtha: Vidya and Avidya. The Destructible and the Indestructible. 'When Jiva shows no affection for Prakriti and her principles, he then succeeds in beholding the Supreme and having once beheld Him wishes not to fall away from that felicity.' Eloquent lament of the awakened Jiva.

CCCIX
Bhishma: Vasishtha: The Supreme Soul and Jiva. Why Jiva is called 'Budhyamana'. Emancipation.

CCCX
Bhishma quotes the words of a Rishi to King Vasuman: Righteousness.

CCCXI
Bhishma quotes the words of Yajnavalkya to King Daivarati: The eight principles known by the name of Prakriti and the sixteen modifications. The nine kinds of creation.

CCCXII
Bhishma: Yajnavalkya: Creation. Measures of time. The twenty Bhutas.

CCCXIII
Bhishma: Yajnavalkya: The Dissolution of the Universe.

CCCXIV
Bhishma: Yajnavalkya: The subjects of Adhyatma, Adhibhuta, and Adhidaivata in relation to the body. Characteristics of the three gunas.

CCCXV
Bhishma: Yajnavalkya: Different guna-conditions.

CCCXVI
Bhishma: Yajnavalkya: Purusha and Prakriti.

CCCXVII
Bhishma: Yajnavalkya: Yoga Contemplation. Samadhi.

CCCXVIII
Bhishma: Yajnavalkya: Different regions allotted to men according to the part of the body through which the Jiva-soul escapes. Symptoms premonitory of death. How to conquer death.

CCCXIX
Bhishma: Yajnavalkya: Eloquent description of how Yajnavalkya

received the knowledge of the Vedas from Surya and with the aid of the goddess Saraswati who appeared 'adorned with all the vowels and the consonants and having placed the syllable OM in the van'. How Yajnavalkya compiled the Satapatha Brahmanas. The twenty-four questions put to Yajnavalkya by Viswavasu, and an eloquent description of how the answers came: 'The replies then to those questions naturally arose in my mind like butter from curds.'

The Fourth Science 'based on the principles of ratiocinative inference and having Emancipation for its end'. Purusha and Prakriti.

Knowledge.

CCCXX

Bhishma quotes the words of the Rishi Panchasikha to King Janaka: Immortality of the Soul. 'Decrepitude and death are devourers of all creatures, like wolves.'

CCCXXI

Bhishma quotes the discourse in the Satya Yuga between the lady Sulabha and King Dharmadhyaja: Emancipation. Characteristics of speech. Sovereignty. Stages of foetal growth. Atomic or molecular changes.

CCCXXII

Bhishma quotes the words with which Vyasa exhorted his twenty-five-year-old son Suka to follow the path of Righteousness.

CCCXXIII

Bhishma: Acts and their fruits. 'Whatever acts one does, lie down with the doer who lays himself down. Indeed, the sins one does, sit when the doer sits, and run when he runs. The sins act when the doer acts, and in fact follow the doer like his shadow.'

CCCXXIV

Bhishma begins the account of Suka's birth: Vyasa's austerities.

CCCXXV

Bhishma continues: How the illustrious son of Vyasa was born, and why he was called Suka. The Vedas come to him of their own accord.

CCCXXVI

Bhishma continues: Suka's studies. His father sends him to the palace of Janaka, King of Mithila, to learn of Duty and Emancipation.

CCCXXVII

Bhishma continues: Janaka begins to instruct Suka in Emancipation, but soon realises that the young man already has extensive knowledge.

CCCXXVIII

Bhishma continues: Suka goes to the mountains of Himavat (where Vishnu once shook Skanda's dart). Here Vyasa is instructing his four disciples (= Sumantra, Vaisampayana, Jaimini, Paila) in the study and teaching of the Vedas.

CCCXXIX

Bhishma continues: Vyasa's disciples descend from the mountain to teach and officiate at sacrifices. Narada exhorts Vyasa to resume his suspended recitation of the Vedas: 'The stain of the Vedas is the suspension of their recitation. The stain of the Brahmanas is their non-observance of vows. The Valhika race is the stain of the Earth. Curiosity is the stain of women.' A great wind blows, and Vyasa instructs Suka in the names of the winds (all of whom are the sons of Diti) and explains how the Pranas in the body are a direct reflection of the external winds.

CCCXXX

Bhishma continues: Narada speaks to Suka on Emancipation and quotes the words of Sanatkumara. 'Like a silkworm that ensconces itself in its own cocoon, thou art continually ensconcing thyself in a cocoon made of thy own innumerable acts born of stupefaction and error.' Striking picture of the river of life.

CCCXXXI

Bhishma: Narada: Emancipation.

CCCXXXII

Bhishma: Narada: Acts and their fruits. Cycle of birth and death. 'Rising and setting day after day, the Sun, who is himself undecaying, is continually cooking the joys and sorrows of all men.'

CCCXXXIII

Bhishma: On the summit of the Kailasa Mountain, Suka prepares to enter the Sun.

CCCXXXIV

Bhishma: Suka soars through the welkin, breaks through the conjoined summits of Himavat and Meru, rises up and up, and disappears, fully emancipated. The monosyllable 'Bho' and the echo in mountainous regions.

CCCXXXV

Bhishma quotes the words of Narayana to Narada (in the Krita Age of the Epoch of Manu): Kshetrajna is the Highest of the Highest. The names of the 21 Prajapatis.

CCCXXXVI

Bhishma: Narada goes to Meru, whence he views the White Island, whose strange denizens are described.

Bhishma now begins a narrative which he calls 'the essence of all narratives': Once the seven great Rishis compiled a treatise 'which is the eternal origin of all duties and observances'. Narayana was most pleased with this treatise, but he said that it would disappear on the death of King Uparichara (= Vasu).

CCCXXXVII

Bhishma continues: In the Krita Age King Uparichara holds a sacrifice at which Vrihaspati officiates. Narayana invisibly takes his share, and Vrihaspati becomes enraged. The Rishis Ekata, Dwita, and Trita explain that only the purest beings can see Narayana: they recount their stay on White Island — Narayana could be seen by the strange denizens but not by the Rishis themselves. Death of King Uparichara.

CCCXXXVIII

Bhishma continues: Dispute over the word 'Ajas'. Why King Uparichara was cursed, and how he was released from the curse.

CCCXXXIX

Bhishma: Narada goes to White Island. Narada's hymn to Narayana.

CCCXL

Bhishma: Narayana appears to Narada.

Description of Narayana's form. Narayana speaks about himself and the universe.

'Creation and destruction succeed each other even as sunrise and sunset in this world.' Narayana discloses his 'ancient appearances and future ones also'.

Distinction between Narayana and Brahma(n).

The importance of this narrative — 'really the essence of the hundreds of other narratives that thou hast heard from me' ... 'In days of yore, O monarch, the deities and the Asuras, uniting together, churned the Ocean and raised the Amrita. After the same manner, the Brahmanas, uniting together in days of yore, churned all the scriptures and raised this narrative which resembles nectar.'

'Suta continued, I have now told you all that Vaisampayana recited to Janamejaya.'

CCCXLI

Saunaka asks about the practices called Nivritti and Pravritti and the origins of sacrifice. In reply Suta (= Sauti) quotes the words of Vaisampayana (= disciple of Vyasa) to Janamejaya: What Vyasa said on this subject to his disciples — account of creation, names of the eight Prakritis, names of the seven spiritual sons of Brahma(n), the four Yugas, the Kali Yuga and the Tisya constellation.

CCCXLII

Vaisampayana quotes the words of Krishna to Arjuna: Some of Krishna's names and their meanings.

CCCXLIII

Vaisampayana: Krishna to Arjuna: Creation and dissolution, 'When four thousand Yugas according to the measure of the celestials elapse, the dissolution of the universe comes.' ... 'Day was not. Night was not. Aught was not. Naught was not.' The meaning of Tamas. The origin of Agni and Shoma (= Soma). Origin and status of the Brahmanas. Why Rudra's throat turned blue.

How King Hiranyakasipu dismissed Vasishtha and installed Viswarupa (= Trisiras) as his Hotri. How Trisiras became huge and drank all the sacrificial Soma; how Indra made his thunderbolt and how he slew Trisiras and Vritra; how Indra hid within a lotus stalk and how Nahusha took his place until Indra was restored. How Vishnu received a beautiful whirl [whorl?] on his bosom. Story of Soma and Rohini. Stories showing the power of Brahmanas. Names of Krishna and their meanings. 'The Vedic lexicon called Nighantuka.' ... 'I am He who is the repository of the science of syllables and pronunciation that is treated of in the supplementary portions of the Vedas.' ... 'Galava ... compiled the rules in respect of the division of syllables and words, and those about emphasis and accent in utterance, and shone as the first scholar who became conversant with those two subjects.'

How the combat between Rudra and Narayana came to an end.

CCCXLIV

Sauti to Saunaka: Vaisampayana: description of Nara and Narayana. In praise of Krishna. (Vyasa = the grandfather of the grandfather of Janamejaya.)

CCCXLV

Vaisampayana: In praise of the Self. The pathway to the Paramatman. Narada's devotion to Narayana.

CCCXLVI

Vaisampayana: Nara and Narayana to Narada: Origin of the Pitris and why they are also called Pindas.

CCCXLVII

Vaisampayana: 'Know that the Island-born Krishna, otherwise called Vyasa, is Narayana on Earth. Who else than he, O tiger among kings, could compile such a treatise as the *Mahābhārata*?'

(Bhagavad-Gita = Hari-Gita = Narayana-Gita.)

Sauti: In praise of Krishna.

CCCXLVIII

Sauti: Vaisampayana: Dissolution. How the two Asuras Madhu and Kaitabha stole the Vedas from Brahma. Brahma's hymn to Krishna. How Krishna slays Madhu and Kaitabha and restores the Vedas to Brahma. Striking description of Krishna's equine-headed form. In praise of Krishna. Krishna's pronunciation and the sound of his voice.

CCCXLIX

Vaisampayana: The origin and history of the Religion of Devotion in the Krita and Treta Ages.

CCCL

Vaisampayana: The fatigue felt by Vyasa 'in consequence of the great strain on his energies occasioned by the composition of the *Mahā bhārata*'.

Vyasa to his disciples: Why Narayana decided to appear in different forms from time to time. How the goddess of Intelligence entered Brahma. How the Rishi Saraswat arose from the syllable 'Bho'.

Saraswat (= Apantaratamas) in a later age was born as Vyasa, son of Parasara. 'The promulgator of Sankhya cult is said to be the great Rishi Kapila. The primeval Hiranyagarbha, and none else, is the promulgator of the Yoga system. The Rishi Apantaratamas is said to be the preceptor of the Vedas, some call that Rishi by the name of Prachina-garbha.

The cult known by the name of Pasupata was promulgated by the Lord of Uma, that master of all creatures, viz., the cheerful Siva, otherwise known by the name of Sreekantha, the son of Brahma. The illustrious Narayana is himself the promulgator of the cult, in its entirety, contained in the Pancharatra scriptures. In all these cults, O foremost of kings, it is seen that the puissant Narayana is the one sole object of exposition.'

CCCLI
Vaisampayana quotes the words of Brahma(n) to his son Siva: Purusha. Question of the one and the many.

CCCLII
Vaisampayana: Brahma: Purusha. Question of the one and the many. The Soul.

CCCLIII
Sauti: Vaisampayana: Bhishma prepares to recount to Yudhishthira the story which Narada once told to Indra.

CCCLIV
Bhishma: Indra's story begins: One Brahmana asks a superior Brahmana about the best type of duty.

CCCLV
Bhishma continues: The superior Brahmana refers to the virtues of a Naga called Padmanabha.

CCCLVI
Bhishma continues: The other Brahmana, delighted, resolves to visit Padmanabha.

CCCLVII
Bhishma continues: Finding that the Naga will be away for fifteen days pulling the chariot of Surya, the Brahmana resides in the adjacent forest, pending his return.

CCCLVIII
Bhishma continues: Despite the solicitations of the Naga's relatives, the Brahmana observes a strict fast.

CCCLIX
Bhishma continues: The Naga returns home.

CCCLX

Bhishma continues: The Naga is persuaded to go to see the Brahmana in the forest.

CCCLXI

Bhishma continues: The Naga goes to the Brahmana, whose name is Dharmaranya.

CCCLXII

Bhishma continues: The Naga speaks about Surya and the rain. 'What, again, can be more wonderful than this, that the mighty Wind, emanating from Surya, takes refuge in his ray and thence yawns over the universe?' How a great Being became one with Surya.

CCCLXIII

Bhishma continues: Surya declares that the great Being is a Brahmana who has observed the Unccha vow.

CCCLXV (sic)

Bhishma concludes: Dharmaranya adopts the Unccha observance.

END OF SANTI PARVA

ANUSASANA PARVA

I

Bhishma, to console Yudhishthira, tells the story of Mrityu, Gautami, Kala, the fowler, and the serpent. Actions and their ultimate cause. Karma.

II

Bhishma to Yudhishthira: How Sudarsana (= son of Agni) overcame Death while leading the life of a householder, and how his wife (= Oghavati) became the River Oghavati.

III

Yudhishthira asks how the Kshatriya Viswamitra became a Brahmana. The constellation of the Great Bear. The Pole Star.

IV

Bhishma: Why Aswatirtha is so called. The birth of Viswamitra, and how he became a Brahmana.

V

Bhishma: The story of 'The Fowler, the Parrot, and the Tree'.

VI

Bhishma quotes the words of Brahma to Vasishtha: Exertion, Destiny, Karma.

VII

Bhishma: Acts and their fruits.

'Whatever actions are performed by particular corporeal beings, the fruits thereof are reaped by the doers while endued with similar corporeal bodies; for example, the fruits of actions done with mind are enjoyed at the time of dreams, and those of actions performed physically are enjoyed in the working state physically. In whatever states creatures perform good or evil deeds, they reap the fruits thereof in similar states of succeeding lives. No act done with the five organs of sensual perception is ever lost.

'The five sensual organs and the immortal soul, which is the sixth, remain its witnesses.'

VIII

Bhishma: The status of Brahmanas. 'I like those regenerate persons whose highest wealth is Brahman, whose heaven consists in the knowledge of the soul, and whose penances are constituted by their diligent study of the Vedas.'

'To do good to the Brahmanas is the most sacred of all sacred acts.'

'To a woman, verily, the husband is the deity and he is the highest end after which she should strive. As the husband is to the wife, even so are the Brahmanas unto Kshatriyas.'

'A woman, in the absence of her husband, takes his younger brother for her lord; even so the Earth, not having obtained the Brahmana, made the Kshatriya her lord.'

IX

Bhishma: the story of the jackal and the ape.

X

Bhishma: The story of the Rishi and the Sudra, illustrating the wrongfulness of imparting instruction to a low-born person.

'That instruction which is imparted in barter for money always pollutes the instructor.'

XI

Bhishma quotes the eloquent words of Sree, goddess of Prosperity. 'I do not reside with those women also that do not attend to household furniture and provisions scattered all around the house, and that always utter words contrary to the wishes of their husbands.'

XII

Bhishma: Why King Bhangaswana became a lady. 'In acts of congress, the pleasure that women enjoy is always much greater than what is enjoyed by men.'

XIII

Bhishma: Conduct.

XIV

Krishna *(sic)* quotes the words of the Rishi Upamanyu: In praise of Mahadeva. 'When the unrighteous or sinful Kali Yuga comes, one should never pass a moment without devoting his heart upon Mahadeva.' Description of Mahadeva. Description of the bow called the Pinaka. Description of the Pasupata weapon. Description of the Sula weapon. Description of Mahadeva's battleaxe.

'Verily, Brahma and Narayana and Sakra — those three high-souled deities — shone there like three sacrificial fires. In their midst shone the illustrious god like the Sun in the midst of his corona, emerged from autumnal clouds.' Upamanyu's magnificent hymn to Mahadeva. 'Thou art he that hadst created from thy right side the Grandsire Brahma, the Creator of all things. Thou art he that hadst created from thy left side Vishnu for protecting the Creation. Thou art that puissant Lord who didst create Rudra when the end of the Yuga came and when the Creation was once more to be dissolved.'

Krishna tells of his own meeting with Mahadeva: description of Mahadeva. Krishna's hymn to Mahadeva.

XV

Krishna: The sixteen boons granted to me by Mahadeva and his spouse Uma.

XVI

Krishna: Upamanyu quotes Tandi's splendid hymn to Mahadeva. 'Thou art Adhi-Purusha, thou art Adhyatma, thou art Adhibhuta, and Adhi-Daivata, thou art Adhi-loka, Adhi-Vijnanam and Adhi-Yajna.'

XVII

Krishna: Upamanyu: Some of the names of Mahadeva, listed here in 'the king of all hymns', composed by Brahma, then 'conveyed from the region of Brahman to heaven, the region of the celestials. Tandi then obtained it from heaven. Hence it is known as the hymn composed by Tandi. From heaven Tandi brought it down on Earth. It is the most auspicious of all auspicious things, and is capable of cleansing the heart from all sins however heinous.'

'Thou art possessed of teeth that are exceedingly sharp (since thou art competent to chew innumerable worlds even as one munches nuts and swallows them speedily).'

'Thou art the *Mahābhārata* and other histories of the kind. Thou art the treatises called Mimansa. Thou art Gautama (the founder of the science of dialectics). Thou art the author of the great treatise on Grammar that has been named after the Moon.'

'Thou art the point (in the alphabet) which indicates the nasal sound. Thou art the two dots, i.e. Visarga.'

'Thou art that wind which rises at the time of the universal dissolution and which is capable of churning the entire universe even as the staff in the hands of the dairymaid churns the milk in the milkpot.'

'Thou art he who having put forth three feet covered all the universe with two and wanted space for the remaining one.'

'When a creature becomes cleansed of all his sins in course of millions of births in diverse orders of being, it is then that devotion springs up in his heart for Mahadeva.'

XVIII

Vaisampayana: Yudhishthira hears of numerous examples of Mahadeva's grace.

'Garga said — "O son of Pandu, gratified with me in consequence of mental sacrifice which I had performed, the great god bestowed upon me, on the banks of the sacred stream Saraswati, that wonderful science, viz., the knowledge of Time with its four and sixty branches."'

XIX

Bhishma begins the story of the Rishi Ashtavakra and how he was tested.

XX

Bhishma continues the story of Ashtavakra.

XXI

Bhishma concludes the story of Ashtavakra: how he married Suprabha (= daughter of the Rishi Vadanya).

XXII

Bhishma answers miscellaneous questions on morality.

XXIII

Bhishma: How to tell a good Brahmana from a bad one.

XXIV

Bhishma: When a person is guilty of Brahmanicide without actually slaying a Brahmana.

XXV

Bhishma quotes the words of Angiras: Tirthas and the merits they confer.

XXVI

Bhishma, quoting a Rishi, gives an eloquent tribute to the River Ganga (= Bhagirathi). 'Ganga is the daughter of Himavat, the spouse of Hara, and the ornament of both Heaven and Earth. She is the bestower of everything auspicious, and is competent to confer the six well-known attributes beginning with lordship or puissance. Verily, O king, Ganga is the one object of great sanctity in the three worlds and confers merit upon all. Truly, O monarch, Ganga is Righteousness in liquefied form. She is energy also running in a liquid form over the Earth.'

XXVII

Bhishma begins the story of Matanga and the She-Ass: Matanga, born a Chandala, wishes to become a Brahmana. Indra tells Matanga that it is impossible for one of low birth to become a Brahmana.

XXVIII

Bhishma continues the story: Indra re-affirms the impossibility of becoming a Brahmana.

XXIX

Bhishma concludes the story: Matanga's death, and the boons he received from Indra.

XXX

Bhishma: How the royal sage Vitahavya (= Haihaya) attained to the status of a Brahmana.

XXXI

Bhishma quotes Narada: The kinds of men that are worthy of worship.

XXXII

Bhishma: The story of King Vrishadarbha, 'The Pigeon, and the Hawk'.

XXXIII

Bhishma: The sublime status of Brahmanas. 'One cannot seize the wind with one's hands. One cannot touch the Moon with one's hand. One cannot support the Earth on one's arms. After the same manner, O king, one is not able to vanquish the Brahmanas in this world.'

XXXIV

Bhishma quotes the words of the Earth to Vasudeva: The duty of reverencing the Brahmanas.

XXXV

Bhishma: The sublime status of Brahmanas. 'The element of space or ether is incapable of being touched. The Himavat mountains are incapable of being moved from their site. The current of Ganga is incapable of being resisted by a dam. The Brahmanas are incapable of being subjugated. Kshatriyas are incapable of ruling the Earth without cultivating the good will of the Brahmanas. The Brahmanas are high-souled beings. They are the deities of the very deities.'

XXXVI

Bhishma: How Samvara rose to pre-eminence among the Asuras, and how Sakra rose to pre-eminence among the deities.
Reverence towards Brahmanas.

XXXVII

Bhishma: Morality.

XXXVIII

Bhishma quotes the words of the Apsara Panchachuda to the Rishi Narada: The disposition of women.

XXXIX

Yudhishthira: Why do men still attach themselves to women? Can women be restrained within the prescribed bounds?

XL

Bhishma: The disposition of women. 'There is no creature more sinful, O son, than women. Woman is a blazing fire. She is the illusion, O king, that the Daitya Maya created. She is the sharp edge of the razor. She is poison. She is a snake. She is fire. She is, verily, all these united together.' Why women were created. The story of the ascetic Devasarman, his wife Ruchi, and his disciple Vipula. The forms that can be assumed by Indra. How Vipula entered the body of Ruchi to protect her from Indra's advances.

XLI

Bhishma continues with a dramatic account of how Vipula restrained the lady and spoke through her mouth before moving back to his own body. Indra vanishes in terror!

XLII

Bhishma continues the story: Vipula becomes aware of his sin.

XLIII

Bhishma concludes the story: Devasarman, Ruchi and Vipula go to heaven. Disposition of women.

XLIV
Bhishma: Marriage. Types of marriage. Dowry.

XLV
Bhishma: Marriage and morality.

XLVI
Bhishma: The duty of men to honour and worship women.

XLVII
Bhishma: Marriage. Inheritance.

XLVIII
Bhishma: Inter-marriage. The names given to the offspring of cross-breeding.

XLIX
Bhishma: Inter-marriage. Different kinds of son.

L
Bhishma begins the story of Chyavana, the Rishi who dwelt in the confluence of the Ganga and the Yamuna. Chyavana gets dragged up by fishermen.

LI
Bhishma concludes the story: The purchase price for Chyavana. Eloquent praise of kine.

LII
Bhishma begins the story of the Rishi Chyavana and King Kusika.

LIII
Bhishma continues the story: How the king and queen are tested by serving the Rishi.

LIV
Bhishma continues the story: How Chyavana is gratified with the king and queen.

LV
Bhishma continues the story: Chyavana tells Kusika that his grandson will become a Brahmana.

LVI

Bhishma concludes the story: 'How the Bhrigus and the Kusikas became connected with each other by marriage ... The birth of Rama (of Bhrigu's race) and of Viswamitra (of Kusika's race) happened in the way that Chyavana had indicated.'

LVII

Bhishma: Acts and their fruits.

LVIII

Bhishma: The merits attached to the digging of tanks and the planting of trees.

LIX

Bhishma: Gifts. Reverence for Brahmanas.

LX

Bhishma: Gifts to Brahmanas.

LXI

Bhishma: Giving as a kingly duty.

LXII

Bhishma: 'The gift of Earth.' Importance of land. In praise of the Earth.

LXIII

Bhishma: The gift of food. In praise of food.

LXIV

Bhishma: Under what conjunctions particular gifts should be made.

LXV

Bhishma: Gifts.

LXVI

Bhishma: The gift of kine.

LXVII

Bhishma: The gift of drink.

LXVIII

Bhishma: The gift of water, of sesame, and of lamps. The story of Yama.

LXIX
Bhishma: The gift of kine.

LXX
Bhishma: The story of King Nriga and Krishna.

LXXI
Bhishma: The story of the Rishi Uddalaki, his son Nachiketa, and Yama. Gifts.

LXXII
Bhishma begins the dialogue between Sakra and the Grandsire (= Brahma(n)). The gift of kine.

LXXIII
Bhishma: The Grandsire's words to Sakra: The gift of kine.

LXXIV
Bhishma: The Grandsire's words to Sakra: The gift of kine. Dakshina. In praise of gold.

LXXV
Bhishma: Self-restraint. Practice of Brahmacharya. In praise of heroes. In praise of Truth. 'A thousand horse-sacrifices and Truth were once weighed in the balance. It was seen that Truth weighed heavier than a thousand horse-sacrifices.'

LXXVI
Bhishma: The gift of kine.

LXXVII
Bhishma: The gift of kine. How the cow called Surabhi was created, and how the Kapila cows were produced from her. How Rudra adopted the sign of the bull.

LXXVIII
Bhishma quotes the words of Vasishtha: In praise of kine.

LXXIX
Bhishma quotes the eloquent words of Vasishtha: The gift of kine.

LXXX
Bhishma quotes the words of Vasishtha: In praise of kine.

LXXXI

Bhishma quotes the words of Vyasa: In praise of kine. The gift of kine.

LXXXII

Bhishma: 'The glory of the dung of kine.' The story of Sree and the kine.

LXXXIII

Bhishma quotes the words of Brahman to Indra: In praise of kine.

LXXXIV

Bhishma begins a complex account of the merits of gold. He quotes the words of Vasishtha to Rama of Bhrigu's race. In praise of gold. How Rudra was persuaded not to procreate, and how Uma cursed the gods, that they should have no offspring.

LXXXV

Bhishma continues the story: Because Taraka is afflicting the three worlds, the gods seek Agni to help them. (Agni is able to have offspring, since he was not present when Uma uttered her curse.) How the frogs lost their tongues; how the elephants' tongues were bent back; how the parrots' tongues were turned up; how Agni casts his seed into the womb of Ganga; how Ganga casts the foetus onto Mount Meru; and why the child was called Kartikeya or Skanda or Guha. 'It was in this way that gold came into existence as the offspring of the deity of blazing flames.' In praise of gold. 'Verily, gold is said to have for its essence Agni and Soma.' (Agni is identified with Rudra.)

Bhishma tells another story: Once Rudra held a great sacrifice. 'The Rig-Veda also came there, adorned with the rules of orthoepy. The Lakshanas, the Suras, the Niruktas, the Notes arranged in rows, and the syllable OM, as also Nigraha and Pragraha, all came there and took their residence in the eye of Mahadeva.' The origin of all mobile creatures; of all immobile creatures; of Bhrigu; of Angiras; of Kavi; of Marichi; of Kasyapa; of the Valakhilyas; of Atri; of the Vaikhanasas; of the twin Aswins; of the Prajapatis; of the Rishis; of Chhandas; of Mind. How Kartikeya grew up and slew Taraka.

LXXXVI

Bhishma: Details of the upbringing of Kartikeya (= Kumara) and how he slew Taraka.

LXXXVII
Bhishma: The times for the performance of the Sraddha ritual (in honour of the Pitris).

LXXXVIII
Bhishma: Types of food to be offered at the Sraddha ritual. The constellation Magha.

LXXXIX
Bhishma: The names of the various constellations under which one may perform the Sraddha ritual.

XC
Bhishma: Those Brahmanas that should be invited to Sraddhas, and those that should not be invited. 'Utterers of Brahma say that even a single person that happens to be the descendant of sires who were teachers of the Veda and that is himself a Vedic teacher, sanctifies full seven miles around him.'

XCI
Bhishma: How the Sraddha was first conceived.

XCII
Bhishma: Further ordinances about the Sraddha. How the Pitris and the deities got indigestion and how they were cured.

XCIII
Bhishma: Standards of morality for Brahmanas. The story of King Vrishadarbhi and the Rishis: how the Rishis practised self-denial, and how they had to give explanations of their names to the Raskasi *(sic)* Yatudhani. The curses uttered by the Rishis.

XCIV
Bhishma: The story of the Rishis and the stolen lotus-stalks. The curses uttered by the Rishis. 'Let him chant the Vedas, offending at each step against the rules of orthoepy.'

XCV
Bhishma: The origin of the custom of giving umbrellas and sandals, contained in the story of Jamadagni, his wife Renuka, and Surya.

XCVI
Bhishma concludes the story of Jamadagni, Renuka and Surya.

XCVII
Bhishma quotes the words of the goddess Earth to Vasudeva: The duties of the householder.

XCVIII
Bhishma quotes the words of Sukra (= Kavi) to Vali: The gift of flowers; the gift of incense; the gift of lights.

XCIX
Bhishma begins the story of Nahusha and Agastya and Bhrigu: How Nahusha's pride on becoming the chief of the gods caused him to harness Rishis to his chariot.

C
Bhishma concludes the story: How Nahusha, cursed by Bhrigu, was transformed into a snake, until freed by Yudhishthira. How Indra was reinstated as chief of the celestials.

CI
Bhishma tells the story of the Chandala and the Kshatriya: The sin of pride.

CII
Bhishma tells the story of Indra (disguised as King Dhritarashtra), the ascetic Gautama, and the elephant. Description of various celestial regions.

CIII
Bhishma quotes the words of Bhagiratha to Brahman: How Bhagiratha attained the region 'which transcends that of the deities, of kine, and of the Rishis', through observing the 'vow of fast'.

CIV
Bhishma: A short life results from bad conduct, a long life from good conduct. 'One should wake up from sleep at the hour known as the Brahma Muhurta and then think of both religion and profit.' ... 'There is nothing that shortens life so effectually as sexual congress with other people's wives. For as many thousand years shall the adulterer have to live in Hell as the number of pores on the bodies of the women with whom he may commit the offence.'

Details of practical morality. Particular constellations connected with the Sraddha.

CV

Bhishma: Duties of the eldest brother and the youngest brother. Supremacy of the mother.

CVI

Bhishma quotes the words of the Rishi Angiras: The observance of fasts. Names of the months.

CVII

Bhishma: Fasts and their fruits.

CVIII

Bhishma: The spiritual significance of tirthas. 'Those ablutions which one performs with a blazing mind in the waters of the knowledge of Brahma in the tirtha called Manasa, are the true ablutions of those that are conversant with Truth.'

CIX

Bhishma: The observance of fasts and the worship of Krishna.

CX

Bhishma: Very detailed astronomical signs of when to begin the vow called Chandravrata.

CXI

Vrihaspati now appears and answers Yudhishthira's questions: How the vital seed originates; the different forms that have to be inhabited on account of sin.

CXII

Vrihaspati: Righteous actions and their fruits.

CXIII

Vrihaspati speaks of universal compassion and then departs.

CXIV

Bhishma: Abstention from meat.

'As the footprints of all other animals are engulfed in those of the elephant, even so all other religions are said to be comprehended in that of compassion.'

CXV

Bhishma: Abstention from meat.

CXVI

Bhishma: Abstention from meat. 'While dwelling in the uterus, all creatures are cooked in the fluid juices, that are alkaline and sour and bitter, of urine and phlegm and faeces — juices that produce painful sensations and are difficult to bear. There in the uterus, they have to dwell in a state of helplessness and are even repeatedly torn and pierced. They that are covetous of meat are seen to be repeatedly cooked in the uterus in such a state of helplessness.' Etymology of the word 'mansa', meaning 'flesh'.

CXVII

Bhishma begins the story of 'Vyasa and the Worm that retained its Memory'.

CXVIII

Bhishma continues: How the grace of Vyasa transforms the worm into a Kshatriya.

CXIX

Bhishma concludes: How the Kshatriya became a Brahmana.

CXX

Bhishma quotes the words of Vyasa to Maitreya: The supremacy of gift. Why Vyasa laughed.

CXXI

Bhishma quotes the words of Maitreya to Vyasa: The status of Brahmanas.

CXXII

Bhishma quotes the words of Vyasa to Maitreya: 'As filth is washed away from the body with water, as darkness is dispelled by the splendour of fire, even so is sin washed off by gifts and penances.'

CXXIII

Bhishma quotes the striking words of Sandili to Sumana: The conduct of a lady.

CXXIV

Bhishma tells the story of the Brahmana and the Rakshasa, to indicate the power of conciliation.

CXXV
Bhishma begins to quote a discussion that once took place at the Court of Indra: Ways of gratifying the Pitris.

CXXVI
Bhishma continues: Ways of gratifying Vishnu and the Pitris. The constellation Magha. The constellation Rohini.

CXXVII
Bhishma continues: Ways of gratifying the deities and the Pitris. New moon. Full moon. Purity of heart.

CXXVIII
Bhishma continues: Vayu tells how to gratify the Pitris and the deities.

CXXIX
Bhishma continues: Lomasa tells how to gratify the Pitris and the deities.

CXXX
Bhishma continues: Arundhati (= wife of Vasishtha) and Yama and Surya speak of good actions and bad actions.

CXXXI
Bhishma continues: The Pramathas speak of good practices and bad practices.

CXXXII
Bhishma continues: The elephants upholding the Earth speak of good practices.

CXXXIII
Bhishma continues: Maheswara speaks of the importance of kine.

CXXXIV
Bhishma concludes his account of the conference in the court of Indra: Skanda and Vishnu speak of good practices.

CXXXV
Bhishma: From whom food may be accepted.

CXXXVI
Bhishma: Expiation.

CXXXVII

Bhishma lists a number of kings who have gone to heaven through sacrifice and gifts.

CXXXVIII

Bhishma: Five kinds of gift.

CXXXIX

Bhishma begins an ancient story of Krishna: How Krishna underwent a vow to obtain a son; how fire proceeded out of Krishna's mouth; and how Krishna restored the creatures that had been consumed by the fire.

CXL

Bhishma continues: Narada addresses Krishna and gives a beautiful account of an even earlier occasion when Mahadeva developed his third eye.

CXLI

Bhishma: Narada: Mahadeva tells Uma why he has four faces; why he carries the Pinaka; why his throat is blue; why his abode is a crematorium. Mahadeva speaks of duty; the respective duties of the four orders of men; the religion of Pravritti and the religion of Nivritti.

CXLII

Bhishma: Narada: Mahadeva expounds the duties of forest recluses and ascetics.

CXLIII

Bhishma: Narada: Mahadeva to Uma: Duty, conduct, and how a man may move up or down through the four orders of men.

CXLIV

Bhishma: Narada: Mahadeva to Uma: The words that bind and the words that release; the thoughts that bind and the thoughts that release; the deeds that bind.

CXLV

Bhishma: Narada: Mahadeva to Uma: The deeds that release, and further deeds that bind.

CXLVI

Bhishma: Narada: Uma to Mahadeva: The duties of women.

CXLVII
Bhishma: Narada: Mahadeva to the Rishis: In praise of Krishna. The ancestors of Krishna.

CXLVIII
Bhishma: In praise of Krishna.

CXLIX
Bhishma: The Thousand Names of Krishna.

CL
Bhishma: The Savitri Mantras. The eleven Rudras; the twelve Adityas; the eight Vasus; the two Aswins; the Rishis known as Manavas; the seven Ritwiks of Yama; the seven Ritwiks in the sacrifice of Varuna; the seven Ritwiks of the Lord of Treasures; the seven upholders of the world.

CLI
Bhishma: The high status of Brahmanas.

CLII
Bhishma begins the story of Pavana and Arjuna (= King Kartavirya). Arjuna's pride.

CLIII
Bhishma continues the story: The god of Wind tells Arjuna of the prowess of the Brahmanas.

CLIV
Bhishma continues: The god of Wind tells Arjuna how the spirit of Kasyapa maintained the Earth for thirty thousand celestial years; and how Utathya (= Angiras) drank the ocean to recover his wife Bhadra from the clutches of Varuna.

CLV
Bhishma continues: The god of Wind tells Arjuna how Agastya consumed the Danavas and rescued the deities; and how Vasishtha rescued the deities from the Danavas.

CLVI
Bhishma continues: The god of Wind tells Arjuna how Atri protected the gods and how Chyavana forced the gods to grant the twin Aswins a share of the Soma.

CLVII

Bhishma concludes: Arjuna, humbled by all these accounts, comes to worship the Brahmanas.

CLVIII

Bhishma: In praise of Krishna.

CLIX

Krishna: The high status of Brahmanas. How Krishna once gratified the Rishi Durvasa, who yoked Krishna's wife Rukmini to his carriage.

CLX

Krishna: In praise of Mahadeva.

CLXI

Krishna: In praise of Mahadeva.

CLXII

Bhishma: Authority. Righteousness. Use of the word 'Tvam'.

CLXIII (wrongly numbered CLXVIII)

Yudhishthira: Exertion and destiny. 'One may be seen to be without any knowledge of the science of morals and policy even after one has studied all the treatises on that science.' ... 'One, again, may be seen appointed as the prime minister of a king without having at all studied the science of morals and policy.'

CLXIV

Bhishma: The power of Time. Righteousness. 'All men are equal in respect of their physical organism. All of them, again, are possessed of souls that are equal in respect of their nature. When dissolution comes, all else dissolves away. What remains is the inceptive will to achieve Righteousness.'

CLXV

Bhishma: Recital of the names of the gods, the names of learned Brahmanas, and the names of the principal kings.

CLXVI

Vaisampayana: 'When Bhishma became silent, the entire circle of kings (who were seated around him) became perfectly silent. Indeed, they all sat motionless there, like figures painted on canvas.' Yudhishthira and his followers return to Hastinapura.

CLXVII

Vaisampayana: After fifty days Yudhishthira and his followers come back to Bhishma, who has now spent fifty-eight days on his bed of arrows. Bhishma obtains Krishna's permission to leave the body.

CLXVIII

Vaisampayana: How Bhishma left the body. 'The life-breaths of Bhishma, piercing through the crown of his head, shot up through the welkin like a large meteor and soon became invisible.'

Cremation. Ganga's tribute to Bhishma and her lament for him. Krishna consoles Ganga, and everyone departs.

END OF ANUSASANA PARVA

ASWAMEDHA PARVA

I
Vaisampayana: Yudhishthira is stricken with grief at Bhishma's death, and Dhritarashtra is filled with repentance.

II
Krishna and Vyasa seek to guide the stricken Yudhishthira into the right path.

III
Vyasa exhorts Yudhishthira to prepare to offer sacrifices.

IV
Vyasa begins the story of King Marutta.

V
Vyasa continues: How Indra became envious of Marutta and dissuaded Vrihaspati from acting as priest to Marutta.

VI
Vyasa continues: Narada advises the discomfited Marutta to engage Samvarta as his priest.

VII
Vyasa continues: The irascible Samvarta agrees to be Marutta's priest.

VIII
Vyasa continues: Samvarta tells Marutta how to obtain gold. A list of the names of Mahadeva. Vrihaspati becomes grieved at the prosperity of Marutta and Samvarta.

IX
Vyasa continues: Indra sends Agni to Marutta to inform Marutta that Vrihaspati should be reinstated as his priest. Marutta curtly dismisses Agni.

X
Vyasa concludes: Indra sends the Gandharva Dhritarashtra to sway

Marutta with threats, but Samvarta's power gratifies Indra, who then partakes of Marutta's sacrifice.

Vyasa urges Yudhishthira to collect and use the gold left after Marutta's sacrifice.

XI

Vaisampayana: To comfort Yudhishthira, Krishna tells the story of the conflict between Indra and Vritra: how Vritra transferred himself from one element to another, until eventually he was slain within Indra's own body.

XII

Krishna tells Yudhishthira the essence of physical health and disease and the essence of mental health and disease. Krishna instructs Yudhishthira in the steps that lie ahead: 'The time has now arrived, when thou must fight the battle which each must fight single-handed with his mind. Therefore, O chief of Bharata's race, thou must now prepare to carry the struggle against thy mind; and by dint of abstraction and the merit of thine own Karma, thou must reach the other side of the mysterious and unintelligible (mind).'

XIII

Krishna: Desire. Renunciation. 'The word with two letters is Mrit-yu (death of the soul or perdition), and the word with three letters is Sas-wa-ta (Brahman) or the eternal spirit. The consciousness that this or that thing is mine, or the state of being addicted to worldly objects, is Mrityu and the absence of that feeling is Saswatam. And these two, Brahman and Mrityu, O king, have their seats in the souls of all creatures, and remaining unseen, they, without doubt, wage war with each other.'

The eloquent Kamagita.

XIV

Vaisampayana: Yudhishthira begins to rule the Earth again.

XV

Krishna and Arjuna enjoy the time of peace.

XVI

Krishna begins to tell Arjuna the story of Kasyapa and a very great ascetic.

XVII

Krishna continues: The ascetic to Kasyapa: How the Jiva leaves the body.

Actions and their fruits. 'Even as men possessed of eyes behold the firefly appearing and disappearing amid darkness, men possessed of the eye of knowledge and crowned with success of penances, behold, with spiritual vision, Jiva as he leaves the body, as he is reborn, and as he enters the womb.'

XVIII

Krishna continues: The ascetic to Kasyapa: How Jiva enters the womb. Facts about Pradhana. 'That person who looks upon pleasure and pain as inconstant, which, indeed, is the correct view, who regards the body as an unholy conglomeration, and destruction as ordained in action, and who remembers that what little of pleasure there is, is really all pain, will succeed in crossing this terrible ocean of worldly migration that is so difficult to cross.'

XIX

Krishna concludes: The ascetic to Kasyapa: Emancipation.

XX

Krishna quotes the words of a Brahmana to his wife: The Pranas and the sevenfold creation.

XXI

Krishna continues to quote: The goddess Word, the Pranas, and the Mind.

XXII

Krishna continues to quote the words of the Brahmana: 'The nose, the eye, the tongue, the skin, and the ear numbering the fifth, the mind, and the understanding — these are the seven sacrificing priests standing distinctly from one another. Dwelling in subtle space, they do not perceive one another.'

XXIII

Krishna continues to quote: The five Pranas: 'the five sacrificing priests'.

XXIV

Krishna continues to quote: The five Pranas.

XXV

Krishna continues to quote: 'The agent, the instrument, the action and Emancipation — these, O beautiful lady, are the four sacrificing priests by whom the universe is enveloped.' The Soul.

XXVI

Krishna continues to quote: The One. 'Unto them that enquired about what is highly beneficial, the holy one uttered only the word OM, which is Brahman in one syllable.'

XXVII

Krishna continues to quote: 'Having crossed that impassable fastness (the world) which has purposes for its gadflies and mosquitoes, grief and joy for its cold and heat, heedlessness for its blinding darkness, cupidity and diseases for its reptiles, wealth for its one danger on the road, and lust and wrath its robbers, I have entered the extensive forest of (Brahman).'

Eloquent description of this forest. The Kshetrajna.

XXVIII

Krishna continues to quote: Nature and Desire.

The conversation between a Yati and an Adhwaryu: The Indestructible and the Destructible. The Kshetrajna.

XXIX

Krishna: The Brahmana begins a story:

Why Rama (= son of Jamadagni) slew King Karttaviryya-Arjuna and all his followers.

XXX

Krishna: The Brahmana concludes his story:

The Pitris tell Rama the story of King Alarka — how he tried to shoot arrows at the sense-organs and the mind, and how he came to find joy in Yoga.

XXXI

Krishna continues to quote the words of the Brahmana: 'There are three foes in the world.'

The song of King Amvarisha: The necessity of overcoming cupidity. Sovereignty.

XXXII

Krishna continues to quote: The story of King Janaka:

The question of what is mine and what is not mine.

XXXIII

Krishna continues to quote: Reality.

XXXIV

Krishna continues to quote: Of Brahman. Krishna equates his own mind with the Brahmana and his own understanding with the Brahmana's wife and himself with Kshetrajna.

XXXV

Krishna quotes the words of another Brahmana to his disciple:

Truth, Brahman. Emancipation. Adhyatma. 'Understanding properly that great tree which has the unmanifest for its seed sprout, and the understanding for its trunk, and high consciousness of self for its branches, and the senses for the cells whence its twigs issue, and the (five) great elements for its flower buds, and the gross elements for its smaller boughs, which is always endued with leaves, which always puts forth flowers, and upon which all existent objects depend, whose seed is Brahman, and which is eternal — and cutting all topics with the sharp sword of knowledge, one attains to immortality and casts off birth and death.'

XXXVI

Krishna continues to quote the words of the Brahmana, who in turn is quoting the words of Brahma to the Rishis:

The dark manifestations of Tamas in human life.

XXXVII

Krishna: The Brahmana: Brahma: The manifestations of Passion (Rajas) in human life.

XXXVIII

Krishna: The Brahmana: Brahma: The manifestations of Goodness (Sattwa) in human life.

XXXIX

Krishna: The Brahmana: Brahma: The three qualities exist together in everything. 'Beholding the Sun rising, men of evil deeds become inspired with fear. Travellers on their way become afflicted with heat, and suffer distress. The Sun is Goodness developed; men of evil deeds represent Darkness; the heat which travellers on their way feel is said to be the quality of Passion; the shading (or eclipse) of the Sun on Parvana days should be known to represent Darkness. Even thus, the three qualities exist in all luminous bodies.'

XL

Krishna: The Brahmana: Brahma: The Great Soul (or Mahat).

XLI
Krishna: The Brahmana: Brahma: Egoism.

XLII
Krishna: The Brahmana: Brahma: Ahankara, the five elements, the five senses, the five organs of action; the fourfold mode of birth; Adhyatma; Emancipation.

'It is settled that the body has fire for colour, water for blood and other liquids, wind for sense of touch, earth for hideous holder of mind (viz., flesh and bones, etc), space (or ether) for sound; that it is pervaded by disease and sorrow; that it is overwhelmed by five currents; that it is made up of the five elements; that it has nine doors and two deities; that it is full of passion; that it is unfit to be seen (owing to its unholy character); that it is made up of three qualities; that it has three constituent elements (viz., wind, bile, and phlegm); that it is delighted with attachments of every kind; that it is full of delusion.'

XLIII
Krishna: The Brahmana: Brahma: The foremost trees. The foremost mountains. Creatures in which Rajas predominates. The senses and sensory perception. The Kshetrajna.

XLIV
Krishna: The Brahmana: Brahma: A list of 'firsts': e.g. 'The syllable OM is the first of all the Vedas, and the life-wind Prana is the first of all winds.'

XLV
Krishna: The Brahmana: Brahma: Striking picture of the wheel of life.

XLVI
Krishna: The Brahmana: Brahma: The life of the regenerate man.

XLVII
Krishna: The Brahmana: Brahma: Emancipation.

XLVIII
Krishna: The Brahmana: Brahma: Purusha, the Kshetrajna, and Nature.

XLIX
Krishna: The Brahmana: The Rishis ask Brahma what the highest duty is.

L

Krishna: The Brahmana: Brahma: Nature, the Kshetrajna, and Purusha. The elements, the senses. The names of the seven musical notes. The 'twelve varieties in colour'.

LI

Krishna: The Brahmana: Brahma: The Kshetrajna. Purusha.
   Krishna reveals: 'I am the preceptor, O mighty-armed one, and know that the mind is my pupil.'

LII

Vaisampayana: Arjuna utters the praises of Krishna. Krishna obtains Yudhishthira's permission to visit his father.
   (Hastinapura = Nagapura.)

LIII

On the journey Krishna meets the Rishi Utanka, who threatens to curse him for not having rescued the Kauravas.

LIV

Vasudeva speaks of himself to Utanka.

LV

Utanka worships Krishna and is granted a sight of Krishna's universal form. The origin of Utanka-clouds.

LVI

The story of Utanka: His devotion to his preceptor Gautama and how he promised to bring celestial earrings for Ahalya (= Gautama's wife).

LVII

The story of Utanka continues: How he meets King Saudasa (who has become a cannibal through Vasishtha's curse) whose wife Madayanti owns the celestial earrings.

LVIII

The story of Utanka concludes: How he obtains the earrings, how these are stolen and then recovered and presented to Ahalya.

LIX

Krishna reaches the city of Dwaravati, where the festival of Raivataka is running its merry course.

LX

Krishna gives his father (= Vasudeva) a summary of the battle.

LXI

Krishna gives his father an account of the death of Abhimanyu (= grandson to Vasudeva and son to Subhadra, who is sister to Krishna).

LXII

The obsequial rites of Abhimanyu are performed. Vyasa announces that Abhimanyu's son (as yet unborn) will be a great and righteous king. (This unborn child becomes the father of Janamejaya.)

LXIII

King Yudhishthira and his followers set off to bring back the wealth deposited by Marutta. The constellation Dhruba.

LXIV

The expedition reaches the mountains and camps for the night.

LXV

After worshipping Mahadeva, the expedition excavates the wealth and begins to convey it to Hastinapura.

LXVI

Meanwhile Parikshit is born (but without life on account of the blade of grass thrown by Aswatthaman) to Uttara.

LXVII

Subhadra pleads with Krishna to give life to the stillborn child.

LXVIII

Uttara (= grandmother to Janamejaya) makes a similar plea to Krishna.

LXIX

Uttara (= daughter to Virata) laments over her dead son. Krishna revives the child.

LXX

Rejoicing! Meaning of the name Parikshit.

LXXI

The expedition returns with the wealth, and plans are made for the horse-sacrifice.

LXXII
Yudhishthira appoints Arjuna to protect the horse as it roams the Earth.

LXXIII
After Yudhishthira's initiation, Arjuna sets off to protect the horse.

LXXIV
Following the horse, Arjuna subjugates the Trigartas.

LXXV
Arjuna begins a furious encounter with King Vajradatta (= son to Bhagadatta).

LXXVI
After three days Arjuna vanquishes Vajradatta.

LXXVII
Arjuna encounters the Saindhavas in battle.

There are portents as they appear to overwhelm Arjuna: 'Rahu swallowed up both the Sun and the Moon at the same time.'

LXXVIII
Arjuna vanquishes the Saindhavas. Their queen, Dussala, is the daughter of Dhritarashtra.

LXXIX
Arjuna is slain by his son Vabhruvahana (= son of Chitrangada and stepson (?) to Ulupi the daughter of the Snake-king) the King of Manipura.
(Ulupi also = wife to Arjuna.)

LXXX
Arjuna is revived by a special gem brought by Ulupi.

LXXXI
Ulupi explains that Arjuna had been slain on account of a curse pronounced by the Vasus when Arjuna slew Bhishma 'by unrighteous ways'.

LXXXII
Arjuna vanquishes Meghasandhi (= ruler of Magadha and son to Sahadeva).

LXXXIII
Arjuna vanquishes Sarabha (= son of Sisupala) and many others.

LXXXIV
Arjuna vanquishes the son of Sakuni.

LXXXV
Meanwhile preparations for the sacrifice are being made.

LXXXVI
Yudhishthira receives the news that the sacrificial horse and Arjuna are returning.

LXXXVII
Yudhishthira wants to know why Arjuna always leads a life of hardship, and Krishna explains: 'I do not see any censurable feature in this prince, except that the cheek bones of this lion among men are a little too high. It is in consequence of this that the foremost of men has always to be on the road.'

Arjuna returns.

LXXXVIII
More preparations are made for the sacrifice.

LXXXIX
The sacrificial animals are slain and cooked, the central part being the marrow of the horse. Yudhishthira gives the whole Earth to Vyasa; Vyasa returns it; Yudhishthira gives the Brahmanas the price of the Earth in gold. 'It was like a great festival, full of rejoicing and contented men.'

XC
A mongoose appears and deprecates the sacrifice. The mongoose tells the story of the Brahmana and his family who gave away their last food to a guest who turned out to be the deity of Righteousness.

XCI
The merits of different types of sacrifice. The question whether animals should be slain for sacrifice.

XCII
The story of Agastya and his sacrifice. How the Rishi Jamadagni overcame Anger.

END OF ASWAMEDHA PARVA

ASRAMAVASIKA PARVA

I
Vaisampayana to Janamejaya: How Yudhishthira ruled the kingdom, and how the utmost respect was paid to Dhritarashtra and Gandhari.

II
Yudhishthira endears himself to Dhritarashtra and to all the people.

III
For fifteen years Dhritarashtra is stung by the hostile feelings which Bhima harbours against him. The old king expresses his desire to lead a life of penance in the forest. Yudhishthira's grief.

IV
Vyasa instructs Yudhishthira to comply with Dhritarashtra's wishes.

V
Dhritarashtra instructs Yudhishthira in the art of kingship.

VI
Dhritarashtra continues to instruct Yudhishthira in the art of kingship.

VII
Dhritarashtra concludes his statements on the art of kingship.

VIII
Preparations for Dhritarashtra's departure.

IX
Dhritarashtra bids farewell to the citizens.

X
The shocked citizens bid farewell to Dhritarashtra. Destiny.

XI
Before leaving, Dhritarashtra wishes to perform the Sraddha-sacrifice for his dead sons and relatives, but Bhima objects.

XII
Yudhishthira gives every encouragement to Dhritarashtra to proceed with the Sraddha.

XIII
Dhritarashtra prepares to hold the Sraddha 'on the day of the full moon in the month of Kartika'.

XIV
Dhritarashtra performs the Sraddha.

XV
Dhritarashtra and Gandhari set off for the forest.

XVI
Much to the distress of the Pandavas, Kunti has resolved to go to the forest to care for Dhritarashtra and Gandhari.

XVII
Kunti explains her decision to her sons.

XVIII
Accompanied by Brahmanas, Dhritarashtra and Gandhari and Kunti spend their first night in the forest.

XIX
The three forest dwellers take up their abode in the retreat of the royal sage Satayupa.

XX
In the forest retreat Narada speaks of other royal sages who earned great merit through penances. Narada says that after three years Dhritarashtra and Gandhari will be highly honoured in the regions of Kuvera.

XXI
The Pandavas are left disconsolate.

XXII
The Pandavas decide to visit the forest dwellers.

XXIII
The royal entourage sets off.

XXIV
The Pandavas are reunited with Dhritarashtra, Gandhari and Kunti.

XXV
Sanjaya describes the royal visitors as he introduces them to the assembled ascetics. Description of Yudhishthira, Bhima, Arjuna, Sahadeva, Nakula, Krishna (the lady), Ulupi, etc.

XXVI
Yudhishthira hears that Vidura is practising severe penances. He finds Vidura alone in the forest. Striking account of how Vidura enters the body of Yudhishthira, who 'felt that he himself had become stronger than before and that he had acquired many additional virtues and accomplishments. Possessed of great learning and energy, O monarch, Pandu's son, King Yudhishthira the just, then recollected his own state before his birth among men.'

XXVII
The following morning everyone assembles at the forest retreat.

XXVIII
Vyasa speaks of the high nature of Vidura and of Yudhishthira:
'Through the curse of Mandavya, the deity of Righteousness became born as Vidura ... At the command of the Grandsire, and through my own energy, Vidura of great intelligence was procreated by me upon a soil owned by Vichitraviryya. A deity of deities, and eternal, he was, O king, thy brother. The learned know him to be Dharma in consequence of his practices of Dharana and Dhyana ... From that deity of Righteousness, through Yoga-puissance, the Kuru King Yudhishthira also took his birth. Yudhishthira, therefore, O king, is Dharma of great wisdom and immeasurable intelligence.'
'He that is Dharma is Vidura; and he that is Vidura is the (eldest) son of Pandu.'

XXIX
Vyasa wishes to grant a boon. Dhritarashtra expresses his anxiety about the fate of his dead sons and relatives and the other heroes slain in the battle.

XXX
Kunti gives an account of the birth of Karna. Vyasa assures Kunti that no fault is ascribed to her.

XXXI

Vyasa gives the true identity of Dhritarashtra, Pandu, Kshattri, Yudhishthira, Duryodhana, Sakuni, Dussasana, Bhima, Arjuna, Krishna, Sahadeva and Nakula, Karna, Abhimanyu, Dhrishtadyumna, Sikhandin, Drona, Aswatthaman, Bhishma.

XXXII

Vyasa causes all the dead heroes to arise from the waters of the Bhagirathi.

'Dhritarashtra, beholding all those heroes, with his celestial vision obtained through the grace of that sage, became full of joy.'

XXXIII

Happy union between the living and the dead. The dead return to their respective regions, and, at Vyasa's invitation, the Kshatriya widows plunge into the Bhagirathi in order to be with their lords.

XXXIV

Vaisampayana: 'Acts done without exertion are true and foremost, and bear real fruit. The soul, united however with such acts as require exertion for their accomplishment, enjoys pleasure and pain. Though united so (that is, with pleasure and pain), yet it is a certain inference that the soul is never modified by them, like the reflection of creatures in a mirror. It is never destroyed. As long as one's acts are not exhausted (by enjoyment or endurance of their fruits good and bad), so long does one regard the body to be oneself.' ... 'As regards creatures, they appear from an invisible state, and once more disappear into invisibleness.'

XXXV

Sauti: At King Janamejaya's request, Vyasa brings King Parikshit and others down from heaven to be seen by Janamejaya and his followers assembled for the sacrifice.

XXXVI

Sauti: Vaisampayana to Janamejaya: Dhritarashtra is now perfectly happy, and the royal visitors depart.

XXXVII

Vaisampayana: Two years later Narada visits Yudhishthira and tells him how Dhritarashtra and Gandhari and Kunti met death in a forest conflagration.

XXXVIII

Yudhishthira's laments.

XXXIX

The Pandavas perform the funeral rites. 'King Yudhishthira, after the death of his uncle, became very cheerless. Deprived of his kinsmen and relatives, he somehow bore the burthen of sovereignty.'

END OF ASRAMAVASIKA PARVA

MAUSALA PARVA

I

Vaisampayana: In the thirty-sixth year after the battle there are grave portents everywhere. All of the Vrishnis, except Krishna and Rama, are slain by the iron bolt. Prohibition on the manufacture of wines and spirits.

II

The power of Time.

III

Vaisampayana describes how the Vrishnis quarrelled with each other. Satyaki slays Kritavarman. Satyaki, Samva, Charudeshna, Pradyumna, Aniruddha, and Gada are all slain. Krishna exterminates the Vrishnis and the Andakas.

IV

Rama and Krishna leave the body.

V

Arjuna goes to the lamenting city of Dwaraka.

VI

Krishna's father (= Vasudeva = Anakadundubhi = Arjuna's uncle) asks Arjuna to protect the Vrishni kingdom and Krishna's sixteen thousand widows.

VII

Krishna's father leaves the body.

Arjuna escorts the remnants of the Vrishnis, the Andhakas, and the Bhojas to Hastinapura. On the way the company is attacked by robbers and Arjuna is appalled at being incapable of stopping them from carrying off wealth and women.

VIII

Arjuna reports everything to Vyasa, who consoles him and says, 'The time has come, O Bharata, for you all to attain to the highest goal.'

END OF MAUSALA PARVA

MAHAPRASTHANIKA PARVA

I

The five sons of Pandu, accompanied by Draupadi and a dog, set off, resolved to retire from the world. ('Parikshit will rule in Hastinapura, while the Yadava prince, Vajra, will rule in Sakraprastha.')

Arjuna returns to Varuna the bow Gandiva and the two inexhaustible quivers.

II

As they walk on, Draupadi falls to the ground, followed by Sahadeva, then Nakula, then Arjuna, then Bhima.

III

Sakra appears and offers to take Yudhishthira to heaven, but Yudhishthira will not abandon the devoted dog, which then reveals itself as Dharma. Yudhishthira now expresses his desire to go where Draupadi and his brothers have gone.

END OF MAHAPRASTHANIKA PARVA

SWARGAROHANIKA PARVA

I

On his arrival in Heaven, Yudhishthira (still in human form) is shocked to find Duryodhana enjoying a place of high honour. Yudhishthira refuses to stay: he wishes to see his relatives and friends.

II

Yudhishthira is shown a view of Hell [strongly paralleled by parts of Dante's 'Inferno']. As the messenger is about to take him back, Yudhishthira hears the voices of his friends and relatives, who have been comforted by his presence. Yudhishthira refuses to leave.

III

All the gods arrive to praise Yudhishthira. Sakra says: 'Hell, O son, should without doubt be beheld by every king ... He who enjoys first the fruits of his good acts must afterwards endure Hell. He, on the other hand, who first endures Hell, must afterwards enjoy Heaven ... Thou hadst, by a pretence, deceived Drona in the matter of his son. Thou hast, in consequence thereof, been shown Hell by an act of deception.'

Dharma is delighted that Yudhishthira has passed the third test put to him.

IV

Everything has become celestial. Yudhishthira sees many of his friends and their celestial counterparts.

V

The divine nature and celestial counterpart of others in the narrative.

Janamejaya's sacrifice now ends, the interval between rituals having been filled by the narrative told by Vaisampayana.

In praise of the *Mahābhārata*: Its composition, its recitation, and its essence.

VI

In praise of the *Mahābhārata*: By whom and how it should be recited; the merits of reciting it and of hearing it recited; the gifts that should be made during the recitation. 'The "Bharata", O chief of the Bharatas, is the foremost of all scriptures.'

END OF SWARGAROHANIKA PARVA

PART TWO

WHERE'S WHAT IN THE MAHĀBHĀRATA

		Parva	Section
Absolute		SAN	CCI
Accidents		U	XLVI
Action		B	XXVIII, XXIX
	nature of	U	XXXIV
	action and non-attachment	B	XXVI
	action and renunciation of action	SAN	CCLXIX
	organs of action	SAN	CCLXXV
		ASW	XLII
	who is really the actor?	SAN	CCXXVII
Acts	good acts	AN	CXXXII, CXXX, CXXXIV
	good and bad acts	AN	CXXX, CXXXI
	acts that bind and acts that release	AN	CXLV
	righteous acts and their fruits	AN	CXXII
	acts and their ultimate cause	AN	I
	causes and results of acts	SAN	XXXII
	Krishna speaks of human acts	U	LXXVII
	human affairs and their mainspring	U	LXXIX
	'The person cast into the funeral pyre is followed only by his own acts.'	U	XL
Acts and their Fruits		AD	LXXXIX
		ST	II, III
		SAN	IX, XLII, CLXXXI, CCI, CCLXXIX, CCII, CCXCI, CCXCII, CCXCIX, CCCXXIII
		AN	VII, LVII
		ASW	XVII
		ASR	XXXIV
Adhyatma		SAN	CXCIV, CCXLVII
		ASW	XXV, XLII
	science of adhyatma	SAN	CCLXXXVI
Ahankāra		ASW	XLII
Akshauhini	constitution of	AD	II
Amaravati	i.e. the city of Indra	VA	XLII
	description	VA	XLIII

Amrita		U	CII
	Narayana advises gods to churn Ocean for Amrita	AD	XVII
	Amrita given to Narayana for safekeeping	AD	XIX
	how Garuda obtained the Amrita	AD	XXXIII
	Amrita quaffed in city of Patalam	U	XCIX
	how Amrita comes from the Ocean	AD	XVIII
Anger	Yudhishthira speaks on anger and forgiveness	VA	XXIX
	Brahma's anger begins to burn universe	D	I
	how Rishi Jamadagni overcame anger	ASW	XCII
Architecture	*see* **Assembly Houses, Palaces**		
Arts	Viswakarman is founder of all arts	AD	LXVI
Assembly	function of assembly with regard to righteousness	U	XCV
Assembly Houses	Narada describes assembly houses of:		
	Sakra	SAB	VII
	Yama	SAB	VIII
	Varuna	SAB	IX
	Kuvera	SAB	X
	Brahma	SAB	XI
	see also **Palaces**		
Astronomy		U	XLVIII
		B	II, III, XVII
	'Day when star Varga-Daivata (Purva-phalguni) would be ascendant'	AD	VIII
	origin of quarrel between Rahu's head and Surya and Soma. 'And to this day it swalloweth Surya and Soma.'	AD	XIX
	why Surya decided to consume the world	AD	XXIV
	the wives of Soma (the Nakshatras)	AD	LXVI
	Druva's son (Kala-time)	AD	LXVI
	Soma's son	AD	LXVI
	when Yudhishthira was born	AD	CXXIII
	'Moon in conjunction with five-starred constellation Hasta'	AD	CXXXVII
	'Pandavas set out on 8th day of Phalguna'	AD	CXLVII
	'This day Moon has entered constellation called Pushya'	AD	CC
	'When constellation Magha was in ascendant'	AD	CCXII

Astronomy *cont*	why Arundhati becomes a little star	AD	CCXXXV
	Krishna 'set out at excellent moment of lunar day of auspicious stellar conjunction'	SAB	II
	'Those versed in chronology say that thou (Sun) art beginning and end of day of Brahma, which consisteth of a full thousand Yugas.'	VA	III
	'These ... are virtuous persons stationed in their respective places. It is these whom thou hast seen ... as stars, from the Earth.'	VA	XLII
	'The day following the full moon of Agrahayana in which constellation Pushya was ascendant'	VA	XCIII
	Mount Vindhya addresses the Sun: 'As thou every day goest round Meru ... dost thou even the same by me, O maker of light!'	VA	CIV
	'O Bharata, dividing time into day and night, Kala and Kashtha, that Lord, the Sun, dealeth life and motion to all created things.'	VA	CLXII
	Mandara, Mahameru and the work of Sun and Moon	VA	CLXII
	auspicious times connected with constellations	VA	CLXLIX
	conjunction of Sun, Moon and Agni	VA	CCXXIII
	movements of Sun, Moon and constellations	U	CX
	constellations; Swati, Sun, Moon, Luminaries	U	CXI
	Parigha	B	CXIII
	Purvabhadra, Uttarabhadra	U	CXIV
	Punarvasu	K	XLIX
		SAN	XLIV
	Chitra	K	LXXVI
	Magha	AN	LXXXVIII, CXXVI
	Rohini	AN	CXXVI
		K	XCIV
	Dhruba	ASW	LXIII
	Revati	B	XI
	constellation of the Great Bear; Pole Star	AN	III
	dimensions of planet Swarbhanu, Moon, Sun	B	XII
	comparisons between combatants and heavens: Rahu, Sun, Moon, Planets, Budha and Sukra (Mercury and Venus)	B	CII
	permanent presence of Lakshmi in the Moon	D	II

Astronomy *cont*	planets and constellations named	U	CXLIII
	Rahu, Surya	B	XI
	Budha	D	LXXXIV
	Venus	D	CLXVIII
	Mars	K	XV
	Sukra	D	LXXXIV
		K	XVII
	Mercury	D	CLXVIII
		K	XV, XIX, XCIV
	Rahu	B	XII
		K	LXXXVII
	Vrihaspati	K	XVII
	headless planet Ketu	K	XVIII, LXXXVII
	Soma	B	XI
		D	LXXXIV
	Jupiter	K	XCIV
	'seven great planets including the Sun seemed to proceed against one another (for combat)'	K	XXXVII
	Sun is eclipsed by Ketu	K	XLVI
	'the Sun himself between months of Jyaishtha and Ashadha, within his bright corona'	K	LXXIX
	conjunction of Venus, Mars, Mercury	SAL	XI
	Saturn	SAL	XVI
	Rama says: 'Two and 40 days have passed since I left home. I set out under constellation Pushya and have come back under Sravana.'	SAL	XXXIV
	Rama set out under Pushya, under conjunction of asterism called Maitra	SAL	XXXV
	story of Soma and 27 daughters of Daksha	SAL	XXXV
	Rahu swallowed the Sun most untimely ...	SAL	LVI
	'gladdening that great host, divine Chandramas rose before it in the firmament, once more inspiring with moisture, by his own force, the terrestrial herbs and plants whose juice had been sucked up by the Sun'	SAN	LII
	astronomy and army tactics and manoeuvres	SAN	C
	planet Vrihaspati began to move in a retrograde course and Soma, abandoning his own orbit, receded towards the south	SAN	CXLI

Astronomy *cont*	16 portions of Jiva, compared to the 16 portions of Chandramas	SAN	CCCV
	Kali Yuga and the Tisya constellation	SAN	CCCXLI
	Surya and the rain	SAN	CCCLXII
	how a great Being became one with Surya	SAN	CCCLXII
	under what conjunctions particular gifts should be made	AN	LXIV
	names of various constellations under which one may perform the Sraddha ritual	AN	LXXXIX
	very detailed astronomical signs of when to begin the vow called Chandravrata	AN	CX
	new moon, full moon	AN	CXXVII
	'Rahu swallowed up both Sun and Moon'	ASW	LXXVII
	see also **Time, Wheel of Time, Zodiac, Sun, Moon**		
Asylum	the absolute pre-eminence of Asylum called Vadari	VA	XC
Atheism	virtue and atheism	VA	XXXI
Austerities	practised by Arjuna	VA	XXXVIII
	Death for billions of years	D	LII
	Vyasa	SAN	CCCXXIV
	austerities of Chyavana, who became an anthill	VA	CXXII
	austerities of Yavakri, to gain knowledge of Vedic lore	VA	CXXXV
	Visvamitra ... only person to rise from lower order to Brahmana by ascetic austerities	U	CVI
Authority		AN	CLXII
Battles	*see* **Warfare**		
Beauty	signs of feminine beauty	U	CXVI
Bhagavadgita	begins	B	XXV
	ends	B	XLII
Bharatvarsha	and its rivers and provinces	B	IX
Bhikshu	mode of life	SAN	LXIII

Bhogavati	Narada takes Matali to city of Bhogavati	U	CIII
Biology	information *see also* **Physiology, Medicine, Birth, Body**	VA	CCXII
Birds	Narada shows Matali the region of birds whose principal names are given. Their guardian deity is Vishnu. They all subsist on snakes and have no compassion	U	CI
Birth	fourfold mode of	ASW	XLII
Body	description of	ASW	XLII
	the three attributes of	SAN	XVI
Boons	Janamejaya grants Astika a boon	AD	LVI
	Shiva has granted Gandhari boon of 100 sons	AD	CX
	Mahadeva promised five husbands to Rishi's daughter	AD	CLXXI
	Indra's boon to Arjuna and Krishna	AD	CCXXXVI
	boon of Dhritarashtra to Draupadi	SAB	LXX
	boon granted to Hanuman	VA	CXLVII
	Utanka obtains boon from Vishnu	VA	CC
	Skanda grants Swaha boon	VA	CCXXX
	Duryodhana receives boon from Muni Durvasa	VA	CCLX
	Savitri receives five boons from Yama	VA	CCLXV
	Rudra grants Amva boon that she will slay Bhishma	U	CXC
	Two boons granted to Bhishma by his father	B	CXX
	boon conferred on Jayadratha by Mahadeva	D	XL
	16 boons granted to Krishna by Mahadeva	AN	XV
	Vyasa's boon to Dhritarashtra	ASR	XXXII
Botany	origins of many botanical species	AD	LXVI
Brahmacharya	practice of	AN	LXXV
Brahma	attainment of	SAN	CCV
Brahmanas	nature of	VA	CLXXIX
	greatness of	VA	CLXLI

Brahmanas	status of	AN	VIII, CXXI
cont	sublime status of	AN	XXXIII
	high status of	AN	CLI, CLIX
	Brahmanas dutiful and neglectful	SAN	LXXVI
	origin and status of the Brahmanas	SAN	CCCXLIII
	duty of reverencing the Brahmanas	AN	XXXIV
	reverence towards Brahmanas	AN	XXXVI, LIX
	standards of morality for Brahmanas	AN	XCIII
	gifts to Brahmanas	AN	LX
	names of learned Brahmanas	AN	CLXV
	importance of a priest to a king	AD	CLXXII
	importance of the priest	AD	CLXXV
	need for Kshatriyas to be associated with Brahmanas	VA	XXVI
	four modes of life laid down exclusively for Brahmanas Vanaprastha, Bhaikshya, Garhasthya, Brahmacharya	SAN	LXI
	qualities of a priest	SAN	LXXIX
	how Brahmanas should behave in times of distress	SAN	CXXXII
	how to tell a good Brahmana from a bad one	AN	XXIII
	sublime status of Brahmanas ... deities of deities	AN	XXXV
	those Brahmanas that should and should not be invited to Sraddhas	AN	XC
	see also **Four Orders of Men**		
Brahmanicide	how Indra was purified from Brahmanicide	SAL	XLIII
	Janamejaya commits Brahmanicide	SAN	CL
	how Grandsire took Brahmanicide from Indra and divided her equally among Agni, Vegetation, the Apsaras and water	SAN	CCLXXXII
	when a person is guilty of Brahmanicide without actually slaying a Brahmana	AN	XXIV
Chariots	Arjuna receives marvellous chariot made by Viswakarman	AD	CCXXVII
	wonderful chariot made by the celestials using all the parts of the universe	K	XXXIV
	see also **Warfare**		

Chastisement	rod of	SAN	XV, XXIII
	importance of	SAN	XX
	respective punishment for four orders of men	SAN	XV
	the many names and multiform appearance of Chastisement and his wife Morality. 'This eternal universe is impartial Chastisement's self'	SAN	CXXI
	if science of chastisement disappears, Vedas will disappear	SAN	LXIII
	how Saraswati created Danda-niti (science of chastisement); line of descent of rod of chastisement from Kshupa to the Kshatriyas	SAN	CXXII
	see also **Punishment**		
Chetana		SAN	CCCIII
China	reference to	U	LXXXVI
Churning	how the gods churned the Ocean	AD	XVIII
Clouds	origin of Utanka clouds	ASW	LV
	clouds called Kundadhara	SAN	CCLXXI
Colours	the three colours	SAN	CCCIII
	the four colours associated with four orders of men	SAN	CLXXXVIII
	how the six colours proceed from different guna mixtures, with white as foremost colour; how the Jiva may pass from Dark Colour to White during a period measured in thousands of Kalpas	SAN	CCLXXX
	the 12 varieties in colours	ASW	L
Compassion	compassion universal	AN	CXIII
	universal compassion	AN	CXIV
Conches	Krishna's conch is called Gigantes and Arguna's Theodotes	B	I
	names of Pandava conches	B	XXV, LI
	Panchajanya will emit shrill Rishava note (the 2nd note of the Hindu gamut)	D	LXXIX
Conciliation	power of	AN	CXXIV

Conduct		SAN	CXXIX, CXCIII, CCLIX
		AN	XIII
	good conduct	SAN	CCLXX
	good and bad conduct	AN	CIV
	conduct of a lady	AN	CXXIII
	conduct and duty	AN	CXLIII
	purity of conduct	U	CXIII
	how a person may overcome all difficulties	SAN	CX
	how to behave when abused by the ignorant	SAN	CXIV
	the supreme importance of conduct	SAN	CXXIV
	the man of self restraint	SAN	CLX
	how to overcome grief	SAN	CLXXIV
	how to behave when one sees that Death and Decrepitude are assailing everything	SAN	CLXXV
	the malevolent person	SAN	CLXIV
	self-restraint	SAN	CCXX
	how to become a truly regenerate person	SAN	CCLI
	the life of the regenerate man	ASW	XLVI
Consciousness	states of	SAN	CCLXXV
	the three states of	SAN	CCIII
Contemplation		B	XXX
	according to Yoga doctrine	SAN	CCXL
	Yoga contemplation Samadhi	SAN	CCCXVII
Contentment		SAN	CLXXX
	contentment is highest heaven ... highest bliss. There is nothing higher than contentment	SAN	XXI
Covetousness	as the source of sin	SAN	CLVIII
Creation		SAN	CCLXXX
	account of	SAN	CLXVI, CLXXXII, CCII, CCVII, CCVIII, CCX, CCXXXII, CCCXLI

Creation *cont*	account of creation from the mighty egg	AD	I
	what happened when creation came to its end. A striking account of inter-creation activity	VA	CCII
	Garuda speaks of the creation	U	CXIV
	Krishna speaks of Siva and creation	SAU	XVII
	creation of the elements	SAN	CLXXXIII
	all the classes of created beings, beginning with the Prajapatis; the eternal creation and the creation produced by the Great Rishis	SAN	CLXXXVIII
	the Primary Creation and the Secondary Creation	SAN	CCV
	the eight constituents of primordial Prakriti	SAN	CCX
	the 16 constituents of a creature	SAN	CCX
	the process of withdrawal of creation when the night of Brahma comes	SAN	CCXXXIII
	hierarchy of created beings	SAN	CCXXXVII
	question of existence and non-existence	SAN	CCXXXVIII
	Creation and Dissolution	SAN	CCCXLIII
	the origin of all mobile and immobile creatures	AN	LXXXV
	origin and destruction of all creatures	SAN	CCLXXV
	Destructible and the Indestructible	SAN	CCCVIII
		ASW	XXVIII
	an account of creation	SAN	CCCIII
	the nine kinds of creation	SAN	CCCXI
	the 20 Bhutas	SAN	CCCXII
	Pranas and the seven-fold creation	ASW	XX
	'as regards Creatures, they appear from an invisible state and once more disappear into invisibleness'	ASR	XXXIV
Cremation		AN	CLXVIII
Cupidity	the necessity of overcoming cupidity	ASW	XXXI
Curses	why Bhrigu decides to curse Agni	AD	VI
	how brothers of Janamejaya are cursed by Sarama	AD	III
	how the Rishi Sahasrapat was changed into a snake by a Brahmana, and how he regained his human form	AD	X
	why Kadru cursed her snake-sons	AD	XX
	Sringin curses Parikshit	AD	XLI

Curses *cont*	Sukra puts the curse of decrepitude upon Yayati	AD	LXXXIII
	the curse upon Pandu	AD	XCV
	how an Apsara became a fish	AD	LXIII
	why King Mahabhisha was cursed in heaven	AD	XCVI
	why the Vasus were cursed ... by Vasishtha	AD	XCVI
	... by the Rishi Apava	AD	XCIX
	why the god of Justice was cursed	AD	CVII
	why Dirghatamas was cursed with blindness	AD	CIV
	why a deer cursed Pandu	AD	CXVIII
	how Vasishtha frees Kalmashapada from his curse	AD	CLXXIX
	Arjuna releases the Apsaras from their curse	AD	CCXIX
	how King Kalmashapada was cursed by Saktri	AD	CLXXVIII
	Urvasi curses Arjuna	VA	XLVI
	five crocodiles are Apsaras under a Brahmana's curse	AD	CCXVIII
	Nala frees a snake from a curse	VA	LXVI
	the curse laid upon Kuvera by the Rishi Agastya is lifted by Bhima	VA	CLX
	Ashtavakra is cursed by his father Kahoda	VA	CXXXII
	the Rishi Maitreya curses Duryodhana	VA	X
	a snake is really the royal sage Nahusha, cursed by Agastya	VA	CLXXVIII
	Nahusha is freed from his curse	VA	CLXXX
	a fowler is really a Brahmana under Rishi's curse	VA	CCXIV
	why Nahusha became a snake	U	XVII
	Vriddhakshatra suffers from his own curse	D	CXLV
	the two curses put upon Karna	K	XLII
	Karna suffers the Brahman's curse	K	XC
	Saraswati is freed from curse of Viswamitra	SAL	XLIII
	Krishna's curse upon Aswatthaman	SAU	XVI
	Gandhari curses Krishna	ST	XXV
	why Arjuna, son of Kritavirya, was cursed by the Rishi Apava	SAN	L
	how Rama frees an Asura from the curse of being a worm	SAN	III
	Narada and Parvata curse and free each other	SAN	XXX
	Yudhishthira curses all the women of the world; 'henceforth no woman shall succeed in keeping a secret'	SAN	VI

Curses *cont*	curse uttered by the Rishis, one curse being: 'Let him chant the Vedas, offending at each step against the rules of orthoepy.'	AN	XCIII, XCIV
	why King Uparichara is cursed and how he is freed	SAN	CCCXXXVIII
	King Saudasa has become a cannibal through Vasishtha's curse	ASW	LVII
	the curse upon Arjuna	ASW	LXXXI
	Nahusha, cursed by Bhrigu, becomes a snake until freed by Yudhishthira	AN	C
Dakshina		AN	LXXIV
	the southern direction, '2nd door of Yama' ... 'It is here that the periods allotted to men are calculated in Trutis and Lavas.' ... 'This region ... is the goal of the acts of the dead.'	U	CIX
Dancing	Arjuna learns dance from Chitrasena	VA	XLIV
Death	portrayed as lady emerging from Brahma's pent-up wrath	D	LI
	origin and nature of disease and death	D	III
	death is depicted as lady in red and black	SAN	CCLVII
	institution of birth and death	SAN	CCLVII
	different regions allotted to men according to part of body through which Jiva escapes	SAN	CCCXVIII
	how to conquer death	SAN	CCCXVIII
	how Bhishma left the body	AN	CLXVIII
	symptoms premonitory of death	SAN	CCCXVIII
Demonic Nature	described by Krishna	B	XL
Desire		B	XXVII
		ASW	XIII
	how Desire leads to Ignorance	VA	II
	the Extirpation of Desire	SAN	CLXXVII
	Desire and Emancipation	SAN	CCXVII
	Desire and Wrath, used by death to stop the life-breaths	SAN	CCLVIII
		ASW	XXVIII

Devadatta	the conch given by Maya to Arjuna	SAB	III
Devotion		B	XXVIII, XXX, XXXVI
	the devotion of Savitri to Satyavan	VA	CCLXV
	devotion to Truth	SAN	CCLXXVII
	origin and history of Religion of Desire in Krita and Treta Ages	SAN	CCCXLIX
Dharana	seven kinds of Dharana (one-pointed attention)	SAN	CCXXXVI
Diadem	manufacture and history of Arjuna's diadem	K	XC
Disease	*see* **Medicine**		
Dog	the dog who is really Dharma	MAH	I, II, III
Dreams	the nature of	SAN	CCXVI
Duty		B	XXVII
		SAN	CCXCIII
	duty of the four orders of men	VA	CCVI
		SAN	LX, CCXCIV
		AN	CXLI
	respective	U	XL
	in society	VA	CXLIX
	wifely duty	VA	CCXXXI, CCXXXII
	duty of women	AN	CXLVI
	Krishna speaks of duty of four castes and duty of a king	U	XXIX
	duty of a king	SAN	XXV, LVI, LXXV, XCIII
	duty and nature of a king	SAN	LXVIII
	miscellaneous duties of a king, including espionage, warfare, internal and external policies and the great science of chastisement	SAN	LXIX
	kingly duty	SAN	XIV, LXVI
	giving as a duty	AN	LXI
	a summary of duties	SAN	CXX
	duties of kings: 'Happiness of their subjects, observance of truth and sincerity of behaviour are the eternal duties of kings.'	SAN	LVII
	prime duty is protection of subjects	SAN	LVIII

Duty *cont*	duty in times of distress and at other times	U	XXVIII
	duty of Kshatriyas	SAN	XXII, XXIII, XXXII, LV, CXXXIV
		U	LXXIII
	importance of duty of Kshatriyas	SAN	LXIII
	duty of Brahmanas	SAN	XIV, XXII, CCXXXIV, CCXXXV
	Bhishma: 'The worship of mother, father and preceptor is most important according to me ... They are the three worlds ... the three modes of life ... the three Vedas ... the three sacred fires.'	SAN	CVIII
	the foremost of all duties	SAN	CCL
	duty of men to honour and worship women	AN	XLVI
	duty of the householder	AN	XCVII
	duty of forest recluses and ascetics	AN	CXLII
	duty and conduct	AN	CXLIII
Earth	nature of	B	IV
	how the goddess Earth was given to Kasyapa	VA	CXIV
	how the Earth sank in Krita Yuga and was lifted up again by Vishnu	VA	CXLI
	'Earth, if its resources are properly developed according to its qualities and prowess, is like an ever-yielding cow, from which the three-fold fruits of virtue, profit and pleasure, may be milked.' ... 'If Earth be well looked after, it becometh the father, mother, children, firmament and heaven of all creatures.'	B	IX
	how the Earth was milked	D	LXIX
	Rama's gift of the Earth to Kasyapa	D	LXX
	how the Earth oppressed by the weight of the creatures, came to the court of Indra	ST	VIII
	how King Dilipa gave away the entire Earth	SAN	XXIX
	why the Earth came to be called Urvi	SAN	L
	'The gift of Earth'; importance of land; in praise of the Earth	AN	LXII
	how the spirit of Kasyapa maintained the Earth for 30 thousand celestial years	AN	CLIV
	Yudhishthira gives the whole Earth to Vyasa, who returns it; Yudhishthira then gives the Brahmanas the price of the Earth in gold	ASW	LXXXIX

Echo	the monosyllable 'Bho' and the echo in mountainous regions	SAN	CCCXXXIV
Economics	righteous community living in the Krita Age	AD	LXIV
	the people live righteously while Dushmanta is king	AD	LXVIII
	description of a well-run society	AD	CIX
	the state of a country under good rule	SAB	XXXII
	natural law and free land	VA	CLIII
	'Earth, if its resources are properly developed ...' (*see* full quote under **Earth**)	B	IX
	the Utopian conditions in Rama's kingdom	D	LIX
	'when anarchy sets in on Earth, the weak are oppressed by the strong and no man is master of his own property'	SAN	L
	'there is no evil greater than anarchy'	SAN	LXVII
	how Manu, in a time of anarchy, set men to their respective duties	SAN	LXVII
	the men that make good legislators, ministers of war, courtiers, generalissimos and counsellors	SAN	LXXXIII
	what kinds of ministers should be appointed	SAN	LXXXV
	the administration of justice	SAN	LXXXV
	the internal administration of a kingdom	SAN	LXXXVII
	taxation	SAN	LXXXVIII
	levies at times of invasion	SAN	LXXXVII
	and the true source of royal revenue	SAN	LXXI
	how the king should treat ... the Vaisyas	SAN	LXXXVII
	... his various subjects	SAN	LXXXVIII
	'Agriculture, cattle-rearing and trade, provide all men with the means of living. A knowledge of the Vedas, however, provides them with the means of obtaining heaven. They, therefore, that obstruct the study of the Vedas and cause of Vedic practices, are to be regarded as enemies of society. It is for the extermination of these that Brahman created Kshatriyas.'	SAN	LXXXIX
	how the king should fill his treasury	SAN	CXXXVI
	importance of appointing ministers to right offices	SAN	CXIX
	king's treasury ... treatment of robbers	SAN	CXXXIII
	qualities a king's servants should have	SAN	CXV
	powerful description of how society degenerates: characteristics of each state through which it passes	SAN	CCXXXVIII

Economics *cont*	slavery, ploughing, agriculture importance of land; in praise of the Earth *see also* **Duty, Government, Kingship, Morality**	SAN AN	CCLXII LXII
Egoism		ASW	XLI
Elements		VA SAN	CCX CCXXXIX, CCXLVII, CCLXXV, CCLXXXVI
	the creation of the five elements	ASW SAN B SAN ASW	L CLXXXIII V CXCIV, CCII, CCXIX XLII
	as constitution of all creatures Bhrigu distinguishes the living agent from the five elements which compose the body the elements and the senses mastery over the elements elements and their properties	SAN SAN SAN SAN SAN	CLXXXIV CLXXXVII CCXXXII, CCLII CCXXXVI CCLV
Elephants	how the celestial elephant Airavata comes from the Ocean elephants mentioned: Supratika, Airavata, Vamana, Kumuda, Anjana the four princely elephants the elephants upholding the Earth speak of good practices	AD U B AN	XVIII XCIX XII CXXXII
Emancipation		SAN ASW	CXCIV, CCI, CCVI, CCXII, CCXIII, CCXVI, CCXIX, CCXLIX, CCLI, CCLXX, CCLXXIII, CCLXXVI, CCLXXXVII, CCLXXXIX, CCCIX, CCCXXI, CCXXX, CCXXXI XIX, XXXV, XLII, XLVII

Emancipation *cont*	the means to emancipation	SAN	CCXV, CCXXIX, CCLXXIV
	emancipation according to the Sankhya system and according to the Yoga system	SAN	CCXXXVI
Etymologies	of 'Mansa', meaning 'flesh'	AN	CXVI
	meaning of the root 'Diksha'	U	XLIII
	meaning of words 'Kshatriya' and 'Raja'	D	LXIX
	'Rajan', 'Vrishala', 'Dharma'	SAN	XC
	'Dharma'	SAN	CIX
Excellence	the pursuit of	SAN	CCLXXXVIII
Exertion		VA	XXXII
		U	CXXXV
		SAN	LVIII
		AN	VI
	also	AN	CLXIII (wrongly numbered CLXVIII)
Expiation		AN	CXXXVI
	the method of expiation for various sins, especially if committed by Brahmanas	SAN	CLXV
Faith		SAN	CCLXIV
Fame	Karna's words on fame	VA	CCLXVIII
Family	duties of the eldest and youngest brother	AN	CV
Fasting		SAN	CCXXI
	fasts and their fruits	AN	CVII
	the observance of fasting	AN	CVI, CIX
Fate		SAL	II, LXIII
		SAU	IX
		AN	VI
		ASR	X
	the power of fate	D	CLI
	Dhritarashtra speaks of the inevitability of the decrees of fate	SAB	LVI

Fate *cont*	the evil spirits that mould the destinies of men, including spirits that cause abortion, and 'the evil spirits presiding over the destinies of young children, and until children attain their 16th year; these spirits exercise their influence for evil, and after that, for good.'	VA	CCXXIX
	Draupadi's thoughts on Destiny	VI	XX
	fate, free-will and sanskara	U	CLX
	'All men are subjected to and governed by these two forces – Destiny and Exertion.'	SAU	II
	the power of Time and Destiny	SAN	XXVIII
	Destiny and Exertion	SAN	CLXXVII
		AN	CLXIII (wrongly numbered CLXVIII)
	see also **Providence**		
Firsts	a list of, e.g. 'the syllable OM is the first of all the Vedas and the life-wind Prana is the first of all winds'	ASW	XLIV
Flagstaff	how Garuda became Vishnu's flagstaff device	AD	XXXIII
Flower	how Krishna obtained the celestial flower called Parijata	D	XI
Foam	foam-drinkers	U	CII
Food	gift of and in praise of	AN	LXIII
	proof that food is 'instinct with solar energy'	VA	III
	food and the question of flesh-eating	VA	CCVII
	Krishna speaks of the three kinds of food	B	XLI
	the types of food reserved for Rakshasas and to be avoided by men	SAL	XLIII
	food suitable for Brahmanas	SAN	XXXVII
	vegetarianism	SAN	CCXXI
	abstention from meat	AN	CXIV, CXV, CXVI
	from whom may be accepted	AN	CXXXV

Forgiveness		VA	XXVIII, XXIX
	the power of forgiveness	U	XXXIII
Four Modes of Life		SAN	CXCI, CCXLII-CCXLV
Four Orders of Men		SAU	III
		SAN	CCXXXVIII
	origin of	B	XXVIII
	and their duties	SAN	CCXCIV
	origin and function of	K	XXXII
	respective punishments for	SAN	XV
	creation and duties of	SAN	LXXII
	respective qualities of	SAN	CLXXXIX
	the creation of	SAN	CCVII
	origin and duties of	SAN	CCXCVII
	respective duties of	AN	CXLI
	how a man may move up and down through the ...	AN	CXLIII
	the four colours associated with ... How the ... are all Brahmanas in pursuit of varied activities	SAN	CLXXXVIII
	how the different orders of men should act in changing circumstances	SAN	LXXVIII
Freedom from Attachments		B	XXIX
		SAN	CLXXVIII
	see also **Emancipation**		
Friendship		U	X
		SAN	CLXXIII
	the value of friendship	U	XXXVI
	those one should and should not have as friends	SAN	CLXVIII
Funeral Rites	Yudhishthira holds funeral rites for all the dead	ST	XXVI
Gambling	Vidhura speaks of the evils of gambling	SAB	LXII
	the pros and cons of gambling	SAB	LVIII
	Krishna speaks of the evils of dice-gaming	VA	XIII
Genealogy	'the genealogy of all the principal creatures'	AD	LXVI

266   WHERE'S WHAT IN THE MAHĀBHĀRATA

Genealogy *cont*	descent of all human beings from Prachetas	AD	LXXV
	a full genealogy from Daksha to Arguna's great-great-great grandson	AD	XCV
Gifts		AN	LIX LXV, LXXI
	the practice of making gifts	VA	CLXLIX
	Vyasa's words on charity	VA	CCLVII
	gifts to Brahmanas	AN	LX
	gifts as a kingly duty	AN	LXI
	under what conjunction particular gifts should be made	AN	LXIV
	the origin of custom of giving umbrellas and sandals	AN	XCV
	the supremacy of gifts	AN	CXX
	gifts and sacrifice	AN	CXXXVII
	five kinds of gift	AN	CXXXVIII
	the gift that should be made during the recitation of the *Mahābhārata*	SW	VI
	the gift of ... food	AN	LXIII
	... kine	AN	LXVI, LXIX, LXXII, LXXIII, LXXIV, LXXVI, LXXVII, LXXIX, LXXXI
	... drink	AN	LXVII
	... water, sesame, lamps	AN	LXVIII
	... flowers, incense, lights	AN	XCVIII
Gods	names of	AN	CLXV
	description of	VA	LVII
	why the gods become incarnate	AD	LXIV
	numerous occasions when gods disguised themselves to overcome their foes	VA	CCCXIII
	Indra assigns sovereignty over ... the Yakshas and all the wealth of the world to Kuvera; ... the Pitris to Yama; ... the waters to Varuna	U	XVI
	a list of gods with their consorts	U	CXVII
	long list of gods and powers in creation	SAL	XLV
	Bhishma 'saw with his physical eyes all the gods with Indra at their head'	SAN	XXXVIII
	how the goddess of Intelligence entered Brahma	SAN	CCCL

Gold	in praise of	AN	LXXIV
	merits, praise and origin of gold	AN	LXXXIV, LXXXV
	Yudhishthira gives Brahmanas price of the Earth in gold	ASW	LXXXIX
Government	the righteous government of Yudhishthira, who always said: 'Give unto each what is due to each.'	SAB	XIII
Grace	numerous examples of the grace of Mahadeva	AN	XVIII
Grief	and its remedy	SAN	CCV
	'It should be known that sorrow springs from the very fact of acceptance of body (in the womb).'	SAN	CCXIII
Gunas		SAN	CCLXXXVI
	Gunas and their influence upon men	VA	CCXI
	the three Gunas	SAN	CXCIV
	characteristics linked to three Gunas	SAN	CCXIII, CCCXIV
	qualities of three Gunas	SAN	CCXIX
	characteristics associated with each of the Gunas	SAN	CCXLVII
	Gunas in relation to the six colours	SAN	CCLXXX
	different Gunas – conditions	SAN	CCCXV
	the meaning of Tamas	SAN	CCCXLIII
	the dark manifestation of Tamas in human life	ASW	XXXVI
	manifestation of Rajas in human life	ASW	XXXVII
	manifestation of Sattwa in human life	ASW	XXXVIII
	the three qualities exist together in everything	ASW	XXXIX
	creatures in which Rajas predominates	ASW	XLIII
	characteristics of the three Gunas	SAN	CCXII
Hands		SAN	CLXXX
Happiness	as the highest object of acquisition	SAN	CXC
	true happiness	VA	CCXV
	Vyasa speaks of happiness and misery	VA	CCLIX
	Vyasa's words on happiness and misery	VA	CCLVII

Harmlessness	the practice of	SAN	CCLXII, CCLXV, CCLXXII
Heaven	advantages and disadvantages of heaven	VA	CCLIX
	description of various celestial regions	AN	CII
Hell		SW	II
	of Bhauma	AD	XC
Heroism	in praise of heroes	AN	LXXV
	'there is nothing higher in the three worlds than heroism'	SAN	XCIX
Himalayas	description of	VA	CVIII
Hiranyapura	city of	U	C
	aerial city destroyed by Arjuna	VA	CLXXII
Hiranya-Sringa	peak where Mahadeva has his abode	SAB	III
Himavat	region called 'the other world' to north of Himavat	SAN	CXCII
Hope		SAN	CXXV-CXXVIII
Horses	how the celestial horse Uchchaishravas comes from the Ocean	AD	XVIII
	Uchchaishravas	U	CII
	why horses are without teats	K	XXXIV
	names of Krishna's horses	SAU	XIII
Human Form		SAN	CLXXX
Humour	knockabout comedy from Arjuna	VI	XXXVII, XXXVIII
	Krishna chaffs Bhima for his new-found mildness	U	LXXV
Hymns	see **In Praise of**		
Ignorance		SAN	CCXII
	ignorance and relation to covetousness	SAN	CLIX
Imagery		U	XCIV
		D	CLXXXIV
	'Man's corporeal self has been compared to a chariot, his soul to a character and his senses to horses'	VA	CCX

Imagery *cont*	'One's body, O king, is one's car; the soul within is the driver and the senses are its steeds.'	U	XXXIV
	extended analogy between battlefield and river	D	XIV
	striking similes	D	XX
	striking metaphor of the Drona-ocean	SAU	X
	picture of ... body as chariot etc	U	XLVI
	... the two Krishnas painted by many literary images and similes	D	C
	... chariot, steeds, traces and driver plus different picture of chariot of man's soul	ST	VII
	... the body as a city	SAN	CCLIV
	... Desire as a tree in heart of man	SAN	CCLIV
Immortality	of the soul	B	XXVI
		VA	CCVIII
	Vaka answers question 'What are sorrows and joys of those that lead deathless lives?'	VA	CLXLII
	see also **Soul**		
Incarnation	Vishnu and all celestials are incarnated on Earth to bring about Ravana's downfall	VA	CCLXXIV
	Krishna promised that for the good of the Universe he would take his birth among mankind in the family of Vasudeva	B	LXVI
In Praise of	the *Mahābhārata*	AD	II, LXII
		SW	V, VI
	the twin Aswins	AD	III
	Garuda	AD	XXIII
	Indra	AD	XXV
	Parikshit	AD	XLIX
	Janamejaya	AD	LV
	Krishna	AD	LXIII
		SAB	XXXVII
		U	LXXI, LXXXVI
		B	LXVII
		D	XI, CXLVIII
		SAN	XLIV, XLVIII, LI, CX, CCIX, CCCXLIV, CCCXLVII, CCCXLVIII,

In Praise of cont	Krishna *cont*	AN	CXLVII-CXLIX, CLVIII
		ASW	LII
	Krishna (a hymn uttered by Brahma)	B	LXV
	wives, sons, Truth	AD	LXXIV
	Agni	AD	CCXXXIV
		SAB	XXX
	the Sun	VA	III
	sons	VA	IX
	Mahadeva	VA	XXXIX
		D	LXXX
		SAL	XXXVIII
		AN	XIV, XVI, CLX, CLXI
	Mahadeva (the 'king of all hymns')	AN	XVII
	Sthanu	K	XXXIII
	Saraswati	SAL	XLII, LIV
	Vishnu	VA	CC
		SAN	CCLXXX
	Durga	VI	VI
		B	XXIII
	Arjuna	B	CXXIII
	Siva	SAU	VII
	Siva, the 1,008 names of, foremost of all hymns	SAN	CCLXXXV
	the life of domesticity	SAN	XII
	ascetic penances	SAN	XIX
	contentment	SAN	XXI
	Bhishma	SAN	LI
		AN	CLXVIII
	a good wife	SAN	CXLIV
	a good husband	SAN	CXLVIII
	Narada	SAN	CCXXX
	father, mother	SAN	CCLXVI
	the knowledge contained in Sankhya system	SAN	CCCII
	Narayana	SAN	CCCXXXIX
	the Self	SAN	CCCXLV
	the River Ganga	AN	XXVI
	kine	AN	LI, LXXVIII, LXXX, LXXXIII
	the dung of	AN	LXXXII
	Earth	AN	LXII
	food	AN	LXIII
	gold	AN	LXXIV, LXXXIV, LXXXV
	heroes, Truth	AN	LXXV

Instruction	on Brahman; primary seed called Mahayasas; accidents; creature-Soul, (Iswara); Apana; Prana; will; intellect; picture of the body as chariot, etc	U	XLVI
	Sanat-sujata … instructing Dhritarashtra in ascetism, Vedas, Chhandas and knowledge of Brahman	U	XLIII
	… discourses on 'mada'	U	XLIII, XLV
	… discourses on the four steps of Brahmacharya and on nature of Brahman	U	XLIV
	Yudhishthira speaks of prosperity and poverty; sin, hell, salvation; stages of a dogfight	U	LXXII
	Krishna speaks of … his higher and lower nature; man of knowledge; Adhyatma; Adhibhuta; Adhidaiva; Adhiyajna	B	XXXI
	… death; Prana, devotion; day and night of Brahman; bright and dark path	B	XXXII
	… his universal nature	B	XXXIV
	… his higher nature and worship	B	XXXIII
	renunciation and abandonment and their three-fold nature; five causes for completion of all actions; three-fold nature of knowledge, action, agent, constancy, intellect, happiness; respective duties of the four orders of men	B	XLII
	'This body … is called Kshetra. Him who knoweth it, the learned call Kshetrajna.'	B	XXXVII
	'That instruction which is imparted in barter for money always pollutes the instructor.'	AN	X
Intellect		U	XLVI
Intelligence		SAN	CXCIV
Island	of Sudarsana	B	V, VI
Jewels	how the gem Kaustubha comes from the Ocean	AD	XVIII
	gem Kaustubha	U	CII
	Vyasa asks Aswatthaman to give to Pandavas the gem (properties described) which was in his head at birth	SAU	XV
	Arjuna is revived by special gem brought by Ulupi	ASW	LXXX

Jiva		SAN	CCXLI
	nature of, when invested with ignorance	SAN	CCCV
	the 16 portions of Jiva compared to 16 portions of Chandramas	SAN	CCCV
	lament of the awakened Jiva	SAN	CCCVIII
	the Supreme Soul and Jiva	SAN	CCCIX
	why Jiva is called 'Budhyamana'	SAN	CCCIX
	how the Jiva leaves the body	ASW	XVII
	how Jiva enters the womb	ASW	XVIII
Karma		VA	CCVII, CCVIII
		AN	I, VI
Khandava	how forest of Khandava is burned	AD	CCXXVIII
Khandavaprastha	becomes capital city of the Pandavas	AD	CCIX
Kine	in praise of	AN	LXXVIII, LXXX
	importance of	AN	CXXXIII
	Surabhi is 'mother of all kine'; her principal offspring	U	CII
	how Surabhi was created and how the Kapila cows were produced from her; how Rudra adopted the sign of the bull	AN	LXXVII
Kingship		VI	IV
		SAN	CCCXXI
		ASW	XXXI
	art of	SAB	V
		ASR	V-VII
	importance of	AD	XLI
	advice on becoming a king	AD	LXXXVII
	duties of a king	AD	CXLII
	kingly duty	VA	CLXL
	names of the principal kings	AN	CLXV
	Truthfulness in Santanu's kingdom. 'And during the rule of the best of Kurus – of that king of kings – speech became united with truth and the minds of men were directed towards liberality and virtue.'	AD	C
	magnificence of Yudhishthira's reign	AD	CCXXIV
	Yudhishthira morning devotions as a king	D	LXXXII

Kingship *cont*	kingship and the titles of kings	VA	CLXXXIV
	Gandhari's words on kingship	U	CXXIX
	Krishna's words on kingship	U	CXXXII
	Arjuna discourses on wealth, kingship, and 'the great path called Dasaratha'	SAN	VIII
	Bhishma: There was no sovereignty at first, but it began in the Krita Age when righteousness and the Vedas were lost	SAN	LIX
	Prithu is cited as the ideal king	SAN	LIX
	'If the functions of royalty are disturbed, all creatures are overtaken by evil.'	SAN	LXIV
	the duties and nature of a king. 'No one should disregard the king by taking him for a man, for he is really a high divinity in human form.' How the king assumes the forms of Agni, Aditya, Mrityu, Yama and Vaisravana to meet different occasions. 'The king is the heart of his people; he is the great refuge; he is their glory; and he is their highest happiness.'	SAN	LXVIII
	the king is responsible for the actions of his subjects	SAN	LXXVII
	the king's ministers, four friends	SAN	LXXX
	'Refusal to trust anyone has been said to be one of highest mysteries of kingcraft.'	SAN	LXXXV
	kings, righteousness and pride. 'When the king does not restrain vice, a confusion of castes follows, and sinful Rakshasas, and persons of neutral sex, and children destitute of limbs or possessed of thick tongues, and idiots, begin to take birth, even in respectable families.'	SAN	XC
	awesome responsibilities of the king	SAN	XCI
	kings and righteousness	SAN	XCII
	how a king should behave towards his foe	SAN	CIII
	the king and his ministers	SAN	CXVIII
	conduct of a king who has lost his kingdom	SAN	CIV, CV CVI
	relationship between aristocracy and monarchy	SAN	CVII
	how a king may act in times of distress	SAN	CXXX
	actions open to a weak king oppressed by foe	SAN	CXXXI
	how a king should behave in times of distress. 'It is better, O monarch, that a king should blaze up for a moment like charcoal of ebony wood than that he should smoulder and smoke like chaff for many years.'	SAN	CXL

Knowledge		B	XXVIII
		SAN	CCXLI, CCLXXXVI, CCCXIX
	Knowledge of Truth	SAN	CXCIV
	Knowledge of the Soul	SAN	CCXLIX
	the knowledge called 'Trayi'	SAN	CCXXXV
	instantaneous realization for man of Knowledge	AD	XCII
	Krishna: 'When thou, O Bhishma, wilt leave this world for that, all Knowledge, O hero, will expire with thee.'	SAN	LI
	Vidya and Avidya	SAN	CCCVIII
Kshatriyas	greatness of the royal Kshatriyas	VA	CLXLIII
	how Rama began to exterminate the Kshatriyas	SAN	L
	how a Kshatriya should die	SAN	XCVII
Kshetrajna		ASW	XXVII, XXVIII, XLIII, XLVIII, L, LI
Kurukshetra	'The space between the Tarantuka and the Arantuka, and the lakes of Rama and Shamachakra, is known as Kurukshetra.' ... 'The very dust of Kurukshetra, borne away by the wind, shall cleanse persons of wicked acts and bear them to heaven.'	SAL	LIII
Kusa Grass	why it is holy	AD	XXXIV
Lady	conduct of	AN	CXXIII
Lamentations	of Draupadi	SAB	LXVIII, LXIX
		VA	XII, XXVII
		VI	XVIII-XX
	of Yudhishthira	SAU	X
		SAN	I, VII
		ASR	XXXVIII
	of Yudhishthira for Abhimanyu	D	XLIX
	of Arjuna for Abhimanyu	D	LXXII
	of Subhadra for Abhimanyu	D	LXXVIII

Lamentations *con*	of Duryodhana	SAL	LXIV
	of the citizens of Kurujangala	VA	XXIII
	of Dhritarashtra	ST	I
	... for Bhishma	B	XIV
	... for his dead sons	SAL	II
	of the Kuru ladies	ST	XVI, XXII-XXV
	of Gandhari for ... Duryodhana	ST	XVII
	... her dead relatives	ST	XIX
	of Uttara for her husband Abhimanyu	ST	XX
	of Karna's wives for their husband	ST	XXI
	of Kunti for Karna	ST	XXVII
	of the awakened Jiva	SAN	CCCVIII
	of Ganga for Bhishma	AN	CLXVIII
Language	Bhishma hymns Krishna: 'Roots with all kinds of affixes and suffixes are thy limbs. The Sandhis are thy joints. The consonants and the vowels are thy ornaments. The Vedas ... have declared thee to be the divine word. Salutations to thee in thy forms as the word!'	SAN	XLVIII
	'Thou art the author of the great treatise on Grammar that has been named after the Moon.' ... 'Thou art the point (in the alphabet) which indicates the nasal sound. Thou art the two dots (i.e. Visarga).'	AN	XVII
	Rudra's sacrifice: 'The Rig-Veda also came there, adorned with the rules of orthoepy. The Lakshanas, Suras, Niruktas, Notes arranged in rows, and the syllable OM, as also Nigraha and Pragraha, all came there and took their residence in the eye of Mahadeva.'	AN	LXXXV
Laughter	why Vyasa laughed	AN	CXX
Law		SAN	CXXI
Lies	the destructive power of lies, the worst being lying for the sake of land	U	XXXV
Mahābhārata	summary of	AD	LXI
	abridged and detailed forms	AD	I

Mahābhārata cont	how Ganesa was commissioned to write down the *Mahābhārata*	AD	I
	picture of the *Mahābhārata* as a tree	AD	I
	study of the *Mahābhārata*	AD	I
	value of the *Mahābhārata*	AD	I
	the *Mahābhārata* compared with the Vedas	AD	I
	two summaries of the *Mahābhārata*	AD	II
	its value as a source	AD	II
	how Vyasa composed 100 Parvas which Santi redistributed into 18 Parvas	AD	II
	number of slokas in each Parva	AD	II
	Saunaka wants to hear 'that sacred history called the *Mahābhārata*, spreading the fame of the Pandavas, which Krishna-Dwaipayana, asked by Janamejaya, caused to be duly recited after the completion of the sacrifice.'	AD	LIX
	Vaisampayana speaks in Praise of the *Mahābhārata*	AD	LXII
	fatigue felt by Vyasa 'in consequence of the great strain on his energies occasioned by the composition of the *Mahābhārata*'	SAN	CCCL
	composition, recitation, essence of *Mahābhārata*	SW	V
	by whom and how the *Mahābhārata* should be recited	SW	VI
	the merits of reciting it and hearing it	SW	VI
	gifts that should be made during recitation	SW	VI
Mahat		SAN	CCXXXII
Man	Yudhishthira points out that 'the gods, Pitris, Siddhas, Rishis, Gandharvas, brutes, and even worms and ants depend for their lives on men'	VA	CLVI
	see also **Four Orders of Men**		
Mandara	*see* **Mount Mandara**		
Manliness		U	CXXXIII, CXXXIV
Mantras	used to give victory in battle	D	XCIII
	the Savitri mantra	AN	CL
	'those mantras which are recited in the beginning of the Atharvan Veda' and which can put any deity under power of the speaker	VA	CCCIII

Mantras *cont*	Yudhishthira has been made whole by surgeons using mantras and drugs	K	LXXXIX
	the Brahmanas slay Charvaka with the mantra Hun	SAN	XXXIX
	see also **Meditation**		
Marriage	constitution of	D	LIII
	marriage and morality	AN	XLV
	marriage and inheritance	AN	XLVII
	the eight kinds of marriage	AD	LXXIII
	ordinance of marriage as established by Swetaketu	AD	CXXII
	why a husband and wife protect each other	VA	XII
	'the husband is the wife's god and he is her refuge'	VA	CCXXXI
	why a wife is called 'Jaya'	VI	XXI
	the marriage ceremony between Princess Uttara and Abhimanu	VI	LXXII
	types of marriage dowry	AN	XLIV
	inter-marriage … names given to offspring of cross-breeding	AN	XLVIII
	… different kinds of son	AN	XLIX
Medicine	the three attributes of the body; … mind	SAN	XVI
	what the sensible physician does first	VA	II
	skilled surgeons are brought to Bhishma, but he dismisses them	B	CXXII
	Bhishma cures Duryodhana's wound with a herb	B	LXXXII
	origin and nature of disease and death	D	LII
	King Mandhatri was delivered surgically by the twin Aswins from womb of his father (*sic*)	D	LXII
	gestation and birth	ST	IV
	Yudhishthira has been made whole by surgeons using mantras and drugs	K	LXXXIX
	treatment prescribed for madness	SAN	XIV
	causes and nature of mental and physical diseases	SAN	XVI
	passing references to medicine and chemistry	SAN	XXVIII
	'persons conversant with the scriptures do not take into account the sins that women may commit at heart. Whatever their sins (of this description) they are cleansed by their menstrual course like a metallic plate that is scoured with ashes.'	SAN	XXXVI

Medicine *cont*	human diseases depicted as the tears of Death	SAN	CCLVIII
	how the Pitris and the deities got indigestion, and how they were cured	AN	XCII
	the essence of health and disease – physical and mental *see also* **Physiology**	ASW	XII
Meditation		SAN	CXCV
	Meditation and 'silent Reciters of sacred mantras'	SAN	CXCVI
	Yudhishthira describes Krishna in a state of	SAN	XLVII
Merits	attached to the digging of tanks and the planting of trees	AN	LVIII
Meru	*see* **Mount Meru**		
Mind		SAN	CXCIV, CCXLVIII, CCLXXXVI
		ASW	XXI
	origin of	AN	LXXXV
	the three attributes of the mind	SAN	XVI
	'the struggle against thy mind'	ASW	XII
Moksha		VA	CCXII
Moon	how the Moon comes from the Ocean	AD	XVII
Morality		VA	CLXLIX
		U	XLV
		SAU	I, II, III, V
		SAN	CXXXII, CCLIX, CCC
		AN	XXII, XXXVII
	questions of morality	SAB	LXVII
	'Sahadeva obtained the whole science of morality and duties from (Vrihaspati) the spiritual chief of celestials.'	AD	CXLI
	Valarama asks Krishna: 'Why are the virtuous suffering while the vicious flourish?'	VA	CXIX
	Kuvera speaks on 'propriety regarding place and time'	VA	CLXI

Morality	injury and non-injury	VA	CCVII
	morality and righteousness	VA	CCLXV
	what happens if one abandons a person seeking protection	U	XII
	morality in times of distress and at other times	U	XXVIII
	principles of social morality: kings, masters, servants	U	XXXVII
	treatment of guests: administration of households and kingdoms	U	XXXVIII
	epigrams on morality; the importance of a right attitude towards one's relatives	U	XXXIX
	high standards of morality shown in the combat between Bhishma and Rama of Bhrigu's race	U	CLXXXII
	profound teaching on death, Yama, vice, virtue, rebirth, attainment of celestial regions, knowledge, ignorance	U	XLII
	'For the sake of a family a member may be sacrificed; for the sake of a village a family may be sacrificed; for the sake of a province a village may be sacrificed; and for the sake of one's soul the whole Earth may be sacrificed.'	U	CXXVIII
	morality on the battlefield	D	CXLII
	battle morality	D	CXCIX
	to cause Drona's downfall, Bhima and Yudhishthira, encouraged by Krishna, tell untruths	D	CXCI
	immorality, intoxication, theft, adultery, abortion	K	XLV
	Krishna speaks of five kinds of sinless falsehood	K	LXIX
	Krishna favours deception	SAL	LVIII
	Krishna supports use of 'contrivances and means', citing actions of gods as antecedents	SAL	LXI
	Morality, Profit, Pleasure: Krishna lists the six kinds of advancement a person may have	SAL	LX
	acts that require expiation and that incur no sin	SAN	XXXIV, XXXV
	how various sins may be expiated. 'Women, by leading a regulated life for one year, become cleansed of all their sins.'	SAN	XXXVI

Morality *cont*	the words of Manu on many aspects of morality	SAN	XXXVII
	the characteristics of the wicked man	SAN	CIII
	questions of truth, falsehood, morality, righteousness	SAN	CIX
	morality spoken of as wife of Chastisement	SAN	CXXI
	Yudhishthira expresses stupefaction at the paradoxical standards of morality suggested by Bhishma's words	SAN	CXLII
	the fine morality of Kayavya the robber	SAN	CXXXV
	the rise and fall of morality	SAN	CCXCV
	morality and marriage	AN	XLV
	standards of morality for Brahmanas	AN	XCIII
	details of practical morality	AN	CIV
Mothers	long list of mothers who become Skanda's companions	SAL	XLVI
Mountains	Gandhamadana Mountain	VA	CXLV
		B	VI
	Meru Mountain	AD	XVII
		B	VI
	Kolahala Mountain	AD	LXIII
	Kailasa Mountain	VA	CXLIV
	Rishabha Mountain	U	CXIII
	Malyavat Mountain	B	VII
	Krauncha Mountain	SAL	XLVI
	the foremost mountain	ASW	XLIII
	how the gods churned the Ocean with Mandara Mountain	AD	XVIII
	Vindhya Mountain is jealous of Meru Mountain	VA	CIV
	description of flora, fauna, minerals on Gandhamadana Mountain	VA	CLVII
Munis	characteristics of	AD	XCI
Music	names of musical instruments	D	LXXXII
	the seven kinds of sound (i.e. the seven original notes: their seven names)	SAN	CLXXXIV
		ASW	L
	from Chitrasena Arjuna learns 'the instrumental music that is current among the celestials and which existeth not in the world of men'	VA	XLIV
	Panchajanya will emit the shrill Rishava note (2nd note of the Hindu gamut)	D	LXXIX

Music	Viswavasu 'played on his Vina the seven notes according to the rules that regulate their combinations. Such was the character of Viswavasu's music that every creature (whatever he might be) thought that the great Gandharva was playing to him alone.'	SAN	XXIX
Names	the meaning or origin of: Abhimanu	AD	CCXXIII
	Ashtavakra	VA	CXXXII
	Astika	AD	XLVIII
	Aswatirtha	AN	IV
	Aswatthaman	AX	CXXI
		D	CXCVII
	Aurva	AD	CLXXXI
	Bharata	AD	LXXIV
	Bhishma	AD	C
	Chirakarin	SAN	CCLXVI
	Dhristadyumna	AD	CLXIX
	Dhritarashtra	AD	CVI
	Drona	AD	LXIII, CXXXI
	Durga	B	XXIII, VI VI
	Gargasrota	SAL	XXXVII
	Garuda	AD	XXX
	Ghatotkacha	AD	CLVII
	Jarasandha	SAB	XVII, XVIII
		D	CLXXXI
	Karna	AD	CXI
		VA	CCCVIII
	Krauncha, Mount	SAL	XLVI
	Kripa	AD	CXXX
	Kshatriya	SAN	XXIX
	Kurukshetra	SAL	LIII
	Mandhata	VA	CXXVI
	Narayana	VA	CCLXX
	Nishadas	SAN	LIX
	Pandu	AD	CVI
	Parikshit	ASW	LXX
	Pinaka	SAN	CCXC
	Prabhasa	SAL	XXXV
	Prativindhya	AD	CCXXIII
	Prithivi	SAN	LIX
	Prithu	SAN	XXIX
	Raja	SAN	XXIX
	Ravana	VA	CCLXXIII
	Rishyasringa	VA	CX

Names			
cont	Salya	K	XXXII, XXXV
	Santanu	AD	XCV, XCVII
	Santanika	AD	CCXXIII
	Soma	SAL	XLIII
	Srutakarman	AD	CCXXIII
	Srutasena	AD	CCXXIII
	Subhumika	SAL	XXXVII
	Suka	SAN	CCCXXV
	Sutasoma	AD	CCXXIII
	Suvarnashthivin	D	LIII
	Tamas	SAN	CCCXLIII
	Tilottama	AD	CCXIII
	Tirthas	VA	LXXXII-LXXXV
	Vaikartana	D	CLXXX
	Vasishthapavaha	SAL	XLII
	Vinasana	SAL	XXXVII
	Vrisha	D	CLXXX
	Vyasa	AD	LXIII
	Yayata	SAL	XLI
	why Siva is called Nilakantha	AD	XVIII
	why Garuda is called Suparna	AD	XXXIII
	names of principal snakes that perished in Janamejaya's sacrifice	AD	LVII
	why Vasu was also called Uparichara	AD	LXIII
	why Vyasa is called ... Dwaipayana	AD	LXIII
	... Krishna	AD	CV
	names of celestial beings and their earthly counterparts	AD	LXVII
	names of Dhritarashtra's 100 sons	AD	LXVII
	... in order of birth	AD	CXVII
	the heroic kings in Puru's line	AD	XCIV
	why Karna is called Vasusena	AD	CXI
	names of the months	AN	CVI
	Arjuna's ten names and their origins	VI	XLIV
	why Arjuna is called ... Tapatya	AD	CLXXIII
	... Savyasachin	AD	CLXLIX
	why Asmaka was also called Parasara	AD	CLXXX
	Agni's other names and the reasons for some of them	SAB	XXX
	the 108 names of the Sun	VA	III
	why a wife is called Jaya	VA	XII
	why King Kuvalaswa changed his name to Dhundhumara	VA	CC
	descendants of Angiras	VA	CCXVII, CCXVIII
	genealogies of fire-gods	VA	CCXX
	the many names of Skanda	VA	CCXXX

Names *cont*	names of Krishna	U SAN AN	LXX CCCXLII, CCCXLIII CXLIX
	how Krishna came to be called Madhusudana	SAN	CCVII
	names of Krishna's steeds	U SAU	LXXXIII XIII
	names of the principal birds	U	CI
	names of famous Nagas	U	CIII
	meanings of names of the four quarters (N, S, E and W)	U	CXI
	list of gods with their consorts	U	CXVII
	why a man is called Purusha	U	CXXXIII
	names of the seven Varshas	B	VI
	Bhishma lists heroes in the Kuru ranks and in the Pandava army	U	CLXVI-CLXXIII
	Ganga and the names of her streams	B	VI
	names of Mahadeva	AN ASW	XVII VIII
	meanings of many of the names of Mahadeva	D	CCII
	why Sthanu came to be called Mahadeva	K	XXXIV
	why the tirtha Usanasa is also called Kapalamochana	SAL	XXXIX
	long lists of gods and powers in creation	SAL	XLV
	long list of mothers who become Skanda's companions	SAL	XLVI
	why Indra is also called Satakratu	SAL	XLIX
	why the Ocean was also called Sagara	SAN	XXIX
	why the Earth came to be called Urvi	SAN	L
	pedigrees of the Prajapatis; of the deities that rule the three worlds; of the great Rishis	SAN	CCVIII
	names of Narayana	SAN	CCLXXIX
	the 1,008 names of Siva	SAN	CCLXXXV
	why Jiva is called Budhayamana	SAN	CCCIX
	names of the winds	SAN	CCCXXIX
	names of the 21 Prajapatis	SAN	CCCXXXV
	names of the eight Prakritis	SAN	CCCXLI
	names of the seven spiritual sons of Brahman	SAN	CCCXLI
	why the Pitris are also called Pindas	SAN	CCCXLVI
	other names for the 'Bhagavad-Gita'	SAN	CCCXLVII

Names *cont*	names of the gods, of learned Brahmaas and of the principal kings	AN	CLXV
Nature	the work of nature	ASW SAN	XLVIII, L CCXXII
Night	equals the goddess of Divination	U	XIII
Nobility	the attributes of high families	U	XXXVI
Number	Vidura's words related to number	U	XXXIII
Ocean	description of	AD	XXI, XXII
	Narayana advises the gods to churn the Ocean to obtain Amrita	AD	XVII
	from the Ocean come the Moon, Lakshmi, Soma, the steed Uchchaishravas, the gem Kaustubha, Dhanwantari holding the vessel of Amrita, the elephant Airavata and the poison called Kalakuta	AD	XVIII
	the Ocean is swallowed by Agastya	VA	CV
	how Ganga refills the Ocean	VA	CIX
	the milky Ocean	U	CII
	why Ocean created the region called Surparaka	SAN	L
	how Utathya drank the Ocean to recover his wife	AN	CLIV
One	the One	ASW	XXVI
Palaces	of Vaisravana *see also* **Assembly Houses**	VA	CLIX
Parabrahma	the supreme abode of Vishnu	VA	CCLIX
Paschima	the West, described by Garuda	U	CX
Patalam	the city in the very centre of the world of the Nagas. 'From here Vishnu fills the universe with sound.'	U	XCIX
Penances		SAN	LXXIX, CLXI, CCXCVI
	true penances	SAN	CCXXI
	penances of body, speech, mind	B	XLI

Physiology		SAN	CCXXXIX
	the nine kinds of scent	SAN	CLXXXIV
	the six kinds of taste	SAN	CLXXXIV
	the 16 kinds of form constituting the property of vision	SAN	CLXXXIV
	the 11 properties appertaining to the wind	SAN	CLXXXIV
	the seven kinds of sound	SAN	CLXXXIV
	the Pranas and their respective functions within the body ...	SAN	CLXXXV
	... motion	SAN	CLXXXV
	... digestion	SAN	CLXXXV
	... heat	SAN	CLXXXV
	... circulation	SAN	CLXXXV
	origin of the vital seed	SAN	CCXIV
		AN	CXI
	the ten principal ducts of the body	SAN	CCXIV
	stages of foetal growth	SAN	CCCXXI
	life in the uterus	AN	CXVI
	see also **Medicine, Senses**		
Pilgrimage	begins of Yudhishthira, Bhima, Nakula and Sahadeva	VA	XCIII
Pitris	origin of and why they are also called Pindas	SAN	CCCXLVI
	ways of gratifying the Pitris	AN	CXXV
	Vishnu and the Pitris	AN	CXXVI, CXXIX
Poison	how the poison called Kalakuta comes from the Ocean and is held in Siva's throat	AD	XVIII
Portents		SAB	LXXX
		VI	XLVI
		B	I-III, XVII, XIX, LXXI, C
		U	LXXIII, LXXXIV, CXXXVIII
		D	VII, LXXVII, CXCIII
		K	XXXVII, XLVI, XCIV
		SAL	XI, XXIII, LVI, LVIII, LXIV,
		SAN	XC
		ASW	LXXVII

Portents *cont*	good portents	D	LXXXIV
	portents in the celestial regions	AD	XXX
	omens of battle	VA	CLIV
		U	CXLIII
	fierce omens of calamity	U	CLVII
	grave portents everywhere in the 36th year after the battle	MAU	I
Possession	the question of what is and is not mine	ASW	XXXII
Powerful Passages		U	XLVI
	description of ... a forest	AD	LXX
	... the Ocean	AD	XXI, XXII
	... Hanuman	VA	CXLV
	... the enormous chariot made by Rudra	D	CCII
	... battle as sacrifice	SAN	XCVIII
	... the body as a chariot	SAN	CCXXXVI
	... 'the extensive forest of Brahman'	ASW	XXVII
	how Garuda defeated the gods and extinguished the fire around the Amrita	AD	XXXII
	the precarious position of Jaratkaru's ancestors	AD	XLV
	Astika asks for the snake-sacrifice to be stopped	AD	LVI
	the five Indras	AD	CLXLIX
	Bhima's lament over his sleeping mother and brothers	AD	CLIII
	Damayanti's eloquent lament for Nala	VA	LXIV
	debate between Vandin and ten-year-old Ashtavakra	VA	CXXXIV
	a lady's discourse on Virtue	VA	CCV
	account of inter-creation activity	VA	CCII
	Karna's words on fame	VA	CCLXVIII
	Savitri, Satyavan and Yama	VA	CCLXV
	the river of ... blood	VI	LXII
	... life	SAN	CCL, CCCXXX
	... milk	SAN	CCLXXXIV
	the ocean of life	SAN	CCCII
	the wheel of life	ASW	XLV
	Desire as a tree in the heart of man	SAN	CCLIV
	Krishna ... travels in pomp to the royal court	U	XCIV
	... sets out to slay Bhishma	B	LIX
	... describes the battlefield after sunset	D	CXLVII
	... describes the whole battlefield	K	LVIII

Powerful Passages *cont*	Krishna's equine-headed form	SAN	CCCXLVIII
	Bhishma encounters Rama of Bhrigu's race	U	CLXXXII
	Bhishma's hymn to Krishna	SAN	XLVIII
	Dhritarashtra's lament for his father Bhishma	B	XIV
	the battlefield at dusk; the carrion creatures	D	XLVIII
	Aswatthaman on the reverses wrought by Time	SAL	LXV
	the Kuru ladies lament	ST	XXIII, XXIV
	Gandhari laments Duryodhana	ST	XVII
	Vidura gives a striking statement about gestation and birth and about the difficulties which beset one in this life	ST	IV
	the importance of Time	SAN	XXV
	the words of Asma to King Janaka	SAN	XXVIII
	the striking words of Pangala when she awoke	SAN	CLXXIV
	how society degenerates: characteristics of each phase	SAN	CCXXVIII
	account of the creation of the elements (given originally to Rishis in the Brahmakalpa)	SAN	CLXXXIII
	Vali's words	SAN	CCXXVII
	Desire as a tree in the heart of man	SAN	CCLIV
	how the Soul surrounds itself with multifarious illusions	SAN	CCCIV
	the words of Sree, goddess of Prosperity	AN	XI
	the awakened Jiva laments	SAN	CCCVIII
	how the answers arose when Viswavasu put 24 questions to Yajnavalkya	SAN	CCCXIX
	how Yajnavalkya received the knowledge of the Vedas from Surya and with the aid of the goddess Saraswati	SAN	CCCXIX
	praise of kine	AN	LI
	conduct of a lady	AN	CXXIII
	how Mahadeva developed his 3rd eye	AN	CXL
	the Kamagita	ASW	XIII
	how Vidura enters the body of Yudhishthira	ASR	XXVI
	Yudhishthira's insight into Hell	SW	II

Pradhana	facts about	ASW	XVIII
Prajapatis	names of 22 Prajapatis	SAN	CCCXXXV
Prakriti		SAN	CCCIII
	Prakriti and Purusha	SAN	CCCXIX, CCCXVI
	the names of the eight Prakriti	SAN	CCCXLI
	the eight principles known by the name of Prakriti and the 16 modifications	SAN	CCCXI
Pranas		VA	CCXII
		B	XXVIII
		ASW	XXI
		U	XLVI
	the five Pranas	ASW	XXIII, XXIV
		SAN	CLXXXIV
	the Pranas and their respective functions within the body	SAN	CLXXXV
	how the Pranas in the body are a direct reflection of the external winds	SAN	CCCXXIX
	the Pranas and the seven-fold creation	ASW	XX
Procreation	the different methods of procreation in the four ages	SAN	CCVII
Prophecy	Vyasa prophesies the destruction of all the Kshatriyas	SAB	XLV
	Vyasa promises Yudhishthira: 'On the 5th day from this, the Earth will be thine.'	D	CLXXXIII
	the destruction of the Kurus is foretold	SAB	LXXIX
	Krishna decrees that the battle will occur in seven days, the day of the new moon ' for that day ... is presided over by Indra'	U	CXLII
	Bhishma predicts the future of the Pandavas: 'Living happily as long as the creation lasts, all of you at the next new creation will be admitted among the gods, and enjoying all kinds of felicities ye will at last be numbered among the Siddhas.'	SAN	CCLXXX

Providence	Krishna speaks of Providence *see also* **Fate**	U	LXXVII
Punishment	Crime and punishment in society throughout the ages, with particular reference to capital punishment *see also* **Chastisement**	SAN	CCLXVII
Purity	of heart	AN	CXXVII
Purusha		SAN	CCCLI, CCCLII
		ASW	XLVIII, L, LI
	Krishna speaks of the Supreme Purusha	B	XXXVII
	Purusha and Prakriti	SAN	CCCXVI, CCCXIX
Purva	the eastern quarter. All the wonderful events connected with it, e.g.: 'It was here that the divine Creator of the Universe first sang the Vedas ... Here first grew the 100 different branches of OM!'	U	CVIII
Rasatala	'the 7th stratum below the Earth'	U	CII
Reality		ASW	XXXIII
Realisation	instantaneous realisation for the man of knowledge	AD	XCII
	description of the realised man	B	XXXVIII
Rebirth		AD	XC
		SAN	CCII, CCXIII, CCLXXV, CCXCVIII, CCIV
	different forms that have to be inhabited on account of sin	AN	CXI
Reflection		SAN	CCL
Religion	of Pravritti and Nivritti	AN	CXLI
	Asita-Devala adopts the Moksha religion	SAL	L

Religion *cont*	Manu describes 'the best of all religions'	SAN	XXI
	the 'auspicious religion called Pasupata'	SAN	CCLXXXV
	the origin and history of the Religion of Devotion in the Krita and Treta Ages	SAN	CCCXLIX
Renunciation		SAN	CLXXVI, CLXXXIX, CCCLXXIII
		ASW	XIII
	the life of Renunciation as means to Emancipation	SAN	CCLXXVIII
Rhetoric	*see* **Powerful Passages, Speech**		
Righteousness		SAN	CCLIX, CCLXXIII, CCCX
		AN	CLXII, CLXIV
	righteousness and the king	SAN	XC, XCII
	'Righteousness (Dharma) is so called because it upholds all creatures.'	SAN	CIX
Rishis	origin of	AN	LXXXV
Rituals	the Sraddha rites for those dead in the battle	SAN	XLIII
	further ordinances about the Sraddha	AN	XCII
	how the Sraddha was first conceived	AN	XCI
	types of food to be offered at the Sraddha	AN	LXXXVIII
	the times for performance of the Sraddha	AN	LXXXVII
	names of the various constellations under which one may perform the Sraddha	AN	LXXXIX
	particular constellations connected with the Sraddha	AN	CIV
	Dhritarashtra performs the Sraddha	ASR	XIV
	the obsequial rites of Abhimanyu are performed	ASW	LXII
	the Pandavas perform the funeral rites	ASR	XXXIX

RELIGION | SACRIFICE

Ritwiks	the seven Ritwiks ... of Yama	AN	CL
	... of the Lord of Treasures	AN	CL
	... in the sacrifice of Varuna	AN	CL
Rivers	Suktimati	AD	LXIII
	why the Saraswati moved her course eastwards during the Krita Age	SAL	XXXVII
	how the Saraswati came to have seven forms	SAL	XXXVIII
	Lomasa conducts the exiles to the Vaitarani	VA	CXIV
	Payosini	VA	CXXI
	'Here flow before thee the seven Gangas'	VA	CXXXIX
	origin of the Aruna, a tributary of the Saraswati	SAL	XLIII
	origin of the Oghavati	AN	II
Sacrifice		B	XXVII, XXVIII
	nature of	SAN	CCLXIII
	importance of	SAN	LX
	sacrifice and gifts	AN	CXXXVII
	sacrifice and wealth	SAN	XX
	fire and sacrifice	VA	CCXIX
	the sacrifice associated with fire-gods	VA	CCXX
	the four kinds of sacrifice	SAU	XVIII
	the Viswarij Sacrifice	SAN	XXIX
	the 17 limbs of sacrifice	SAN	CCLXVIII
	Krishna speaks of the three kinds of sacrifice	B	XLI
	how Parasara, until stopped by Pulastya, performed a sacrifice for the destruction of Rakshasas	AD	CLXXXIII
	Yudhishthira begins the Rajasuya Sacrifice	SAB	XXXIV
	Vidura's words to Dhritarashtra: 'For the sake of a family a member may be sacrificed; for the sake of a village a family may be sacrificed; for the sake of a province a village may be sacrificed; and for the sake of one's soul the whole Earth may be sacrifced.'	SAB	LXI
	why Rudra receives the best portions of sacrifce	VA	CXIV

Sacrifice *cont*	Duryodhana celebrates the Vaishnava Sacrifice	VA	CCLIV
	a horse-sacrifice is made to wipe out Indra's sin of Brahmanicide	U	XIII
	question of giving Dakshina at a sacrifice	SAN	LXXIX
	Janamejaya performs the horse-sacrifice	SAN	CLII
	the horse-sacrifice held by Yudhishthira	ASW	LXXXIX
	the Merits of different types of sacrifice	ASW	XCI
	whether animals should be slain for sacrifice	ASW	XCI
	Janamejaya's sacrifice now ends; the intervals betwen rituals have been filled by the narrative told by Vaisampayana	SW	V
	see also **Snake-Sacrifice**		
Sakadwipa	Utopian life in Sakadwipa	B	XI
Samantapanchaka	'is the northern (sacrificial) altar of Brahman, the Lord of all Creatures'	SAL	LIII
	formation by Rama of Samantapanchaka, site of the battle between the Kauravas and Pandavas	AD	II
Sankhya	*see* **System**		
Science	of Sanjivani	AD	LXXVI
	of Adhyatma	SAN	CCLXXVI
	of syllables and pronunciation	SAN	CCCXLIII
	sciences called 'Varna' and 'Akshara'	SAN	CCXXXV
	Chakshushi, the science of producing illusions	AD	CLXXII
	Vyasa imparts to Yudhishthira the science called Pratismriti	VA	XXXVI
	Yudhishthira imparts to Arjuna the science called Pratismriti	VA	XXXVII
	Vrihadaswa imparts to Yudhishthira the full science of dice	VA	LXXIX
	Rituparna imparts to Nala the whole science of dice	VA	LXXII
	Nala imparts to Rituparna 'the mysteries of equestrian science'	VA	LXXVII

Science *cont*	'In consequence of one's being able to expound every object (Vyakarana), one is said to be endued with universal knowledge (Vaiyakarana), and indeed the science itself is called Vyakarana owing to its being able to expound every object to its very root (which is Brahman)'	U	XLIII
	a classification of creatures, '24 in all, these are described as Gayatri (Brahma)'	B	IV
	the transmission of system	B	XXVIII
	Krishna declares 'that supernal science of science' ... 'When an observer recognizes none else to be an agent save the qualities, and knows that which is beyond (the qualities), he attaineth to my nature.'	B	XXXVIII
	Sukra first acquired the science of morality	SAN	CCX
	passing references to medicine and chemistry	SAN	XXVIII
	Narada acquired the science of music	SAN	CCX
	Bharadwaja acquired the science of arms	SAN	CCX
	the dark-complexioned son of Atri acquired the science of medicine	SAN	CCX
	other sciences mentioned: Nyaya, Vaiseshika, Sankya, Patanjala, etc	SAN	CCX
	the Fourth Science, 'based on the principles of ratiocinative inference and having Emancipation for its end'	SAN	CCCXIX
	atomic or molecular changes	SAN	CCXXI
	'Thou are Gautama (the founder of the science of dialectics)'	AN	XVII
	how Garga received 'that wonderful science, viz. the knowlege of Time with its 64 branches'	AN	XVIII
Seasons	description of the rainy season and of autumn	VA	CLXXXI
	see also **Wheel of Time**		
Self		SAN	CCII
	in Praise of the Self, Pathway to the Paramatman	SAN	CCCXLV
	'preserve thy own self now, for self is the refuge of everything'	SAL	IV
Self-Restraint		AN	LXXV

Senses		SAN	CXCIV, CCII, CCXIX, CCXXXIX, CCXLVII, CCLXXV, CCLXXXVI
		ASW	I, XLII
	and elements	SAN	CCLII
	and sensory perception	ASW	XLIII
	control of the senses	B	XXVI
	subjugation of the senses	VA	CCX
	sense-organs as the doors of knowledge	U	XXXII
Service	in the royal household	VI	IV
Sin		SAN	CCLXXIII
	of pride	AN	XCIX-CI
	of Brahmanicide	U	X
Snakes	why their tongues are divided in twain	AD	XXXIV
	names of the principal snakes, Sesha being the first-born and Vasuki the second	AD	XXXV
Snake-Sacrifice	origin of King Janamejaya's snake-sacrifice	AD	III
	foretelling of the snake-sacrifice of Janamejaya	AD	XX
	Janamejaya resolves to perform the snake-sacrifice	AD	LI
Sons	the 12 kinds	AD	CXX
	value of a son	VA	IX
Soul		SAN	CXCIV, CCII-CCIV, CCVI, CCXIII, CCXLI, CCXLV, CCXLVI, CCXLVIII, CCLXXXVI, CCCLII
		ASW	XXV
		ASR	XXXIV
	why the Soul is called Purusha	SAN	CCX
	the two Souls	SAN	CCXXXVI
	immortality of the Soul	SAN	CCXI, CCCXX
	how to behold the Soul	SAN	CCLIII
	the Supreme Soul and Jiva	SAN	CCIX

Soul *cont*	The Great Soul (or Mahat)	ASW	XL
	the unity of the Jiva-soul with the Supreme Soul	SAN	CCCVI
	how one may behold the Supreme Soul through Yoga Contemplation and through the Sankhya system; why the Soul is called the Presider and Kshetrajna and Purusha	SAN	CCCVII
	description of the region of the Supreme Soul, compared with which the regions of the gods are hells	SAN	CXCVIII
	'One occupies that much of the Supreme Soul as is commensurate with what is occupied in one's own soul by Vedic sound.'	SAN	CCXXXIX
	'When the Soul becomes endued with vulgar attributes, it comes to be called Kshetrajna. When freed from these attributes, it comes to be called Paramatman or Supreme Soul. Know that Soul. He is inspired with universal benevolence. He resides in the body like a drop of water in a lotus.' ... 'The man of wisdom, living on frugal fare and with a heart cleansed of all sins, devoting himself to Yoga meditation, succeeds every night, before sleep and after sleep, in beholding his Soul by the aid of his Soul.'	SAN	CLXXXVII
	knowledge of the Soul	SAN	CCXLIX
	see also **Immortality**		
Speculations	on existence and non-existence; on cause and effect	SAN	CCXVIII
Speech	characteristics of	SAN	CCCXXI
	how Krishna speaks 'words that were clear, distinct, correctly pronounced and without a single letter dropped'	U	XCI
	'Agreeableness of speech, O Sakra, is the one thing by practising which a person may become an object of regard with all creatures and acquire great celebrity.'	SAN	LXXXIV
	the monosyllable 'Bho'	SAN	CCCXXXIV
	dispute over the word 'Ajas'	SAN	CCCXXXVIII

Speech *cont*	'I am He who is the repository of the science of syllables and pronunciation that is treated of in the supplementary portions of the Vedas.' ... 'Galava ... compiled the rules in respect of the division of syllables and words, and those about emphasis and accent in utterance, and shone as the first scholar who became conversant with those two subjects'	SAN	CCCXLIII
	how the Rishi Saraswat arose from the syllable 'Bho'	SAN	CCCL
	use of the word 'Tvam'	AN	CLXII
	the goddess Word	ASW	XXI
	the words that bind and release	AN	CXLIV
	a footnote states: 'Ladies spoke in Prakrita and not in Sanskrit.'	AN	XLI
	Krishna's pronunciation and the sound of his voice	SAN	CCCXLVIII

Stories Good for Retelling to Children

	A + sign indicates a particularly strong recommendation:	AD	XL-XLIV, LIV-LVII
		VA	XCIX-CIX
	all the stories about Garuda	AD	XXV-XXXIV
	how Kacha thrice came back to life	AD	LXXVI
	Bhima gains the strength of 10,000 elephants	AD	CXXVIII
	+King Parikshit, the frog-princess, Vamadeva and the Vami steeds	VA	CLXLI
	how Drona amazes the young princes	AD	CXXXIII
	why Prince Ekalavya paid a tuition fee of his own right thumb	AD	CXXXIV
	how Arjuna shot the head from the bird	AD	CXXXV
	+the Pandavas are tested by Dharma	VA	CCCIX-CCCXII
	the jackal, tiger, mouse, wolf and mongoose	AD	CXLII
	the House of Lac	AD	CXLVIII-CL
	Bhima slays the Rakshasa Vaka	AD	CLIX-CLXVI
	+the man who fell into a hole in the forest	ST	V
	how Arjuna is chosen by Draupadi	AD	CLXL
	the cat and the mice	U	CLXI
	Mankanaka and the vegetable juice	VA	LXXXIII
	Rama and Rama	VA	CXIX

Stories Good for Retelling to Children

cont

Legend of the fish (cf. Noah and the Flood)	VA	CLXXXVI
Bhima fails to lift Hanuman's tail	VA	CXLVI
Kings – Ashtaka, Pratardana, Vasumanas and Sivi	VA	CLXLVII
the incarnation of the dwarf	VA	CCLXX
the crow and the swan	K	XLI
how Sthanu destroys three cities with one shaft	K	XXXIV
how Indradyumna lost and regained heaven	VA	CLXLVIII;
Soma and the 27 daughters of Daksha	SAL	XXXV
Ekata, Dwita and Trita	SAL	XXXVI
The Rakshasa's head and Mahodara's thigh	SAL	XXXIX
Aswatthaman and Krishna's discus	SAU	XII
how Siva's bow was made and how its string broke	SAU	XVIII
Krishna gives an account of Siva and Creation	SAU	XVII
why Gandari produces a sore nail on Yudhishthira's foot	ST	XV
why Dalvya-Vaka stopped destroying Dhritarashtra's kingdom	SAL	XLI
how the Saraswati obeyed Viswamitra and Vasishtha and why her waters became blood for a year	SAL	XLII
Dhritarashtra destroys an iron statue of Bhima	ST	XII
+the mouse, the cat and the owl	SAN	CXXXVIII
how Likhita was punished for stealing from his brother	SAN	XXIII
The sage, the crow and the king	SAN	LXXXII
the jackal and the tiger	SAN	CXI
the camel and his long neck	SAN	CXII
+the Brahmana, King Ikshvaku, Dharma, Mrityu, Yama and Time	SAN	CXCIX
the Ocean and the Rivers	SAN	CXIII
the Muni and the dog	SAN	CXVI, CXVII
the three Sakula fish	SAN	CXXXVII
how Indra regained his sovereignty	SAN	CXXIV
King Brahmadatta and the bird Pujani	SAN	CXXXIX
the drought, the Rishi and the haunch of dog's meat	SAN	CXLI
Gautama, the Brahmana who lived like a robber	SAN	CLXVIII-CLXXIII

Stories Good for Retelling to Children

cont	the jackal, the vulture and the boy who was restored to life by the great god Sankara	SAN	CLIII
	the fowler and the pigeon	SAN	CXLIV-CXLIX
	the son who was commanded to slay his own mother	SAN	CCLXVI
	how the Grandsire took Brahmanicide from Indra and divided her equally among Agni, vegetation, the Apsaras and water	SAN	CCLXXXII
	Narayana and White Island	SAN	CCCXXXVI, CCCXXXVII
	King Uparichara and the curse	SAN	CCCXXXVIII
	Mrityu, Gautami, Kala, the fowler and the serpent	AN	I
	the fowler, the parrot and the tree	AN	V
	how the royal sage Vitahavya became a Brahmana	AN	XXX
	the king, the pigeon and the hawk	AN	XXXII
	the humbling of Nahusha's pride	AN	XCIX, C
	Chyavana and the fishermen	AN	L, LI
	King Nriga and Krishna	AN	LXX
	Jamadagni, his wife Renuka and Surya	AN	XCV, XCVI
	the worm that retained its memory	AN	CXVII, CXVIII
	how King Alarka tried to shoot arrows at the sense-organs of the mind	ASW	XXX
	Utanka and the celestial earrings	ASW	LVI-LVIII
Study	the fugitives study 'the Rik and the other Vedas and also all the Vedangas, as well as the sciences of morals and politics'	AD	XLVIII
	'the faults of students in the pursuit of learning'	U	XL
	the study comprised by the term 'Agama'	SAN	CCLXIX
	Sanjaya says: 'the fruits that arise from a study of the Vedas arise from a study of this Parva also.'	D	CCII
	Suka's study	SAN	CCCXXXVI
	distinction between Vedic study and Yoga penances	SAN	XXVI
	Vyasa instructs his disciples in the study and teaching of the Vedas	SAN	CCCXXVIII
	see also **Science, Instruction**		
Sun	the 108 names of	VA	III
	hymn of praise to the Sun	VA	III

Supplication	the need to protect a suppliant	SAN	CXLIX
Swastikas		U	CIII
		D	LXXXII
		SAN	XLI
Swayamvara	of Damayanti	VA	LVII
	Yayati holds a Swayamvara for his daughter	UC	XX
System	the Yoga system compared to the Sankhya system	SAN	CCCI
	the Sankhya system	SAN	CCCII
	Adhyatma, Adhibhuta and Adhidaivata in relation to the body	SAN	CCCXIV
	Sankhya, Yogas, Vedas, Pasupata, Pancharatra	SAN	CCCL
	question of the one and the many	SAN	CCCLI, CCCLII
Thoughts	that bind and release	AN	CXLIV
Time	divisions of	AD	XXV
		SAN	CXXXVII
	power of	B	III
		SAL	LXIII
		ST	II
		SAN	XXXIII, XXVIII
		AN	CLXIV
		MAU	I
	importance of	SAN	XXV
	the divisions of	SAN	CXXXVII
	the great River of	SAN	CCXXXV
	measure of	SAN	CCCIII, CCCXII
	the work of	SAN	CCXXXVIII
	the inevitable effects of	ST	IX
	'those versed in chronology say that thou (the Sun) art the beginning and thou art the end of a day of Brahma, which consisteth of a full 1,000 Yugas'	VA	III
	Janaka says: 'He alone is a truly learned man who understandeth the significance of the thing that hath 30 divisions, 12 parts, 24 joints and 360 spokes', references to the divisions of time and their calculation	VI	LII

Time *cont*	reference to 'ever-fleeting Time'	U	LI
	specific reference to the season, month, hour	U	LXXXIII
	the day and night of Brahman	B	XXXII
	Aswatthaman speaks of the reverses wrought by Time	SAL	LXV
	'Time possessing the seeds of both destruction and growth, was made the sovereign of all creatures, as also of the four portions of death (viz. weapons, diseases, Yama and acts), and lastly of grief and joy.'	SAN	CXXII
	'Time cooks everything.'	SAN	CCXXIV
	'Time, of its own power, cooks all entities within itself. No one, however, knows That in which Time, in its turn, is cooked.'	SAN	CCXXXIX
	a new way to calculate the length of the life of one creation	SAN	CCLXXX
	how Garga received 'that wonderful science, viz. the knowledge of Time with its 64 branches'	AN	XVIII
	the names of the months	AN	CVI
	the divisions of Time – all things are being cooked in Time's 'cauldron'	SAN	CCXXVII
	including the lengths of the Yugas in celestial years	SAN	CCXXXI
	power of	SAN	LXII
	see also **Wheel of Time**		
Tirthas	Spiritual significance of	AN	CVIII
	enumerated by Dhaumya	VA	LXXXVIII-XC
	and the merits they confer	AN	XXV
	the sacred lake Dwaitavana	VA	XXIV
	the merits attaching to tirthas	VA	LXXXII-LXXXV
	cleansing power of Prithudaka tirthas	SAN	CLII
Tranquillity		SAN	CLXXIX
Treatises	the Grandsire composed 'a treatise consisting of 100,000 chapters', of encyclopaedic breadth and dealing with 'the histories of all past events, the origin of the great Rishis, the holy waters, the planets and stars and asterisms, the		

Treatises *cont*	duties in respect of the four orders of men, and the four branches of learning,' etc, etc. This treatise was repeatedly abridged by gods and Rishis until it was reduced to 1,000 lessons. The various names of this treatise are Dandaniti, Vaisalakasha, Vahudantaka and Varhaspatya	SAN	LIX
	the great Rishis once compiled a treatise 'which is the eternal origin of all duties and observances'. Narayana was most pleased with this treatise, but said that it would disappear on the death of King Uparichara	SAN	CCCXXXVI
Trees	as constituted by the five elements	SAN	CLXXXIV
	'whose seed is Brahman'	ASW	XXXV
	the foremost trees	ASW	XLIII
	story of Pavana and the huge Salmali tree	SAN	CLIV-CLVII
	Krishna speaks of the eternal Aswatta tree	B	XXXIX
	the huge Jamvu tree	B	VII
	description of a mighty jujube tree	VA	CXLIV
Triple Aggregate	(i.e. Virtue, Wealth, Pleasure)	VA	XXXIII
Truth		ASW	XXX
	in praise of	AN	LXXV
	and its 13 forms	SAN	CLXII
	Truth and Untruth	SAN	CXC
	'In Truth is immortality'	SAN	CLXXV
	'when the soldiers that compose Death's army are on their march, nothing can resist them, except that one thing, viz. the power of Truth, for in Truth alone immortality dwells.'	SAN	CCLXXVII
	Bhishma declares his allegiance to Truth	AD	CIII
	to Yudhishthira 'truth seems to be the first consideration, above that of my sovereign power itself.'	VA	CXX

Truth *cont*	'our mental faculties have their proper play when their foundation is laid in Truth'	VA	CCVI
	'this whole universe, unconquerable everywhere and abounding in great elements, is Brahma and there is nothing higher than this.'	VA	CCIX
	Karna says: 'Death itself is not fraught with such terrors for me as Untruth.'	VA	CCC
	interrelations of Power, Righteousness and Truth	SAN	CXXXIV
	'there is nothing which contributes so much to the success of kings as Truth'	SAN	LVI
Understanding		SAN	CCXLVIII, CCXLIX, CCLXXXVI
	levels of	SAU	III
	the 60 properties of the Understanding	SAN	CCLV
Universe	description of	SAN	CLXXXII
	dissolution of	SAN	CCCXIII
	creation and destruction of	SAN	CLCIV
	Narayana speaks about himself and the universe. An important narrative, 'really the essence of the hundreds of other narratives that thou hast heard from me.'	SAN	CCCXL
Uttara	Madhyama; the North, described by Garuda; here dwell Krishna, Jushnu, Brahman, Maheswara	U	CXI
Vadari	hermitage of Nara and Narayana	VA	CLV
Vadavamukha	a marine shape like a horse's head, formed from the fire of Aurva's wrath	AD	CLXXXII
Vanity	the sin of	AD	XC
Varshas	seven more Varshas	B	XII
Vedas		SAN	CCX
	come to Suka of their own accord	SAN	CCCXXV
	distinction between Vedic study and Yoga penances	SAN	XXVI

Vedas	'If the science of chastisement disappears, the Vedas will disappear.'	SAN	LXIII
	how Arshtishema acquired mastery of the Vedas in the Krita Age	SAL	XL
	how Saraswat taught the Vedas to 60,000 Rishis who had forgotten the scriptures	SAL	LI
	'This discourse, O son, intended for thy instruction, is the essence of all the Vedas.'	SAN	CCXLVI
	how Yajnavalkya received the knowledge of the Vedas from Surya	SAN	CCCXIX
	Vyasa instructs his disciples in the study and teaching of the Vedas	SAN	CCCXXVIII
	'the stain of the Vedas is the suspension of their recitation'	SAN	CCCXXIX
	'the Vedic lexicon called Nighantuka: 'I am He who is the repository of the science of syllables and pronunciation that is treated of in the supplementary portions of the Vedas.'	SAN	CCCXLIII
	how the Vedas are stolen by two Asuras and restored by Krishna	SAN	CCCXLVIII
Vice	the 13 vices; their origin and how they may be subdued	SAN	CLXIII
	see also **Virtue**		
Virtue		VA	CXL, CLVI, CLXLIX
	virtue and atheism	VA	XXXI
	virtue and vice	VA	XCIV, CCIX
	the words of Saraswati on virtue	VA	CLXXXV
	Narada speaks of virtuous conduct	VA	CLXLIII
	the establishment of virtue in the new age	VA	CLXL
	virtuous conduct	VA	CLXLVII, CCVI
	Vyasa's words on virtue	VA	CCLVII
	a lady's beautiful discourse on virtue	VA	CCV
	characteristics of self-restraint	U	LXIII
	the four cardinal virtues are ascetic penances, truth, compassion, liberality	D	LIII
	the virtue of a life of domesticity	SAN	XI
	kingly virtue	SAN	XIII

Virtue *cont*	how virtue accrues to the dutiful king	SAN	LXVI
	the 36 virtues which a king should observe	SAN	LXX
	description of the virtuous person	SAN	CLVIII
	Virtue, Wealth, Pleasure and their connection with Will, Emancipation, Knowledge of Self	SAN	CXXIII
	Virtue, Wealth, Desire, Emancipation	SAN	CLXVII
Vishnupada	the footprint of Vishnu: a place in the Northern quarter	U	CXI
Vows	called Chandravrata	AN	CX
	description of the vow called 'Go'	U	XCIX
	Yudhishthira vows he will starve to death	SAN	XXVII
	the Unccha vow	SAN	CCCLXIII, CCCLXV
	the 'vow of fast'	AN	CIII
Warfare	the three causes of victory	SAB	XVI
	details of fortification and defensive works	VA	XV
	speaking of Jamadagni: 'To him, rivalling in lustre the author of light, came spontaneously and without instruction the knowledge of the entire military art and of the four-fold missile arms.'	VA	CXV
	celestial warfare studied for five years by Arjuna	VA	CLXIII
	terrific battle between the gods and the Danavas	VA	CCXXX
	mighty encounter between Gandharvas and the Kurus	VA	CCXXXIX
	battle between ... Gandharvas and the Pandavas	VA	CCXLII, CCXLIII
	... the Pandavas and Jayadratha's army	VA	CCLXVIII
	... the Trigartas and Virata's army	VI	XXXII
	the attack on Lanka	VA	CCLXXXII-CCLXXXVIII
	Karna learns arms from Drona	VA	CCCVII
	duel between Arjuna and Karna	VI	LIV
	encounter between Arjuna and ... Kripa	VI	LVII
	... Drona	VI	LVIII
	... Aswatthaman	VI	LIX
	... Karna	VI	LX
	... Bhishma	VI	LXIII, LXIV

VIRTUE | WARFARE

Warfare *cont*	Sanjaya ... describes the chariots and steeds of the Pandavas	U	LVI
	... shows how each division in the enemy ranks has been assigned a particular target	U	LVII
	description of chariots ... Krishna's	U	LXXXIII
	... Alamvusha's	D	CLXVII
	... Ghatotkacha's	D	CLXXV
	historical background to the great battle	U	CXLVIII
	the Kuru battle array, men, beasts, tackle, weapons; names of units and companies (e.g. Pattis, Gulmas, Ganas)	U	CLVI
	the secret of victory ...	U	CLVII
	... truth, compassion, righteousness, energy	B	XXI
	single combat between Bhishma and Rama of Bhrigu's race	U	CLXXXII–CLXXXVIII
	combat regulations	B	I
	signs of a victorious army and of an army in rout	B	III
	the Kuru battle standards and their devices	B	XVII
	the battle array known as Vajra and the reason for this array	B	XIX
	the great battle begins	B	XLIV
	the Pandava army forms a very special battle array known as Krauncharuma	B	L
	the Pandavas form arrays ... Makara	B	LXXV
	... Vajra	B	LXXXII
	... Sringataka	B	LXXXVIII
	... Krauncha	D	VII
	... Madhyama	SAL	XVIII
	the Kurus have a battle array called Makara, while the Pandavas form 'that invincible and prince of arrays called the Syena'	B	LXIX
	the Kurus form ... the array called Garuda and the Pandavas make a counter-array in the form of the half-moon	B	LVI
	... the Mandala array	B	LXXXII
	... the Sakata array	D	VII
	... the Sarvatobhadra array	B	C
	... the Garuda array	D	XX
	Dhritarashtra describes his army: training, qualities, weapons	B	LXXVI
	the Suchimukha array	B	LXXVII
	a perfectly matched mace-combat between Bhima and Salya	D	XV
	mace-combat between Bhima and Duryodhana	SAL	LVII

Warfare *cont*	description of the horses and standards belonging to the Pandavas	D	XXIII
	the chariot and standard of Jayadratha	D	XLI
	Drona puts his forces into an array part Sakata and part a circle 'full 48 miles long and the width of its rear measured 20 miles' ... 'In the rear of that array was another impenetrable array of the form of a lotus. And within that lotus was another dense array called the needle.'	D	LXXXVII
	Sanjaya describes Arjuna's standard and nine standards belonging to Kuru heroes	D	CIV
	Karna puts his troops into the Makara array; the Pandavas form the half-moon	K	XI
	how Rama received all the celestial weapons from Maheswara and passed the whole science of weapons to Karna	K	XXXIV
	Krishna describes Karna's chariot and standard	K	LXXXVI
	fortification of citadels	SAN	LXXXVI
	rules of combat ... 'Manu himself, the son of the Self-born (Brahman), has said that battles should be fought fairly.'	SAN	XCV
	... how the king should conduct himself towards his foes	SAN	XCVI
	magnificent description of battle as sacrifice	SAN	XCVIII
	army tactics and manoeuvres; combat linked to constellations and planets	SAN	C
	characteristics of fighters linked to their physical appearance	SAN	CI
	indications of the future success of an army ... the use of severity and mildness	SAN	CII
	see also **Weapons**		
Water	'the whole universe is composed of water. Water is the form of all embodied creatures. In that water is the Soul which is displayed in the Mind.'	SAN	CLXXXVII
Weakness	amazing power of	SAN	XCI
Wealth	and sacrifice	SAN	XX
	Garuda speaks of the function of wealth	U	CXIV
	Duryodhana describes the wealth of the Pandavas	SAB	L-LII
	Arjuna discourses on Wealth, Kingship and 'the great path called Dasaratha'	SAN	VIII

Wealth *cont*	the faults inherent in the possession of wealth	SAN	XXVI
Weapons	Drona teaches the science of arms to the Kauravas and the Pandavas	AD	CXXXI
	Agneya	AD	CXXXVII
		U	CLXXXIII
		D	XCVII, CLVI, CCI
	Varuna	AD	CXXXVII, CCXXIX
		U	CLXXXIII
		D	XCVII, CLVI
		K	LXXXIX
	Vayavya	AD	CXXXVII
		U	CLXXXIII
		D	CLV, CLX, CLXI, CLXXV, CLXXXVIII
		K	LXXXIX, XCI
	Parjanya	AD	CXXXVII
	Bhauma, Parvatya, Antardana	AD	CXXXVII
	Kshura, Naracha, Vala, Vipatha	AD	CXLI
	Arjuna receives Gandiva; Krishna receives the discus and a mace called Kaumodaki	AD	CCXXVII
	weapons of the gods: Yama (mace), Kuvera (spiked club), Varuna (noose and missile), Skanda (lance), Dhatri (bow), Jaya (club)	AD	CCXXIX
	Yama gives Arjuna his mace; Varuna gives Arjuna some Varuna weapon; Kuvera gives Arjuna his Antarddhana weapon	VA	XLI
	Maya gives a marvellous club to Bhima	SAB	III
	the Pasupata weapon given to Arjuna by Mahadeva	VA	XL
	how Twashtri made the Vajra weapon	VA	C
	Raudra	VA	CLXXII
	weapon of the Pandavas	VI	XLII, XLIII
	history of Gandiva	VI	XLIII
	Sanmohana	VI	LXV
	Sthur-karna	U	XLVIII

Weapons *cont*	Brahma	U	XLVIII
		D	CLVI, CLXXXVIII, CXCI, CXCII, CCI
		K	LXXXIX, XCI
	Arjuna's weapons named: Suka, Kakudika, Naka, Asyamodaka, Akshisantarjana, Santana, Nartana, Ghora	U	XCVI
	'That knotty bow that was created for the destruction of the world,' from which Arjuna's bow has taken its name	U	XCVIII
	the three celestial bows (Gandiva, Sarnga, Vijaya) and the gods associated with them	U	CLIX
	the four types of weapon in the science of arms	U	CLXXXI
	Guhyaka	U	CLXXXIII
	Praswapa, Samvodhana	U	CLXXXVI
	Arjuna releases the Mahendra	B	LIX
	the Brahma weapon is used	U	CLXXXVII
	Arjuna ... invokes the Aindra	B	LXXXII
		D	CXLV
	... wields the Vayavya	D	XIX
	... shoots the Brahma weapon	D	XXV
	... uses the Jyotishka and the Aditya	D	XXVIII
	... learns how to use the Pasupata	D	LXXXI
	... invokes the Varuna	D	CXLIV
	Drona wields the Saila	B	CIII
	Sikhandin wields the Varuna	B	LXXXVI
	how Krishna obtained the discus called Sudarsana	D	XI
	names of bows: Vayavya (Bhima), Vaishnava (Nakula), Aswina (Sahadeva), Paulastya (Ghatotkacha), Raudra, Agneya, Kauverya, Yamya, Girisa (the five sons of Draupadi)	D	XXIII
	Bhagadatta hurls the Vaishnava	D	XXVII
	Abhimanyu uses the Gandharva	D	XLIII
	the bow of Siva is called Ajagava or Pinaka	D	LXIX
	Krishna's mace, Kaumodaki	D	LXXIX
	description of Arjuna's arrows	D	XCVIII
	Drona and Yudhishthira both invoke the Brahma	D	CV

Weapons *cont*	Bhima uses the Tvashtri	D	CVII
	Yamya, Varuna, Savitra, Prajapatya, Mahendra	D	CLVI
	the infallible weapon called Naikartana	D	CLXXIX
	Aindra	D	CLVI, CLXXXVIII
		K	XXVII, LIII, LXIV
	Pasupata	U	XLVIII
		D	CLXXXVIII
	Tvashtra	D	CLVI CLXXXVIII
	Yamya	D	CLXXXVIII
	types of arrow regarded as improper	D	CXC
	how Aswatthaman was given the Narayana	D	CXCVI
	Aswatthaman invokes the Narayana	D	CC
	Karna's bow, Vijaya: its manufacture and history	K	XXXI
	Karna invokes the Brahma	K	XLIX
	Naga, Sauparna	K	LIII
	Bhargava	K	LXIV, LXXXIX
	the snaky weapon the Brahma	K	XC
	Anjalika	K	XCI
	description of Bhima's mace	SAL	XI
	Brahmasira	SAU	XII, XIII
	Yudhishthira slays Salya with a special dart forged by Tashtri	SAL	XVII
	how Dadicha gave his bones (as weapons) to Sakra for vanquishing the Asuras	SAL	LI
	how Siva's bow was made and how its strings broke	SAU	XVIII
	origin of the sword; the eight names of the sword. 'Of all weapons, O son of Madravati, the sword is the foremost'; the bow was created by Prithu	SAN	CLXVI
	origin of Mahadeva's Pinaka, and why it is so called	SAN	CCXC
	descriptions of the bow called Pinaka, the Pasupata, the Sula, Mahadeva's battleaxe	AN	XIV
	Arjuna returns to Varuna the bow Gandiva and the two inexhaustible quivers	MAH	I

Wheel of Time		U	LI
	with seasons and the signs of the Zodiac; Utanka's vision of the Wheel of Time	AD	III
	'the upraised Wheel of Time'	U	LIV
	'Endued with divine attributes, Kesava, by the power of his soul, causeth the Wheel of Time, the wheel of the Universe and the wheel of the Yuga to revolve incessantly.'	U	LXVIII
	see also **Time**		
Wheel of Birth and Death		SAN	CCCXXXII
	see also **Rebirth**		
White Island	and its strange denizens	SAN	CCCXXXVI
Will		U	XLVI
Winds	names of	SAN	CCCXXIX
Wine	origin of wine called Varuni	U	CII
Wisdom		SAN	CCXXXVII
	attributes of wisdom and foolishness	U	XXXIII
	the wise man never regards himself as the actor	SAN	CCXXVI
Women	disposition of	SAN	XLIII
		AN	XXXVIII, XL
	duties of	AN	CXLVI
	why women were created	AN	XL
	'Indeed, women are like frightful mantra-powers. They stupefy persons reft of wisdom. They are sunk in the attribute of Passion. They are the eternal embodiment of the senses.'	SAN	CCXIII
	why do men still attach themselves to women? Can women be restrained within the prescribed bounds?	AN	XXXIX
Work		B	XXVII
	Krishna speaks of the significance of work	U	XXIX

Worship	of Krishna	AN	CIX
	why Indra is worshipped around a pole planted in the ground	AD	LXIII
	Krishna and Arjuna adore the goddess Twilight	D	LXXII
	the kinds of men that are worthy of worship	AN	XXXI
Yawn	origin of	U	IX
Yoga-Nidra	is described as 'the deep sleep under the spell of spiritual meditation'	AD	XXI
Yugas	and their characteristics	SAN	CCXXXII
	and universal dissolution	VA	CXXXVII
	the Krita Yuga	VA	CLXI
		SAU	XVIII
		SAN	XL
	righteous community living in the Krita Age	AD	LXIV
	how Arshtishema acquired mastery of the Vedas in the Krita Age	SAL	XL
	'After the expiry of this, the Krita Age, a confusion will set in regarding the different modes of life, and innumerable Bhikshus will appear with sectarian marks of different kinds.'	SAN	LXV
	how Rama formed Samantapanchaka in the interval between the Treta and Dwapara Yuga	AD	II
	how the Kauravas fought the Pandavas in the interval between the Dwapara and Kali Yuga	AD	II
	how the Ocean 'becomes the bed of the lotus-naveled Vishnu when, at the termination of every Yuga, that deity of immeasurable power enjoys Yoga-nidra, the deep sleep under the spell of spiritual meditation.'	AD	XXI
	'the truth is that the king makes the age. When the king ... rules with a complete and strict reliance on the science of chastisement, the foremost of ages called Krita is then said to set in; ... relies upon only three of the four parts of the science of chastisement,		

Yugas *cont*	leaving out a fourth, the age called Treta sets in; … observes the great science by only a half, leaving out the other half, then the age that sets in is called Dwapara; … abandoning the great science totally, oppresses his subjects by evil means of diverse kinds, the age that sets in is called Kali.' Characteristics of the four ages; what happens to the king who produces the four ages	SAN	LXIX
	the words of Narayana spoken in the Krita Age of the Epoch of Manu	SAN	CCCXXXV
	Lomasa says 'this period is the junction between the Treta and the Kali Age'	VA	CXXI
	how the Earth sank in the Krita Yuga and was lifted up again by Vishnu	VA	CXLI
	Hanuman teaches Bhima the characteristics of the four Yugas	VA	CXLVIII
	teaching on the Yuga given by a boy whose stomach contains all creation	VA	CLXXXVIII
	signs of the end of the Yuga; how Kalki, 'commissioned by Time … will inaugurate a new Yuga'	VA	CLXXXIX
	cycle of the ages and the 'interval' between cycles	VA	CCLXX
	Bhima considers Duryodhana as typical of the vile individuals that spring up at the end of each Yuga	U	LXXIV
	Krishna's words on the Yuga: 'It is the king that createth the Krita, Treta or Dwapara Age. Indeed, it is the king that is the cause of also the fourth Yuga (viz. the Kali).'	U	CXXXII
	Krishna says, referring to the coming battle: 'All signs of the Krita, Treta and Dwapara Ages will disappear (but, instead, Kali embodied will be present).'	U	CXLII
	Krishna says: 'Know that the Kali Age is at hand.'	SAL	LX
	respective qualities of the four Yugas, including the measures of life	B	X
	the installation, in a former Kalpa, of Varuna as Lord of all aquatic creatures	SAL	XLVII

Yugas *cont*	Bhishma speaks of Krishna: 'He it is who, towards the close of the Dwapara Yuga and the beginning of the Kali Yuga, is sung of with Sankarshana, by believers with devotion. It is that Vasudeva that createth, Yuga after Yuga, the worlds of the gods and the mortals, all cities girt by the sea, and the region of human habitation.'	B	LXVI
	Bhishma tells a story set 'towards the end of the Treta and the beginning of Dwapara'	SAN	CXLI
	Bhishma quotes a discourse from the Satya Yuga	SAN	CCCXXI
	Narada says of Rama: 'Rooting out all evils from the Earth, he caused the primeval Yuga to set in.'	D	LXX
	different methods of procreation in the four ages	SAN	CCVII
	cycle of celestial Yuga	SAN	CCX
	lengths of the Yuga in celestial years	SAN	CCXXXI
	characteristics of the four Yugas: 'The men of the Treta, Dwapara and Kali Yugas are inspired with doubts.'	SAN	CCXXXVIII
	crime and punishment in society throughout the ages, with particular reference to capital punishment	SAN	CCLXVII
	the four Yugas, the Kali Yuga and the Tisya constellation	SAN	CCCXLI
	'When 4,000 Yugas, according to the measure of the celestial elapse, the dissolution of the universe comes.'	SAN	CCCXLIII
	origin and history of the Religion of Devotion in the Krita and Treta Ages	SAN	CCCXLIX
	'When the unrighteous or sinful Kali Yuga comes, one should never pass a moment without devoting one's heart upon Mahadeva.'	AN	XIV
Zodiac	*see* **Wheel of Time**		
Zoology	origins of many zoological species	AD	LXVI
	why animals of the bovine species have cloven hooves	K	XXXIV

PART THREE

WHO'S WHO IN THE MAHĀBHĀRATA

Name	Aspect	Parva	Section
Abhaya	(son to Dhritarashtra)		
	slain by Bhima	D	CXXVI
Abhimanyu	earthly counterpart of Varchas	AD	LXVII
	son of Arjuna through Subhadra	AD	CCXXIII
	nephew of Krishna	AD	CCXXIII
	naming, why so called	AD	CCXXIII
	marries Uttara, daughter of King Virata	VI	LXXII
	prowess of	B	LXI, LXXIX, LXXX, CI
		D	XIV
	vanquishes Rakshasa Alavusha	B	CII
	'regarded superior to Krishna or Partha one and a half times in battle'	D	XXIII
	slain	D	XXXI
	qualities	D	XXXII
	penetrates/holds in check the entire Kuru army	D	XXXV
	slays Sushena, Drighalochana, Kundavedhin, and the ruler of the Asmakas	D	XXXV
	slays Salya's younger brother	D	XXXVI
	slays Karna's younger brother	D	XXXIX
	slays Vasatiya	D	XLII
	slays Rukmaratha	D	XLIII
	slays Lakshmana and the son of Kratha	D	XLIV
	slays Vrindaraka and Vrihadvala	D	XLV
	slays the ruler of the Magadhas, Aswaketu, the Bhoja Prince of Martikavata, Satrunjaya, Chandraketu, Mahamegha, Suvarchas and Suryabhasa	D	XLVI
	slain by Duhsasana's son	D	XLVII
	lamented by Yudhishthira	D	XLIX
	lamented by his father	D	LXXII
	lamented by his mother	D	LXXVIII
	funeral rites	ASW	LXII
	Vyasa announces that his son (as yet unborn) will be a great and righteous king. [This child becomes the father of Janameya]	ASW	LXII
	his true identity	ASR	XXXI
Achala	(son to the King of Gandhara)		
	(brother to Vrishaka)		
	slain by Arjuna	D	XXVIII

Achyutayus	slain by Arjuna	D	XCII
Adharma	birth	AD	LXVI
	always destroys every creature	AD	LXVI
	begets the Rakshasa called Nairitas upon his wife Niriti	AD	LXVI
Adhiratha	(charioteer) (husband to Radha) adopts Karna	VA	CCCVII
Aditi	his sons are the celestials	AD	LXIV
	his 12 sons (the 12 Adityas)	AD	LXV
Aditya	name of the Sun	D	CLXXXVII
Adityaketu	(son of Dhritarashtra) slain by Bhima	B	LXXXIX
Adityas	the twelve Adityas	AN	CL
Adrisyanti	(daughter-in-law to Vasishtha) mother of Asmaka	AD	CLXXIX
Agastya	Rishi	VA	XCVI
	slays Vatapi	VA	XCVI
	marries Lopamudra	VA	XCVII
	obtains wealth from the Asura Ilwala	VA	XCIX
	father to Dridhasyu through Lopamudra	VA	XCIX
	prevents the expansion of Mt Vindhya	VA	CIV
	drinks the Ocean and enables the gods to vanquish the Asuras	VA	CV
	curses Kuvera	VA	CLX
	turns Nahusha into a snake	VA	CLXXVIII
	consumes the Danavas and rescues the gods	AN	CLV
	his sacrifice	ASW	XCII
Agni	cursed by Bhrigu	AD	VI
	withdraws from all places until comforted by Brahma	AD	VII
	(portion of) the celestial counterpart of Dhristadyumna	AD	LXVII
	drinks clarified butter for 12 years	AD	CCXXV
	with assistance from Arjuna and Krishna burns the forest of Khandava	AD	CCXXVIII-CCXXX
	agrees to spare the Sarngaka birds	AD	CCXXXI-CCXXXIV

Agni *cont*	praised	AD	CCXXXIV
		SAB	XXX
	gratified	AD	CCXXXVI
	marries daughter of King Nila	SAB	XXX
	other names, and reason for some of them	SAB	XXX
	appears to King Usinara in the form of a pigeon	VA	CXXXI
	accepts Angiras as his son	VA	CCXVI
	history of his great race	VA	CCXVI-CCXXI
	begets Skanda upon the disguised Swaha	VA	CCXXIV
	attributes, enumerated by Vrihaspati	U	XVI
	finds the hidden Indra	U	XVI
	hides in the entrails of the Sami wood	SAL	XLVII
	located within the stomach of living beings	SAN	CCXXXIX
	origin	SAN	CCCXLIII
	casts his seed into the womb of Ganga, the result being Skanda	AN	LXXXV
Agnivesya	receives special mantras from Vrihaspati and gives them to Drona	D	XCIII
Ahalya	(wife to Gautama)		
	offered celestial earrings	ASW	LVIII
Ailavila	name for Kuvera	U	CXI
Airavata	(celestial elephant)		
	proceeds from the Ocean	AD	XVIII
Ajagara	speaks to King Prahlada on Tranquillity	SAN	CLXXIX
Ajaka	celestial counterpart of Salwa	AD	LXVII
Ajatasatru	name of Yudhishthira	AD	CLXLIII
Akampana	(King)		
	(father to Hari)		
	comforted by Narada	D	L-LII
Akritavrana	speaks to the exiled Pandavas	VA	CXV-CXVII
	friend to Rama	U	CLXXVIII
Alamvusha I	(Rakshasa)		
	(son of Rishyasringa)		
	wreaks havoc among the Pandavas	B	CI
	vanquished by Abhimanyu	B	CII
	fights Bhima	D	CVII
	slain by Ghatotkacha	D	CVIII

Alamvusha II	(Rakshasa) (son to Jatasura)		
	vanquished by Arjuna	D	CLXVII
	slain by Ghatotkacha	D	CLXXIV
Alamvusha III	(King)		
	slain by Satyaki	D	CXXXIX
Alarka	(King)		
	tries to shoot arrows at sense-organs and mind finds joy in Yoga	ASW	XXX
Alayudha	(Rakshasa)		
	fights Bhima	D	CLXXVII
	slain by Ghatotkacha	D	CLXXVIII
Alolupa	(son of Dhritarashtra)		
	slain by Bhima	K	LXXXIV
Amartarayas	father to King Gaya	D	LXVI
Ambalika	marries Vichitravirya	AD	CII
Ambika	marries Vichitravirya	AD	CII
Amitaujas	earthly counterpart of Ketumat	AD	LXVII
Amva	(eldest daughter to the ruler of Kasi)		
	seized by Bhishma	U	CLXXIV
	released by Bhishma and rejected by the man she loves (Salwa, King of the Salwas)	U	CLXXVI
	causes combat between Rama and Bhishma	U	CLXXX-CLXXXVIII
	still seeking to destroy Bhishma, half of her becomes a crooked river and the other half lives as a maiden	U	CLXXXIX
	walks into her own funeral pyre	U	CXC
	is born to King Drupada, who treats her like a son; her name is now Sikhandin	U	CXCI
Amvalika	*see also* **Ambalika**	U	CLXXIV
Amvika	*see also* **Ambika**	U	CLXXIV

Amvarisha	(King) (son to Nabhaga)		
	even he had to die	D	LXIV
	gives away a million kings (*sic*)	SAN	XXIX
	goes to heaven and finds that his generalissimo is enjoying higher regions of felicity than he himself	SAN	XCVIII
	sings of the necessity of overcoming cupidity	ASW	XXXI
Anadhriti	(son of Dhritarashtra)		
	slain by Bhima	B	XCVII
Angada	(monkey envoy to Ravana)		
	abused by Ravana	VA	CCLXXXII
Angaraparna	(King of the Gandharvas)		
	overpowered by Arjuna	AD	CLXXII
	his discourses	AD	CLXXII-CLXXXIV
Angaristha	King	SAN	CXXIII
Angiras	(Rishi)		
	his three sons	AD	LXVI
	accepted as the son of Agni	VA	CCXVI
	offspring begotten on his wife Subha	VA	CCXVII
	other descendants	VA	CCXVIII
	speaks of tirthas and the merits they confer	AN	XXV
	origin	AN	LXXXV
	speaks of the observance of fasts	AN	CVI
	drinks the ocean to recover his wife Bhadra from the clutches of Varuna	AN	CLIV
Anjanaparvan	(son of Ghatotkacha) (grandson of Bhima)		
	slain by Aswatthaman	D	CLV
Ansumat	made the 'lord of all herbs'	SAN	CXXII
Anuhlada	celestial counterpart of Dhrishtaketu	AD	LXVII
Anukampaka	(King in the Krita Age)		
	his son Hari is slain	SAN	CCLVI
	instructed by Narada	SAN	CCLVI
Anuvinda I	(brother to Vinda)		
	slain by Arjuna	D	XCVIII

Anuvinda II	(son of Dhritarashtra) slain by Bhima	D	CXXVI
Anuvinda III	(of the Kaikayas) slain by Satyaki	K	XIII
Apantaratamas	name for Saraswat	SAN	CCCL
Aparajita	(son to Dhritarashtra) slain by Bhima	B	LXXXIX
Apava	(Rishi) curses Arjuna of the thousand arms	SAN	L
Arishtanemi	speaks to Sagara on Emancipation	SAN	CCLXXXIX
Arjuna I	son of Pandu, real father is Indra	AD	LXIII
	begotten upon Pritha by Indra	AD	CXXIII
	specially devoted to Drona and to the science of arms	AD	CXXXIV
	receives extra tuition from Drona	AD	CXXXIV
	'And amongst all the princes, Arjuna alone became an Atiratha'	AD	CXXXIV
	shoots the head from the bird	AD	CXXXV
	receives the Brahmasira weapon from Drona	AD	CXXXV
	displays his prowess at the tournament	AD	CXXXVII
	is told the fee he must one day pay to Drona: 'O sinless one, thou must fight with me when I fight with thee.'	AD	CXLI
	overpowers Angaraparna, King of the Gandharvas	AD	CLXXII
	why addressed as 'Tapatya' by Angaraparna	AD	CLXXIII-CLXXV
	strings the great bow, hits the mark, is chosen by Draupadi	AD	CLXL
	overpowers Karna	AD	CLXLII
	why called Savyasachin	AD	CLXLIX
	breaks the pact and lives in forest for 12 years	AD	CCXV
	spends a night with Ulupi	AD	CCXVI
	begets a son (Vabhruvahana) upon Chitrangada	AD	CCXVII
	releases five Apsaras who have become crocodiles	AD	CCXVIII
	falls in love with Bhadra	AD	CCXXI
	seizes Bhadra for himself	AD	CCXXII

Arjuna I cont	marries (Su)bhadra and begets Abhimanyu	AD	CCXXIII
	father to Srutakarman through Draupadi	AD	CCXXIII
	receives the bow Gandiva and the marvellous chariot made by Viswakarman	AD	CCXXVII
	enables Agni to consume Forest of Khandava	AD	CCXXVIII-CCXXX
	with Krishna, routs the celestials	AD	CCXXIX
	asks Indra for all of his weapons	AD	CCXXXVI
	receives the conch Devadatta from Maya	SAB	III
	conquers the North	SAB	XXV
	receives the knowledge of Pratismriti from Yudhishthira	VA	XXXVII
	meets Indra	VA	XXXVII
	practises austerities	VA	XXXVIII
	has single combat with Mahadeva	VA	XXXIX
	sings praise to Mahadeva	VA	XXXIX
	is embraced by Mahadeva	VA	XXXIX
	receives the Pasupata weapon from Mahadeva	VA	XL
	receives Yama's mace, some Varuna weapons from Varuna and Kuvera's Antarddhana weapon	VA	XLI
	rides in Indra's chariot to the city of Indra	VA	XLII
	shares Indra's seat	VA	XLIII
	spends five years in heaven from Chitrasena learns dancing and celestial music	VA	XLIV
	resists Urvasi's wiles	VA	XLVI
	cursed by Urvasi	VA	XLVI
	reunited with his brothers	VA	CLXIV
	relates his adventures in heaven	VA	CLXVI-CLXXIII
	begins to display his celestial weapons, with devastating effect on all creatures	VA	CLXXIV
	plans to disguise himself as one of the neuter sex called Brihannala and as an instructor to women in singing and dancing	VI	II
	indulges in knockabout comedy	VI	XXXVII, XXXVIII
	his ten names and their origins	VI	XLIV
	duel with Karna, who eventually retires	VI	LIV
	vanquished Kripa	VI	LVII
	forces Drona to withdraw	VI	LVIII
	overcomes Aswatthaman	VI	LIX

Arjuna I	forces Karna to retreat	VI	LX
cont	creates a great river of blood	VI	LXII
	forces Bhishma to retreat	VI	LXIII, LXIV
	uses the Sanmohana weapon	VI	LXV
	gives all the glory to Uttara!	VI	LXVI
	chooses Krishna as a non-combatant charioteer	U	VII
	identified as Nara	U	XLIX, XCVI
	auspicious marks on feet	U	LIX
	as Jishnu, dwells in the north	U	CXI
	instructed and exhorted by Krishna	B	XXVI-XLII
	fights Bhishma	B	LII, LX
	prowess of	B	LXXXII, CXVIII
		D	XXVIII, XCIX
	fights Drona	B	CIII
	fights Dussasana	B	CXI
	with three arrows fashions a fitting pillow for Bhishma	B	CXXII
	provides a special jet of water for Bhishma	B	CXXIII
	praised by Bhishma	B	CXXIII
	slays thousands	D	XIX
	slays 14,000 opponents	D	XXV
	slays King Bhagadatta and his elephant Supratika	D	XXVII
	slays Vrishaka and Achala	D	XXVIII
	slays Satrunjaya and Vipatha	D	XXX
	qualities	D	XXXII
	adores the goddess Twilight	D	LXXII
	mourns for Abhimanyu	D	LXXII
	vows to slay Jayadratha	D	LXXIII
	his dream	D	LXXX, LXXXI
	wreaks havoc among the Kurus	D	LXXXVIII, LXXXIX
	slays Sudakshina	D	XCI
	slays Srutayus, Achyutayus and Srutayus (*sic*)	D	XCII
	slays Vinda and Anuvinda	D	XCVIII
	holds the entire opposition at bay and at the same time creates an arrowy hail and a lake to water the steeds	D	XCVIII
	physical description	D	CXXV
	vanquishes Karna	D	CXLIV
	cuts off Jayadratha's head and sends it into the lap of Vriddhakshatra	D	CXLV

Arjuna I *cont*	drives Kripa and Aswatthaman from battlefield	D	CXLVI
	vows to slay Karna	D	CXLVII
	vanquishes Karna	D	CXLVIII
	vanquishes Alamvusha	D	CLXVII
	fights Drona	D	CLXXXVIII
	upbraids Yudhishthira for his untruth to Drona	D	CXCVII
	identified as Nara	D	CCI
	meets Vyasa and tells him that another person continually preceded him in battle and actually defeated the foe. Vyasa declares this person to be Mahadeva	D	CCII
	slays Karna	K	I
	fights Aswatthaman	K	XVI
	slays Dandadhara and his brother Danda	K	XVIII
	wreaks havoc among the Kurus	K	XIX
	slays Satyasena, King Satrunjaya, son of Susruta, Chandradeva, Chitravarman, Mitrasena and thousands more!	K	XXVII
	stunned by Susarman	K	LIII
	slays 27,000 warriors and 3,000 elephants	K	LIII
	held in check, with Krishna, by Aswatthaman	K	LVI
	vanquishes Aswatthaman	K	LVI
	rescues Dhrishtadyumna from Aswatthaman	K	LIX
	causes great carnage	K	LXIV
	accused of cowardice by Yudhishthira	K	LXVIII
	the heavenly words spoken of him seven days after his birth	K	LXVIII
	draws his sword to slay Yudhishthira!	K	LXIX
	restrained by Krishna	K	LXIX
	upbraids Yudhishthira	K	LXX
	reconciled to Yudhishthira	K	LXXI
	again vows to slay Karna	K	LXXI
	prowess of	K	LXXVII, LXXIX, LXXX, LXXXI
	receives Gandiva, chariot, steeds, inexhaustible quivers, conch, weapons	K	LXXIX
	shows his prowess with the mace	K	LXXXI
	slays Vrishasena	K	LXXXV
	with Krishna, identified with Nara and Narayana	K	LXXXVII
	fights Karna	K	LXXXIX, XC

Arjuna I *cont*	slays Aswasena	K	XC
	strikes off Karna's armour	K	XC
	slays Karna	K	XCI
	fights Aswatthaman	SAL	XIV
	decides to exterminate the opposition	SAL	XXIV
	slays Satyakarman, Susarman and Satyeshu	SAL	XXVII
	has curly hair	SAN	XXIII
	with Krishna, enjoys the time of peace	ASW	XV
	sings the praises of Krishna	ASW	LII
	appointed to protect the roving horse	ASW	LXXII
	sets off to protect the horse	ASW	LXXIII
	subjugates the Trigartas	ASW	LXXIV
	vanquishes King Vajradatta	ASW	LXXVI
	vanquishes the Saindhavas	ASW	LXXVIII
	slain by his son Vabhruvahana	ASW	LXXIX
	revived by a special gem brought by Ulupi	ASW	LXXX
	slain on account of a curse pronounced by the Vasus when he slew Bhishma 'by unrighteous ways'	ASW	LXXXI
	vanquishes Meghasandhi	ASW	LXXXII
	vanquishes Sarabha and many others	ASW	LXXXIII
	vanquishes the son of Sakuni	ASW	LXXXIV
	Krishna's comment on Arjuna: 'I do not see any censurable feature in this prince, except that the cheekbones of this lion among men are a little too high. It is in consequence of this that that foremost of men has always to be on the road.'	ASW	LXXXVII
	returns	ASW	LXXXVII
	true identity	ASR	XXXI
	asked to protect the Vrishni kingdom and Krishna's 16,000 widows	MAU	VI
	appalled at being incapable of stopping some robbers	MAU	VII
	returns to Varuna the bow Gandiva and the two inexhaustible quivers	MAH	I
	falls to the ground	MAH	II
Arjuna II	name for King Kartavirya	AN	CLII
	'the mighty lord of the Haihaya tribe'	VA	CXVI
	his combat with Rama	VA	CXVI
	emperor	SAN	L
	thousand-armed son to Kritavirya	SAN	L
	cursed by the Rishi Apava	SAN	L
	arms lopped off by Rama	SAN	L

Arka	celestial counterpart of Rishika	AD	LXVII
Arshtishena	(royal sage)		
	receives the exiled Pandavas at his hermitage	VA	CLVII
	promises Yudhishthira that he will rule the Earth	VA	CLVIII
	acquires mastery of the Vedas in the Krita Age	SAL	XL
Artayani	name of Salya	K	XXXII
Aruna	(son to Kasyapa and Vinata)		
	prevents disaster by becoming Surya's charioteer	AD	XXIV
Arundhati	wife to Vasishtha	AD	CLXXVI
	insults Vasishtha and becomes a little star	AD	CCXXXV
	cooks jujubes for 12 years	SAL	XLVIII
	speaks of actions good and bad	AN	CXXX
Aruni	(disciple to Ayoda-Dhaumya)		
	how he comes to be called Uddalaka	AD	III
Arushi	(mother to Aurva by Chyavana)		
	daughter to Manu	AD	LXVI
Arvavasu	(son to the sage Raivya)		
	by austerities restores to life his father and Bharadwaja and Yavakri	VA	CXXXVIII
Aryaka	(father to Chikura)		
	grandfather to Sumukha	U	CIV
Ashtaka	(King)		
	son to Viswamitra through Madhavi	U	CXIX
	converses with Narada	VA	CLXLVII
Ashtavakra	(Rishi)		
	(son to Kahoda)		
	(nephew to Swetaketu)		
	cursed by his father for being crooked in eight parts of his body	VA	CXXXII
	at age of ten defeats Vandin in superb debate	VA	CXXXIV
	all his limbs made straight	VA	CXXXIV
	tested: marries Suprabha	AN	XIX-XXI

Asita-Devala	(ascetic)		
	adopts the Moksha religion	SAL	L
	speaks to Narada on the origin and destruction of all creatures	SAN	CCLXXV
Asma	his marvellous words to King Janaka	SAN	XXVIII
Asmaka	(son to Adrisyanti) (grandson to Vasishtha)		
	why also called Parasara	AD	CLXXX
	until stopped by Pulastya, performs a sacrifice for the destruction of Rakshasas	AD	CLXXXIII
Asoka	earthly counterpart of Aswa	AD	LXVII
Astaka	(royal sage)		
	converses with Yayati	AD	LXXXIX-XCII
	gives his merits to Yayati	AD	XCII
Astika	(son to the Rishi Jaratkaru through Jaratkuru, sister to Vasuki)		
	why so called	AD	LXVIII
	studies the Vedas with Chyavana	AD	LXVIII
	frustrates Janamejaya's snake-sacrifice	AD	XV
	praises Janamejaya	AD	LV
	receives a boon; asks for sacrifice to be stopped	AD	LVI
	stops the sacrifice and saves Takshaka	AD	LVIII
Asuras, The	fight the gods for the possession of Lakshmi and the Amrita	AD	XIX
	make the Ocean their fortress	VA	CI
	terrorize the universe	VA	CII
	vanquished by the gods with help from Agastya	VA	CV
	fight the gods for 32,000 years	SAN	XXXIII
	deserted by Sree	SAN	CCXXVIII
Aswa	celestial counterpart of Asoka	AD	LXVII
Aswagriva	celestial counterpart of Rochamana	AD	LXVII
Aswaketu	slain by Abhimanyu	D	XLVI
Aswapati I	celestial counterpart of Hardikya	AD	LXVII

Aswapati II	(King)		
	father to Savitri	VA	CCLXLI
	receives 100 sons through intercession of Savitri	VA	CCLXLV
Aswasena	(snake)		
	becomes united with Karna's most terrible weapon and is fired at Arjuna	K	XC
	removes Arjuna's diadem	K	XC
	slain by Arjuna	K	XC
Aswatthaman	(son to Kripa by Drona)		
	(grandson to Gautama)		
	nephew to Kripa	AD	LXIII
	why so called	AD	CXXXI
	receives extra tuition from Dron	AD	CXXXIV
	severs bowstring of Gandiva	VI	LIX
	retreats before Arjuna	VI	LIX
	shows his prowess	B	LXXIII
	slays Nila	D	XXIX
	vanquishes Ghatotkacha	D	CLV
	slays Anjanaparvan	D	CLV
	slays a full Akshauhini of Rakshasa troops	D	CLV
	slays Suratha, Satrunjaya, Valanika, Jayanika, Jaya, Prishdhra, Chandrasena, Srutayus, and the ten sons of Kuntibhoja	D	CLV
	vanquishes Dhrishtadyumna	D	CLIX
	fights Ghatotkacha	D	CLXV
	vows to slay Dhrishtadyumna	D	CXCVI
	meaning of his name	D	CXCVII
	wreaks havoc among the Pandavas	D	CC
	fights Bhima	D	CCI
	vanquishes Satyaki	D	CCI
	slays Sudarshana and Paurava and the ruler of the Chedis	D	CCI
	meets Vyasa and learns the truth about Arjuna and Krishna	D	CCI
	in a former life 'endued with great wisdom and equal to a god'	D	CCI
	now has the highest regard for Krishna	D	CCI
	fights Bhima	K	XV
	fights Arjuna	K	XVI
	slays Pandya	K	XX
	holds Arjuna and Krishna in check!	K	LVI
	vanquished by Arjuna	K	LVI
	vows to slay Dhristadyumna	K	LVII
	physical description	SAL	VI

Aswatthaman	other qualities	SAL	VI
cont	fights Arjuna	SAL	XIV
	slays Suratha	SAL	XIV
	vows to slay the Pandavas	SAL	LXV
	installed as generalissimo	SAL	LXV
	one of the three survivors of the Kuru army	SAU	I
	conceives the idea of slaying the sleeping Pandavas	SAU	I
	his way to the sleeping Pandavas is barred by a huge figure	SAU	VI
	offers a hymn to Siva, who enters his body	SAU	VII
	slays Dhristadyumna, Uttamaujas, Yudhamanyu, Prativindhya, Sutasoma, Satanika, Srutakarman, Srutakirti and Sikhandin	SAU	VIII
	with Kripa and Kritavarman, slays everyone in the Pandava camp, including the sons of Draupadi	SAU	VIII
	is unable to budge Krishna's discus	SAU	XII
	censured by Vyasa	SAU	XV
	throws his celestial weapon into the wombs of the Pandava women	SAU	XV
	gives to Yudhishthira the gem which was in his head at birth	SAU	XVI
	cursed by Krishna	SAU	XVI
	true identity	ASR	XXXI
Aswins,	praised	AD	III
the Twin	fathers to Nakula and Sahadeva	AD	LXIII
	sons to Savitri by Tvashtri	AD	LXVI
	bestow youth and beauty on Chyavana	VA	CXXIII
	obtain the right to the Soma juice	VA	CXXV
	origin	AN	LXXXV
	granted a share of the Soma	AN	CLVI
Atithi	father to King Suhotra	SAN	XXIX
Atri	praises King Vainya	VA	CLXXXIV
	origin	AN	LXXXV
	protects the gods	AN	CLVI
Aurva	son to Chyavana through Arushi	AD	LXVI
	father to Richika	AD	LXVI
	Brahmana baby who blinded some Kshatriyas	AD	CLXXX

Aurva *cont*	begged by the Pitris not to consume the three worlds	AD	CLXXXI
	casts his wrath into the sea, where it becomes 'like a large horse's head which persons conversant with the Vedas call by the name of Vadavamukha'	AD	CLXXXII
Avikshit	father to King Marutta	D	LIII
Ayobhuja	(son to Dhritarashtra) slain by Bhima	D	CLVI
Ayoda-Dhaumya	Rishi	AD	III
Ayu	father to Nahusha	VA	CLXXIX
Bhadra I	name of Subhadra		
Bhadra II	becomes mother to seven children by the corpse of her husband King Vyushitaswa	AD	CXXI
Bhadra III	(wife to Angiras) rescued from the clutches of Varuna	AN	CLIV
Bhagadatta	(King of the Pragjyotishas)		
	earthly counterpart of Vashkala	AD	LXVII
	strickes Bhima senseless	B	LXIV
	shows his prowess	B	LXXXIV
	shows his prowess	B	XCVI
	wreaks havoc among the Pandavas	D	XXIV
	slays Ruchiparvan	D	XXIV
	slain by Arjuna	D	XXVII
Bhagiratha	(of Ikshvaku's race) (King)		
	requests Ganga to refill the Ocean	VA	CIX
	adopted by Ganga as his father	D	LX
	even he had to die	D	LX
	Bhagiratha and Ganga	SAN	XXIX
	obtains a transcendental region through the 'vow of fast'	AN	CIII
Bhangaswana	(King) becomes a lady	AN	XII
Bhanudatta	(brother to Sakuni) slain by Bhima	D	CLVI

Bhanusena	(son to Karna)		
	slain by Bhima	K	XLVIII
Bharadwaja	(Rishi)		
	(father to Drona and Yavakri)		
	converses with King Satrunjaya on the behaviour of a king in times of distress	SAN	CXL
	acquires the science of arms	SAN	CCX
	grieved by Yavakri's death, enters fire	VA	CXXXVII
	restored to life by Arvavasu	VA	CXXXVIII
Bharata I	(son to Dushmanta through Sakuntala)		
	why so called	AD	LXXIV
	founder of the Bharata race: 'It is that Bharata from whom have emanated so many mighty achievements.'	AD	LXXIV
	even he had to die	D	LXVIII
	his sacrifices	SAN	XXIX
Bharata II	(son to Queen Kaikeyi)		
	becomes ruler of Ayodhya	VA	CCLXXV
Bhimaratha	(brother to Duryodhana)		
	slays Salya	D	XXIII
Bhimasena	(often known as 'Bhima')		
	son to Pandu; real father is Marut or Vayu	AD	LXIII
	begotten upon Pritha by Vayu	AD	CXXIII
	born same day as Duryodhana	AD	CXXIII
	shows his prowess in sporting with the sons of Dhritarashtra	AD	CXXVIII
	poisoned and cast into the river	AD	CXXVIII
	gains the strength of 10,000 elephants	AD	CXXVIII
	has tournament mace-combat with Duryodhana	AD	CXXXVII
	utters eloquent lament over his sleeping mother and brothers	AD	CLIII
	slays the Rakshasa Hidimva	AD	CLVI
	begets Ghatotkacha upon the Rakshasa woman Hidimva (*sic*)	AD	CLVII
	slays the Rakshasa Vaka	AD	CLXVI
	father to Sutasoma through Draupadi	AD	CCXXIII
	receives marvellous club from Maya	SAB	III
	wrestles with King Jarasandha for thirteen days	SAB	XXIII
	slays Jarasandha	SAB	XXIV
	releases the kings imprisoned by Jarasandha	SAB	XXIV

Bhimasena			
cont	conquers the East	SAB	XXV
	vows to slay Dussasana	SAB	LXVII
	vows to break Duryodhana's thighs	SAB	LXX
	slays the Rakshasa Kirmira	VA	XI
	to please Draupadi, scours the Gandhamadana Mountain for particular species of flower: encounters his brother Hanuman	VA	CXLV
	cannot so much as lift Hanuman's tail	VA	CXLVI
	hears story of Rama from Hanuman	VA	CXLVI
	receives guidance and support from Hanuman	VA	CL
	vanquishes Kuvera's guards around the lotus lake and gathers the lotuses for Draupadi	VA	CLIII
	slays the Rakshasa Jatasura	VA	CLVI
	clears the whole area of Rakshasas and destroys the Rakshasa Maniman	VA	CLIX
	frees Kuvera from the curse of Agastya	VA	CLX
	seized and overpowered by mighty snake	VA	CLXXVII
	released	VA	CLXXX
	plans to disguise himself as a cook and wrestler named Vallabha	VI	II
	slays Kichaka	VI	XXII
	rescues Draupadi from Kichaka's relatives	VI	XXIII
	description, exploits, prowess, mace	U	LI
	takes on, single-handed, whole division of the Kalingas	B	LIV
	tackles 10,000 elephants	B	LXII
	wreaks havoc upon the entire Kuru army	B	LXIII
	also known as Satyaki	B	LXIV
	struck senseless by Duryodhana and again by Bhagadatta	B	LXIV
	shows his prowess	B	LXXVII, LXXVIII, CXIV
	wounds Duryodhana	B	LXXX
	slays these sons of Dhritarashtra: Aparajita, Kundadhara, Panditaka, Visalaksha, Mahodara, Adityaketu, Vahvasin	B	LXXXIX
	slays these sons of Dhritarashtra: Vyudoraksha, Kundalin, Anadhriti, Kundabhedin, Virata, Dirghalochana, Dirghavahu, Suvahu, Kanykadhyaja	B	XCVII
	mace-combat with Salya	D	XV

Bhimasena *cont*	fights Duryodhana	D	XXIV
	fails to overcome Bhagadatta's elephant Supratika	D	XXIV
	slays the ruler of the Angas	D	XXIV
	qualities	D	XXXII
	fights the Rakshasa Alamvusha	D	CVII
	slays these sons of Dhritarashtra: Kundabhedin, Sushena, Dirghanetra, Vrindaraka, Abhaya, Raudrakarman, Durvimochana, Vinda, Anuvinda, Suvarman, Sudarsan	D	CXXVI
	vanquishes Karna	D	CXXVIII–CXXX
	fights Karna	D	CXXXI
	slays Durjaya, son to Dhritarashtra	D	CXXXII
	vanquishes Karna	D	CXXXIII
	slays Durmukha, son to Dhritarashtra	D	CXXXIII
	slays these sons of Dhritarashtra: Durmarshana, Duhsaha, Durmada, Durdhara and Jaya	D	CXXXIV
	slays six sons of Dhritarashtra: Chitra, Upachitra, Charuchitra, Sarasan, Chitrayudha and Chitravarman	D	CXXXV
	slays seven sons of Dhritarashtra: Satrunjaya, Satrusaha, Chitra, Chitrayudha, Dridha, Chitrasena and Vikarna	D	CXXXVI
	fights Karna	D	CXXXVII, CXXXVIII, CLXXXVIII
	slays the son of the ruler of the Kalingas and his brother Dhruva	D	CLIV
	slays two sons of Dhritarashtra: Durmada and Dushkarna	D	CLIV
	slays Valhika	D	CLVI
	slays nine sons of Dhritarashtra: Nagadatta, Dridharatha, Viravahu, Ayobhuja, Dridha, Suhasta, Viragas, Pramatha and Ugrayayin	D	CLVI
	slays Satachandra and Sakuni's five brothers: Gavaksha, Sarabha, Bibhu, Subhaga, Bhanudatta	D	CLVI
	vanquishes Duryodhana	D	CLXV
	fights the Rakshasa Alayudha	D	CLXXVII
	encouraged by Krishna, tells untruths	D	CXCI
	has the Narayana weapon fall upon his head!	D	CC

Bhimasena *cont*	rescued from the Narayana weapon by Krishna and Arjuna	D	CCI
	fights Aswatthaman	D	CCI
		K	XV
	slays Kshemadhurti	K	XII
	slays Bhanusena	K	XLVIII
	vanquishes Karna	K	L
	slays five sons of Dhritarashtra: Vivitsu, Vikara, Saha, Nanda and Upananda	K	LI
	shows his prowess	K	LXXVII
	vanquishes Sakuni	K	LXXVII
	stunned by Dussasana	K	LXXXII
	slays Dussasana and quaffs his blood	K	LXXXIII
	(here called Partha) slays ten sons of Dhritarashtra: Nishangin, Kavachin, Pasin, Dundadhara, Dhanurgraha, Alolupa, Saha, Shanda, Vatavega, Suvarchasas	K	LXXIV
	slays 25,000 opponents	K	XCIII
	mace-combat with Salya ends in double knockout	SAL	XII
	causes Duryodhana to faint	SAL	XVI
	slays 21,000 foot-soldiers	SAL	XIX
	slays eleven sons of Dhritarashtra: Durmarshana, Srutanta, Jayatsena, Jaitra, Ravi, Bhurivala, Durvimochana, Dushpradharsha, Sujata, Durvishaha, Srutarvan	SAL	XXVI
	slays Sudarsana, son to Dhritarashtra	SAL	XXVII
	has mace-combat with Duryodhana	SAL	LVII
	fractures Duryodhana's thighs	SAL	LVIII
	true identity	ASR	XXXI
	falls to the ground	MAH	II
Bhishma	born in the womb of Ganga through King Santanu	AD	LXIII
	also called Devavrata	AD	XCV
	background to his birth begins	AD	XCVI
	is really Dyu (one of the Vasus) who has to live on Earth as Ganga's child	AD	XCIX
	also called Gangadatta and Gangeya	AD	XCIX
	relinquishes his right to the throne and vows to die childless, in order that his father might marry Satyavati	AD	C
	why so called	AD	C
	praises Krishna	SAB	XXXVII
	forced to retreat by Arjuna	VI	LXIII, LXIV

Bhishma cont			
	brother to Vichitravirya	U	CXLVII
	uncle to Vidura	U	CXLVIII
	grandson to Pratipa	U	CXLVIII
	appointed as commander of the Kuru forces	U	CLVII
	quarrels with Karna	U	CLXIX
	carries off three sisters: Amva, Amvika, Amvalika	U	CLXXIV
	releases Amva, who then seeks his death	U	CLXXV-CXC
	defeats Rama in single combat	U	CLXXXII-CLXXXVIII
	his mother also called Kali, Gandhavati and Bhagirathi	U	CLXXVI, CLXXXVIII
	refuses to harm Sikhandin (once the lady Amva)	U	CXCV
	slain by Sikhandin	B	XIII
	slays Sweta	B	XLVIII
	fights Arjuna	B	LII, LX
	nearly slain by Krishna	B	LIX
	extols Krishna's infinite glories	B	LXVII
	cures Duryodhana's wound with a herb	B	LXXXVII
	fights Yudhishthira	B	LXXXVII
	displays his prowess	B	CIV, CXVII
	wreaks havoc among the Pandavas	B	CVII
	nearly slain by Krishna	B	CVII
	tells Krishna and the five Pandavas that he can be slain only by Arjuna shielded by Sikhandin	B	CVIII
	falls, but will hold to life until the northern declension	B	CXX
	receives respects from both Kurus and Pandavas	B	CXXI
	dismisses the skilled surgeons	B	CXXII
	praises Arjuna's qualities	B	CXXIII
	reconciled to Karna	B	CXXIV
	gives balanced appraisal of Karna's character	B	CXXIV
	sees 'with his physical eyes all the gods with Indra at their head'	SAN	XXXVIII
	details of birth and life	SAN	XXXVIII
	qualities	SAN	XLVII
	offers long and marvellous hymn to Krishna	SAN	XLVIII
	speaks in praise of Krishna	SAN	LI
	has 56 days to live	SAN	LI

Bhishma *cont*	granted a clear mind and full alleviation of pain	SAN	LII
	gives instruction on his deathbed	SAN	LV-CCCXL, CCCLIII-CCCLXV
		AN	I-XIII, XIX-CX, CXIV-CLXV
	obtains Krishna's permission to leave the body	AN	CLXVII
	leaves the body: 'The life-breaths of Bhishma, piercing through the crown of his head, shot up through the welkin like a huge meteor and soon became invisible.'	AN	CLXVIII
	cremated	AN	CLXVIII
	his tribute from Ganga	AN	CLXVIII
	true identity	ASR	XXXI
Bhishmaka	father to King Rukmi	U	CLIX
Bhrigu	why he decides to curse Angi	AD	VI
	son to Brahman	AD	LXVI
	father to Sukra and Chyavana	AD	LXVI
	turns Dansa into a worm	SAN	III
	his words to Bharadwaja	SAN	CLXXXII-CXCII
	origin	AN	LXXXV
	turns Nahusha into a snake	AN	C
Bhrigus, The	become connected with the Kusikas by marriage	AN	LVI
Bhuminjaya	(name for Uttara)		
Bhuri	slain by Satyaki	D	CLXV
Bhuridyumna	son to King Viradyumna	SAN	CXXVII
Bhurisravas	(son to Somadatta)		
	slays the ten sons of Yuyudhana	B	LXXIV
	cuts off the goad in Krishna's hand	D	CIII
	has right arm lopped by Arjuna	D	CXLI
	takes to an ascetic way of life, but is slain by Satyaki	D	CXLII
Bhurivala	(son to Dhritarashtra)		
	slain by Bhima	SAL	XXVI

Bhutakarman	(also called Sabhapati)		
	slain by Satanika	D	XXIII
Bhuti	name for Sree	SAN	CCXXV
Bibhu	(brother to Sakuni)		
	slain by Bhima	D	CLVI
Brahma(n)	commands the gods to become incarnate and strive against the Asuras	AD	LXIV
	names of his six spiritual sons	AD	LXV
	father to Manu	AD	LXVI
	father to Dhatri and Vidhatri and their sister Lakshmi	AD	LXVI
	father to Vasishta	AD	CLXXVI
	his assembly house described	SAB	XI
	appears as a great fish	VA	CLXXXVI
	dwells in the north	U	CXI
	his hymn to Krishna	B	LXV
	his anger begins to burn the universe	D	L
	from his wrath emerges a lady called Death	D	LI
	creates the priest Kshupa	SAN	CXXII
	in the form of a golden swan, speaks to the Sadhyas about Morality	SAN	CCC
	speaks to his son Siva about Purusha	SAN	CCCLI-CCCLII
	speaks to Vasishtha about Exertion, Destiny and Karma	AN	VI
	his words to Indra	AN	LXXII-LXXIV
	speaks to Indra in praise of kine	AN	LXXXIII
Brahmadatta	(King)		
	Brahmadatta and the Pujani	SAN	CXXXIX
Brihannala	pseudonym for Arjuna	VI	II
Chandra	celestial counterpart of Chandravarman	AD	LXVII
Chandradeva	slain by Arjuna	K	XXVII
Chandrahantri	celestial counterpart of Sunaka	AD	LXVII
Chandraketu	slain by Abhimanyu	D	XLVI
Chandramas	name for Soma	SAL	XXXV
	'made the King of Stars and constellations'	SAN	CXXII

Chandrasena	slain by Aswatthaman	D	CLV
Chandravarman	earthly counterpart of Chandra	AD	LXVII
Chandravinasana	celestial counterpart of Janaki	AD	LXVII
Charuchitra	(son to Dhritarashtra) slain by Bhima	D	CXXXV
Charvaka	(Rakshasa) (friend to Duryodhana) slain by the sound 'Hun'	SAN	XXXIX
Chekitana	slain by Duryodhana	SAL	XII
Chirakarin	why so called	SAN	CCLXVI
	commanded by his father to slay his own mother	SAN	CCLXVI
Chirakura	(son to Aryaka) (father to Sumukha) devoured by Garuda	U	CIV
Chitra I	(son to Dhritarashtra) slain by Bhima	D	CXXXV
	slain by Bhima	D	CXXXVI
Chitra II	slain by Prativindhya	K	XIV
Chitra III	slain by Karna	K	LVI
Chitrangada I	(son to Santanu through Satyavati) brother to Vichitravirya	AD	CI
	becomes king, but is killed by a Gandharva also called Chitrangada	AD	CI
Chitrangada II	(daughter to King Chitravahana) conceives a son (Vabhruvahana) from Arjuna	AD	CCXVII
Chitrasena I	instructs Arjuna in dancing and heavenly music	VA	XLIV
Chitrasena II	King of the Gandharvas	VA	CCXXXIX
	takes Duryodhana captive	VA	CCXL
	friend of Arjuna	VA	CCXLIII

Chitrasena III	(son to Dhritarashtra) slain by Bhima	D	CXXXVI
Chitrasena IV	slain by Srutakarman	K	XIV
Chitrasena V	(brother to Karna) slain by Yudhamanyu	K	LXXXIII
Chitrasena VI	slain by Nakula	SAL	X
Chitravarman	earthly counterpart of Virupaksha	AD	LXVII
Chitravarman I	(son to Dhritarashtra) slain by Bhima	D	CXXXV
Chitravarman II	slain by Arjuna	K	XXVII
Chitrayudha I	(son to Dhritarashtra) slain by Bhima	D	CXXXV, CXXXVI
Chitrayudha II	slain by Karna	K	LVI
Chyavana	(Rishi)		
	son to Bhrigu	AD	VI
	why so called	AD	VI
	studies the Vedas with Astika	AD	XLVIII
	father to Aurva through Arushi	AD	LXVI
	practises austerities and becomes an anthill	VA	CXXII
	eyes pierced by the Princess Sukanya	VA	CXXII
	marries Sukanya	VA	CXXII
	receives youth and beauty from the twin Aswins	VA	CXXIII
	paralyzes Indra's arm and creates a huge demon called Mada	VA	CXXIV
	gains his request	VA	CXXV
	dragged up by fishermen	AN	L
	his purchase price	AN	LI
	tests King Kusika and his queen	AN	LIII
	forces the gods to grant the twin Aswins a share of the Soma	AN	CLVI
Dadhicha	(Rishi) (son to Bhrigu)		
	strongest creature in the world	SAL	LI
	gives his bones to make the Vajra weapon for conquering the Asuras	VA SAL	C LI

Daityas, The	defeated by the gods	AD	XIX
Daksha	son to Prachetas	AD	LXXV
	grandfather to Vivaswat (the Sun)	AD	LXXV
	great-grandfather to Manu	AD	LXXV
	his thirteen daughters	AD	LXV
	his fifty daughters	AD	LXV
	his twenty-seven daughters and Soma	SAL	XXXV
	thirteen daughters married to Kasyapa	SAN	CCVII
	ten daughters married to Dharma	SAN	CCVII
	twenty-seven daughters married to Soma	SAN	CCVII
	his sacrifice destroyed by Siva's wrath	SAN	CCLXXXIV
	his prayer	SAN	CCLXXXIV
	sings the hymn which contains the 1,008 names of Siva	SAN	CCLXXXV
Dalvya-Vaka	(great ascetic)		
	begins to destroy Dhritarashtra's kingdom	SAL	XLI
	why he stops	SAL	XLI
Damayanti	(Princess)		
	the story of her love for King Nala is told by the Rishi Vrihadaswa	VA	LIII-LXXIX
Dambhodbhava	(King)		
	his pride curbed by Nara and Narayana	U	XCVI
Danavas, The	defeated by the gods	AD	XIX
Danayu	her four sons	AD	LXV
Danda	(brother to Dandadhara)		
	earthly counterpart of Krodhahantri	AD	LXVII
	slain by Arjuna	K	XVIII
Dandadhara	(brother to Danda)		
	earthly counterpart of Krodhavardhana	AD	LXVII
	slain by Arjuna	K	XVIII
Dandadhara	(son to Dhritarashtra)		
	slain by Bhima	K	LXXXIV
Dansa	(Asura)		
	turned into a worm by Bhrigu	SAN	III
	bites Karna	SAN	III
	freed by Rama	SAN	III

Danu	his 40 sons	AD	LXV
Darada	earthly counterpart of Surya	AD	LXVII
Daruka	charioteer to Krishna	D	LXXIX
Dasaratha	father of Rama, who is Vishnu incarnate	VA	XCIX
Devadhipa	earthly counterpart of Nikumbha	AD	LXVII
Devaki	mother to Krishna by Vasudeva	AD	LXIII
	gives birth to Krishna from a black hair of Narayana's body	AD	CLXLIX
Devapi	slain by Karna	K	LVI
Devasarman	(ascetic)		
	(husband to Ruchi)		
	preceptor to Vipula	AN	XL
	goes to heaven	AN	XLIII
Devasena	(daughter to Prajapati)		
	asks for an invincible husband	VA	CCXXIII
	marries Skanda	VA	CCXXVIII
	other names: Shashthi, Lakshmi, Asa, Sukhaprada, Sinivali, Kuhu, Saivritti, Aparajita	VA	CCXXVIII
Devashtana	speaks to Yudhishthira about wealth, sacrifice and contentment	SAN	XX, XXI
Devayani	(daughter to Sukra)		
	quarrels with Sarmishtha	AD	LXXVIII
	becomes mistress of Sarmishtha and her thousand maids	AD	LXXX
	marries King Yayati	AD	LXXXI
	mother to Yadu and Turvasu	AD	LXXXIII
Dhanurgraha	(son to Dhritarashtra)		
	slain by Bhima	K	LXXXIV
Dhanwantari	holds the vessel of Amrita	AD	XVIII
Dharma	cursed by the Rishi Animandavya, 'was born a Sudra in the form of the learned Vidura'	AD	LXIII
	= Yama, god of Justice	AD	LXIII

Dharma *cont*	father to Yudhishthira	AD	LXIII
	his ten wives	AD	LXVI
	son to Brahma(n)	AD	LXVI
	his three sons	AD	LXVI
	cursed by Mandvya and obliged to be born in the Sudra order	AD	CVII, CVIII
	appears to the Pandavas as a Yaksha	VA	CCCX, CCCXI
	grants the Pandavas the boon of non-recognition in their thirteenth year of exile	VA	CCCXII
	husband to ten daughters of Daksha	SAN	CCVII
	appears as a dog	MAH	I-III
Dharmaranya	(Brahmana)		
	decides to adopt the Unccha observance	SAN	CCCLVI-CCCLXV
Dharmadhyaja	(King)		
	converses with Sulabha	SAN	CCCXXI
Dhatri	(god)		
	(son to Brahma(n))		
	brother to Vidhatri and Lakshmi	AD	LXVI
	his weapon is the bow	AD	CCXXIX
Dhaumya	appointed as a priest to the fugitive Pandavas	AD	CLXXXV
	lists tirthas and 'sacred asylums'	VA	LXXXVII-XC
	instructs Yudhishthira in 'geography' referring to Mandara, Maha-meru, and the work of the Sun and Moon	VA	CLXII
	tells the Pandavas of numerous occasions when the gods disguised themselves in order to overcome their foes	VA	CCCXIII
Dhirghajihva	celestial counterpart of Kasiraja	AD	LXVII
Dhrishtadyumna	(son to Drupada)		
	(brother to his twin sister Krishna)		
	born from the sacrifical fire	AD	LXIII
	earthly counterpart of a portion of Agni	AD	LXVII
	why so called	AD	CLXIX
	'This prince hath been born for the destruction of Drona' – celestial voice	AD	CLXIX

Dhrishtadyumna cont	lists some of the great kings assembled for Draupadi's hand	AD	CLXXXVIII
	learns true identity of the five Pandavas disguised as Brahmanas	AD	CLXLIV
	elected generalissimo to the Pandava forces	U	CLI
	fights Drona	B	LIII
	his devotion to Bhima	B	LXXVII
	shows his prowess	D	XCIV
	rescued from Drona by Satyaki	D	XCVI
	fights Drona	D	CXXI
	vanquished by Asmatthaman	D	CLIX
	slays Drumasena	D	CLXX
	vanquished by Drona	D	CXCII
	brings about the fall of Drona	D	CXCIII
	vanquished by Kripa	K	XXVI
	vanquishes Duryodhana	K	LVI
	rescued from Aswatthaman by Arjuna	K	LIX
	slays Salwa's huge elephant	SAL	XX
	slain by Asmatthaman	SAU	VIII
	true identity	ASR	XXXI
Dhrishtaketu	earthly counterpart of Anuhlada	AD	LXVII
	son to Sisupala	D	CXXIV
	slays Viradhanwan	D	CVI
	slain by Drona	D	CXXIV
Dhritarashtra	begotten by Vyasa upon Amvika	AD	CVI
	why so called	AD	CVI
	married Gandhari	AD	CX
	his hundred sons are born in pots	AD	CXV
	begets Yuyutsu upon one of Gandhari's maids	AD	CXV
	names of his sons in order of birth	AD	CXVII
	installs Yudhishthira as heir apparent	AD	CXLI
	'sentiments towards the Pandavas became suddenly poisoned'	AD	CXLI
	suggests that the Pandavas go to Varanavata	AD	CXLV
	gives half the kingdom to the Pandavas	AD	CCIX
	seeks to dissuade Duryodhana from the dice match	SAB	XLIX
	yields weakly to Duryodhana and orders construction of gaming house	SAB	LV
	offers Draupadi a boon	SAB	LXX

Dhritarashtra *cont*	gives the Pandavas leave to return to Khandavaprastha with their wife and wealth	SAB	LXXII
	is persuaded to summon the Pandavas back for a second dice game	SAB	LXXII
	seeks for peace with the Pandavas	U	XXI-XXVI
	disowns Duryodhana for disobedience	U	LVIII
	offers hymn of praise to Krishna and seeks his protection	U	LXXI
	birth	U	CXLVII
	mourns for his father Bhishma	B	XIV
	laments	ST	I
	consoled by Vidura	ST	II
	longs to slay Bhima, but instead destroys an iron statue of Bhima	ST	XII
	reproved by Krishna	ST	XIII
	becomes fully reconciled to the five sons of Pandu	ST	XIII
	filled with repentance at Bhishma's death	ASW	I
	father to Queen Dussala	ASW	LXXVIII
	stung for 15 years by Bhima's hostile feelings, desires to live penitently in the forest	ASR	III
	instructs Yudhishthira in the art of kingship	ASR	V-VII
	performs the Sraddha for his dead sons and relatives	ASR	XIV
	sets off for the forest with Gandhari	ASR	XV
	true identity	ASR	XXXI
	overjoyed to see all the dead heroes rise from the waters of the Bhagirathi	ASR	XXXII
	dies in forest fire	ASR	XXXVII
Dhriti	celestial counterpart of Madri	AD	LXVII
Dhruva I	father to Kala, i.e. Time	AD	LXVI
Dhruva II	slain by Bhima	D	CLIV
Dhundhu	(Danava chief) (son to Madhu and Kaitabha)		
	plans to conquer the celestials and the three worlds	VA	CCI
	slain by Kuvalaswa	VA	CCIII
Dhundhumara	(name of Kuvalaswa)		

Dilipa	(also called Khattanga) (King) (son to Ilavila)		
	even he had to die	D	LXI
	gives away the entire Earth	SAN	XXIX
Dirghalochana	(son to Dhritarashtra)		
	slain by Bhima	B	XCVII
Dirghanetra	(son to Dhritarashtra)		
	slain by Bhima	D	CXXVI
Dirghaprajna	earthly counterpart of Vrishaparvan	AD	LXVII
Dirghatamas	while still in the womb of Mamata, is cursed with blindness by Brihaspati	AD	CIV
	becomes a great Rishi and perpetuates the royal line of Vali	AD	CIV
Dirghavahu	(son to Dhritarashtra)		
	slain by Bhima	B	XCVII
Diti	father to the Daityas	AD	LXIV
	father to Hiranyakasipu	AD	LXV
Divodasa	(King of the Kasis)		
	helps Galava in his quest	U	CXVII
Draupadi	(also known as Krishna)		
	born from the sacrificial altar	AD	LXIII
	earthly counterpart of a portion of Sachi	AD	LXVII
	daughter to Drupada	AD	CLXIX
	sister to Dhrishtadyumna	AD	CLXIX
	identified by Vyasa as being previously a Rishi's daughter to whom Mahadeva once promised five husbands	AD	CLXXI
	refuses Karna	AD	CLXXXIX
	chooses Arjuna	AD	CLXL
	becomes common wife to the five Pandavas	AD	CLXLIII
	incarnation of Sri	AD	CLXLIX
	marries the five sons of Pandu	AD	CC
	mother to Prativindhya by Yudhishthira	AD	CCXXIII
	mother to Sutasoma by Bhima	AD	CCXXIII
	mother to Srutakarman by Arjuna	AD	CCXXIII
	mother to Satanika by Nakula	AD	CCXXIII
	mother to Srutasena by Sahadeva	AD	CCXXIII

Draupadi *cont*	dragged into gaming house and insulted	SAB	LXVI
	has hundreds of robes pulled from her by Dussasana	SAB	LXVII
	laments	SAB	LXVIII, LXIX
	chooses the freedom of her five husbands	SAB	LXX
	speaks of the perverse ways of God to man	VA	XXX
	speaks of Exertion	VA	XXXII
	becomes faint on the journey, nursed by the Pandavas and Brahmanas	VA	CXLIII
	sends Bhima in search of a particular flower	VA	CXLV
	speaks of wifely duty	VA	CCXXXI-CCXXXII
	prays to Krishna when faced with 10,000 hungry visitors	VA	CCLXI
	outraged by Jayadratha's offer of marriage	VA	CCLXV
	abducted by Jayadratha	VA	CCLXVI
	rescued by her husbands	VA	CCLXVII-CCLXIX
	plans to act as waiting woman to Queen Sudeshna	VI	III
	obtains the protection of an invisible Rakshasa	VI	XV
	exhorts Bhima to avenge her upon Kichaka	VI	XVII, XXI
	falls to the ground	MAH	II
Dridha	(son to Dhritarashtra) slain by Bhima	D	CXXXVI, CLVI
Dridharatha	(son to Dhritarashtra) slain by Bhima	D	CLVI
Dridhasyu	(also called Idhmavaha) son to the Rishi Agastya through Lopamudra	VA	XCIX
Drighalochana	slain by Abhimanyu	D	XXXV
Drona	why so called	AD	LXIII, CXXXI
	earthly counterpart of portion of Vrihaspati	AD	LXVII

Drona cont	teaches the science of arms to the Kauravas and Pandavas	AD	CXXXI
	son to Bharadwaja	AD	CXXXI
	birth	AD	CXXXI
	marries Kripi and begets Aswatthaman	AD	CXXXI
	receives from Rama, son to Bhrigu, all his weapons	AD	CXXXI
	repulsed by Drupada, King of the Panchalas	AD	CXXXII
	amazes the young princes by bringing up a ball and a ring from the bottom of a dry well	AD	CXXXIII
	receives special devotion from Arjuna	AD	CXXXIV
	gives extra tuition to Arjuna and Aswatthaman	AD	CXXXIV
	receives Prince Ekalavya's right thumb	AD	CXXXIV
	receives Drupada as his preceptorial fee from the Pandavas!	AD	CXL
	spares Drupada's life, but takes half his kingdom	AD	CXL
	demands this fee of Arjuna: 'O sinless one, thou must fight with me when I fight with thee.'	AD	CXLI
	forced to retreat by Arjuna	VI	LVIII
	virtues described by Arjuna	VI	LVIII
	fights Dhrishtadyumna	B	LIII
	shows his prowess	B	LXXV, LXXVII
		D	VIII, XIV, XXI, XCI, XCIV
	slays Sankha	B	LXXXIII
	fights Arjuna	B	CIII
	accepts leadership of the Kuru forces	D	VII
	slain by Dhrishtadyumna	D	VIII
	his virtues listed by Dhritarashtra	D	IX
	slays Vyaghradatta, Singhasena and Kumara	D	XVI
	slays Satyajit, Satanika, King Kshema, Vasudeva and the Prince Panchala	D	XXI
	fastens Duryodhana'a armour with special mantras	D	XCIII
	fights Yudhishthira	D	CV
	vanquished by Satyaki	D	CXVI
	slays Viraketu	D	CXXI
	fights Dhrishtadyumna	D	CXXI
	slays Vrihatkshatra, Dhrishtaketu, the son of Jarasandha, Kshatradharman, and the son of Dhrishtaketu. 'The venerable Drona, full five and eighty years of age, dark in hue and with white locks descending to his ears, careered in battle like a youth of sixteen.'	D	CXXIV

Drona *cont*	slays King Sivi	D	CLIV
	fights Yudhishthira	D	CLVI, CLXI
	slays the three grandsons of Drupada, Drupada himself and Virata	D	CLXXXVI
	fights Arjuna	D	CLXXXVIII
	vanquishes Dhrishtadyumna	D	CXCII
	falls by the hand of Dhrishtadyumna	D	CXCIII
	body burned on funeral pyre	ST	XXIII
	true identity	ASR	XXXI
Druma	earthly counterpart of Sivi	AD	LXVII
Drumasena	earthly counterpart of Garishtha	AD	LXVII
	slain by Dhrishtadyumna	D	CLXX
Drupada	(also called Prishata and Yajnasena) (King of the Panchalas)		
	repudiates Drona's offer of friendship	AD	CXXXII
	is paid to Drona as the preceptorial fee of the Pandavas	AD	CXL
	gains his life, but loses half his kingdom to Drona	AD	CXL
	obtains a twin boy and girl (Dhrishtadyumna and Krishna)	AD	CLXIX
	makes joyous alliance with the Pandavas	AD	CCI
	father to Sikhandin		
	treats his daughter Sikhandin like a son	U	CXCI
	slain, with his three grandsons, by Drona	D	CLXXXVI
Duhsaha	(son to Dhritarashtra)		
	slain by Bhima	D	CXXXIV
Duhsala	(appears to be the same as Dussala)		
	daughter to Gandhari	AD	CXVI
	marries Jayadratha	AD	CXVII
Duhsasana	(son to Dhritarashtra)		
	vanquished by Satyaki	D	CXXII
	fights Sahadeva	D	CLXXXVIII
Duhshaha	name for Sree	SAN	CCXXV
Durdhara	(son to Dhritarastra)		
	slain by Bhima	D	CXXXIV
Durga	other names: Kali, Mahakali, Uma, Sakambhari, Swaha, Swadha, Kala, Kashta, Saraswati, Savitra, Savitri	B	XXIII

Durga *cont*	(goddess) (wife to Kapala)		
	mother to Skanda	B	XXIII
	offered a beautiful prayer by Yudhishthira	VI	VI
	meaning of name	VI	VI
	promises protection to the exiled Pandavas	VI	VI
	offered prayer by Arjuna	B	XXIII
	assures Arjuna of victory	B	XXIII
Durjaya	(son to Dhritarashtra)		
	slain by Bhima	D	CXXXII
Durmada	(son to Dhritarashtra)		
	slain by Bhima	D	CXXXIV, CLIV
Durmarshana	(son to Dhritarashtra)		
	slain by Bhima	D	CXXXIV
		SAL	XXVI
Durmukha	(son to Dhritarashtra)		
	slain by Bhima	D	CXXXIII
Durvasa	(Rishi; irascible Muni)		
	gives Pritha a mantra for invoking the gods	AD	CXI
	sets test for Mudgala	VA	CCLVIII
	grants boon to Duryodhana	VA	CCLX
	visits the exiled Pandavas with 10,000 disciples, all of whom are fed by the Lord Krishna	VA	CCLXI
	yokes Krishna's wife to his carriage	AN	CLIX
Durvimochana	(son to Dhritarashtra)		
	slain by Bhima	D	CXXVI
		SAL	XXVI
Durvishaha	(son to Dhritarashtra)		
	slain by Bhima	SAL	XXVI
Duryodhana	(son to Dhritarashtra)		
	'As soon as Duryodhana was born, he began to cry and bray like an ass.'	AD	CXV
	born on the same day as Bhima	AD	CXXIII
	begins hostilities against Bhima	AD	CXXVIII
	has tournament mace-combat with Bhima	AD	CXXXVII
	begins to plot	AD	CXLIII
	orders house of lac to be built at Varanavata	AD	CXLVI

Duryodhana burns with jealousy and is laughed at
cont   for his mistakes in Yudhishthira's
      assembly room   SAB XLVI
    gets the idea of the dice match from Sakuni   SAB XLVII
    describes the wealth of the Pandavas   SAB L-LII
    insults Draupadi   SAB LXX
    intends to slay the exiled Pandavas, but
      is forbidden by Vyasa   VA VII
    cursed by the Rishi Maitreya   VA X
    taken captive by the Gandharvas   VA CCXL
    also known as Suyodhana
    set free by the Pandavas   VA CCXLIV
    resolves to starve to death   VA CCXLVII-CCXLIX
    summoned to the infernal regions by the
      Daityas and Danavas   VA CCXLIX
    persuaded to return to Hastinapura in
      magnificent procession   VA CCL
    the Earth is re-conquered for him by Karna   VA CCLII
    celebrates the Vaishnava sacrifice   VA CCLIV
    receives general acclaim   VA CCLV
    delighted to have ten crores of Narayanas
      on his side   U VII
    disowned by Dhritarashtra for
      disobedience   U LVIII
    directly responsible, with Karna, for the
      impending calamity   U XCIII
    strikes Bhima senseless   B LXIV
    begins to 'regard highly both Kesava and
      those mighty car-warriors, viz., the
      sons of Pandu'   B LXVIII
    shows his prowess   B LXXVIII
        D CLII
    wounded by Bhima   B LXXX
    cured by Bhishma with a herb   B LXXXII
    fights Ghatotkacha   B XCII
    fights Bhima   D XXIV
    fights Satyaki   D CXV
    fights Yudhamanyu and Uttamaujas   D CXXIX
    vanquished by Bhima   D CLXV
    vanquished by Satyaki   D CLXXI
    vanquishes Nakula   D CLXXXVII
    vanquished by Yudhishthira, who spares
      his life   K XXIX
    vanquished by Dhrishtadyumna   K LVI
    alone fights all the Pandavas united
      together   K XCIII

Duryodhana *cont*	shows his prowess	SAL	III, XXII
	slays Chekitana	SAL	XII
	becomes the sole surviving son to Dhritarashtra	SAL	XXVII
	his army exterminated, he takes refuge in a lake	SAL	XXIX
	emerges from the lake	SAL	XXXII
	has mace-combat with Bhima	SAL	LVII
	thighs fractured by Bhima	SAL	LVIII
	bitterly accuses his foes of using unfair means	SAL	LXI
	his lamentations	SAL	LXIV
	dies	SAU	IX
	true identity	ASR	XXXI
	enjoys a place of high honour in heaven	SW	I
Dushkarna I	slain	B	LXXX
Dushkarna II	(son to Dhritarashtra)		
	slain by Bhima	D	CLIV
Dushmanta	father to King Bharata	AD	LXXIV
		D	LXVIII
	founder of Paurava line	AD	LXVIII
	goes hunting	AD	LXIX
	welcomed at the sacred asylum of Kasyapa	AD	LXX
	meets Sakuntala	AD	LXXI
	marries Sakuntala	AD	LXXIII
	finally acknowledges Sakuntala and child	AD	LXXIV
Dushpradharsha	son to Dhritarashtra		
	slain by Bhima	SAL	XXVI
Dussala	(appears to be the same as Duhsala)		
	(Queen of the Saindhavas)		
	(daughter of Dhritarashtra)		
	vanquished by Arjuna	ASW	LXXVIII
Dussasana	insults Draupadi	SAB	LXVI
	pulls hundreds of robes from Draupadi	SAB	LXVII
	fights Arjuna	B	CXI
	vanquished by Sahadeva	K	XXIII
	stuns Bhima	K	LXXXII
	slain by Bhima, who quaffs his blood	K	LXXXIII
	true identity	ASR	XXXI

Dwapara	(i.e. the third Yuga) celestial counterpart of Sakuni	AD	LXVII
Dwita	(son to Gautama) brother to Ekata and Trita	SAL	XXXVI
Dyu	The Vasu who lives on Earth as Bhishma	AD	XCIX
Dyumatsena	(King) father to Satyavan	VA	CCXLV
	father to Satyavat	SAN	CCLXVII
	receives sight and kingdom through the intercession of Savitri	VA	CCXLV
Ekachakra	celestial counterpart of Pritivindhya	AD	LXVII
Elalavya	(Prince) pays his own right thumb as tuition fee to Drona	AD	CXXXIV
Ekata	(son to Gautama) brother to Dwita and Trita	SAL	XXXVI
Elapatra	tells the other snakes that the virtuous snakes will be rescued by Astika	AD	XXXVIII
Gada	younger brother to Krishna	SAN	XLIX
Gadhi	(also called Kausika) father to Viswamitra	SAL	XL
Galava	obstinate disciple of Visvamitra	U	CVI
	given a very difficult mission, which is accomplished with the help of Garuda	U	CXIV-CXIX
	compiles 'the rules in respect of the division of syllables and words, and those about emphasis and accent in utterance, and shone as the first scholar who became conversant with those two subjects'	SAN	CCCXLIII
Gandhari	born from Suvala	AD	LXIII
	earthly counterpart of Mati	AD	LXVII
	sister to Sakuni	AD	CX
	marries Dhritarashtra	AD	CX
	obtains from Siva a boon that she will have 100 sons	AD	CX

Gandhari *cont*	how her daughter Duhsala is born	AD	CXVI
	seeks in vain to dissuade Dhritarashtra from summoning the Pandavas to a second dice game	SAB	LXXIV
	pleads with Duryodhana; speaks of kingship	U	CXXIX
	produces a sore nail on Yudhishthira's foot	ST	XV
	reconciled to the five sons of Pandu	ST	XV
	her lament for Duryodhana	ST	XVII
	her lament for her daughters-in-law	ST	XVIII
	her lament for her dead relatives	ST	XIX
	curses Krishna	ST	XXV
	sets off for the forest with Dhritarashtra dies in forest fire	ASR	XV, XXXVII
Ganesa	commissioned to write down the *Mahābhārata*	AD	I
Ganga	(mother to Bhishma by King Santanu)		
	has to be reborn on Earth	AD	XCVI
	marries Santanu	AD	XCVIII
	throws her first seven children into the river	AD	XCVIII
	is prevented by Santanu from throwing in the eighth, who will be called Gangadatta	AD	XCVIII
	leaps from heaven, to refill the Ocean	VA	CIX
	origin	U	CXI
	adopts King Bhagiratha as her father	D	LX
	praised	AN	XXVI
	mother to Skanda by Agni	AN	LXXXV
	mourns for Bhishma	AN	CLXVIII
	consoled by Krishna	AN	CLXVIII
Garga	receives 'the knowledge of Time with its four and sixty branches'	AN	XVIII
Gargya	acquires the history of the celestial Rishis	SAN	CCX
Garishtha	celestial counterpart of Drumasena	AD	LXVII
Garuda	born to Vinata	AD	XVI
	birth	AD	XXIII
	praised	AD	XXIII
	carries Kadru's snake-sons near the Sun	AD	XXV
	seeks the Amrita	AD	XXVIII
	seizes an enormous elephant and a gigantic tortoise	AD	XXIX
	eats said elephant and tortoise	AD	XXX
	origin of his name	AD	XXX

Garuda *cont*	story behind his birth	AD	XXXI
	defeats the gods and extinguishes the fire around the Amrita	AD	XXXII
	obtains the Amrita	AD	XXXIII
	becomes Vishnu's flagstaff device	AD	XXXIII
	becomes immortal	AD	XXXIII
	struck by Indra's thunderbolt	AD	XXXIII
	comes to be called Suparna	AD	XXXIII
	given snakes for his food	AD	XXXIV
	deceives the snakes	AD	XXXIV
	devours Chikura and threatens his son Sumukha	U	CIV
	boasts of his prowess before Vishnu	U	CV
	humbled by weight of Vishnu's right arm	U	CV
	reconciled to everlasting friendship with Sumukha	U	CV
	describes the eastern quarter (Purva)	U	CVIII
	decribes the southern direction (Dakshina)	U	CIX
	describes the west (Paschima)	U	CX
	describes the north (Uttara or Madhyama)	U	CXI
	sets off eastwards with Galava	U	CXII
	younger brother to Aruna	U	CXII
	also called Tarkhya	U	CXII
	loses his wings and regains them	U	CXIII
	enables Galava to accomplish his mission	U	CXIV-CXIX
Gautama I	'From the seed of Gautama, fallen upon a clump of reeds were born two that were twins, the mother of Aswatthaman (called Kripi) and Kripa of great strength.'	AD	LXIII
Gautama II	father of Ekata, Dwita and Trita	SAL	XXXVI
Gautama III	(Brahamana who lived as a robber) slain, restored to life, and cursed	SAN	CLXVIII-CLXXIII
Gautama IV	'founder of the science of dialectics'	AN	XVII
Gautama V	ascetic story of Gautama, the elephant and the disguised Indra	AN	CII
Gautama VI	(husband to Ahalya) preceptor to Utanka	ASW	LVI
Gavaksha	(brother to Sakuni) slain by Bhima	D	CLVI

Gavalgana	father to Sanjaya	U	XXIII
Gaya	(King) (son to Amartarayas (or Amurtarayas))		
	even he had to die	D	LXVI
	his sacrifices	SAN	XXIX
Ghatotkacha	son to Bhima through the Rakshasa woman Hidimva	AD	CLVII
	why so called	AD	CLVII
	carries the exiles to the hermitage of Nara and Narayana	VA	CCXLIV
	fights Duryodhana	B	XCII
	wreaks havoc among the Kurus	B	XCIII
	slays the Rakshasa Alamvusha	D	CVIII
	vanquished by Aswatthaman	D	CLV
	fights Aswatthaman	D	CLXV
	slays the Rakshasa Alamvusha	D	CLXXIV
	fights Karna	D	CLXXV
	slays the Rakshasa Alayudha	D	CLXXVIII
	slain by Karna	D	CLXXIX
	as he falls, slays a full Akshauhini of foes by his sheer weight	D	CLXXIX
	truth about him stated by Krishna	D	CLXXXI
	mourned by Yudhishthira	D	CLXXXIII
Gods, The	The 33 gods are the 8 Vasus, 11 Rudras, 12 Adityas and Prajapati and Vashatkara	AD	LXVI
	seek to destroy Skanda	VA	CCXXV-CCXXVI
	succumb to Skanda and make him their general	VA	CCXXVI, CCXXVIII
	win battle over the Danavas	VA	CCXXX
	at Brahma(n)'s request, Vishnu and all the celestials are incarnated on Earth to bring about Ravana's downfall	VA	CCLXXIV
	fight the Asuras for 32,000 years	SAN	XXXIII
	their pedigrees	SAN	CCVIII
Gotama	converses with Yama	SAN	CXXIX
Granthika	pseudonym for Nakula	VI	III
Gunakesi	daughter to Matali through Sudharma	U	XCVII
Haihaya	name for Vitahavya	AN	XXX

Hanuman	lies across the way of his brother Bhima	VA	CXLV
	his tail cannot be lifted by Bhima	VA	CXLVI
	tells story of Rama	VA	CXLVI
	recounts his leap across the Ocean	VA	CXLVII
	allowed to live as long as Rama's fame	VA	CXLVII
	teaches Bhima characteristics of the four Yugas	VA	CXLVIII
	reveals something of the mighty form he had at the time of his great leap	VA	CXLIX
	instructs Bhima on the duties of the four orders of men	VA	CXLIX
	gives guidance and support to Bhima	VA	CL
	discovers Sita in Lanka	VA	CCLXXX
Hara	(god)		
	celestial counterpart of Suvahu	AD	LXVII
	grants boon to King Jayadratha	VA	CCLXX
Hardikya	earthly counterpart of Aswapati	AD	LXVII
Hari I	son to King Akampana		
	slain in battle	D	L
Hari II	slain by Karna	K	LVI
Haryyaswa	King of Ayodhya	U	CXV
	helps Galava in his quest	U	CXVI
Hayagriva	dutiful king	SAN	XXIV
Hidimva I	(Rakshasa)		
	slain by Bhima	AD	CLVI
Himdiva II	(sister to Himdimva I)		
	falls in love with Bhima	AD	CLIV
	mother to Ghatotkacha by Bhima	AD	CLVII
Hiranyagarbha	'promulgator of the Yoga system'	SAN	CCCL
Hiranyakasipu I	son to Diti	AD	LXV
	his five sons	AD	LXV
	celestial counterpart of Sisupala	AD	LXVII
Hiranyakasipu II	(King)		
	dismisses Vasishtha and installs Viswarupa (Trisiras) as his Hotri	SAN	CCCXLIII

Hiranyaroman	(name of Rukmi)		
Hiranyvarman	(King of the Dasarnakas)		
	declares war when he discovers that his daughter has married a lady (Sikhandin)	U	CXCII
	mollified when Sikhandin is found to be a male!	U	CXCV
Hotravahana	(royal sage)		
	grandfather to Amva	U	CLXXVIII
Hridika	father to Kritavarman	D	CXIII
Ilavila I	father to King Dilipa	D	LXI
Ilavila II	(Asura)		
	(elder brother to Vatapi)		
	gives wealth to the Rishi Agastya	VA	XCIX
Indra	(other names: Vasava, Purandara, Sakra)		
	praised	AD	XXV
	causes a downpour of rain	AD	XXVI
	frightened after insulting some Rishis whose bodies were of the measure of a thumb	AD	XXXI
	strikes Garuda with his thunderbolt	AD	XXXIII
	makes friends with Garuda	AD	XXXIV
	father to Arjuna	AD	LXIII
	the five Indras, identified by Vyasa as the Pandavas	AD	CLXLIX
	offers boons to Arjuna and Krishna	AD	CCXXXVI
	description of his assembly room	SAB	VII
	orders Urvasi to use her wiles upon Arjuna	VA	XLV
	decrees that Urvasi's curse will operate on Arjuna only for the 13th year of exile	VA	XLVI
	instructs Lomasa to guide and protect Yudhishthira and his brothers	VA	XLVII
	forbids Chyavana to offer Soma juice to the Aswins	VA	CXXIV
	arm paralyzed by Chyavana; threatened with destruction	VA	CXXIV
	quickly gives the Aswins the right to the Soma	VA	CXXV
	puts his forefinger into a baby's mouth, saying, 'He will suck me.'	VA	CXXVI

Indra cont	appears to King Usinara as a hawk	VA	CXXXI
	visits the exiled Pandavas	VA	CLXV
	meets the royal sage Vaka	VA	CLXLII
	appears as a hawk	VA	CLXLVI
	slays the Asura Kesin	VA	CCXXII
	offers Skanda his own position	VA	CCXXVIII
	exchanges an infallible weapon for Karna's mail and earrings	VA	CCCVIII
	overpowered by the sin of Brahmanicide	U	X
	hides in the fibres of a lotus-stalk	U	XIV
	assigns to Kuvera, Yama and Varuna their respective sovereignty	U	XVI
	reinstated as chief of the celestials	U	XVIII
	presides over the new moon	U	CXLII
	receives special mantras from Siva and gives them to Angiras	D	XCIII
	purified from Brahmanicide by bathing in the Aruna	SAL	XLIII
	disguises himself as the Rishi Vasishtha	SAL	XLVIII
	why also called Satakratu	SAL	XLIX
	his conversation with Mandhatri	SAN	LXIV
	made the ruler of the deities	SAN	CXXII
	regains his sovereignty from Prahlada	SAN	CXXIV
	speaks, in the form of a jackal, to Kasyapa	SAN	CLXXX
	divides the portions of Sree among the Earth, the Waters, Fire, and good men	SAN	CCXXV
	located in the arms of living creatures	SAN	CCXXXIX
	slays Vritra and becomes afflicted by the personified form of Brahmanicide	SAN	CCLXXXII
	makes his thunderbolt and slays Viswarupa and Vritra; hides in a lotus-stalk	SAN	CCCXLIII
	rises to pre-eminence among the deities	AN	XXXVI
	the forms he can assume	AN	XL
	makes advances to Ruchi, but flees in terror!	AN	XL, XLI
	addressed by the Grandsire	AN	LXXII-LXXIV
	disguises himself as King Dhritarashtra	AN	CII
	his conflict with Vritra, described by Krishna	ASW	XI
Indradyumna	(King)		
	loses and regains heaven	VA	CLXLVIII
Indrajit	(son to Ravana)		
	slain by Lakshmana	VA	CCLXXXVII

Indrasena I	son to Nala through Damayanti	VA	LVII
Indrasena II	daughter to Nala through Damayanti	VA	LVII
Indrota	(also called Saunaka) (son to Sunaka) against all tradition, helps to cleanse King Janamejaya from Brahmanicide	SAN	CLI-CLII
Iravat	son to Arjuna through the daughter of the King of the Nagas his prowess and death	B B	XCI XCI
Ishupa	celestial counterpart of Nagnajita	AD	LXVII
Jaigishavya	(ascetic) speaks to Asita-Devala on Emancipation	AN	CCXXIX
Jaimini	disciple to Vyasa	SAN	CCCXXVIII
Jaitra	(son to Dritarashtra) slain by Bhima	SAL	XXVI
Jajali	(proud ascetic) allows a family of birds to be reared on his head instructed by the trader Tuladhara	SAN SAN	CCLXI CCLXII-CCLXIV
Jamadagni	(son to Richika) father to Rama	AD SAN	LXVI L
	birth: 'to him, rivalling in lustre the author of light, came spontaneously and without instruction the knowledge of the entire military art and of the fourfold missile arms' marries Renuka, has five sons, and dies his strange birth Jamadagni, Renuka and Surya overcomes Anger	VA VA SAN AN ASW	CXV CXVI L XCV, XCVI XCII
Janaka	decides to adopt a life of mendicancy, while his wife pleads for him to remain king King of Mithila lays heaven and hell before his troops on the eve of battle	SAN SAN SAN	XVIII XCIX XCIX

Janaka *cont*	speaks of Freedom from Attachments	SAN	CLXXVIII
	instructs Suka in Emancipation	SAN	CCCXXVII
	the question of what is mine and what is not	ASW	XXXII
Janaki	earthly counterpart of Chandravinasana	AD	LXVII
Janamejaya	The *Mahābhārata* recited at his snake-sacrifice	AD	I
	crowned after King Parikshit's death	AD	XLIV
	marries Vapushtama	AD	XLIV
	hears how Takshaka slew Parikshit	AD	LI
	resolves to perform the snake-sacrifice	AD	LI
	conquers the whole world in three nights	SAN	CXXIV
	commits Brahmanicide and is purified	SAN	CL-CLII
	great-great-grandson to Vyasa	SAN	CCXLIV
	sees Parikshit and other brought down from heaven by Vyasa	ASR	XXXV
	his sacrifice ends	SW	V
Jishnu	slain by Karna	K	LVI
Jishnukarman	slain by Karna	K	LVI
Jyotsnakali	(daughter to Soma)		
	chooses Pushkara as her husband	U	XCVIII
Kacha	(Brahman)		
	killed and revived three times	AD	LXXVI
	learns science of re-vivification	AD	LXXVII
Kadru	(wife to Kasyapa)		
	mother to 1,000 snakes	AD	XVI
	curses her snake-sons	AD	XX
	puts her sister into slavery	AD	XXIII
	her sons	AD	LXV
Kahoda	curses his son Ashtavakra	VA	CXXXII
	defeated in debate by Vandin	VA	CXXXII
	drowned	VA	CXXXII
	restored to life	VA	CXXXIV
Kaikeyi	(Queen)		
	(mother to Bharata)		
	causes Rama's exile	VA	CCLXXV

Kaitabha	Danava	VA	CCII
	Asura	SAN	CCCXLVIII
	mother to Dundhu	VA	CCII
	slain by Hari at the end of creation	VA	CCII
	steals the Vedas from Brahma	SAN	CCCXLVIII
	slain by Krishna	SAN	CCCXLVIII
Kala	(Time)		
	son to Dhruva	AD	LXVI
Kalakavrikshiya	(sage)		
	story of Kalakavrikshiya, his crow, and the King of Kosala	SAN	LXXXII
	speaks to Kshemadarsin on the conduct of a king who has lost his kingdom	SAN	CIV-CVI
Kalakirti	earthly counterpart of Mayura	AD	LXVII
Kalaneni	celestial counterpart of Kansa	AD	LXVII
Kali	(god)		
	ruins King Nala	VA	LVIII-LXXII
Kalmashapada	(King)		
	cursed by Saktri, becomes a Rakshasa	AD	CLXXVIII
	liberated by Vasishtha	AD	CLXXIX
	appoints Vasishtha to beget a son upon his queen	AD	CLXXXIV
Kamandaka	(Rishi)		
	his words to King Angaristha	SAN	CXXIII
Kanika	advises Dhritarashtra on the duties of a king	AD	CXLII
Kanka	pseudonym for Yudhishthira	VI	I
Kansa	earthly counterpart of Kalanemi	AD	LXVII
Kanwa	(Rishi)		
	foster father to Sakuntala	AD	LXXI, LXXII
Kanykadhyaja	(son to Dhritarashtra)		
	slain by Bhima	B	XCVII

Kapila	(Rishi)		
	said to be 'the promulgator of the Sankhya cult'	SAN	CCCL
	Kapila and the cow and the Rishi Syumarasmi	SAN	CCLXVIII-CCLXX
Karna	begotten upon Kunti by Surya	AD	LXIII, CXI
	brought up by Radha and her husband	AD	CXI
	why so called	AD	CXI
	why also called Vasusena	AD	CXI
	emulates Arjuna's feats; sides with Duryodhana	AD	CXXXVIII
	strings the great bow, but is rejected by Draupadi	AD	CLXXXIX
	overpowered by Arjuna	AD	CLXLII
	sets out to re-conquer the Earth for Duryodhana	VA	CCLI
	subdues the Earth and raises Duryodhana's hopes	VA	CCLII
	vows to slay Arjuna	VA	CCLV
	utters notable words on fame	VA	CCLXLVIII
	exchanges his earrings for an infallible weapon	VA	CCCVIII
	born cased in mail and adorned with earrings	VA	CCCVI
	brought up by the charioteer Adhiratha and his wife Radha	VA	CCCVII
	also known as Vrisha	VA	CCCVII
	learns arms from Drona	VA	CCCVII
	origin of name	VA	CCCVIII
	vanquished by Arjuna	VI	LIV
	forced to retreat by Arjuna	VI	LX
	directly responsible, with Duryodhana, for the impending calamity	U	XCIII
	shows a level-headed side to his character	U	CXLI
	is informed of his true mother	U	CXLV
	quarrels with Bhishma	U	CLXIX
	reconciled to Bhishma	B	CXXIV
	balanced account of his character given by Bhishma	B	CXXIV
	still feels he has to fight, and obtains Bhishma's permission to fight	B	CXXIV
	pays tribute to Bhishma	D	II
	vanquished by Bhima	D	CXXVIII
	fights Bhima	D	CXXX, CXXXI
		D	CXXXVII, CXXXVIII, CLXXXVIII

Karna *cont*	vanquished by Arjuna	D	CXLIV, CLVIII
	fights Satyaki	D	CXLVI, CLXX
	vanquishes Sahadeva	D	CLXVI
	wreaks havoc among the Pandavas	D	CLXXIII
	fights Ghatotkacha	D	CLXXV
	slays Ghatotkacha with his infallible weapon	D	CLXXIX
	made commander-in-chief to the Kurus	K	I
	slain two days later by Arjuna	K	I
	vanquishes Nakula and spares his life	K	XXIV
	shows his prowess	K	XXIV
	vows to slay Arjuna the next day	K	XXXI
	receives entire science of weapons from Rama	K	XXXIV
	has two curses upon him: one from Rama, one from a Brahmana	K	XLII
	vanquishes Yudhishthira	K	XLIX
	vanquished by Bhima	K	L
	slays Jishnu, Jishnukarman, Devapi, Chitra, Chitrayudha, Hari, Singhaketu, Rochamana and Salabha	K	LVI
	wreaks havoc with the Bhargava weapon	K	LXIV
	assessed by Krishna	K	LXXII
	shows his prowess	K	LXXVIII
	his sober estimate of Arjuna	K	LXXIX
	slays Visoka and the son of Dhrishtadyumna	K	LXXXII
	fights Arjuna	K	LXXXIX, XC
	armour struck off by Arjuna	K	XC
	chariot sinks according to the Brahmana's curse. When he heaves up his chariot, the whole Earth rises 'with her seven islands and her hills and waters and forests'. Asks for time to raise his chariot	K	XC
	slain by Arjuna	K	XCI
	tribute: 'He left the world, taking away with him that blazing glory of his own which he had earned on Earth by fair fight ... When Karna fell, the rivers stood still.'	K	XCIV
	mourned by his wives	ST	XXI
	birth	SAN	II
	gains favour with Rama	SAN	II
	cursed by the Brahmana whose cow he has slain	SAN	II

Karna	deceives Rama	SAN	II
cont	obtains from Rama a knowledge of weapons	SAN	II
	bitten by a worm which is really an Asura	SAN	III
	told by Rama that when death is at hand he will have no control over the Brahma weapon	SAN	III
	his might enables Duryodhana to carry off a princess	SAN	IV
	combat with Jarasandha	SAN	V
	factors contributing to his death	SAN	V
	true identity	ASR	XXXI
Kartavirya	(also called Arjuna) (King)		
	his pride humbled by Pavana	AN	CLII-CLVII
Kartikeya	(also called Kumara)		
	grows up and slays Taraka	AN	LXXXV, LXXXVI
Kasiraja	earthly counterpart of Dhirghajihva	AD	LXVII
Kasyapa	in the Golden Age grants boons to his two wives, Kadru and Vinata	AD	XVI
	hopes to obtain wealth by protecting Parikshit, but instead accepts the wealth offered by Takshaka	AD	XLIII
	son to Marichi	AD	LXVI
	father to the gods and the Asuras	AD	LXVI
	father to Vivaswat (the Sun) through a daughter of Daksha	AD	LXXV
	grandfather to Manu	AD	LXXV
	the Earth is given to him	VA	CXIV
	also called Marichi	D	LXX
	given the Earth by Rama	D	LXX
	sage who gathers the reamining Kshatriyas	SAN	L
	speaks of the mutual trust between king and priest	SAN	LXXIII
	married to 13 daughters of Daksha	SAN	CCVII
	origin	AN	LXXXV
	his spirit maintains the Earth for 30,000 celestial years	AN	CLIV
	Kasyapa and the great ascetic	ASW	XVI-XIX
Kausika	(also named Gadhi) (Brahmana)		
	destroys a she-crane which has fouled him	VA	CCV

Kausika *cont*	learns from a fowler the duty of serving one's parents and the secret of happiness	VA	CCVI-CCXV
Kavachin	(son to Dhritarashtra) slain by Bhima	K	LXXXIV
Kavi	name for Usanas	SAN	CCXC
	origin	AN	LXXXV
Kavya	= Sukra = Usanas	AD	LXXVI
Kayavya	robber with a fine morality	SAN	CXXXV
Kesin	(Asura) slain by Indra	VA	CCXXII
Ketumat	celestial counterpart of Amitaujas	AD	LXVII
Khattanga	(name for Dilipa)		
Kichaka	(commander of Virata's forces)		
	makes advances to Draupadi	VI	XIV
	slain by Bhima	VI	XXII
Kindama	Muni in the form of a deer	AD	CXVIII
	curses Pandu	AD	CXVIII
Kirmira	(Rakshasa) (brother to Vaka) slain by Bhima	VA	XI
Kotika	son to King Jayadratha	VA	CCLXII
Kratha I	celestial counterpart of Parvateya	AD	LXVII
Kratha II	earthly counterpart of Rahu (?)	AD	LXVII
Krathana	celestial counterpart of Suryaksha	AD	LXVII
Kratu	his sons	AD	LXVI
Kripa	(son to Gautama) (brother to Kripi) (uncle to Aswatthaman)		
	'of great strength'	AD	LXIII
	appointed as preceptor to the Kuru princes	AD	CXXIX
	birth	AD	CXXX
	why so called	AD	CXXX
	vanquished by Arjuna	VI	LVII
	vanquishes Sikhandin	D	CLXIX

Kripa *cont*	vanquishes Drishtadyumna	K	XXVI
	slays Suketu	K	LIV
	one of the three survivors of the Kuru army	SAU	I
Kripi	(daughter to Gautama)		
	sister to Kripa	AD	LXIII
	wife to Drona	AD	CXXXI
	mother to Aswatthaman	AD	LXIII, CXXXI
Krishna I	begotten by Vasudeva upon Devaki	AD	LXIII
	praised	AD	LXIII
	born from a black hair of Narayana's body	AD	CLXLIX
	gives wedding presents to the Pandavas	AD	CCI
	brother to Subhadra	AD	CCXXI
	uncle to Abhimanyu	AD	CCXXII
	receives the discus and a mace called Kaumodaki	AD	CCXXVII
	enables Agni to consume the forest of Khandava	AD	CCXXVIII
	with Arjuna, routs the celestials	AD	CCXXIX
	asks Indra for eternal friendship with Arjuna	AD	CCXXXVI
	is offered the Arghya at Yudhishthira's Rajasuya sacrifice	SAB	XXXV
	praised	SAB	XXXVII
	slays King Sisupala	SAB	XLIV
	his feats in former lives, recited by Arjuna	VA	XII
	slays King Salwa and destroys his city of Saubha	VA	XXII
	promises to be Arjuna's charioteer and to restore the kingdom to Yudhishthira	VA	LI
	leader of the Vrishnis	VA	CXVIII
	visits the exiled Pandavas	VA	CXVIII
	visits the exiled Pandavas with his consort Satyabhama	VA	CLXXXII
	brother to Vabhru, King of Kasi	U	XXVIII
	catalogue of past exploits	U	XLVIII
	identified as Narayana	U	XLIX, XCVI
	description of person and of discus	U	LXVIII
	his names and their meanings	U	LXX
	offered hymn of praise by Dhritarashtra	U	LXXI
	acts as peace envoy to the Kurus	U	LXXXIII-CXXXI
	attributes and chariot described	U	LXXXIII

Krishna I cont			
	attributes	U	LXXXV
	again praised by Dhritarashtra	U	LXXXVI
	how he speaks	U	XCI
	dwells in the north	U	CXI
	assumes a terrible form	U	CXXXI
	instructs Arjuna	B	XXVI-XLII
	sets out to slay Bhishma, but is restrained by Arjuna	B	LIX
	praised by Brahma	B	LXV
	promises that for the good of the Universe he will take his birth among mankind in the family of Vasudeva	B	LXVI
	qualities and titles	B	LXVI
	infinite glories extolled by Bhishma	B	LXVII
	what Narada, Markandeya and Bhrigu say about him	B	LXVIII
	prepares to slay Bhishma, but is restrained by Arjuna	B	CVII
	displays his skill as a charioteer	B	CVII
	qualites and achievements listed by Dhritarashtra	D	XI
	obtains conch, discus and celestial flower	D	XI
	becomes 'covered with sweat, and much weakened'	D	XIX
	adores the goddess Twilight	D	LXXII
	resolves to fight	D	LXXIX
	picture of the two Krishnas, painted with many literary images and similes	D	C
	produces illusion of darkness	D	CXLV
	offered hymn of praise by Yudhishthira	D	CXLVIII
	encourages Bhima and Yudhishthira to lie	D	CXCI
	identified as Narayana	D	CCI
	left arm pierced by Satyasena's lance	K	XXVII
	assesses Karna	K	LXXII
	presses Arjuna's chariot one cubit into the Earth	K	XC
	favours deception in Bhima's mace-combat with Duryodhana	SAL	LVIII
	prevents Rama from attacking Bhima	SAL	LX
	supports the use of 'contrivances and means'	SAL	LXI
	comforts Gandhari	SAL	LXIII
	his discus cannot be moved by Aswatthaman	SAU	XII
	names of his horses	SAU	XIII
	curses Aswatthaman	SAU	XVI
	gives an account of Siva and creation	SAU	XVII, XVIII

Krishna I cont	presents a statue of Bhima for Dhritarashtra to destroy	ST	XII
	reproves Dhritarashtra	ST	XIII
	cursed by Gandhari	ST	XXV
	offered hymn of praise by Yudhishthira	SAN	XLIV
	his state of meditation described by Yudhishthira	SAN	XLVII
	offered marvellous hymn by Bhishma	SAN	XLVIII
	younger brother to Baladeva and elder brother to Gada	SAN	XLIX
	speaks in praise of Bhishma	SAN	LI
	grants the stricken Bhishma a clear mind and full alleviation from pain	SAN	LII
	praised by Bhishma	SAN	CX
	how he comes to be called Madhusudana	SAN	CCVII
	qualities and prowess	SAN	CCIX
	in the form of a boar, conquers the Daityas and Danavas	SAN	CCIX
	attributes	SAN	CCX
	speaks to Ugrasena about Narada's good qualities	SAN	CCXXX
	some of his names and their meanings	SAN	CCXLII, CCCXLIII
	speaks to Arjuna of creation and dissolution	SAN	CCXLIII
	his praises sung	SAN	CCCXLIV, CCCXLVII
	slays Madhu and Kaitabha and restores the Vedas to Brahma	SAN	CCCXLVIII
	his equine-headed form described	SAN	CCCXLVIII
	his praises sung	SAN	CCCXLVIII
	his pronunciation and the sound of his voice	SAN	CCCXLVIII
	meets Mahadeva and sings his praises	AN	XIV
	granted 16 boons by Mahadeva	AN	XV
	Krishna and King Nriga	AN	LXX
	undergoes a vow to obtain a son	AN	CXXXIX
	fire proceeds from his mouth	AN	CXXXIX
	restores the creatures consumed by the fire	AN	CXXXIX
	praised by Mahadeva	AN	CXLVII
	his ancestors	AN	CXLVII
	praised by Bhishma	AN	CXLVIII
	his thousand names	AN	CXLIX
	praised by Bhishma	AN	CLVIII
	gratifies the Rishi Durvasa	AN	CLIX
	consoles Ganga on the death of Bhishma	AN	CLXVIII

Krishna I *cont*	tells the story of the conflict between Indra and Vritra	ASW	XI
	instructs Yudhishthira	ASW	XII
	enjoys the time of peace with Arjuna	ASW	XV
	tells Arjuna story of Kasyapa and the ascetic	ASW	XVI-XIX
	quotes the words of a Brahmana to his wife	ASW	XX-XXXIV
	quotes the words of another Brahmana to his disciple	ASW	XXXV-LI
	praises sung by Arjuna	ASW	LII
	obtains Yudhishthira's permission to visit his father	ASW	LII
	threatened by the Rishi Utanka	ASW	LIII
	speaks of himself	ASW	LIV
	worshipped by Utanka	ASW	LV
	gives his father a summary of the battle	ASW	LX
	tells his father of the death of Abhimanyu	ASW	LXI
	revives the stillborn Parikshit	ASW	LXIX
	true identity	ASR	XXXI
	exterminates the Vrishnis and the Andakas	MAU	III
	leaves the body	MAU	IV
Krishna II	(name for Draupadi)		
Kritavarman	(son to Hridika)		
	shows his prowess	D	CXIII
	fights Satyaki	D	CXV
	vanquishes Yudhishthira	D	CLXIV
	vanquishes Sikhandin	K	XXVI
	vanquished by Satyaki	SAL	XVII
	fights Satyaki	SAL	XXI
	one of the three survivors of the Kuru army	SAU	I
	slain by Satyaki	MAU	III
Kriti	father to Ruchiparvan	D	XXIV
Krodhahantri	celestial counterpart of Danda	AD	LXVII
Krodhavardhana	celestial counterpart of Dandadhara	AD	LXVII
Kshatradharman	slain by Drona	D	CXXIX

Kshema	(King) slain by Drona	D	XXI
Kshemadarsin	(King of Kosala) story of Kshemadarsin, Kalakavrikshiya, and his crow	SAN	LXXXII
Kshemadhurti I	slain by Vrihatkshatra	D	CVI
Kshemadhurti II	(King of the Kulutas) slain by Bhima	K	XII
Kshemakirti	(King) slain by Satyaki	SAL	XXI
Kshupa	(priest) created by Brahman	SAN	CXXII
Kukshi	celestial counterpart of Parvatiya	AD	LXVII
Kumara I	slain by Drona	D	XVI
Kumara II	name of Kartikeya	AN	LXXXVI
Kumbhakarna	long-sleeping brother to Ravana	VA	CCLXXXIV
	awakened by Ravana	VA	CCLXXXIV
	slain by Lakshmana	VA	CCLXXXV
Kundabhedin	(son to Dhritarashtra) slain by Bhima	B	XCVII, CXXVI
Kundadhara	(son to Dhritarashtra) slain by Bhima	B	LXXXIX
Kundalin	(son to Dhritarashtra) slain by Bhima	B	XCVII
Kundavedhin	slain by Abhimanyu	D	XXXV
Kuni-Garga	(Rishi) his daughter gives half of her ascetic merits to the man who will marry her	SAL	LII
Kunti	(name of Pritha)		
Kuntibhoja	marries Pritha	AD	LXVII

Kupatha	celestial counterpart of Suparswa	AD	LXVII
Kuru	son to Samvarana through Tapati	AD	CLXXV
	tills the plain	SAL	LIII
Kurus, The	a clear account of the origin and early history of the Kuru race	U	CXLIX
Kusika	(King)		
	tested by the Rishi Chyavana	AN	LIII
	told that his grandson (Visvamitra) will become a Brahmana	AN	LV, LVI
Kusikas, The	become connected with the Bhrigus by marriage	AN	LVI
Kuvalaswa	(King)		
	of Ishvaku's race	VA	CC
	son to King Vrihadaswa	VA	CCII
	slays Dhundhu, a Danava chief	VA	CCIII
	known henceforth as Dhundhumara	VA	CCIII
Kuvera	(also called Vaisravana and Ailavila)		
	his weapon: spiked club	AD	CCXXIX
	his assembly house described	SAL	X
	gives his Antarddana weapon to Arjuna	VA	XLI
	'the Lord of Treasures'	VA	CLIX
	'Lord of the Rakshasas'	VA	CLIX
	description of his palace	VA	CLIX
	is freed by Bhima from the curse of Agastya	VA	CLX
	promises full support to the Pandavas	VA	CLXI
	receives sovereignty over the Yakshas and all the wealth of the world	U	XVI
	abides in the north	U	CXI
	made the Lord of Treasures and of all Rakshasas	SAN	CXXII
Lakshmana I	(brother to Rama)		
	slays Kumbhakarna	VA	CCLXXXV
	slays Indrajit	VA	CCLXXXVII
Lakshmana II	(grandson to Dhritarashtra)		
	slain by Abhimanyu	D	XLIV
Lakshmi	(also known as Devasena)		
	(daughter to Brahman)		

Lakshmi *cont*	a name for Sree	SAN	CCXXV
	proceeds from the Ocean	AD	XVIII
	sister to Dhatri and Vidhatri	AD	LXVI
	abides in the Moon	D	II
Likhita	brother to Sankha, from whom he steals	SAN	XXII
	punished by King Sudyumna	SAN	XXII
Lomapada	(King)		
	(father to Santa)		
	how the drought ceases in his country	VA	CXIII
Lomasa	(Rishi)		
	instructed by Indra to guide and protect Yudhishthira and his brothers	VA	XLVII
	tells the four Pandavas how Arjuna fares in heaven	VA	XCI
	conducts the four brothers on a pilgrimage to tirthas	VA	XCIII-CXLIV
	tells how to gratify the Pitris and the deities	AN	CXXIX
Lopamudra	marries the Rishi Agastya	VA	XCII
	mother to Dridhasyu by Agastya	VA	XCIX
Mada	huge demon created by Chyavana to devour Indra	VA	CXXIV
	distributed piecemeal by Chyavana 'in drinks, in women, in gambling, and in field sports'	VA	CXXV
Madayanti	(wife to King Saudasa)		
	owns celestial earrings	ASW	LVII
Madhava	name of Satyaki	D	CXV
Madhavi	(daughter to King Yayati)		
	given to Galava to accomplish his quest	U	CXV-CXIX
	gives sons to three kings, each time becoming a maiden again	U	CXVI-CXVIII
	mother to Sivi by Usinara	U	CXVIII
	mother to Ashtaka by Viswamitra	U	CXIX
	chooses the forest as her husband and devotes herself to ascetic austerities	U	CXX

Madhu	(father to Dhundhu)		
	Danava	VA	CCII
	Asura	SAN	CCCXLVIII
	slain by Hari at the end of creation	VA	CCII
	steals the Vedas from Brahma	SAN	CCCXLVIII
	slain by Krishna	SAN	CCCXLVIII
Madri	(sister to the King of Madra)		
	earthly counterpart of Dhriti	AD	LXVII
	accompanies Pandu in his life as a hunter	AD	CXIV
	dies	AD	CXXV
	funeral rites	AD	CXXVII
Maghavat	gives gold to King Suhotra	SAN	XXIX
Mahabhisha	(King)		
	why cursed in heaven	AD	CXVI
	reborn as Santanu	AD	XCVII
Mahadeva	promises five husbands to a Rishi's daughter	AD	CLXXI
	how he comes to have four faces and 1,000 eyes	AD	CCXIII
	abides on the peak called Hiranya-sringa	SAB	III
	has single combat with Arjuna	VA	XXXIX
	praised	VA	XXXIX
	embraces Arjuna	VA	XXXIX
	gives Arjuna the Pasupata weapon	VA	XL
	identified by Vyasa as the person continually preceding Arjuna and actually defeating the foe	D	CCII
	some of his names, with meanings	D	CCII
	conquers the Asuras in their triple city	D	CCII
	hymned by the celestials	K	XXXIII
	destroys the three cities with one shaft	K	XXIV
	hymned by Mankanaka	SAL	XXXVIII
	'made the lord of the Rudras'	SAN	CXXII
	husband of Uma		
	obtains a share in sacrificial offerings	SAN	CCLXXXIII
	Fever arises from one drop of sweat on his body	SAN	CCLXXXIII
	hymned by Upamanyu	AN	XIV
	description	AN	XIV
	battleaxe described	AN	XIV
	again hymned by Upamanyu	AN	XIV
	hymned by Krishna	AN	XIV
	meets Krishna	AN	XIV

Mahadeva *cont*	second description	AN	XIV
	grants 16 boons to Krishna and Uma	AN	XV
	hymned by Tandi	AN	XVI
	some of his names	AN	XVII
	'the king of all hymns' addressed to him	AN	XVII
	numerous examples of his grace	AN	XVIII
	develops his third eye	AN	CXL
	why he has four faces; why he carries the Pinaka; why his throat is blue; why his abode is a crematorium	AN	CXLI
	speaks of duty and action	AN	CXLI-CXLV
	praises Krishna	AN	CXLVII
	praised	AN	CLX
	hymned by Krishna	AN	CLXI
	list of his names	ASW	VIII
Mahamegha	slain by Abhimanyu	D	XLVI
Maheswara	dwells in the north	U	CXI
	speaks of the importance of kine	AN	CXXXIII
Mahisha	(leader of the Danava forces) slain by Skanda	VA	CCXXX
Mahodara I	(son to Dhritarashtra) slain by Bhima	B	LXXXIX
Mahodara II	(great Rishi) his thigh and a Rakshasa's head	SAL	XXXIX
Maitravaruni	name for Vasishtha	SAN	CCCIII
Maitreya	(Rishi)		
	curses Duryodhana	VA	X
	speaks to Vyasa about the status of Brahmanas	AN	CXXI
Mamata	mother to Dirghatamas	AD	CIV
Mandapala	(Rishi) father to the Sarngaka birds through Jarita	AD	CCXXXI
Mandavya	curses Dharma	AD	CVII, CVIII
Mandhata	why so called born to his own father Yuvanaswa becomes a mighty and virtuous king *see* next entry	VA	CXXVI

Mandhatri	(King)		
	even he had to die	D	LXII
	born in the stomach of his father Yuvanaswa sucks Indra's finger	SAN	XXIX
	his conversation with Indra	SAN	LXIV
	conquers 'the whole world in the course of only one night'	SAN	CXXIV
	see previous entry		
Maniman	(Rakshasa)		
	slain by Bhima	VA	CLIX
Manimat	earthly counterpart of Vritra	AD	LXVII
Mankanaka	son of the wind-god and Sukanya; from him and Saraswati sprang seven Rishis, and from these Rishis sprang the 49 Maruts	VA	LXXXIII
	emits vegetable juice from his finger	SAL	XXXVIII
	praises Mahadeva	SAL	XXXVIII
Manki	speaks of the Extirpation of Desire	SAN	CLXXVII
Manu	son to Brahma(n)	AD	LXVI
	father to Prajapati	AD	LXVI
	son to Vivaswat (the Sun)	AD	LXXV
	grandson to Kasyapa	AD	LXXV
	father to all human beings	AD	LXXV
	father to Ila	AD	LXXV
	grandfather to Pururavas	AD	LXXV
	great-grandfather to Ayus	AD	LXXV
	great-great-grandfather to Nahusha	AD	LXXV
	great-great-great-grandfather to Yayati	AD	LXXV
	great-great-great-great-grandfather to Puru	AD	LXXV
	Manu, universal flood, and salvation in an ark pulled by a great fish	VA	CLXXXVI
	'Manu will create (again) all beings,' says the fish	VA	CLXXXVI
	self-create	SAN	XXI
	his words on 'the best of all religions'	SAN	XXI
	what he said to an assembly of Rishis in the Krita Age	SAN	XXXVII
	in a time of anarchy, Manu sets men their respective duties	SAN	LXVII
	speaks of the embodiment of righteousness	SAN	CXXI
	speaks to his disciple Vrihaspati on Emancipation	SAN	CCI
	speaks of the Soul	SAN	CCII-CCVI

Maricha	(friend of Ravana) disguised as golden deer, lures away Rama	VA	CCLXXVI
Marichi	name of Kasyapa	D	LXX
	father of Kasyapa	AD	LXVI
	origin	AN	LXXXV
Markandeya	Rishi and deathless sage	VA	CLXXXII
	visits the exiled Pandavas	VA	XXV
		VA	CLXXXII
	speaks of the universal dissolution which he has witnessed, and of the boy whose stomach contains all creation	VA	CLXXXVII
	instructs Yudhishthira in kingly duty	VA	CLXL
Marut	(wind-god) father to Bhima	AD	LXIII
Maruts, The	their origin	U	CX
	the 49 Maruts spring from the seven Rishis	SAL	XXXVIII
Marutta	(King) (son to Avikshit)		
	even he had to die	D	LIII
	the Viswarij sacrifice	SAN	XXIX
	his story told by Vyasa	ASW	IV-X
	has left gold which Vyasa urges Yudhishthira to use	ASW	X
Matali	(husband to Sudharma) (father to Gunakesi)		
	charioteer to Indra	VA	XLII
	seeks a fit son-in-law	U	XCVII
	eventually chooses a Naga called Sumukha	U	CIII, CIV
Matanga	Chandala who wishes to become a Brahmana	AN	XXVII
	receives boons from Indra and dies	AN	XXIX
Matariswan	god of Winds speaks of the creation and duty of the four orders of men	SAN	LXXII
Mati	celestial counterpart of Gandhari	AD	LXVII

Maya	Asura	AD	CCXXX
	Daitya	AN	XL
	escapes from blazing forest of Khandava	AD	CCXXX
	constructs a marvellous palace for the Pandavas	SAB	I
	gives Bhima a marvellous club and Arjuna the conch Devadatta; completes the palace	SAB	III
	creator of Woman	AN	XL
Mayura	celestial counterpart of Kalakirti	AD	LXVII
Medhavi	(son to Valadhi)		
	dies when the mountains which are the instruments of his life are shattered by buffaloes	VA	CXXXV
Medhavin	speaks to his father on how to behave when one sees that Death and Decrepitude are assailing everything	SAN	CLXXV
	speaks to his father about devotion to Truth	SAN	CCLXXVII
Meghasandhi	(son to Sahadeva)		
	(King of Magadha)		
	vanquished by Arjuna	ASW	LXXXII
Menaka	(Apsara)		
	mother to Sakuntala by Viswamitra	AD	LXXI, LXXII
Mitrasena	slain by Arjuna	K	XXVII
Mritapa	celestial counterpart of Pascimanupaka	AD	LXVII
Muchukunda	(King)		
	joins forces with his priest Vasishta in order to rule the Earth	SAN	LXXIV
Mudgala	passes the test set by the Muni Durvasa	VA	CCLVIII
Muni	his sons	AD	LXV
Munjakesa	earthly counterpart of Suhtra	AD	LXVII
Nabhaga	father to King Amvarisha	D	LXIV
	conquers the whole world in seven nights	SAN	CXXIV

Nachiketa	(son to the Rishi Uddalaki)		
	Nachiketa and Yama	AN	LXXI
Nagadatta	(son to Dhritarashtra)		
	slain by Bhima	D	CLVI
Nagas, The	their realm	U	XCVIII
	Patalam, their central city	U	XCIX
Nagnajita	earthly counterpart of Ishupa	AD	LXVII
Nahusha	(royal sage)		
	turned into snake by Agastya's curse	VA	CLXXVIII
	ancestor to the Pandavas	VA	CLXXIX
	son to Ayu 'and fifth in descent from the Moon'	VA	CLXXIX
	freed by Yudhishthira, returns to heaven	VA	CLXXX
	temporarily appointed King of the Gods	U	XI
	follows unrighteous ways and becomes a snake	U	XVII
	temporarily fills Indra's position	SAN	CCCXLIII
	proud	AN	XCIX
	cursed by Bhrigu. Becomes a snake until freed by Yudhishthira	AN	C
Nairitas, The	those Rakshasas begotten upon Niriti by Adharma	AD	LXVI
Naishadha	(name of Nala)		
Nakula	(son to Pandu)		
	twin brother to Sahadeva: real fathers are the twin Aswins	AD	LXXIII
	begotten upon Madri	AD	CXXIV
	father to Satanika through Draupadi	AD	CCXXIII
	conquers the West	SAB	XXV
	plans to disguise himself as Granthika and look after the horses of King Virata	VI	III
	with Sahadeva, vanquishes his maternal uncle Salya	B	LXXXIV
	qualities	D	XXXII
	vanquishes Sakuni	D	CLXIX
	vanquished by Duryodhana	D	CLXXXVII
	vanquished by Karna, who spares his life	K	XXIV
	fights Vrishasena	K	LXXXIV
	shows his prowess	K	LXXXIV
	slays Chitrasena, Satyasena and Sushena	SAL	X

Nakula *cont*	true identity falls to the ground	ASR MAH	XXXI II
Nala I	(King) the beautiful story of his love for Damayanti is told by Rishi Vrihadaswa	VA	LIII-LXXIX
Nala II	(monkey) (son to Tashtri) builds bridge for the monkeys to cross the Ocean	VA	CCLXXXI
Namuchi	his words to Indra: the wise man never regards himself as the actor	SAN	CCXXVI
Nanda	(son to Dhritarashtra) slain by Bhima	K	LI
Nandini	(cow belonging to Vasishtha) protects herself against Viswamitra	AD	CLXXVII
Nara	description of Nara and Narayana *see also* **Narayana**	SAN	CCCXLIV
Narada	(Rishi) his attainments	SAB	V
	solves problem for King Suhotra and King Sivi	VA	CLXLIII
	speaks to four kings about virtuous conduct	VA	CLXLVII
	takes Matali on a long tour in search of a fit son-in-law for Matali	U	XCVIII-CIV
	obtains length of days for Sumukha	U	CIV
	comforts King Akampana	D	L-LII
	given Srinjaya's daughter and cursed by the Rishi Parvata	D	LIII
	comforts Srinjaya	D	LIII
	stands with Vyasa between the two celestial weapons fired by Aswatthaman and Arjuna	SAU	XIV
	uncle to Parvata		
	curses and frees Parvata		
	marries Sukumari	SAN	XXX
	restores Suvarnashthivin to life	SAN	XXXI
	converses with Vasudeva	SAN	LXXXI
	acquires the science of music	SAN	CCX
	qualities	SAN	CCXXX

Narada *cont*	speaks to King Anukampaka about the origin of Death	SAN	CCLVI
	speaks to Galava about the pursuit of excellence	SAN	CCLXXXVIII
	instructs Suka in Emancipation	SAN	CCCXXX-CCCXXXII
	goes to Meru and views White Island	SAN	CCCXXXVI
	goes to White Island	SAN	CCCXXXIX
	praises Narayana, who appears to him	SAN	CCCXXXIX-CCCXL
	devoted to Narayana	SAN	CCCXLV
	tells a story to Indra	SAN	CCCLIII-CCCLXV
	speaks of the kinds of men worthy of worship	AN	XXXI
	addresses Krishna	AN	CXL-CXLVII
Naraka	slain by Vishnu	VA	CXLI
Narayana	advises the gods to churn the Ocean	AD	XVII
	beheads Rahu	AD	XIX
	with Nara, leads the gods to victory the Asuras	AD	XIX
	is given the Amrita in custody	AD	XIX
	portion of Narayana is celestial counterpart of Vasudeva	AD	LXVII
	from a black hair of his body is born Krishna	AD	CLXLIX
	from a white hair of his body is born Valadeva	AD	CLXLIX
	the Pandavas reach hermitage of Nara and Narayana	VA	CXLIV
	meaning of name	VA	CCLXX
	ancient exploits of Nara and Narayana	U	XLIX
	Nara and Narayana identified as Arjuna and Krishna	U	XLIX
		U	XCVI
		D	CCI
		K	LXXXVII
	Nara arises from Narayana's asceticism	D	CCI
	speaks to Narada in the Krita Age of the Epoch of Manu	SAN	CCCXXXV
	invisibly takes his share of Uparichara's sacrifice	SAN	CCCXXXVII
	can be seen by none but the purest beings	SAN	CCCXXXVII

Narayana *cont*	praised by Narada	SAN	CCCXXXIX
	appears to Narada	SAN	CCCXL
	his form; speaks of himself, the universe, and his 'ancient appearances and future ones also'	SAN	CCCXL
	distinction between himself and Brahma(n)	SAN	CCCXL
	how his combat with Rudra ends	SAN	CCCXLIII
	description of Nara and Narayana	SAN	CCCXLIV
	his words to Narada	SAN	CCCXLVI
	why he decides to appear in different forms from time to time	SAN	CCCL
	'promulgator of the cult, in its entirety, contained in the Pancharatra scriptures'	SAN	CCCL
Nikumbha	celestial counterpart of Devadhipa	AD	LXVII
Nila	slain by Aswatthaman	D	XXIX
Niriti	(wife to Adharma) mother to the Rakshasas called Nairatas	AD	LXVI
Nishangin	(son to Dhritarashtra) slain by Bhima	K	LXXXIV
Nivata-Kavachas, The	(Danavas) 30,000,000 defeated by Arjuna	VA	CLXVII-CLXXI
Nriga	story of King Nriga and Krishna	AN	LXX
Oghavati	(wife to Sudarsana) becomes the River Oghavati	AN	II
Padma	name of Sree	SAN	CCXXVIII
Padmanabha	virtuous Naga	SAN	CCLV-CCLXII
	pulls Surya's chariot for 15 days	SAN	CCCLVII-CCCLIX
Paila	disciple to Vyasa	SAN	CCCXXVIII
Panchachuda	(Apsara) speaks to Narada on the disposition of women	AN	XXXVIII

Panchala	(Prince)		
	slain by Drona	D	XXI
Panchasikha	(Rishi)		
	speaks to King Janaka on the immortality of the Soul	SAN	CCCXX
Pandavas, The	(i.e. the five sons of Pandu)		
	set out for Varanavata	AD	CXLV
	live in the house of lac	AD	CXLVIII
	escape from burning house	AD	CL
	cross the Ganga	AD	CLI
	study 'the Rik and the other Vedas and also all the Vedangas as well as the sciences of morals and politics'	AD	CLVIII
	live with a Brahmana in Ekachakra	AD	CLIX
	appoint Dhaumya as their priest	AD	CLXXXV
	journey to Panchala	AD	CLXXXVI
	defend Drupada and Draupadi against the enraged monarchs	AD	CLXLI
	have Draupadi as their common wife	AD	CLXLIII, CC
	identified by Vyasa as the five indras	AD	CLXLIX
	make alliance with King Drupada	AD	CCI
	receive wedding gifts from Krishna	AD	CCI
	receive half the kingdom from Dhritarashtra and establish a magnificent city at Khanavaprastha	AD	CCIX
	make a pact regarding Draupadi	AD	CCXIV
	their wealth described by Duryodhana	SAB	L-LII
	lose second dice game	SAB	LXXV
	prepare for thirteen years of exile	SAB	LXXVI
	visit the sacred lake Dwaitavana	VA	XXIV
	receive visit from the Rishi Markandeya	VA	XXV
	conducted on a tirtha-pilgrimage by Rishi Lomasa	VA	XCIII-CXLIV
	worship Rama before starting their southern journey	VA	CXVII
	visited by Valarama and Krishna	VA	CXVIII
	reach hermitage of Nara and Narayana	VA	CXLIV
	have been in the woods for four years	VA	CLVII
	reunited with Arjuna	VA	CLXIV
	blessed with short visit from Indra	VA	CLXV
	spend four years at Kuvera's abode (total of ten years exile)	VA	CLXXV
	begin return journey; spend a year in Visakhayupa Forest	VA	CLXXVI

Pandavas, The *cont*	subdue the Gandharvas and release Duryodhana	VA	CCXLIII, CCXLIV
	move from the Dwaita woods to the forest of Kamyakas, near Lake Trinavindu	VA	CCLVI
	visited by Vyasa	VA	CCLVII-CCLIX
	rescue Draupadi from King Jayadratha	VA	CCLXVII-CCLXIX
	move from the woods of Dwaitavana to the woods of Kamyaka	VA	CCCIX
	four of them die and are restored to life	VA	CCCX-CCCXI
	meet Dharma	VA	CCCXII
	prepare for the year of non-recognition	VA	CCCXIII
	decide to spend 13th year in the city of Virata	VI	I
	after year of non-discovery, join Virata's forces against the invaders	VI	XXXI
	bring victory to Virata's forces	VI	XXXIII
	Bhishma predicts their future: 'Living happily as long as the creation lasts, all you at the next new creation will be admitted among the gods, and enjoying all kinds of felicities ye will at last be numbered among the Siddhas.'	SAN	CCLXXX
	reunited with Dhritarashtra, Gandhari and Kunti, in the forest	ASR	XXIV
	each one described by Sanjaya	ASR	XXV
	perform the funeral rites of Dhritarashtra, Gandhari and Kunti	ASR	XXXIX
	accompanied by Draupadi and a dog, decide to retire from the world	MAH	I
	fall to the ground one by one	MAH	II
Panditaka	(son to Dhritarashtra) slain by Bhima	B	LXXXIX
Pandu	son to Vyasa	AD	I, LXIII
	his five sons, and their real fathers: Yudhishthira – Dharma, Bhima – Marut, Dhananjaya – Indra, Nakula, Sahadeva – the twin Aswins	AD	LXIII

Pandu cont	the curse upon him; his death	AD	XCV
	begotten by Vyasa upon Ambalika	AD	CVI
	why so called	AD	CVI
	why he becomes king	AD	CIX
	marries Pritha	AD	CXI
	chosen as husband by Pritha	AD	CXII
	description	AD	CXII
	marries Madri	AD	CXIII
	subjugates many countries	AD	CXIII
	leads the life of a hunter in the woods	AD	CXIV
	cursed by a deer which is really a Muni called Kindama	AD	CXVIII
	with his two wives, decides to undergo penances in the woods	AD	CXIX
	feels he will not be admitted to heaven	AD	CXX
	dies	AD	CXXV
	funeral rites	AD	CXXVII
	birth	U	CXLVII
	true identity	ASR	XXXI
Pandya	slain by Aswatthaman	K	XX
Parasara	Rishi		
	begets Vyasa upon Satyavati	AD	LXIII
	speaks to King Janaka about acts and their fruits	SAN	CCXCI-CCXCIX
	see also **Asmaka**		
Paravasu	(son to the sage Raivya)		
	accidentally kills his father	VA	CXXXVIII
Parikshit	(King)		
	insults the Rishi Samika by placing a dead snake across his shoulders	AD	XL
	takes defensive measures against Sringin's curse	AD	XLII
	killed by Takshaka	AD	XLIII
	praised	AD	XLIX
	will be born as grandson to Arjuna; will rule the Earth for 60 years	SAU	XVI
	born lifeless (on account of blade of grass thrown by Aswatthaman) to Uttara	ASW	LXVI
	revived by Krishna	ASW	LXIX
	meaning of name	ASW	LXX
Parvata	(Rishi)		
	(nephew to Narada)		
	curses Narada	D	LIII
	curses and frees Narada	SAN	XXX

Parvateya	earthly counterpart of Kratha	AD	LXVII
Parvati	name of Uma	SAN	CCLXXXIII
Parvatiya	earthly counterpart of Kukshi	AD	LXVII
Pascimanupaka	earthly counterpart of Mritapa	AD	LXVII
Pasin	(son to Dhritarashtra) slain by Bhima	K	LXXXIV
Paundramatsyaka	earthly counterpart of Valina	AD	LXVII
Paurava	(King)		
	earthly counterpart of Sarabha	AD	LXVII
	even he had to die	D	LVII
	slain by Aswatthaman	D	CCI
Paushya	King	AD	III
Pavaka	(name for Agni)		
Pavana	god of the Wind		
	Pavana and the huge Salmali tree	SAN	CLIV-CLVII
	humbles the proud King Kartavirya	AN	CLII-CLVII
Pingala	her words on awakening	SAN	CLXXIV
Prabhasa	father to Viswakarman	AD	LXVI
Prachetas	father to Daksha great-grandfather to Visvaswat (the Sun)		
	great-great-grandfather to Manu	AD	LXXV
Prachina-Garbha	name for Saraswat	SAN	CCCL
Pradyumna	(son to Krishna)		
	fights King Salwa	VA	XVII
	upbraids his charioteer for taking him unconscious from the battlefield	VA	XVIII
Prahlada	his three sons	AD	LXV
	earthly counterpart of Salabha	AD	LXVII
	speaks of forgiveness to his grandson Vali	VA	XXVIII

Prahlada *cont*	(Daitya chief) has to give Indra back his sovereignty	SAN	CXXIV
	speaks to Indra about the nature of action	SAN	CCXXII
Prajapati	(son to Manu)		
	father to the eight Vasus	AD	LXVI
	one of the thirty-three gods	AD	LXVI
Prajapatis, The	their pedigrees	SAN	CCVIII
	names of the twenty-one Prajapatis	SAN	CCCXXXV
	origin	AN	LXXXV
Pramatha	(son to Dhritarashtra)		
	slain by Bhima	D	CLVI
Pramathas, The	speak of practices good and bad	AN	CXXXI
Prasena	(son to Karna)		
	slain by the grandson of Sivi	K	LXXXII
Pratardana	(King) (one of four brothers)		
	converses with Narada	VA	CLXLVII
	gives his merits to Yayati	AD	XCII
Pratipa I	(King) (father to Santanu)		
	grandfather to Bhisma	AD	XCVII
		U	CXLVIII
Pratipa II	(father to Valhika)		
	grandfather to Somadatta	D	CLVI
Prativindhya	(son to Yudhishthira through Draupadi)		
	why so called	AD	CCXXIII
	slays Saumadatti	D	CVII
	slays Chitra	K	XIV
	slain by Aswatthaman	SAU	VIII
Prishdhra	slain by Aswatthaman	D	CLV
Pritha	(also called Kunti) (daughter to Sura) (sister to Vasudeva)		
	mother to Karna by Surya	AD	LXIII
	earthly counterpart of Siddhi	AD	LXVII

Pritha	marries Kuntibhoja	AD	LXVII
cont	mother to Karna by Surya	AD	LXVII
	marries Pandu	AD	CXI
	chooses Pandu as her husband	AD	CXII
	accompanies Pandu in his life as a hunter	AD	CXIV
	tells Pandu of the mantra given her by Durvasa	AD	CXXII
	mother to Yudhishthira by Dharma	AD	CXXIII
	mother to Bhima by Vayu	AD	CXXIII
	mother to Arjuna by Sakra	AD	CXXIII
	promises to help the Brahmana family doomed by the Rakshasa Vaka	AD	CLXIII
	summons Surya	VA	CCCIV
	gives birth to Karna	VA	CCCVI
	tells Karna that she is his mother	U	CXLV
	accompanies Gandhari and Dhritarashtra to the forest	ASR	XVI
	tells the story of Karna's birth	ASR	XXX
	assured by Vyasa that no fault is ascribed to her	ASR	XXX
	dies in forest fire	ASR	XXXVII
Prithu	(King)		
	(son to Vena)		
	even he had to die	D	LXIX
	his name	SAN	XXIX
	cited as the ideal king	SAN	LIX
	creator of the bow	SAN	CLXVI
Pritivindhya	earthly counterpart of Ekachakra	AD	LXVII
Pulaha	his sons	AD	LXVI
Pulastya	his sons	AD	LXVI
	stops Asmaka sacrifice aimed at destruction of Rakshasas	AD	CLXXXIII
	speaks of tirthas and their merits	VA	LXXXI-LXXXV
Puloma I	wife to Bhrigu	AD	V
Puloma II	Rakshasa who carried off Bhrigu's wife Puloma	AD	V
	dies	AD	VI
Purochana	constructs house of lac on Duryodhana's orders	AD	CXLVI
	dies in the burning house	AD	CL

Puru	descended from Manu thus: Manu – Ila – Pururavas – Ayus – Nahusha – Yayati – Puru	AD	LXXV
	son to King Yayati through Sarmishtha	AD	LXXXIII
	exchanges his youth for his father's decrepitude	AD	LXXV, LXXXIV
	regains his youth after 1,000 years	AD	LXXV, LXXXV
	is made king	AD	LXXV
	the race adopts his name	AD	LXXV
	'The progeny of Puru are the Pauravas'	AD	LXXXV
Pushkara	son to Varuna		
	chosen as husband by Soma's daughter, Jyotsnakali	U	XCVIII
Pushkaradharini	(wife to the Brahmana Satya)		
	the practice of harmlessness	SAN	CCLXXII
Radha	(wife to Adhiratha)		
	foster mother to Karna	AD	CXI
		VA	CCCVII
Rahu	manages to drink some Amrita	AD	XIX
	is beheaded by Narayana	AD	XIX
	his head rises into the sky. 'And from that time there is a long-standing quarrel between Rahu's head and Surya and Soma. And to this day it swalloweth Surya and Soma.'	AD	XIX
	celestial counterpart of Kratha (?)	AD	LXVII
Raivya	(sage)		
	(father to Paravasu and Arvavasu)		
	kills Yavakri	VA	CXXXVI
	accidently killed by Paravasu	VA	CXXXVIII
	restored to life by Arvavasu	VA	CXXXVIII
Rajadharman	(also called Nadijangha)		
	slain by Gautama and restored to life	SAN	CLXIX-CLXXIII
Rakshasas, The	those called Nairitas are begotten upon Niriti by Adharma	AD	LXVI
Rama	forms Samantapanchaka in the interval between the Treta and the Dwapara Yugas	AD	II

390   WHO'S WHO IN THE MAHĀBHĀRATA

Rama	extirpates the Kshatriyas twenty-one times	AD	LXIV
cont	son to Bhrigu: gives all his weapons to Drona	AD	CXXXI
	(=Vasudeva) born from a white hair of Narayana's body through Rohini	AD	CLXLIX
	son to Dasaratha, and also Vishnu incarnate, humbles Rama of Bhrigu's line	VA	XCIX
	youngest son to Jamadagni through Renuka, slays Renuka		
	and fights Arjuna, lord of the Haihaya tribe	VA	CXVI
	cremates his father's body and wreaks vengeance upon the entire military caste; appears to the exiled Pandavas	VA	CXVII
	story of Rama and Sita told by Hanuman	VA	CXLVI, CXLVII, CL
	story of Rama and Sita told by Markandeya	VA	CCLXXII–CCLXXXIX
	slays Vali	VA	CCLXXVIII
	slays Ravana	VA	CCLXXXVIII
	son to Rohini; visits the Pandavas	U	CLVIII
	= Bhargava (that foremost one of Bhrigu's race) espouses Amva's cause	U	CLXXX
	defeated by Bhishma in single combat	U	CLXXXII–CLXXXVIII
	defeats Ravana; utopian conditions in his kingdom; even he had to die	D	LIX
	son to Jamadagni: 'even he will have to die'. 'Rooting out all evils from the Earth, he caused the primeval Yuga to set in.'	D	LXX
	Gives the Earth to Kasyapa	D	LXX
	son to Jamadagni: vanquishes the assembled Danavas, receives all the celestial weapons from Mahadeva and passes the whole science of weapons to Karna	K	XXXIV
	curses Karna	K	XLII
	(Kesava's elder brother) comes to watch the mace-combat between Bhima and Duryodhana	SAL	XXXIV
	sings hymn about the Saraswati	SAL	LIV
	furious that Bhima has struck Duryodhana below the navel, rushes to attack Bhima, but is prevented by Krishna	SAL	LX
	deceived by Karna	SAN	II
	gives Karna a knowledge of weapons	SAN	II
	frees Dansa from his curse	SAN	III
	(son to Dasaratha); his flourishing reign of 11,000 years	SAN	XXIX
	begotten by Jamadagni	SAN	L

Rama *cont*	lops off the thousand arms of Arjuna, son to Kritavirya	SAN	L
	begins to exterminate the Kshatriyas	SAN	L
	why he slays King Kartaviryya-Arjuna and all his followers	ASW	XXIX
	leaves the body	MAU	IV
Rantideva I	(King) (son to Srinjaya) even he had to die	D	LXVII
Rantideva II	(King) (son to Sankriti) his sacrifices	SAN	XXIX
Raudrakarman	(son to Dhritarashtra) slain by Bhima	D	CXXVI
Ravana	his destruction recounted by Hanuman	VA	CXLVII
	birth	VA	CCLXXIII
	meaning of name	VA	CCLXXIII
	gains sovereignty of Lanka	VA	CCLXXIII
	launches counter-attack against Rama	VA	CCLXXXIII
	wakes his brother Kumbhakarna	VA	CCLXXXIV
	slain by Rama	VA	CCLXXXVIII
Ravi	(son to Dhritarashtra) slain by Bhima	SAL	XXVI
Renuka	marries Jamadagni, by whom she has five sons, of whom Rama is the youngest; dies at Rama's hands; is revived	VA	CXVI
Revati	wife to Valarama	AD	CCXXI
Richika	(son to Aurva) father to Jamadagni	AD	LXVI
Rishabha	Rishi	SAN	CXXVII
Rishika	earthly counterpart of Arka	AD	LXVII
Rishis, The	the seven Rishis spring from Mankanaka and Saraswati	SAL	XXXVIII
	origin	AN	LXXXV

Rishyasringa I	born of a hind	VA	CX
	why so called	VA	CX
	tempted	VA	CXI
	tells his father Vibhandaka of the temptation	VA	CXII
	marries Santa	VA	CXIII
Rishyasringa II	father to the Rakshasa Alamvusha	B	CI
Rituparna	king into whose service Nala enters	VA	LXVII
	imparts to Nala the whole science of dice	VA	LXXII
	receives from Nala 'the mysteries of equestrian science'	VA	LXXVII
Ritwiks, The	the seven Ritwiks of Yama		
	the seven Ritwiks of Kuvera	AN	CL
Rochamana	earthly counterpart of Aswagriva	AD	LXVII
	slain by Karna	K	LVI
Rohini	gives birth to Valadeva (=Rama) from a white hair of Narayana's body	AD	CLXIX
	mother of Rama	U	CLXVIII
	her husband, Soma, and her twenty-six co-wives	SAL	XXXV
	Rohini and Soma	SAN	CCCXLIII
Ruchi	wife to the ascetic Devasarman	AN	XL
	Vipula enters her body to protect her against Indra's advances	AN	XL, XLI
	goes to heaven	AN	XLII
Ruchiparvan	(son to Kriti)		
	slain by Bhagadatta	D	XXIV
Rudra	(also called Kapardin)		
	(appears to be the same as Siva)		
	why he receives the best portions of sacrifices	VA	CXIV
	divine lord of Uma	U	CXC
	grants Amva her wish to slay Bhishma	U	CXC
	persuaded not to procreate	AN	LXXXIV
	holds a great sacrifice	AN	LXXXV
Rudras, The	the eleven Rudras	AN	CL
		AN	LXVI

Rukmaratha	(son to Salya)		
	slain by Abhimanyu	D	XLIII
Rukmi	(also called Hiranyaroman)		
	(King)		
	(son to Bhishmaka)		
	offer of fighting service is rejected by both sides	U	CLIX
Rukmini	(wife to Krishna)		
	earthly counterpart of a portion of Sri	AD	LXVII
	yoked to Durvasa's carriage	AN	CLIX
Ruru	(grandson to Chyavana)		
	due to marry Pramadvara	AD	VIII
	gives half of his own life in order that Pramadvara may live	AD	IX
	vows to kill all serpents	AD	X
Rushangu	casts off his aged body	SAL	XXXIX
Sachi	a portion of Sachi is the celestial counterpart of Draupadi	AD	LXVII
	queen to Indra	U	XI
	seeks refuge with Vrihaspati	U	XI
Sagara	(King)		
	begets 60,000 sons from one wife and one son from another wife	VA	CVII
	how the Ocean appears to Rama	VA	CCLXXXI
	why the Ocean was also called Sagara	SAN	XXIX
Saha	son to Dhritarashtra		
	slain by Bhima	K	LXXXIV
Sahadeva	(son to Pandu)		
	twin brother to Nakula: their real fathers are the twin Aswins	AD	LXIII
	begotten upon Madri	AD	CXXIV
	'Sahadeva obtained with whole science of morality and duties from Vrihaspati'	AD	CXLI
	father to Srutasena through Draupadi	AD	CCXXIII
	conquers the South	SAB	XXV
	praises Agni	SAB	XXX
	plans to act as a royal cowherd under the name of Tantripal	VI	III

Sahadeva *cont*	with Nakula, vanquishes their maternal uncle Salya	B	LXXXIV
	qualities	D	XXXII
	vanquished by Karna	D	CLXVI
	fights Duhsasana	D	CLXXXVIII
	vanquishes Dussasana	K	XXIII
	slays Sakuni and his uncle Uluka	SAL	XXVIII
	true identity	ASR	XXXI
	falls to the ground	MAH	II
Sahasrapat	Rishi who becomes a snake	AD	IX-XII
Saindhavas, The	vanquished by Arjuna	ASW	LXXVIII
Sakra	(name of Indra)		
Saktri	(son to Vasishtha)		
	turns King Kalmashapada into a Rakshasa and is devoured by the Rakshasa	AD	CLXXVIII
Sakuni	(earthly counterpart of Dwapara (= the third Yuga))		
	born from Suvala	AD	LXIII
	brother to Gandhari	AD	CX
	puts idea of dice match into Duryodhana's mind	SAB	XLVII
	plays fateful dice game with Yudhishthira	SAB	LIX-LXIV
	vanquished by Nakula	D	CLXIX
	vanquishes Sutasoma	K	XXV
	slain by Sahadeva	SAL	XXVIII
	true identity	ASR	XXXI
Sakuntala	begotten by Visvamitra upon the Apsara Menaka	AD	LXXI
	brought up by the Rishi Kanwa as his own daughter	AD	LXXI, LXXII
	marries Dushmanta	AD	LXXIII
	rejected, then acknowledged by Dushmanta	AD	LXXIV
	mother to Bharata	AD	LXXIV
Salabha	celestial counterpart of Prahlada	AD	LXVII
	slain by Karna	K	LVI

Salwa I	(King)		
	earthly counterpart of Ajaka	AD	LXVII
	attacks city of Dwaravati	VA	XV
	fights Pradyumna	VA	XVII
	fights Krishna	VA	XX, XXI
	slain by Krishna	VA	XXII
Salwa II	(King of the Salwas)		
	rejects Amva	U	CLXXVI
	slain by Bhimaratha	D	XXIII
Salwa III	(King of the Mlechchhas)		
	slain by Satyaki	SAL	XX
	his huge elephant slain by Dhrishtadyumna	SAL	XX
Salya	(uncle to Yudhishthira)		
	(maternal uncle to Nakula and Sahadeva)		
	earthly counterpart of Samhlada	AD	LXVII
	agrees to be a commander of Duryodhana's armies	U	VIII
	vanquished by them	B	LXXXIV
	also called Artayani	D	XV
	King of the Madras	D	XV
	has mace-combat with Bhima	D	XV
	father to Rukmaratha	D	XLIII
	condescends to be charioteer to Karna	K	XXXII
	meaning of his two names	K	XXXII
	meaning of name	K	XXXV
	agrees to become Karna's charioteer provided that he may speak whatever he wishes	K	XXXV
	speaks harsh words to Karna	D	XXXVII, XXXIX
	becomes commander of the Kuru forces	SAL	VI
	mace-combat with Bhima ends in double knockout	SAL	XII
	shows his prowess	SAL	XIII
	slain, together with his younger brother, by Yudhishthira	SAL	XVII
Samanga	speaks to Narada on Emancipation	SAN	CCLXXXVII
Samlada	celestial counterpart of Salya	AD	LXVII
Samika	(Rishi)		
	(father to Sringin)		
	insulted by King Parikshit	AD	XL
	speaks of the importance of kingship	AD	XLI

Sampaka	speaks of Renunciation	SAN	CLXXVI
Sampati	(elder brother to Jatayu)		
	helps Hanuman to find Sita in Lanka	VA	CCLXXX
Samvara	rises to pre-eminence among the Asuras	AN	XXXVI
Samvarana	father to Kuru through Tapati	AD	CLXXV
Samvarta	irascible priest to King Marutta	ASW	VII-X
Sanatkumara	speaks on sovereignty and the titles of kings	VA	CLXXXIV
	praises Vishnu	SAN	CCLXXX
	speaks of Emancipation	SAN	CCCXXX
Sanat-Sujata	(immortal Rishi)		
	gives Dhritarashtra profound teaching	U	XLII-XLVI
Sandili	(ascetic lady)		
	pardons Garuda and restores his wings	U	CXIII
	speaks to Sumana on the conduct of a lady	AN	CXXIII
Sanjaya	(son to Gavalgana)		
	(son to the Princess Vidula)		
	peace envoy from Dhritarashtra to the Pandavas	U	XXI-XXVI
	spurred into effective action by his mother	U	CXXXIII-CXXXVI
	granted celestial vision by Vyasa	B	II
	speaks of the nature of the Earth	B	IV
	speaks of the five elements	B	V
	speaks of the Island of Sudarsana	B	VI, VII
	speaks of the four Yugas	B	X
	speaks of Sakadwipa	B	XI
	reports the battle to Dhritarashtra	B	XII onwards
	gives the current battle-toll	K	V, VI
	lists the great warriors still alive	K	VII
	taken captive by the Pandavas		
	released on instructions from Vyasa	SAL	XXIX
	loses the celestial vision given by Vyasa	SAU	IX
Sankha I	(son to Virata)		
	slain by Drona	B	LXXXIII
Sankha II	brother to Likhita, who steals from him	SAN	XXIII

Santa	(daughter to King Lomapada)		
	marries Rishyasringa	VA	CXIII
Santanu	(King)		
	son to Pratipa	U	CXLVIII
	father to Bhishma through Ganga	AD	LXIII
	why so called	AD	XCV
	birth	AD	XCVII
	is King Mahabhisha reborn	AD	XCVII
	made king	AD	XCVII
	marries the human form of Ganga	AD	XCVII
	description and virtues	AD	C
	marries Satyavati	AD	C
Sarabha I	(brother to Sakuni)		
	celestial counterpart of Paurava	AD	LXVII
	slain by Bhima	D	CLVI
Sarabha II	(son to Sisupala)		
	vanquished by Arjuna	ASW	LXXXIII
Sarama	(celestial bitch)		
	curses the brothers of Janamejaya	AD	III
Sarasan	(son to Dhritarashtra)		
	slain by Bhima	D	CXXXV
Saraswat	(also called Apantaratamas and Prachinagarbha)		
	(Rishi)		
	born to the Saraswati by the sage Dadhicha		
	teaches the Vedas to 60,000 Rishis	SAL	LI
	'preceptor of the Vedas'	SAN	CCCL
	arises from the syllable 'Bho'	SAN	CCCL
	in a later age is born as Vyasa	SAN	CCCL
Saraswati	speaks of Virtue	VA	CLXXXV
	mother to seven Rishis by Markandeya and grandmother to the 49 Marus	SAL	XXXVIII
	manages to obey both Viswamitra and Vasishtha	SAL	XLII
	why her waters become blood for a year	SAL	XLII
	praised by Vasishtha	SAL	XLII
	freed by Viswamitra's curse	SAL	XLIII
	creates the science of chastisement	SAN	CXXII
	identified as speech and located in the tongue of living creatures	SAN	CCXXXIX

Saraswati *cont*	helps to impart the knowledge of the Vedas to Yajnavalkya	SAN	CCCXIX
	appears 'adorned with all the vowels and the consonants and having placed the syllable OM in the van'	SAN	CCCXIX
	see also **Durga**		
Sarmishtha	(daughter to the Asura chief Vrishaparvan)		
	quarrels with Devayani	AD	LXXVIII
	becomes waiting-maid to Devayani	AD	LXXX
	becomes mother to Drahyu, Anu and Puru by Yayati	AD	LXXXIII
Sarngaka Birds, The	offspring of the Rishi Mandapala and Jarita	AD	CCXXXI
	praise Agni and are spared	AD	CCXXXIV
Sasavindu	(King)		
	(son to Chitrasena)		
	even he had to die	D	LXV
	his sacrifices	SAN	XXIX
Sasin	name of Soma	SAL	XXXV
Satachandra	slain by Bhima	D	CLVI
Satakratu	name for Indra	SAL	XLIX
Satanika I	son to Nakula through Draupadi	AD	CCXXIII
	why so called	AD	CCXXIII
	slays Bhutakarman	D	XXIII
	slain by Aswatthaman	SAU	VIII
Satanika II	(younger brother to King Virata)		
	slain by Drona	D	XXI
Satanika III	(brother to King Virata)		
	slain by the ruler of the Madras	D	CLXVII
Satrunjaya I	(brother to Karna)		
	slain by Arjuna	D	XXX
Satrunjaya II	slain by Abhimanyu	D	XLVI
Satrunjaya III	(son to Dhritarashtra)		
	slain by Bhima	D	CXXXVI
Satrunjaya IV	(son to Drupada)		
	(brother to Suratha)		
	slain by Aswatthaman	D	CLV

Satrunjaya V	(King)		
	slain by Arjuna	K	XXVII
Satrunjaya VI	(King)		
	converses with the Rishi Bharadwaja on the behaviour of a king in times of distress	SAN	CXL
Satrusaha	(son to Dhritarashtra)		
	slain by Bhima	D	CXXXVI
Satwata	name for Satyaki	D	CXV
Satya	(Brahmana)		
	(husband to Pushkaradharini)		
	the practice of harmlessness	SAN	CCLXXII
Satyabhama	consort to Krishna	VA	CLXXXII
Satyajit	left to protect Yudhishthira	D	XVII
	slain by Drona	D	XXI
Satyakarman	slain by Arjuna	SAL	XXVII
Satyaki	(also called Madhava, Satwata, Yuyudhana)		
	(Vrishni hero)		
	(grandson to Sini)		
	rescues Dhrishtadyumna from Drona	D	XCVI
	fights Drona	D	XCVII
	shows his prowess	D	XCVI
	slays Vyaghradatta	D	CVI
	slays Jalasandha	D	CXIV
	fights Duryodhana	D	CXV
	fights Kritavarman	D	CXV
	vanquishes Drona!	D	CXVI
	slays Sudarsana	D	CXVII
	shows amazing prowess, 'surpassing Arjuna himself'	D	CXIX
	vanquishes 'the mountaineers who battle with stones'	D	CXX
	vanquishes Duhsasana	D	CXXII
	slays King Alamvushu	D	CXXXIX
	shows his prowess	D	CXL
	slays Bhurisravas	D	CXLII
	fights Karna	D	CXLVI
	slays Somadatta	D	CLXI
	slays Bhuri	D	CLXV
	fights Karna	D	CLXX

Satyaki *cont*	vanquishes Duryodhana	D	CLXXI
	shows his prowess	D	CXCII
	vanquished by Aswatthaman	D	CCI
	slays Vinda and Anuvinda of the Kaikayas	K	XIII
	vanquishes Kritavarman	SAL	XVII
	slays Salwa	SAL	XX
	slays Kshemakirti	SAL	XXI
	fights Kritavarman	SAL	XXI
	slays Kritavarman	MAU	III
Satyasena I	pierces Krishna's left arm with a lance	K	XXVII
	slain by Arjuna	K	XXVII
Satyasena II	(son to Karna)		
	slain by Nakula	SAL	X
Satyavan	(son to Dyumatsena)		
	marries Savitri	VA	CCLXIII
	dies and is carried away by Yama, but is restored to life by Savitri	VA	CCLXV
Satyavat	(son to King Dyumatsena)		
	converses with his father on crime and punishment	SAN	CCLXVII
Satyavati	born from Vasu's seed in a fish which is really an Apsara under a curse	AD	LXIII
	becomes mother to Vyasa by the Rishi Parasara	AD	LXIII
	the fisherman's supposed daughter	AD	C
	marries Santanu	AD	C
	mother to Chitrangada and Vichitravirya by Santanu	AD	CI
	begs Bhishma to rule and raise a family	AD	CIII
	dies	AD	CXXVIII
Satyeshu	slain by Arjuna	SAL	XXVII
Saudasa	(King)		
	(husband to Madayanti)		
	turned into a cannibal through Vasishtha's curse	ASW	LVII
Saudyumni	(name for Yuvanaswa)		
Saumadatti	(son to Somadatta)		
	slain by the son of Yudhishthira	D	CVII

Saunaka I	(also called Kulapati)		
	it is after his twelve years' sacrifice that Sauti relates the *Mahābhārata*	AD	I
	wants to hear the *Mahābhārata* from Sauti	AD	LIX
Saunaka II	(Brahmana)		
	gives wise teaching to the exiled Pandavas	VA	II
Sauti	(also called Ugrasrava)		
	(son to Lomaharshana)		
	narrates the *Mahābhārata* to a group of sages	AD	I
	sings Krishna's praises	SAN	CCCXLVII
	see also **Suta**		
Savitri I	mother to the twin Aswins by Tvashtri	AD	LXVI
Savitri II	(daughter to King Aswapati)		
	named after the goddess who bestows her	VA	CCLXLI
	marries Satyvan	VA	CCLXLIII
	converses with Yama and regains husband's life	VA	CCLXLV
Seduka	King	VA	CLXV
Senajit	King	SAN	XXV
	king whose son dies	SAN	CLXXIV
Senavindu	earthly counterpart of Tuhunda	AD	LXVII
Sesha	portion of Sesha is the celestial counterpart of Valadeva	AD	LXVII
	firstborn of the snakes	AD	XXXV
	lives 'underneath the Earth, alone supporting the world at the command of Brahman'	AD	XXXVI
	see also **Shesha**		
Shanda	son to Dhritarashtra	K	LXXXIV
	slain by Bhima	K	LXXXIV
Shesha	description	U	CII
	see also **Sesha**		
Shitraketu	father to Suketu	K	LIV

Siddhi	celestial counterpart of Kunti	AD	LXVII
Sikhandin	(was Amva in previous life)		
	earthly counterpart of a Rakshasa	AD	LXVII
	born as a daughter to King Drupada, but treated as a son	U	CXCI
	marries the daughter to King Hiranyavarman	U	CXCII
	changes sex with a Yaksha called Sthunakarna	U	CXCV
	slays Bhishma	B	XIII
	wields the Varuna weapon	B	LXXXVI
	vanquished by Kripa	D	CLXIX
	vanquished by Kritavarman	K	XXVI
	slain by Aswatthaman	SAU	VIII
	true identity	ASR	XXXI
Singhaketu	slain by Karna	K	LVI
Singhasena	slain by Drona	D	XVI
Sini	grandfather to Satyaki	D	XCVII
Sisupala	(King)		
	earthly counterpart of Hiranyakasipu	AD	LXVII
	censures the offering of Arghya to Krishna	SAB	XXXVI
	mocks Bhishma's words	SAB	XL
	his birth, and the prophecy about his death	SAB	XLII
	his harsh words	SAB	XLIII
	slain by Krishna	SAB	XLIV
	father to Dhrishtaketu	D	CXXIV
Sita	story of Rama and Sita told by Markandeya	VA	CCLXXII-CCLXXXIX
	story of Rama and Sita told by Hanuman	VA	CXLVI, CXLVII, CL
Siva	to protect the creation, swallows poison and holds it in his throat; his name Nilakantha	AD	XVIII
	promises offspring to King Sagara	VA	CVI
	breaks Ganga's fall after her leap from heaven	VA	CIX

Siva *cont*	beseeches Brahma to show mercy on the creatures	D	LI
	gives Indra special mantras to overcome Vritra	D	XCIII
	'The Lord Kesava always worshippeth Siva in the phallic emblem as the origin of all creatures.'	D	CCI
	Siva and creation	SAU	XVII
	how his bow is made and how its string breaks	SAU	XVIII
	destroys Daksha's sacrifice in wrath; shows mercy	SAN	CCLXXXIV
	his 1,008 names	SAN	CCLXXXV
	why his throat is blue	SAN	CCCXLIII
	his combat with Narayana ends	SAN	CCCXLIII
	'cheerful'	SAN	CCCL
	'Lord of Uma'	SAN	CCCL
	promulgator of the 'cult known by the name of Pasupata'	SAN	CCCL
	instructed by his father Brahma(n)	SAN	CCCLI, CCCLII
Sivi I	(King)		
	son to King Usinara through Madhavi	U	CXVIII
	gives his merits to Yayati	AD	XCIII
	bars the way of King Suhotra	VA	CLXLIII
	virtues tested and approved by Indra and Agni, who appear as hawk and pigeon	VA	CLXLVI
	even he had to die	D	LVIII
	slain by Drona	D	CLIV
	his sacrifices	SAN	XXIX
Sivi II	celestial counterpart of Druma	AD	LXVII
Skanda	(god)		
	his weapon is a lance	AD	CCXXIX
	begotten by Agni upon various disguised forms of Swaha	VA	CCXXIV
	other names: Guha, Mahasena	VA	CCXXIV
	nursed by the Mothers of the Universe	VA	CCXXV
	subdues the gods	VA	CCXXVI
	his offspring	VA	CCXXVII
	refuses Indra's offer of lordship of the three worlds, but accepts generalship of the celestial forces	VA	CCXXVIII
	marries Devasena	VA	CCXXVIII
	leads the gods to victory over the Danavas	VA	CCXXX

Skanda cont	slays Mahisha, the Danava leader	VA	CCXXX
	his many names and titles	VA	CCXXX
	his appearance and inborn virtues	VA	CCXXVIII
	springs from Maheswara and Agni	SAL	XLIV
	his wonderful powers as a child	SAL	XLIV
	installed as generalissimo to the celestial forces	SAL	XLV
	his companions	SAL	XLV
	the mothers who become his companions	SAL	XLVI
	gifts offered to him	SAL	XLVI
	slays Daityas, Rakshasas and Danavas	SAL	XLVI
	pierces the Krauncha Mountain with his dart	SAL	XLVI
	'made the chief of all the spirits and ghostly beings (that wait upon Mahadeva)'	SAN	CXXII
	speaks of good practices	AN	CXXXIV
Soma	his wives are the Nakshatras	AD	LXVI
	father to Varchas	AD	LXVI
	finds it hard to part with his son and asks that the youth be returned in his 16th year as Abhimanyu	AD	LXVII
	father to Jyotsnakali	U	XCVIII
	other names: Sasin, Chandramas, Virochana	SAL	XXXV
	Rohini and his twenty-six other wives	SAL	XXXV
	Soma and Rohini	SAN	CCCXLIII
Somadatta	(son to Valhika)		
	grandson to Pratipa	D	CLVI
	father to Saumadatti	D	CVII
	slain by Satyaki	D	CLXI
Somaka	(King)		
	has only one son, Jantu	VA	CXXVII
	obtains 100 sons and suffers in hell	VA	CXXVIII
Somasrava	(son to the Rishi Srutasrava)		
	chosen by Janamejaya for his Purohita	AD	III
Sree	(goddess of Prosperity)		
	other names; Duhshaha, Vidhitsa, Bhuti and Lakshmi	SAN	CCXXV
	deserts Vali	SAN	CCXXV
	her portions are divided equally among the Earth, the Waters, Fire and good men	SAN	CCXXV

Sree *cont*	other names: Padma, Swaha and Swadha	SAN	CCXXVIII
	deserts the Asuras and lives with Indra	SAN	CCXXVIII
	description	SAN	CCXXVIII
	her eloquent words	AN	XI
	story of Sree and the kine	AN	LXXXII
Sreekantha	name of Siva	SAN	CCCL
Sri	Portion of Sri is celestial counterpart of Rukmini	AD	LXVII
	becomes incarnate as Draupadi	AD	CLXLIX
Sringin	son to the Rishi Samika, who is insulted by King Parikshit	AD	XL
	curses Parikshit	AD	XLI
Srinjaya	(King)		
	(son to King Switya)		
	(father to Suvarnashthivin)		
	comforted by Narada	D	LIII
	his son restored to life	D	LXXI
	father to King Rantideva	D	LXVII
Srutakarman	(son to Arjuna through Draupadi)		
	why so called	AD	CCXXIII
	slays Chitrasena	K	XIV
	slain by Aswatthaman	SAU	VIII
Srutakirti	slain by Aswatthaman	SAU	VIII
Srutanta	(son to Dhritarashtra)		
	slain by Bhima	SAL	XXVI
Srutarvan	(son to Dhritarashtra)		
	slain by Bhima	SAL	XXVI
Srutasena	(son to Sahadeva through Draupadi)		
	why so called	AD	CCXXIII
Srutayudha	(King)		
	'the son of Varuna, having for his mother that mighty river of cool water called Parnasa'	D	XCI
	slain by his own mace	D	XCI
Srutayus I	slain by Arjuna	D	XCII

Srutayus II	(ruler of the Amvashthas) slain by Arjuna	D	XCII
Srutayus III	slain by Aswatthaman	D	CLV
Srutayush	(King) vanquished by Yudhishthira	B	LXXXV
Sruvavati	(daughter to Bharadwaja) burns her feet to boil five jujubes for the Rishi Vasishtha	SAL	XLVIII
Sthunakarna	(Yaksha) changes sex with Sikhandin	U	CXCV
Subha	wife to Angiras	VA	CCXVII
Subhadra	(also called Bhadra) (sister to Krishna) (wife to Arjuna) mother to Abhimanyu by Arjuna mourns Abhimanyu; 'Alas, O hero, thou has been to me like a treasure in a dream that is seen and lost.'	AD D	CCXXIII LXXVIII
Subhaga	(brother to Sakuni) slain by Bhima	D	CLVI
Sudakshina	Prince of the Kamvojas slain by Arjuna	D	XCI
Surdarsan	(son to Dhritarashtra) slain by Bhima	D	CXXVI
Sudarsana I	slain by Satyaki	D	CXVII
Sudarsana II	(son to Dhritarashtra) slain by Bhima	SAL	XXVII
Sudarsana III	(son to Agni) (husband to Oghavati) overcomes Death while leading the life of a householder	AN	II
Sudarshana	slain by Aswatthaman	D	CCI
Sudeshna	queen to King Virata	VI	III

Sudeva	Brahmana who discovers Damayanti	VA	LXVIII
Sudharma	(wife to Matali) mother to Gunakesi	U	XCVII
Sudyumna	(King) punishes Likhita for stealing from his brother	SAN	XXIII
Sugriva	brother to the monkey-king Vali	VA	CCLXXVII
	becomes ally to Rama	VA	CCLXXVIII
Suhasta	(son to Dhritarashtra) slain by Bhima	D	CLVI
Suhotra	(King) (son to Atithi)		
	bars the way of King Sivi	VA	CLXLIII
	noted for his endless gifts of gold	D	LVI
	even he had to die	D	LVI
	given gold by Maghavat	SAN	XXIX
Suhtra	celestial counterpart of Munjakesa	AD	LXVII
Sujata	(son to Dhritarashtra) slain by Bhima	SAL	XXVI
Suka	(son to Vyasa(		
	taught by his father	SAN	CCXXXI-CCLIV
	birth	SAN	CCCXXIV
	why so called	SAN	CCCXXV
	the Vedas come to him of their own accord	SAN	CCCXXV
	his studies	SAN	CCCXXVI
	instructed by King Janaka	SAN	CCCXXVII
	instructed by Vyasa	SAN	CCCXXIX
	instructed by Narada	SAN	CCCXXX-CCCXXXII
	prepares to enter the Sun	SAN	CCCXXXIII
	soars through the welkin and disappears in full emancipation	SAN	CCCXXXIV
Sukanya	(Princess)		
	pierces Chyavana's eyes	VA	CXXII
	marries Chyavana	VA	CXXII

Suketu	son to Shitraketu	K	LIV
Sukra	(son to Bhrigu)		
	becomes a planet and also the spiritual guide of the Daityas and the gods	AD	LXVI
	also called Kavya and Usanas	AD	LXXVI
	revives Kacha through the science of Sanjivani and is himself revived by Kacha	AD	LXXVI
	father to Devayani	AD	LXXVIII
	curses Yayati with decrepitude	AD	LXXXIII
	first to acquire the science of morality	SAN	CCX
	speaks to Vali about gifts	AN	XCVIII
Sukshma	celestial counterpart of Vrihadratha	AD	LXVII
Sukumari	(daughter to Srinjaya)		
	marries Narada	SAN	XXX
Sulabha	(lady of the Satya Yuga)		
	converses with King Dharmadhyaja	SAN	CCCXXI
Sumantra	disciple to Vyasa	SAN	CCCXXVIII
Sumukha	(Naga)		
	chosen by Matali to be his son-in-law	U	CIII
	marries Matali's daughter Jyotsnakali	U	CIV
	is granted reprieve from Garuda	U	CIV
Sunaka	earthly counterpart of Chandrashantri	AD	LXVII
Sunda	(brother to Upasunda)		
	plan to conquer the three worlds and its failure	AD	CXX-CXXIV
Suparswa	earthly counterpart of Kupatha	AD	LXVII
Suprabha	(daughter to the Rishi Vadanya)		
	marries the Rishi Ashtavakra	AN	XXI
Sura	father to Vasudeva and Pritha	AD	LXVII
Surabhi	'mother of all kine'	U	CII
Suratha	(son to Drupada)		
	(brother to Satrunjaya)		
	slain by Aswatthaman	D	CLV
		SAL	XIV

Surpanakha	(sister to Ravana)		
	mutilated by Rama	VA	CCLXXV
Surya	decides to consume the world	AD	XXIV
	begets Karna upon Kunti	AD	LXIII
	celestial counterpart of Darada	AD	LXVII
	begets Karna upon Kunti	AD	CXI
	'made the lord of all luminous bodies'	SAN	CXXII
	gives the knowledge of the Vedas to Yajnavalkya	SAN	CCCXIX
	speaks of actions good and bad	AN	CXXX
Suryabhasa	slain by Abhimanyu	D	XLVI
Suryaksha	earthly counterpart of Krathana	AD	LXVII
Susarman	(King of the Trigartas)		
	advocates allied invasion of Virata's country	VI	XXX
	stuns Arjuna	K	LIII
	slain by Arjuna	SAL	XXVII
Sushena I	slain by Abhimanyu	D	XXXV
Sushena II	(son to Dhritarashtra)		
	slain by Bhima	D	CXXVI
Sushena III	(son to Karna)		
	slain by Uttamaujas	K	LXXV
Sushena IV	(son to Karna)		
	slain by Nakula	SAL	X
Suta	(also called Sauti)		
	says: 'I have now told you all that Vaisampayana recited to Janamejaya'	SAN	CCCXL
	but continues to quote Vaisampayana's words to Janamejaya	SAN	CCCXLI onwards
Sutasoma I	(son to Bhima through Draupadi)		
	why so called	AD	CCXXIII
Sutasoma II	son to Arjuna	D	XXIII
	vanquished by Sakuni	K	XXV
	slain by Aswatthaman	SAU	VIII

Suvahu I	(son to Dhritarashtra)		
	earthly counterpart of Hara	AD	LXVII
	slain by Bhima	B	XCVII
Suvahu II	king whose family cares for the sorrowing Damayanti	VA	LXV
Suvala	father to Sakuni	D	CLXIX
Suvarchas I	slain by Abhimanyu	D	XLVI
Suvarchas II	(son to Dhritarashtra)		
	slain by Bhima	K	LXXXIV
Suvarman	(son to Dhritarashtra)		
	slain by Bhima	D	CXXVI
Suvarnashthivin	(son to King Srinjaya)		
	why so called	D	LIII
	slain by robbers	D	LIII
	restored to life	D	LXXI
	restored to life by Narada	SAN	XXXI
Suyodhana	(name for Duryodhana)		
Swadha	name for Sree	SAN	CCXXVIII
Swaha	name for Sree	SAN	CCXXVIII
	in love with Agni; assumes the forms of various ladies beloved by Agni		
	result is Skanda	VA	CCXXIV
	given her wish that she may be forever associated with Agni	VA	CCXXX
Swarbhanu	celestial counterpart of Ugrasena	AD	LXVII
Sweta	slain by Bhishma	B	XLVIII
Swetaketu	(son to Uddalaka)		
	uncle to Ashtavakra	VA	CXXXII
	establishes ordinance of marriage	AD	CXXII
Swetaki	(King)		
	at his sacrifice Agni drinks clarified butter for 12 years	AD	CCXXV

Switya	(King) (father to Srinjaya) grandfather to Suvarnashthivin	D	LIII
Syumarasmi	(Rishi) enters the form of a cow	SAN	CCLXVIII-CCLXX
Takshaka	(king of the serpents)		
	steals earrings	AD	III
	slays Janamejaya's father	AD	III
	kills King Parikshit	AD	XLIII
	departs, 'coursing through the blue sky like a streak of the hue of the lotus, and looking very much like the vermilion-coloured line on a woman's crown dividing the dark masses of her hair in the middle'	AD	XLIV
	saved by Astika's intervention	AD	LVIII
Tandi	sings a splendid hymn to Mahadeva	AN	XVI
	obtains from heaven 'the king of all hymns' and brings it down to Earth	AN	XVII
Tantripal	pseudonym for Sahadeva	VI	III
Tanu	(Rishi) consoles King Viradyumna on the loss of his son	SAN	CXXVII
Tapati	(daughter of Vivaswat)		
	meets King Samvarana	AD	CLXXIII
	falls in love with Samvarana	AD	CLXXIV
	marries Samvarana	AD	CLXXV
	mother to Kuru by Samvarana	AD	CLXXV
Taraka	slain by Kartikeya	AN	LXXXV, LXXXVI
Tarksha	questions Saraswati about Virtue	VA	CLXXXV
Tashtri	'the divine artificer of the Universe'	VA	CCLXXXI
	also called Bhaumana *see also* **Tvashtri, Twashtri**	U	LVI
Tilottama	a most beautiful damsel created by Viswakarman	AD	CCXIII
	why so called	AD	CCXIII

Trigartas, The	subjugated by Arjuna	ASW	LXXIV
Trijata	(Rakshasa woman) guards Sita	VA	CCLXXVIII
Trisiras	name of Viswarupa	SAN	CCCXLIII
Trita	(son to Gautama) (brother to Ekata and Dwita) makes an 'imagined' but effective sacrifice	SAL	XXXVI
Tuhunda	celestial counterpart of Senavindu	AD	LXVII
Tuladhara	(trader) instructs the ascetic Jajali	SAN	CCLXII-CCLXIV
Tvashtri	father to the twin Aswins through Savitri *see also* **Tashtri, Twashtri**	AD	LXVI
Twashtri	makes the Vajra weapon	VA	C
	'the lord of creatures and the foremost of celestials'	U	IX
	creates a three-headed son to oppose Indra	U	IX
	creates Vritra to kill Indra *see also* **Tashtri, Tvashtri**	U	IX
Uchchaishravas	(the celestial steed) proceeds from the Ocean	AD	XVIII
Uddalaka	father to Swetaketu	AD	CXXII
	also called Aruni	AD	III
Uddalaki	(Rishi) (father to Nachiketa) story of his son and Yama	AN	LXXI
Ugrasena	earthly counterpart of Swarbhanu	AD	LXVII
Ugrayayin	(son to Dhritarashtra) slain by Bhima	D	CLVI
Uluka	(son to Sakuni) messenger between the two armies	U	CLXI-CLXIV
	vanquishes Yuyutsu	K	XXV
	slain by Sahadeva	SAL	XXVIII

Ulupi	(daughter to the King of the Nagas)		
	spends a night with Arjuna	AD	CCXVI
	revives Arjuna with a special gem	ASW	LXXX
	explains that Arjuna has been slain on account of a curse	ASW	LXXXI
Uma	daughter of Himavat		
	wife to Siva	SAN	CCLXXXIII
	curses the gods	AN	LXXXIV
	tells Mahadeva the duties of women	AN	CXLVI
	see also **Durga**		
Upachitra	(son to Dhritarashtra)		
	slain by Bhima	D	CXXXV
Upamanyu	(Rishi)		
	disciple to Ayoda-Dhaumya	AD	III
	cured of his blindness	AD	III
	twice sings the praises of Mahadeva	AN	XIV
	quotes Tandi's hymn to Mahadeva	AN	XVI
Upananda	(son to Dhritarashtra)		
	slain by Bhima	K	LI
Uparichara	(King)		
	holds a sacrifice in the Krita Age	SAN	CCCXXXVII
	dies	SAN	CCCXXXVII
	cursed and freed from the curse	SAN	CCCXXXVIII
Upasunda	(brother to Sunda)		
	his plan to conquer the three worlds and its failure	AD	CCX-CCXIV
Urvasi	beautiful Apsara	VA	XLV
	ordered by Indra to use her wiles upon Arjuna	VA	XLV
	curses Arjuna	VA	XLVI
Usanas		AD	LXXVI
	preceptor to the Danava Prince Vritra	SAN	CCLXXIX
	enters Mahadeva's stomach	SAN	CCXC
	acquires the name of Sukra	SAN	CCXC
	becomes Uma's son	SAN	CCXC
	see also **Sukra**		
Usinara	(King of the Bhojas)		
	virtues tested and approved by Indra and Agni, who appear as hawk and pigeon	VA	CXXXI
	helps Galava in his quest	U	CXVIII
	father to Sivi through Madhavi	U	CXVIII

Utanka	(Rishi)		
	disciple to Veda	AD	III
	obtains earrings which are stolen from him by Takshaka	AD	III
	exhorts Janamejaya to hold a snake-sacrifice	AD	III
	obtains boon from Vishnu	VA	CC
	beseeches King Vrihadaswa to slay Dhundhu	VA	CCI
	threatens to curse Krishna for not having rescued the Kauravas	ASW	LIII
	worships Krishna and is granted a sight of Krishna's universal form	ASW	LV
	devoted to his preceptor Gautama	ASW	LVI
	promises to bring celestial earrings for Gautama's wife Ahalya	ASW	LVI
	meets King Saudasa	ASW	LVII
	obtains the earrings, loses them, recovers them, presents them	ASW	LVIII
Utathya	speaks to Mandhatri about kingship and righteousness	SAN	XC, XCI
Uttamaujas	slays Sushena	K	LXXV
	slain by Aswatthaman	SAU	VIII
Uttara I	(also called Bhuminjaya)		
	(son to King Virata)		
	becomes the stooge in Arjuna's knock-about comedy	VI	XXXVII, XXXVIII
Uttara II	(daughter to King Virata)		
	marries Abhimanyu	VI	LXXII
	mourns Abhimanyu	ST	XX
	grandmother to Janamejaya	ASW	LXVIII
	mother to Parikshit	ASW	LXVI
Vabhru	(King of Kasi)		
	brother to Krishna	U	XXVIII
Vabhruvahana	son to Arjuna through Chitrangada	AD	CCXVII
	King of Manipura	AD	CCXIX
	slays his father	ASW	LXXIX
Vadanya	(Rishi)		
	father to Suprabha	AN	XXI

Vahuka	pseudonym of King Nala	VA	LXXI-LXXXVI
Vahvasin	(son to Dhritarashtra) slain by Bhima	B	LXXXIX
Vaikanasas, The	origin	AN	LXXXV
Vainya	(King) praised by Atri as 'the foremost of sovereigns'	VA	CLXXXIV
Vaisampayana	disciple to Vyasa	SAN	CCCXXVIII
	recites the *Mahābhārata* at the snake-sacrifice of King Janamejaya	AD	I
	instructed by Vyasa to relate the history of the Kurus and the Pandavas	AD	LX
	gives a summary of the *Mahābhārata*	AD	LXI
	praises the *Mahābhārata* and promises full account	AD	LXII
Vajradatta	(King) (son to Bhagadatta) vanquished by Arjuna	ASW	LXXVI
Vaka I	(Rakshasa) brother to the Rakshasa Kirmira	VA	XI
	slain by Bhima	AD	CLXVI
Vaka II	(Rishi) visits exiled Pandavas	VA	XXVI
Vaka III	(royal sage) meets Indra	VA	CLXLII
Valadeva	(name for Rama) earthly counterpart of a portion of Sesha	AD	LXVII
Valadhi	father to Medhavi	VA	CXXXV
Valaka	Valaka and the blind beast	K	LXIX
Valakhilyas, The	origin	AN	LXXXV
Valanika	slain by Aswatthaman	D	CLV

Valarama	also called Haladhara	AD	CCXXI
	leader of the Vrishnis	VA	CXVIII
	visits the exiled Pandavas	VA	CXVIII
Valhika	(son to Pratipa)		
	(father to Somadatta)		
	slain by Bhima	D	CLVI
Vali I	son to Virochana	AD	LXV
	grandson to Prahlada	VA	XXVIII
	hears Prahlada's words on forgivxeness	VA	XXVIII
	former king, now an ass	SAN	CCXXIII-CCXXV
	deserted by Sree	SAN	CCXXV
	his eloquent words to Indra about the actor	SAN	CCXXVII
Vali II	monkey-king; brother to Sugriva	VA	CCLXXVII
	slain by Rama	VA	CCLXXVIII
Valina	celestial counterpart of Paundramatsyaka	AD	LXVII
Vallabha	pseudonym for Bhima	VI	II
Vamadeva	(Rishi)		
	speaks to King Vasumanas about righteousness and kingship	SAN	XCII-XCIV
Vandin	defeats Kahoda in debate	VA	CXXXII
	defeated in debate by ten-year-old Ashtavakra	VA	CXXXIV
	drowned	VA	CXXXIV
Vapushtama	marries King Janamejaya	AD	XLIV
Varchas	son to Soma	AD	LXVI
	celestial counterpart of Abhimanyu	AD	LXVII
Varuna	god		
	his weapon: noose and missile	AD	CCXXIX
	his assembly house described	SAB	IX
	gives some Varuna weapons to Arjuna	VA	XLI
	receives sovereignty over the waters	U	XVI
	father to Pushkara	U	XCVIII
	father to King Srutayudha	D	XCI
	installed, in a former Kalpa, as lord of all aquatic creatures	SAL	XLVII
	'installed into the sovereignty of the waters and the Asuras'	SAN	CXXII

Vashatkara	one of the 33 gods	AD	LXVI
Vashkala	celestial counterpart of Bhagadatta	AD	LXVII
Vasishtha	(Rishi)		
	curses the Vasus	AD	XCVI
	'Brahma's spiritual (literally mind-born) son and Arundhati's husband'	AD	CLXXVI
	tries in vain to kill himself	AD	CLXXVIII
	frees King Kalmashapada from his curse	AD	CLXXIX
	appointed by King Kalmashapada to beget a son upon his queen	AD	CLXXXIV
	makes the Saraswati obey him	SAL	XLII
	praises the Saraswati	SAL	XLII
	Sakra in disguise	SAL	XLVIII
	'made the lord of the Brahmanas'	SAN	CXXII
	also called Maitravaruni	SAN	CCCIII
	instructs King Karala	SAN	CCCIII-CCCIX
	dismissed by King Hiranyakasipu and replaced by Viswarupa	SAN	CCCXLIII
	praises kine	AN	LXXVIII-LXXX
	praises gold	AN	LXXXIV
	rescues the deities from the Danavas	AN	CLV
Vasu	(King of Chedi)		
	why also called Uparichara	AD	LXIII
	born in the Paurava race	AD	LXIII
	his five sons: Vrihadratha (Maharatha), Pratyagraha, Kusamva (=Manivahana), Mavella and Yadu	AD	LXIII
	marries Girika, who is born from the River Suktimati embraced by the Kolahala Mountain	AD	LXIII
	from his seed a fish (in fact, an Apsara under a curse) gives birth to twins: the girl Satyavati and the boy Matsya	AD	LXIII
	grandfather to Vyasa	AD	LXIII
Vasudeva	(also called Anakadundubhi)		
	father to Krishna through Devaki	AD	LXIII
	uncle to Arjuna; son to Sura and brother to Pritha	AD	LXVII
	earthly counterpart of a portion of Narayana	AD	LXVII
	slain by Drona	D	XXI
	asks Arjuna to protect the Vrishni kingdom and Krishna's 16,000 widows	MAU	VI
	leaves the body	MAU	VII

Vasuhoma	(King)		
	his words to King Mandhatri	SAN	CXXII
Vasuki	is used to help churn the Ocean	AD	XVIII
	secondborn of the snakes	AD	XXXV
	offers his sister to Jaratkaru	AD	XLVI
	King of the Nagas	U	CIII
Vasumanas	(King)		
	one of four brothers	VA	CLXLVII
	converses with Narada	VA	CLXLVII
Vasumat	gives his merits to Yayati	AD	XCIII
Vasumitra	earthly counterpart of Vikshara	AD	LXVII
Vasus, The	the eight sons of Prajapati	AD	LXVI
	the eight Vasus	AN	CL
	cursed by Vasishtha	AD	XCVI
	cursed by the Rishi Apava	AD	XCIX
	why one of them (Dyu) has to live on Earth as Ganga's child, Bhishma	AD	XCIX
Vatapi	(younger brother to the Asura Ilwala)		
	slain by the Rishi Agastya	VA	XCVI
Vatavega	(son to Dhritarashtra)		
	slain by Bhima	K	LXXXIV
Vayu	tells how to gratify the Pitris and deities	AN	CXXVIII
Veda	disciple to Ayoda-Dhaumya	AD	III
Vena	father to King Prithu	D	LXIX
Vibhandaka	father to Rishyasringa	VA	CXII
Vichakhya	(King)		
	speaks of the practice of harmlessness	SAN	CCLXV
Vichitravirya	(son to Santanu through Satyavati) (brother to Chitrangada)		
	becomes king	AD	CI
	marries Ambika and Ambalika	AD	CII
	dies, childless, of phthisis	AD	CII
Vidhatri	(son to Brahma(n))		
	brother to Dhatri and Lakshmi	AD	LXVI

Vidhitsa	name for Sree	SAN	CCXXV
Vidula	(Princess)		
	spurs her faint-hearted son Sanjaya into effective action	U	CXXXIII-CXXXVI
Vidura	(also called Kshatri)		
	Dharma, cursed by the Rishi Animandavya, 'was born a Sudra in the form of the learned Vidura'	AD	LXIII
	son to Vyasa	AD	LXIII
	begotten by Vyasa upon Amvika's maid	AD	CVI
	marries the daughter of King Devaka and begets 'many children like unto himself in accomplishments'	AD	CXIV
	warns the Pandavas about the house of lac	AD	CXLVII
	speaks against the dice match	SAB	XLVIII
	speaks of the evils of gambling	SAB	LXII
	gives farewell blessing to the Pandavas	SAB	LXXVII
	instructs Dhritarashtra in wisdom and foolishness	U	XXXIII-XXXIX
	younger brother to Dhritarashtra	U	CXLVIII
	nephew to Bhishma	U	CXLVIII
	consoles and instructs Dhritarashtra	ST	II-VII, IX
	practises severe penances	ASR	XXVI
	enters Yudhishthira's body	ASR	XXVI
	his high nature described by Vyasa	ASR	XXVIII
	true identity	ASR	XXXI
Vikarna	(son to Dhritarashtra)		
	slain by Bhima	D	CXXXVI
Vikata	(son to Dhritarashtra)		
	slain by Bhima	K	LI
Vikshara	celestial counterpart of Vasumitra	AD	LXVII
Vinata	(wife to Kasyapa)		
	mother to Garuda and to Surya's charioteer	AD	XVI
	lays a wager on Uchchaishravas	AD	XX
	put into slavery by her sister Kadru	AD	XXIII
	freed from slavery	AD	XXXIV
	her sons	AD	LXV
Vinda I	(brother to Anuvinda)		
	slain by Arjuna	D	XCVIII

Vinda II	(son to Dhritarashtra) slain by Bhima	D	CXXVI
Vinda III	(of the Kaikayas) slain by Satyaki	K	XIII
Vipatha	(brother to Karna) slain by Arjuna	D	XXX
Viprachitti	celestial counterpart of Jarasandha	AD	LXVII
Vipula	disciple to the ascetic Devasarman	AN	XL
	enters Ruchi's body to protect her from Indra's advances	AN	XL, XLI
	becomes aware of his sin	AN	XLII
	goes to heaven	AN	XLIII
Viradhanwan	slain by Dhrishtaketu	D	CVI
Viradyumna	(King) (father to Bhuridyumna) consoled by the Rishi Tanu on the loss of his son	SAN	CXXVII
Viragas	(son to Dhritarashtra) slain by Bhima	D	CLVI
Viraketu	(Prince of Panchala) slain by Drona	D	CXXI
Virata I	(King of the Matsyas)		
	the Pandavas decide to spend their 13th year in his city	VI	I
	husband to Sudeshna	VI	III
	delighted by his new 'servants'	VI	XIII
	strikes Yudhishthira on the face	VI	LXVII
Virata II	father to Sankha	B	LXXXIII
Virata III	(son to Dhritarashtra) slain by Bhima	B	XCVII
Virata IV	slain by Drona	D	CLXXXVI
Viravahu	(son to Dhritarashtra) slain by Bhima	D	CLVI

Virochana	name for Soma	SAL	XXV
	father to Vali	AD	LXV
Virupaksha I	celestial counterpart of Chitravarman	AD	LXVII
Virupaksha II	'a mighty king of the Rakshasas'	SAN	CLXX
	slays Gautama	SAN	CLXX-CLXXIII
Visalaksha	(son to Dhritarashtra)		
	slain by Bhima	B	LXXXIX
Vishnu	The Ocean 'becomes the bed of the lotus-naveled Vishnu when at the termination of every Yuga that deity of immeasurable power enjoys Yoga-nidra, the deep sleep under the spell of spiritual meditation.'	AD	XXI
	slays Naraka	VA	CXLI
	in the form of a huge boar with one tusk lifts the sunken Earth	VA	CXLI
	hymned	VA	CC
	slays the Danavas, Madhu and Kaitabha, at the end of creation	VA	CCII
	teaching on Vishnu	VA	CCLXX
	attributes	U	X
	from the city of Patalam, fills the universe with sound	U	XCIX
	guardian deity of birds	U	CI
	makes 'the divine Indra of a thousand eyes the ruler of deities'	SAN	CXXII
	achievements	SAN	CCVII
	located in the feet of living creatures	SAN	CCXXXIX
	praised by Sanatkumara	SAN	CCLXXX
	receives a beautiful mark on his bosom	SAN	CCCXLIII
	gratified	AN	CXXVI
	speaks of good practices	AN	CXXXIV
Visoka	(Kaikaya prince)		
	charioteer to Bhima	K	LXXVI
	slain by Karna	K	LXXXII
Viswakarman	son to Prabhasa through the sister of Vrihaspati	AD	LXVI
	founder of all arts	AD	LXVI
	creates a most beautiful damsel	AD	CCXIII
	makes marvellous chariot, which is given to Arjuna	AD	CCXXVII

Viswamitra	(son to King Gadhi)		
	(grandson to Kusika)		
	father to Sakuntala through Menaka	AD	LXXI
	his great achievements	AD	LXXII
	grandfather to Bharata	AD	LXXIV
	tries to take the cow Nandini from Vasishtha	AD	CLXXVII
	becomes an ascetic	AD	CLXXVII
	the only person we know of to rise from a lower order to become a Brahmana by ascetic austerities	U	CVI
	father to Ashtaka through Madhavi	U	CXIX
	attains Brahmanhood	SAL	XL
	makes the Saraswati obey him	SAL	XLII
	curses Saraswati	SAL	XLIII
	his strange birth	SAN	L
	Visvamitra and the haunch of dog's meat	SAN	CXLI
	Kshatriya who becomes a Brahmana	AN	III, IV
Viswarupa	(also called Trisiras)		
	replaces Vasishtha as Hiranyakasipu's Hotri	SAN	CCCXLIII
	becomes huge and drinks all the sacrificial Soma	SAN	CCCXLIII
	slain by Indra	SAN	CCCXLIII
Viswavasu	(Gandharva)		
	arises from the body of a headless Rakshasa	VA	CCLXXVII
	slain by Rama and Lakshmana	VA	CCLXXVII
	plays on the Vina	SAN	XXIX
Vitahavya	(also called Haihaya)		
	(royal sage)		
	attains to the status of a Brahmana	AN	XXX
Vivaswan	grants Yudhishthira a copper vessel with an inexhaustible supply of food	VA	III
Vivaswat	(the Sun)		
	son to Kasyapa	AD	LXXV
	grandson to Daksha	AD	LXXV
	father to Manu	AD	LXXV
Vivitsu	(son to Dhritarashtra)		
	slain by Bhima	K	LI
Vodhya	speaks of Freedom from attachments	SAN	CLXXVIII

Vriddhakshatra	(father to Jayadratha) dies after dropping his son's head	D	CXLV
Vrihadaswa I	(Rishi) tells the exiles the story of Nala and Damayanti	VA	LIII-LXXIX
	gives Yudhishthira the full science of dice	VA	LXXIX
Vrihadaswa II	(King) (father to Kuvalaswa) devotes himself to asceticism	VA	CCI, CCII
Vrihadratha	(King of the Angas) earthly counterpart to Sukshma	AD	LXVII
	his sacrifices	SAN	XXIX
Vrihadvala	(King of the Kosalas) slain by Abhimanyu	D	XLV
Vrihaspati	uncle to Viswakarman	AD	LXVI
	portion of Vrihaspati is the celestial counterpart of Drona	AD	LXVII
	curses Dirghatamas with blindness	AD	CIV
	'the spiritual chief of celestials'	AD	CXLI
	answers Yudhishthira's questions	AN	CXI-CXIII
	son to Angiras	U	XI
	receives special mantras from his father and gives them to Agnivesya	D	XCIII
	speaks of the nature and duties of a king	SAN	LXVIII
	speaks to Indra about agreeable speech	SAN	LXXXIV
	speaks to Indra on the behaviour of a king towards his foe	SAN	CIII
	first to acquire the branches of the Vedas called the Angas	SAN	CCX
	officiates at the Uparichara's sacrifice	SAN	CCCXXXVII
	enraged when the invisible Narayana takes his share	SAN	CCCXXXVII
Vrihatkshatra	slays Kshemadhurti	D	CVI
	slain by Drona	D	CXXIV
Vrindaraka I	slain by Abhimanyu	D	XLV
Vrindaraka II	son to Dhritarashtra, slain by Bhima	D	CXXVI

Vrishadarba	King	VA	CLXLV
Vrishadarbha	(King) meets the pigeon and the hawk	AN	XXXII
Vrishadarbhi	(King) Vrishadarbhi and the Rishis	AN	XCIII
Vrishaka	(son to the King of Gandhara) (brother to Achala) slain by Arjuna	D	XXVIII
Vrishaparvan	celestial counterpart of Dirghaprajna	AD	LXVII
Vrishaparvan II	(Asura chief) father to Sarmishtha	AD	LXXVIII
Vrishasena	(son to Karna) fights Nakula slain by Arjuna	K K	LXXXIV LXXXV
Vrishnis, The	all slain except Krishna and Rama	MAU	I
Vritra	(Asura) celestial counterpart of Manimat slain by Indra and the Vajra weapon created by Twashtri to kill Indra destroyed with the help of Vishnu Danava prince speaks to his preceptor Usanas about actions and their fruits slain by Indra transfers himself from one element to another, until eventually he is slain within Indra's own body	AD VA U U SAN SAN SAN ASW	LXVII CI IX X CCLXXIX CCLXXIX CCLXXXII XI
Vyaghradatta I	(Prince of the Panchalas) slain by Drona	D	XVI
Vyaghradatta II	'that prince of the Magadhas' slain by Satyaki	D D	CVI CVI
Vyasa	composes the *Mahābhārata* composes the Puranas father to Dhritarashtra, Pandu and Vidura	AD AD AD	I I I

Vyasa	parentage and training	AD	LX
cont	comes to Janamejaya's sacrifice and is asked to relate the history of the Kurus and the Pandavas	AD	LX
	instructs his disciple Vaisampayana to give the narrative	AD	LX
	begotten upon Satyavati by the Rishi Parasara	AD	LXIII
	why so called, and why Dwaipayana	AD	LXIII
	father to Vidura	AD	LXIII
	agrees to raise children to his brother Vichitravirya	AD	CV
	why also called Krishna	AD	CV
	begets Dhritarashtra upon Ambika	AD	CVI
	begets Pandu upon Ambalika	AD	CVI
	begets Vidura upon Amvika's maid	AD	CVI
	advises the Pandavas to dwell in Ekachakra	AD	CLVIII
	tells Drupada the story of the five Indras	AD	CLXLIX
	prophesies destruction of all the Kshatriyas	SAB	XLV
	forbids Duryodhana, Karna etc to slay the exiled Pandavas	VA	VII
	reproves Dhritarashtra	VA	VIII
	gives Yudhishthira the science called Pratismriti	VA	XXXVI
	suggests that Arjuna receive weapons and instruction from the gods	VA	XXXVI
	visits the exiled Pandvas	VA	CCLVII-CCCIX
	grants celestial vision to Sanjaya	B	I
	visits Yudhishthira	D	L-LXXI
	'the abode of Saraswati, the compiler of the Vedas, the habitation of those scriptures, unstained by sin, and of the hue of rain-charged cloud'	D	CCI
	tells Aswatthaman the truth about Krishna and Arjuna	D	CCI
	instructs the Pandvas to release Sanjaya	SAL	XXIX
	comforts Dhritarashtra	SAL	LXIII
	stands with Narada between the two celestial weapons fired by Aswatthaman and Arjuna	SAU	XIV
	censures Aswatthaman	SAU	XV
	teaches his son Suka	SAU	CCXXXI-CCLIV
	exhorts his 25-year-old son Suka to follow the path of Righteousness	SAN	CCCXXII
	instructs Suka in the names of the winds	SAN	CCCXXIX

Vyasa *cont*	instructs his four disciples (Sumantra, Vaisampayana, Jaimini, Paila) in the study and teaching of the Vedas	SAN	CCXXVIII
	grandfather to Janamejaya's grandfather	SAN	CCCXLIV
	'Know that the Island-born Krishna, otherwise called Vyasa, is Narayana on Earth. Who else than he, O tiger among kings, could compile such a treatise as the *Mahābhārata*?'	SAN	CCCXLVII
	feels fatigued 'in consequence of the great strain on his energies occasioned by the composition of the *Mahābhārata*'	SAN	CCCL
	originally the Rishi Saraswat	SAN	CCCL
	praises kine	AN	LXXXI
	Vyasa and the worm that retains its memory	AN	CXVII-CXIX
	speaks to Maitreya about gift	AN	CXX
	why he laughs	AN	CXX
	speaks to Maitreya	AN	CXXII
	seeks to guide the grief-stricken Yudhishthira	ASW	II
	tells the story of King Marutta	ASW	IV-X
	given the whole Earth by Yudhishthira; returns it	ASW	LXXXIX
	gives the true identity of Dhritarashtra, Pandu, Vidura, Yudishthira, Duryodhana, Sakuni, Dussasana, Bhima, Arjuna, Krishna, Sahadeva, Nakula, Karna, Abhimanyu, Dhrishtadyumna, Sikhandin, Drona, Aswatthaman, Bhishma	ASR	XXXI
	causes all the dead heroes to arise from the waters of the Bhagirathi	ASR	XXXIII
	invites the Kshatriya widows to plunge into the Bhagirathi to be with their lords	ASR	XXXIII
	brings King Parikshit and others down from heaven to be seen by King Janamejaya and his followers assembled for the sacrifice	ASR	XXXV
Vyudoroksha	(son to Dhritarashtra)		
	slain by Bhima	B	XCVII
Vyushitaswa	dies of phthisis contracted from sexual excess	AD	CXXI
	his corpse begets seven children upon his wife Bhadra	AD	CXXI

Yajnasena	(name for Drupada)		
Yajnavalkya	instructs King Daivarati	SAN	CCCXI-CCXIX
	receives the knowledge of the Vedas from Surya and with the aid of Saraswati	SAN	CCCXIX
	compiles the Satapatha Brahmanas	SAN	CCCXIX
	answers the 24 questions put by Viswavasu	SAN	CCCXIX
Yama	(god)		
	his weapon is a mace	AD	CCXXIX
	his assembly house described	SAB	VIII
	gives his mace to Arjuna	VA	XLI
	converses with Savitri and grants her five boons, including the life of her dead husband	VA	CCLXV
	other names and titles, with explanations	VA	CCLXV
	receives sovereignty over the Pitris	U	XVI
	made the lord of the Pitris	SAN	CXXII
	speaks of actions good and bad	AN	CXXX
Yatudhani	(Rakshasi)		
	receives explanation of the Rishis' names	AN	XCIII
Yavakri	(son to Bharadwaja)		
	austerities prompted by pride	VA	CXXXV
	killed by the power of the sage Raivya	VA	CXXXVI
	restored to life by Arvavasu	VA	CXXXVIII
Yayati	(King) (son to Nahusha) (father to Madhavi)		
	exchanges his decrepitude for the youth of his son Puru		
	realizes that appetites are insatiable		
	restores Puru's youth		
	makes Puru king, saying: 'In the world shall my race be known by thy name.'	AD	LXXV
	marries Devayani	AD	LXXXI
	father to Yadu and Turvasu through Devayani	AD	LXXXIII
	father to Drahyu, Anu and Puru through Sarmishtha	AD	LXXXIII
	cursed with decrepitude by Devayani's father Sukra	AD	LXXXIII
	practises austerities in the forest and ascends to heaven	AD	LXXXVI
	falls from heaven and hovers in the welkin	AD	LXXXVIII

Yayati *cont*	converses with the royal sage Astaka	AD	LXXXIX-XCII
	receives the merits of As(h)taka, Pratardana, Vasumat and Sivi, and re-ascends to heaven	AD	XCII, XCIII
	gives 1,000 kine to a Brahmana	VA	CLXLIV
	helps Galava in his quest	U	CXV
	dies and goes to heaven, where much later, he is divested of his splendour on account of ignorance, folly and pride	U	CXX
	falls to Earth	U	CXXI
	returns to heaven through the merits of Madhavi and his four grandsons	U	CXXII, CXXIII
	even he had to die	D	LXIII
	his sacrifices	SAN	XXIX
Yudhamanyu	slays Chitrasena	K	LXXXIII
	slain by Aswatthaman	SAU	VIII
Yudhishthira	pictured as a tree	AD	I
	son to Pandu: real father is Dharma	AD	LXIII
	born 'at the eighth Muhurta called Abhijit, of the hour of noon of that very auspicious day of the seventh month (Kartika), viz., the fifth of the lighted fortnight, when the star Jyestha in conjunction with the Moon was ascendant'	AD	CXXIII
	installed as heir apparent by Dhritarashtra	AD	CXLI
	also called Ajatasatru	AD	CLXIII
	father to Prativindhya through Draupadi	AD	CCXXIII
	beneficial influence in the world	AD	CCXXIV
	decides to perform the Rajasuya sacrifice	SAB	XII
	holds the Rajasuya sacrifice	AD	XXXIV, XXXV
	plays fateful dice game with Sakuni	SAB	LIX-LXIV
	receives from Vivaswan a copper vessel with an inexhaustible supply of food	VA	III
	speaks on Anger and Forgiveness	VA	XXIX
	speaks on Virtue and Atheism	VA	XXXII
	receives from Vyasa the science called Pratismriti	VA	XXXVI
	gives the knowledge of Pratismriti to Arjuna	VA	XXXVII
	instructs the Rakshasa Jatasura in Virtue	VA	CLVI

Yudhishthira *cont*	releases Nahusha from Agastya's curse	VA	CLXXX
	spares Jayadratha's life	VA	CCLXX
	answers the Yaksha's riddles	VA	CCCXI
	plans to disguise himself as a dice-loving courtier and Brahmana named Kanka	VI	I
	struck on the face by King Virata	VI	LXVII
	his virtues enumerated by Arjuna	VI	LXX
	vanquishes King Srutayush	B	LXXXV
	his wrath described	B	LXXXV
	fights Bhishma	B	LXXXVII
	his qualities	D	XXXII
	fights Drona	D	CV, CLXI, CLVI
	praises Krishna	D	CXLVIII
	vanquished by Kritavarman	D	CLXIV
	mourns Ghatotkacha	SAB	CLXXXIII
	encouraged by Krishna, tells lies	D	CXCI
	vanquishes Duryodhana and spares his life	K	XXIX
	vanquished by Karna	K	XLIX
	'exceedingly mangled with shafts', retreats to camp	K	LXIII
	accuses Arjuna of cowardice	K	LXVIII
	faces Arjuna's sword-point	K	LXIX
	upbraided by Arjuna	K	LXX
	reconciled to Arjuna	K	LXXI
	made whole by surgeons using mantras and drugs	K	LXXXIX
	vanquishes Salya	SAL	XVI
	slays Salya and his younger brother	SAL	XVII
	challenges Duryodhana to come out of the lake and fight	SAL	XXXI
	reproves Bhima for putting his foot on Duryodhana's head	SAL	LIX
	laments	SAU	X
	holds funeral rites for all the dead	ST	XXVI
	performs the water-rite for the dead	ST	XXVII
	realizes that Karna is Kunti's son	ST	XXVII
	divulges his grief, enormously increased by the knowledge that Karna was his uterine brother	SAN	I
	curses all the women of the world	SAN	VI
	proposes to live as an ascetic	SAN	VII, IX
	vows to starve to death, but is forbidden by Vyasa	SAN	XXVII
	shakes off his grief	SAN	XXXVIII
	receives a royal welcome in Hastinapura	SAN	XXXIX
	installed on the throne	SAN	XLI

Yudhishthira *cont*	performs the Sraddha rites	SAN	XLIII
	offers hymn of praise to Krishna	SAN	XLIV
	frees Nahusha from being a snake	AN	C
	stricken with grief at Bhishma's death	ASW	I-III
	begins to rule the Earth again	ASW	XIV
	sets off for the gold deposited by Marutta	ASW	LXIII
	returns with the gold and plans a horse-sacrifice	ASW	LXXI
	appoints Arjuna to protect the roving horse initiation	ASW	LXXIII
	celebrates the horse-sacrifice. Gives the whole Earth to Vyasa, who returns it. Gives the Brahmanas the price of the Earth in gold	ASW	LXXXIX
	rules the kingdom	ASR	I
	endears himself to Dhritarashtra and to all the people	ASR	II
	instructed by Dhritarashtra in kingship	ASR	V-VII
	Vidura enters his body and he recollects his own state before his birth among men	ASR	XXVI
	his high nature, described by Vyasa	ASR	XXVIII
	true identity	ASR	XXXI
	laments the death of Dhritarashtra, Gandhari and Kunti	ASR	XXXVIII
	will not abandon a devoted dog	MAH	III
	still in human form, reaches heaven	SW	I
	shocked to find Duryodhana enjoying a place of high honour	SW	I
	refuses to stay	SW	I
	shown a view of Hell; hears friends' voices and refuses to leave	SW	II
	praised by all the gods for passing the tests	SW	III
	sees many of his friends and their celestial counterparts	SW	IV
Yuvanaswa	also called Saudyumni		
	father to Mandhata		
	gives birth himself to his own son	VA	CXXVI
Yuyudhana	also called Satyaki	D	XCVII
	his ten sons slain by Bhurisravas	B	LXXIV
Yuyutsu	son to Dhritarashtra through one of Gandhari's maids	AD	CXV
	transfers his allegiance to the Pandavas	B	XLIII
	vanquished by Uluka	K	XXV